What to Do When

When

Practical Guidance Strategies for Challenging Behaviors

Sixth Edition

What to Do When

Practical Guidance Strategies for Challenging Behaviors

SIXTH EDITION

Eva Essa

THOMSON

DELMAR LEARNING

Australia Brazil Canada Mexico Singapore Spain United Kingdom United States

What To Do When...Practical Guidance Strategies for Challenging Behaviors in the Preschool, 6E

Eva Essa

Vice President, Career Education Strategic Business Unit:
Dawn Gerrain

Director of Learning Solutions:
John Fedor

Managing Editor:
Robert L. Serenka, Jr.

Senior Acquisitions Editor:
Erin O'Connor

Editorial Assistant:
Alison Archambault

Director of Production:
Wendy A. Troeger

Production Manager:
Mark Bernard

Content Project Manager:
Angela Iula

Technology Project Manager:
Sandy Charette

Director of Marketing:
Wendy E. Mapstone

Channel Manager:
Kristin McNary

Channel Manager:
Scott Chrysler

Marketing Specialist:
Erica S. Conley

Art Director:
Joy Kocsis

Cover Design:
Joseph Villanova

Library of Congress Cataloging-in-Publication Data

Essa, Eva.
    What to do when ... : practical guidance strategies for challenging behaviors / Eva Essa.—6th ed.
        p. cm.
    Rev. ed. of: A practical guide to solving preschool behavior problems, 2003.
    Includes bibliographical references and index.
    ISBN 1-4180-6716-4 (alk. paper)
    1. Problem children—Education (Preschool) 2. Behavior disorders in children. 3. Social learning. I. Essa, Eva. Practical guide to solving problems of preschool behavior problems. II. Title.

LC4801.E87 2007
649'.15—dc22

2007005134

NOTICE TO THE READER

Contents

Section 4   **Destructive Behaviors**

Section 5   **Emotional and Dependent Behaviors**

Section 6   **Participation in Social and School Activities**

Section 7   **Eating Behaviors**

Section 8   Multiple Challenging Behaviors

Contents

Preface

When I first conceived of this text, formerly called *A Practical Guide to Solving Preschool Behavior Problems,* it was, to a great extent, in response to almost 10 years of teaching early childhood education students. In the course that focused on guidance principles in early childhood, I was often confronted by students who found the existing texts and resource books on the topic interesting but just not specific enough. Their response generally was, "Yes, I understand and appreciate the theory and general principles, but what do I do when . . . ?" As you may guess, this is the source of the new title. My students expressed concern with Tasha, who never seemed to want to interact with other children; with Roger, whose teeth seemed to sink into the body parts of his friends with lightning speed; or with Graciella, whose picky eating behavior caused concern to her parents and teachers. Thus, I began to think about how I might convey information on developmentally appropriate guidance practices in a specific and helpful manner.

In the more than 25 years since publication of the first edition of *A Practical Guide to Solving Preschool Behavior Problems,* I have heard from numerous teachers of young children who have found the practical, behavior-specific approach of this book helpful. As with the first through fifth editions, this sixth edition is intended to help teachers develop appropriate, positive guidance techniques. The text presents a workable method, developed through extensive research, for dealing effectively with children's behavior. The suggested methods match techniques with behaviors. The text is set up to provide step-by-step instructions on dealing with very specific challenging behaviors. A review of the table of contents will show you the wide variety of behaviors that are considered.

One of the main features of *What to Do When. . . . Practical Guidance Strategies for Challenging Behaviors* is that it focuses your attention first on possible underlying causes of the behavior. Before deciding to change a child's challenging behavior, you are directed to examine the child's environment carefully to discern which factors might be provoking the behavior. For example, it is essential to learn as much as possible about the child's home life and about any medical factors that may affect behavior. It is also very important to examine the early childhood environment, including the people in that environment, to find factors that might be reinforcing a particular behavior. This aspect of the book is discussed in each chapter in a section entitled Explore Alternatives.

Particularly in today's changing world, children's behaviors are often a reaction to factors that profoundly affect their lives but that are beyond their control to change. Thus, you, as the teacher, are urged to examine what might be triggering challenging behaviors and to help children cope more effectively with stressful factors in their lives.

Another feature of this book is a focus on working and consulting with the family. Each chapter provides suggestions for consulting with the family of a child about the behavior that is of concern. Some general guidelines for working with the family are also found in Chapter 6, Working with Families. This chapter and the sections in each of the following chapters underscore the importance of involving the parents in finding a resolution to behavior challenges.

The sixth edition has some new content and new features. One revised element in this book has to do with the all-too-frequently used strategy, time-out. As in previous editions, you are encouraged to use this strategy very sparingly. In addition, in this sixth edition, both the name and the approach to this technique have been changed. To reflect what its intent should be, this strategy is called "self-control time." The steps in carrying it out are now less teacher-controlled and more child-directed. Sometimes children need some time away from the bustle and activity of the class to calm down and regain their equilibrium—their self-control. Teachers can help children find such opportunities by providing a quiet place for this purpose. Children, however, are the ones who know when they feel that they are back in control. Thus, in this edition, it is suggested that children be trusted to determine when their self-control time should end. Teachers who have used this approach have found it to be a very effective tool. You will read more about it in Chapter 5 and in the few chapters in which self-control time is a recommended strategy.

One new feature of this sixth edition is a CD-ROM found at the back of the book. This CD contains helpful information for implementing the suggested strategies discussed in this book. Throughout the book you will find the following icon when you should refer to the CD for additional resources. The CD-ROM contains three discrete sections.

- Step-by-step instructions on how to keep effective records of the behavior under discussion. Information on how to keep track of behavior changes through graphs and other record-keeping devices are discussed in detail.
- A section called Your Turn is a set of scenarios intended to help you apply the principles presented in this text to hypothetical situations. The previous edition of this book included some scenarios, but this sixth edition includes a larger number for your consideration. It also includes a checklist to use in preparing for

Family–Teacher Conferences and a suggested activity for applying it to the preceding practice scenarios.

- The final element included in the CD is an expanded list of resources. You will find a listing of pertinent books, articles, and Web sites that can be of help to you as you work with young children. In particular, there are more resources on working with children with disabilities to help you maximize your understanding of each child and the strategies that might be most effective.

The author and Delmar Learning affirm that the Web site URLs referenced herein were accurate at the time of printing. However, because of the fluid nature of the Internet, we cannot guarantee their accuracy for the life of the edition.

My hope is that these changes will provide even more effective practical assistance to those who work with young children on a day-to-day basis. Sensitive support and guidance of individual children, based on an understanding of the children in your class in general and of each child in particular, will contribute to the development of secure and resourceful young people because they have been helped to cope effectively with today's social issues.

The work on this sixth edition has been, as always, supported directly and indirectly by my family and colleagues. The positive work environment provided by colleagues in the Department of Human Development and Family Studies is a mainstay of any endeavor I undertake. Thus, I want to express my gratitude for their support to Sally Martin, Colleen Murray, Sherry Waugh, Melissa Burnham, Leah Sanders, Becky Carter-Steele, and the other members of my department. My deepest appreciation for his never-failing support goes to my husband, Ahmed Essa, without whose encouragement none of these editions would have been written.

Eva L. Essa, Ph.D.
Reno, Nevada
August 2006

ABOUT THE AUTHOR

Eva L. Essa is Foundation Professor and chair of the Department of Human Development and Family Studies at the University of Nevada, Reno, where she has taught for more than 35 years. For 16 years, Dr. Essa served as Director of the Child and Family Research Center, the campus early childhood program. She is author of two other books, *Introduction to Early Childhood Education* (5th ed., Delmar Learning, 2007) and, with Penny Royce-Rogers, *An Early Childhood Curriculum: From Developmental Model to Application* (Delmar Learning, 1992). Dr. Essa also conducted a statewide census of the child care workforce for the state of Nevada, information that has been used to guide statewide policy changes for the improvement of child care. Dr. Essa's research and writing on topics related to early childhood education have been published in a variety of professional journals and books.

REVIEWERS

Judy A. Lindman, M.Ed.
Child Development instructor at community and technical college
Rochester, MN

Pamela Davis, Ph.D.
Professor of Early Childhood & Director of university child center
Arkadelphia, AR

Judy Rose-Paterson
Early Childhood Educator for preschool
Escondido, CA

Pamela E. Chibucos, MS
Professor of Early Childhood Education at community college
Toledo, OH

Mary E. Harder, Ph.D.
Adjunct Early Childhood professor at two-year college
Punta Gorda, FL

Tamara B. Calhoun, MS
Professor of Early Childhood Education at community college
Schenectady, NY

Teresa Frazier, MS
Early Childhood Education Program Head at community college
Hampton, VA

Debbie Stoll, M.Ed.
Instructor of Early Childhood Education at university
Lawton, OK

Julie Bakerlis, M.S.
Instructor of Early Childhood Education at community college
Worcester, MA

SECTION 1
Overview

chapter 1

Introduction: How to Use this Book

This book is intended to help you, as an early childhood teacher, in your most important job of helping young children to learn about and to assimilate the rules and expectations of our society. Because young children are continuously learning what is and what is not acceptable, your reaction to children's behaviors is a significant element in the social learning process. When and how you respond to children not only affects their present behavior but also has implications for their development over time. So when a child engages in challenging behaviors, your choice of a guidance strategy not only addresses the immediate behavior but also contributes to the process of socialization.

This book is intended to provide a guide for dealing with specific behavioral concerns. The techniques outlined in the chapters that focus on discrete behavioral challenges are not proposed as formulas for changing behavior but, rather, are intended as guides. The suggestions are meant to encourage you to think seriously about why a child is behaving as she is and then provide a starting point for systematically dealing with the challenging behavior.

A FEW WORDS ABOUT THEORY

Teachers use a variety of techniques to deal with children's behaviors. Each of these is often based on a specific theory that provides a rationale for why a given technique should work. Many teachers find

3

that a combination of techniques, drawn from a variety of theoretical approaches, works best. The suggestions outlined in this book are drawn from a variety of theoretical approaches. The following discussion provides a brief look at guidance techniques derived from four specific theories—behavioral, psychoanalytic, humanistic, and cognitive—and how these are incorporated into this book.

Behavioral Theory. According to behavioral theory (one of whose main proponents was B. F. Skinner), behavior, whether appropriate or not, is learned as children react to their environment and the people in it. As children interact with peers and adults, they learn ways of responding, reacting, and behaving in social situations. They also learn how others respond and react to their social behaviors. As a result, children adopt behaviors that appear to them to meet the expectations of others.

Both adaptive and challenging behaviors develop in this way. What children do is either reinforced or not reinforced by those around them. Acceptable behavior continues if it is reinforced. Similarly, challenging behavior also continues if it is reinforced. Both kinds of behaviors can be eliminated if they are not reinforced. Children continue many challenging behaviors because they get attention when they so behave, and they discontinue many appropriate behaviors because they are not reinforced.

Challenging behaviors exhibited by young children stem either from patterns that have evolved in their past or from lack of understanding (caused by limited social experience) of what is expected of them. This is normal. With skill, adults can systematically change children's unacceptable behaviors to behaviors that are more suitable.

Because behaviorism attempts to function as a precise science, behavior is defined only by what is observable (for instance, actions or words such as hitting, biting, pouting, and name-calling), rather than by what is not observable (for instance, motives or feelings such as jealousy, anger, and sadness). This focus on the observable is especially relevant for keeping records about how often the behavior happens, and any decrease or increase in the incidence of the behavior. Record-keeping is discussed in more detail in the Record-Keeping section of the CD-ROM.

Social learning, a theory espoused by Albert Bandura, adds to the behavioral approach by suggesting that children also learn how to respond to a wide variety of situations by observing other people and modeling or imitating their behavior. Observational learning occurs often in early childhood classrooms (for instance, when children exhibit traits such as empathy, caring, politeness, and care for materials modeled by teachers and peers). Children are particularly likely to imitate those they admire and like, or those with whom they identify in some way. In addition, certain conditions (for instance, children seeing a behavior being praised) will be more likely to result in imitation of a behavior.

Many of the techniques suggested in this book are based on behavioral theory. For instance, each chapter suggests that teachers carefully identify and define the challenging behavior using observable and measurable criteria. In addition, each chapter also recommends purposeful reinforcement of appropriate behavior, along with various other techniques such as modeling and ignoring.

Psychoanalytic Theory. Psychoanalytic theory, which stems from the work of Sigmund Freud, offers another approach to examining why children behave as they do and to providing techniques for dealing with challenging behaviors. This theory emphasizes the importance of examining underlying factors that might be at the root of a given behavior.

Rudolph Dreikurs, co-author of *Children: The Challenge* (Dreikurs and Soltz 1964), considers that all challenging behavior stems from one of four underlying motives: children may behave as they do because they seek attention, because they are engaged in a struggle for power with an adult, because they want revenge against an adult, or because they feel helpless and unable to accomplish reasonable expectations. Adults must first determine the cause of a behavior before they can effectively deal with it. Dreikurs promotes the use of encouragement and logical consequences rather than rewards and punishments to change challenging behavior.

Another application derived from psychoanalytic theory is based on Erik Erikson's (1963) stages of psychosocial development. Accordingly, it is very important to be sensitive to the needs of children at a given stage and to recognize the task facing them at that point in development. Infants, for instance, need to develop a sense of trust, which is established by providing babies with a consistent, loving environment. Establishment of a strong sense of trust is a fundamental and necessary foundation for positive relationships and guidance.

Toddlers and young preschoolers are struggling to achieve a sense of autonomy evident in the need to assert their fast-developing motor, language, and cognitive abilities. Thus, they need many opportunities to exercise independence within a safe, loving, and reasonable environment. Young children who fail to gain autonomy will continue to the next stage of development with a sense of shame and doubt.

According to Erikson, in their next stage of development, children between the ages of three and five strive to achieve a sense of initiative. They need to be able to explore, satisfy their curiosity, and try new ventures without undue censure and criticism from adults. Otherwise, they develop a sense of guilt and failure.

As children reach the end of the preschool years, they focus more on the development of a sense of industry. They like to plan, carry out, and complete projects. They also lay the foundations for habits of workmanship, persistence, and deeper understanding of social rules. Failure to achieve an adequate sense of industry results in children who settle for mediocrity and a sense of inferiority.

Aspects of the psychoanalytic approach are also incorporated in this book. For instance, throughout the book you will find recommendations that lead you to examine carefully what might be the cause of challenging behavior. So often, children's behavior is a reaction to situations over which they have no control and which they do not understand, such as a divorce, a new sibling, or a health problem. When adults try to fathom what may be triggering a certain behavior, they are in a better position to deal effectively and sensitively with such challenges.

In addition, this book encourages you to take into consideration the psychosocial stages of development of children who may act in challenging ways. The young child who attempts to achieve a sense of autonomy may clash with classroom expectations by grabbing a toy from another child, by biting or hitting when frustrated, or by frequently saying "No!" in response to reasonable requests. The teacher who realizes that such behavior reflects the child's immature expressions of autonomy, rather than deviant behavior, can gently guide, explain, and rechannel the behavior in a positive manner.

Humanistic Theory. Other guidance techniques, for instance those proposed by Thomas Gordon, author of *P.E.T.: Parent Effectiveness Training* (1974), are based on humanistic theory. Humanistic theory builds on the tenet that mutual respect and acceptance between adults and children must underscore all interactions. When a child "owns" a problem, the teacher must respect the child's right and ability to solve the problem. Thus, the teacher does not give advice, moralize, or distract the child. Instead, the teacher uses *active listening,* a technique in which the essence of what a child is conveying is reflected back to the child ("It sounds like you are upset because Ariel and Mary won't let you play with them."). Such a reflective response suggests that adults understand what children are communicating while, at the same time, allowing the children to come to their own resolution of the problem.

When adults own the problem, a different technique is called for. Teachers use *I-messages* to tell children how their actions make the teachers feel ("When I find the blocks all over the floor, I'm afraid someone will trip and get hurt, and that really upsets me."). Teachers do not send a *you-message* ("You are being very irresponsible when you don't clean up the blocks.").

Elements of humanistic theory are incorporated into this book as well. Carefully listening to the child, conveying your own feelings in an honest way, and not belittling are strategies that should be a part of any plan to deal with challenging behavior. Above all, any plan to change a child's challenging behavior must be approached with great care and respect for the child.

Cognitive Theory. Cognitive theory, particularly in its specific focus on moral development, also suggests some guidance techniques. Jean Piaget laid the groundwork for cognitive theory by identifying stages through which children's cognitive development, including moral development, evolve. Children's increasing capacity for logical thought and their growing autonomy are nurtured by teachers who use *inductive reasoning*. Teachers help children understand the consequences of their behavior for other people through logic and reasoning; the focus is on the rights and feelings of others rather than on punitive admonitions or restrictions. In addition, adults allow children many opportunities to make decisions and experience the consequences of those decisions. Inductive reasoning and opportunities for decision-making help children develop self-control. As a result, children's actions will gradually be based more and more on an inner sense of integrity rather than on merely doing what they are told to do (Kamii 1984). Children who have been brought up from the start in a nurturing, respectful atmosphere will be more likely to follow reasonable expectations because these are logical.

Lev Vygotsky's theory also adds suggestions for guidance of young children. In this sociocultural theory, he particularly emphasizes the role of adults and older peers in helping children learn about the expectations and parameters of their culture. He emphasizes the importance of adults' frequent scaffolding of experiences for young children, giving them just enough guidance so they can learn a new skill. This holds true for learning perceptual-motor skills such as putting together a puzzle, gross motor skills such as learning to pedal a tricycle, or social skills such as learning to share items for mutually satisfying play (Berk 1994).

This book draws on cognitive theory as well. When teachers are mindful that children need to develop increasing self-discipline, this understanding is reflected in their interactions with children, their explicit and implicit expectations, and the guidance techniques they use. In this way, children are helped to become increasingly aware of the impact of their behavior on others and to develop socially responsible behaviors. Adults' scaffolding to help children develop skills that are just out of their reach if undertaken alone helps children develop competence in social as well as other developmental skills.

ASSUMPTIONS

The strategies provided in this book are based on some fundamental assumptions about the circumstances and atmosphere in which the suggested strategies should be used. Before teachers seek resolutions to behavioral challenges, they must ensure that some basic conditions are present.

The Environment and the Teachers. The suggestions outlined in this book for dealing with specific behavioral challenges should be carried out only within a child-oriented, developmentally appropriate setting that promotes and facilitates positive interactions and activities. Furthermore, teachers who work with young children must recognize the importance of their role in guiding those children. Teachers must be consistent, objective, and thoughtful. They must also recognize that young children's behaviors are often the result of curiosity and experimentation. Furthermore, they must see that a difficult child is one who is engaging in challenging behavior rather than a "bad" child. In Chapter 2, the setting, including the teacher's role, in encouraging appropriate behavior will be discussed in greater depth.

Why Children Engage in Challenging Behavior. Another assumption on which this book is founded concerns the reasons why children might behave in a way that challenges adults. Teachers must be very careful in examining why a child exhibits certain behaviors. They must never assume that something is wrong with the child or that something has to be done *to* the child to alter the behavior. Often, environmental factors, including the behavior of the teacher, are at the root of behavioral challenges. Each chapter that considers a specific behavior includes a discussion of possible reasons for it. Teachers must eliminate all possible external explanations before they attempt to change the child's behavior. Chapter 3 provides a more thorough discussion of some of the reasons why children might exhibit challenging behaviors.

Rules and Expectations. A third assumption on which this book is based is that children have to understand what is expected of them.

If children are unaware of which behaviors are acceptable and which are not, they cannot be expected to comply. Early childhood programs should have some simple, common-sense rules that the children can help to develop. Most rules for preschoolers should be centered on safety—acts that could result in injury to oneself or others must be prevented. Logical rules are easy to follow. Frequent review of the rules and explanations of the reasons behind them help prevent many challenging behaviors.

In addition, it is important to realize that there may be times when children's behavior is challenging because they simply are not aware that their actions are unacceptable. Although children generally know when they are behaving in a way that adults do not like, this is not always the case. It is important, therefore, that adults help children make the distinction between acceptable and unacceptable behavior. If children are unaware of the effect of their actions, sometimes a simple verbal explanation will suffice. In other circumstances, the expected behavior may have to be modeled or taught in a more systematic way. If, on the other hand, children understand that what they are doing is unacceptable but continue anyway, teachers must consider how to change the behavior, as discussed in the ensuing chapters of this book.

Consistency. The strategies suggested in this book are also based on the assumption that they will be carried out consistently. Successfully changing unacceptable behavior depends on consistent action—to obtain desirable results in changing a child's behavior, it is extremely important to carry out a plan faithfully. When children behave in a particular way over a period of time, it is because the reactions of people around them reinforce such behavior. To change the behavior, reinforcement must be completely omitted.

If an adult ignores challenging behavior most of the time but then periodically pays attention to it, the child becomes confused. Inconsistent reactions will be disconcerting, and the youngster may seek the old, expected reactions by increasing the behavior.

Frequency of the Behavior. Another assumption of this book has to do with how often the behavior occurs. The strategies described are intended for use with behaviors that are repeated consistently. A child may behave in an inappropriate way in isolated circumstances. For example, the child may be tired, a stressful situation may exist at home, or the child may be provoked by a classmate. In such cases, the child should be told quietly that such behavior is not acceptable. At the same time, the cause can be explained. If possible, the situation should be remedied; for instance, you can have the tired child lie down in a quiet area. Not all situations have a solution, but the child can know that the adult is sympathetic. If the same challenging behavior is repeated regularly over a period of time, something in the environment may be reinforcing the behavior. Examine the situation more closely and take systematic steps to remedy it.

Home–School Communications. Finally, this book assumes that working with challenging behavior is, in most cases, enhanced when teachers and parents work together. A teacher who is concerned about a child's repeated challenging behavior should discuss it with the child's parents in an honest, nonthreatening manner. The parents may have a similar concern about the behavior. If they work on the issue together, parents and teachers may find that a combined home–school approach is most effective. It is also possible that the parents feel differently about the child's behavior than does the teacher. In this case, it is important to clarify the underlying values and come to an understanding.

HOW TO USE THIS BOOK

This book is intended to help preschool teachers deal effectively with behaviors that occur in most early childhood settings. If a teacher decides to change a particular behavior that is considered challenging, the behavior that most closely fits the situation should be located in the table of contents. Some of the most common behavioral situations in early childhood settings are covered in the text. The discussion of each specific behavior is dealt with in a self-contained manner. To work on a particular behavior, study the chapter that is most closely related to that behavior.

All chapters are presented in a standardized format. The format material identifies and explains the sections of each chapter, and discusses how to use the information.

STATE THE BEHAVIOR

This section identifies the specific behavior.

OBSERVE THE BEHAVIOR

Before an attempt is made to deal with challenging behavior, all available information about the behavior should be gathered. This section suggests some possible clues as to when, where, how, or why the behavior occurs. Some, but not all, of the suggestions will be relevant to the particular situation. Therefore, to carry out the intent of this section, all teachers in the classroom should carefully watch the child for a few days. Conscious observation often yields some invaluable information and provides the basis for more a more focused approach to changing the behavior. It should be added that not all the suggestions made in this section are related to the outlined approach to changing the behavior. They are presented to help you examine as many aspects of the behavior as possible.

CONSULT WITH THE FAMILY

Each chapter suggests ways of working with the child's family in finding effective strategies to resolve behavioral challenges. As discussed in more detail in Chapter 6, before discussing concerns with family members, it is important to have built a good relationship based on trust and mutual respect. On such a foundation, challenges can be discussed more productively. In discussing your concerns with the family, you have the opportunity to exchange information and to work cooperatively to find a solution to the issue. Family members, for instance, can help you understand whether the child's behavior occurs in circumstances or settings other than at school. Working together in finding a solution and implementing an approach also provides consistency for the child, and will ensure that the resolution is supported both at school and at home. It is also very important to keep the family informed of progress and to share the child's success in learning more appropriate behavioral alternatives.

CONSIDER THE IMPLICATIONS

This section explores what can happen if a challenging behavior is not altered. Teachers sometimes react in self-defeating ways when dealing with unacceptable behavior. These actions may tend to strengthen the challenging behavior, establishing a vicious cycle in which efforts to change the behavior only reinforce it.

EXPLORE ALTERNATIVES

An important consideration in this book is that challenging behavior does not always stem directly from the child. This section examines some alternatives to changing the child's overall behavior in order to eliminate a challenging behavior. Often, the environment encourages a certain behavior. For example, rearranging furniture in a crowded area may eliminate a child's tendency to hit others when in the area. This section should be given careful consideration after making the initial observation. By no means should you begin to plan behavioral change until all other possible alternatives are examined.

STATE THE GOAL

The goal for the child whose behavior you want to change is stated in this section. The goal is a suggestion, and may vary according to the child, the setting, the teachers, and the family's expectations. For one child, it may be desirable to eliminate a certain behavior completely. For another, it may be an accomplishment to simply diminish the behavior. Have a goal in mind before starting so that progress can be measured against it.

APPROACH

This section presents a step-by-step method for changing the specific behavior addressed in the chapter.

DEFINITION

A concise definition of the behavior to be changed is presented. It is important that all adults who are involved with the child have the same concept of the behavior.

STRATEGIES

For each approach, several consecutive or simultaneous steps are outlined. Most of the behaviors discussed in this book suggest reinforcement of an alternative, appropriate behavior as one strategy. In some chapters, a strategy is presented for ignoring a challenging behavior. In other chapters, the approach involves gradual changes over time, with steps provided for increases in expectation within each specified period.

STARTING POINT

Before beginning an approach for changing a child's behavior, it is important to have a sense of the severity or magnitude of the issue. For instance, how often does Sarah hit other children? How many times a day does Pete call other children names? How long do Juan's tantrums last? How many minutes does Alyson stay with an activity before she abandons it and moves on to something new? Having some information about the child's behavior before you begin a systematic approach to change it gives you a base against which change can later be compared. The Record-Keeping section of the CD-ROM provides a more thorough discussion of how to maintain such records in a simple and helpful manner.

MAINTAINING THE CHANGES

Once a goal is reached, it is important to maintain it. Suggestions are given to help the child continue with the appropriate behavior and not go back to the earlier challenging behavior.

CONCLUSION

As you review the instructions for use of this book, you may think that it sounds like a lot of work. It is, therefore, important to realize that if troubling behaviors are not dealt with effectively, you will have to spend considerable time and energy trying to cope with them. The time and energy expended in this way is taken away from positive interactions with the children in your class.

Time management is important. Even more vital is the effect of challenging behavior on the child's self-concept. Adults' reactions to challenging behaviors tend to be, in one way or another, negative. The child who receives such negative attention does not develop good feelings of self-worth.

When a challenging behavior is eliminated, both the teacher and the child benefit. Furthermore, the child learns that appropriate behavior is rewarding.

REFERENCES

Berk, L. E. 1994. Vygotsky's theory: The importance of make-believe play. *Young Children, 50*(1), 30–39.

Dreikurs, R., & Soltz, V. 1964. *Children: The challenge.* New York: Duell, Sloan and Pearce.

Erikson, E. H. 1963. *Childhood and society* (2nd ed.). New York: W. W. Norton.

Gordon, T. 1974. *P.E.T.: Parent effectiveness training.* New York: Peter H. Wyden.

Kamii, C. 1984. Obedience is not enough. *Young Children, 39*(4), 11–14.

chapter 2

Setting a Positive Environment to Encourage Appropriate Behavior

One of the most effective ways to encourage appropriate behavior is to set up an environment that fosters such behavior. A carefully considered, developmentally appropriate environment provides a setting in which children can constructively engage in a wide variety of growth-promoting activities. The early childhood environment, in its broadest sense, includes the arrangement of the physical setting, the materials and activities provided within that setting, the management of time, and the actions and reactions of the adults involved. In this chapter, we will discuss these four elements, considering how each can have a positive effect on children's behaviors.

ARRANGEMENT OF THE PHYSICAL SETTING

Early childhood classrooms typically contain a wide variety of equipment and materials designed to help children develop in physical, cognitive, social, and emotional ways. The environment can be arranged to maximize children's constructive and prosocial behavior. It must show respect for the children by taking their needs and developmental levels into account.

A good early childhood environment, for instance, enhances both fine and gross motor skills through a range of appropriately challenging equipment and materials. The arrangement of the classroom and careful selection of materials also foster cognitive development by providing opportunities for children to classify, find relationships, measure, compare, match, sort, and label items. Positive peer interactions are promoted when the classroom is not crowded, when there are an ample number and variety of items available, and when many of the materials promote cooperation and social play. Children's growing sense of independence is nurtured when they can confidently and competently use equipment appropriate to their abilities and size and when space and materials are arranged so that children can see what is available and make autonomous choices. An appropriate environment also enhances children's self-esteem because it is designed with their needs and development in mind.

Thought and care should be given to arranging the classroom; this task should never be undertaken haphazardly. The beginning of the school year is a good time to consider how best to arrange the classroom. As the year progresses and children change, the room arrangement should be modified to reflect their current abilities, interests, and attention spans.

Messages Sent by the Environment. The way classroom furnishings are placed and grouped communicates many messages to children. For instance, when all the blocks are stored on shelves that surround a well-defined area of the floor out of the flow of traffic, the message clearly is, "This is where you can build with the blocks where they won't be knocked down and where they won't pose a hazard to others." When furniture is arranged so that there are no large, open spaces, the message is, "Inside the classroom, we walk rather than run." When each child has a private space for her belongings, the message is, "Your belongings are valuable, and so are you." When quiet activities are grouped at one end of the room and noisy ones at the other, the message is, "There are places where it's okay to be loud and others where we are more quiet." When the housekeeping area is enclosed to comfortably hold four or five children, the message is, "This is a place where we can play with a few of our friends." When the environment conveys such unspoken messages, appropriate behavior is encouraged.

Some Guidelines for Arranging Space. There are many useful guidelines that can help teachers arrange the classroom to maximize positive behavior. The size and shape of the room or rooms and placement of doors and windows will, to some extent, dictate how a classroom can be arranged. Beyond these fixed features, however, there are many ways to arrange an early childhood center. In setting up the room, it is important that the total arrangement achieve a sense of harmony that is comfortable for children and teachers alike. Colors should be pleasing and coordinated, light from windows or light fixtures should be used to best enhance activities, wall spaces should serve to integrate and complement the room, and furnishings should be arranged in an organized and logical way. Careful use of carpeting and wall covering can decrease noise in the room.

Classroom activity areas should be clearly delineated. Indoor space is usually organized into discrete learning centers or interest areas. Such centers combine materials and equipment around common activities such as art, manipulatives, blocks, dramatic play, music, science, math, language arts, woodworking, cooking, computers, sensory activities such as sand and water play, and a variety of other functions. Learning centers allow children to make choices from available materials, which are arranged in an organized fashion on low shelves. When children can readily see the materials and have easy access to them, they can independently select what they wish to play with and later return the materials to their appropriate places. In addition, pathways through the room should be clear and unobstructed, as should be doorways.

Activity areas should also be grouped in a logical way. Quiet and noisy activities should be separated. Manipulatives, art, language arts, math, and science are generally quieter and should be grouped away from the more noisy areas in which block-building, housekeeping, large motor, or music activities are placed. Activities that have common elements can also be grouped to extend play possibilities. Juxtaposing blocks and dramatic play, for example, can encourage expanded play.

A good early childhood classroom has places for large-group, small-group, and individual activities. Most classroom teachers designate some area where all the children participate in group activities such as story-reading, movement, or music at one or more times during the day. The room should also have a variety of areas in which small groups of children can play together, particularly during self-selected activity times. In addition, private spaces are needed, especially when children spend full days in child care centers; it is important to take into consideration their needs for privacy and comfort. Private, enclosed spaces where a child can occasionally get away from the bustle and activity of the classroom should be available. This might be in a quiet area such as the library, or it could be set up by bringing a small appliance box into the room with one side and the top open to view, and some soft pillows, cuddly toys, and books inside. Children should also have access to cozy, soft places such as beanbag chairs, pillows, or rugs where they can snuggle and find comfort.

One of the most important aspects of the early childhood environment is attention to safety. Safety should, in fact, be an overriding concern in setting up an environment for young children. Any furnishings that are not set against walls should be sturdy and steady so they cannot be knocked over. Electrical outlets should be covered. Sharp edges should be eliminated from all furniture and storage units. A well-organized room with clearly defined boundaries and pathways will minimize safety concerns.

All aspects of the physical environment contribute to children's behavior. When the environment is pleasant, warm, and inviting, it gives children the message that this is a place designed for them. When the environment sets natural boundaries, children find it easier to follow the rules. When the environment tacitly indicates the types of activities that can be carried out, children are more likely to engage in these activities. When the environment shows respect for children, they are more likely to show respect in return.

MATERIALS AND ACTIVITIES

Room arrangement sets the stage, but appropriate materials and activities are imperative in any good early childhood program. These need to fit ages and developmental ability so that children are challenged with an appropriate level of difficulty. If materials and activities are too easy, children may well get bored; if they are too difficult, children will get frustrated. Both boredom and frustration can lead to challenging behavior.

Appropriate Materials. A wealth of appropriate materials—both commercial and homemade—is available for early childhood programs. The selection of these for your particular program must take into account their developmental appropriateness for the children. Also, the materials should encompass a wide range of activities and options. They should enhance all areas of development. One way to ensure that they do is to select a variety of materials to fit into the classroom learning centers discussed above.

For very young preschoolers, play items that encourage vocabulary-building, promote a sense of balance, exercise fingers, and allow for the children's growing sense of independence should be included. A classroom for younger preschoolers generally should be more rudimentary and have fewer items than one for older children, and there should be duplicates of many objects to accommodate young preschoolers' limited social abilities. Older preschoolers, on the other hand, enjoy a more complex, challenging environment with a wider selection of materials that use their more refined skills in all areas of development. Their environment should also provide many materials that promote social play.

All early childhood materials should promote active involvement and exploration. Anything that requires no action on the part of children or does not stretch their imaginations will quickly bore them. One way to ensure active involvement is to provide a wide range of open-ended materials. For example, blocks and props for dramatic play can be used flexibly and do not dictate specifically how they are to be used. Not all materials should be open-ended, of course; puzzles, for instance, have only a single correct outcome.

Appropriate Activities. Within the environmental setting, teachers usually plan a curriculum with a wide range of activities designed to enhance learning and development. Like materials, activities have to be developmentally appropriate to suit the needs and interests of the children. They also must actively involve children; thus, an activity that the teacher carries out while the children passively watch is inappropriate.

Young children's interests and their concrete understanding of the world provide some parameters within which to select appropriate topics for activities. Activities should be derived from the children's life experiences, be based on what is concrete, and be tied to their emerging skills. Activities that enhance and expand understanding of self, family, school, and community are appropriate for preschoolers, who are still very much bound by their immediate world.

Materials and activities also contribute to children's behavior. When these are developmentally appropriate, they give children the message that these materials and activities were designed especially for them. When materials and activities are appropriately challenging, children will participate in productive endeavors. When there is a wide variety of materials and activities to enhance all areas of development and meet all interests, children will find constructive ways to fill their time. When materials and activities are selected to show respect for children, the children are more likely to show respect for the classroom and the people in it.

MANAGEMENT OF TIME

Another aspect of the environment that can dramatically affect children's behavior is the way time is scheduled. The daily schedule of the early childhood program must take into account and be sensitive to the developmental abilities and needs of the children. It has to provide a secure, predictable structure that, at the same time, leaves room for some flexibility. There is no one way to set a schedule; in fact, because the schedule should adapt to the children, it often has to be adjusted somewhat differently for each individual group.

Components of the Daily Schedule. The daily schedule has to balance blocks of time to accommodate the day's activities. Most early childhood programs include large blocks of time for self-selected activities in which the children themselves choose what they would like to do from available materials and activities. There are times for large-group activities in which children and teachers all gather for story-reading, music, movement, or discussion. Sizable blocks of time are devoted to outdoor play. Time for functional activities such as meals, naps or rest, and toileting must also be planned. In addition, it is wise to schedule cleanup times to put the classroom back into order. This conveys to teachers and children that cleaning up is an important component of the program.

Guidelines for Program Scheduling. Arranging the components of the schedule in an effective way include alternating active and quiet times to fit the children's needs for expending energy and for relaxing. Children should have the opportunity to be physically active after they have been in a quiet activity and conversely, to slow down after active involvement. Take into account, therefore, a cycle that balances the more boisterous outdoor play, activity times, and movement exercises with the more sedate story-reading, nap, or snack time.

It is also important to balance child-initiated and teacher-initiated activities throughout the day. Most programs provide large time blocks during which children can make decisions about the activities in which they participate and how they carry them out and times when teachers direct activities. Child-initiated activities help children develop qualities such as autonomy, judgment, independent decision-making, social give-and-take, initiative, exploration, and creativity. Adult-initiated activities encourage compliance with reasonable adult direction and acceptance of the authority and wisdom of adults. A careful balance, with the bulk of activities being child-initiated, will help children develop these qualities.

The schedule also needs to take into account the developmental level of the children. For older preschoolers, who have greater attention spans, you can plan longer time blocks for activities such as story, music, and activity times. Younger preschoolers cannot be expected to sit for more than 5 or 10 minutes for group activities; however, they may need extra time for functional activities such as meals, toileting, naps, and cleanup. Also take into account the general activity level of the children. If a large proportion of the group is particularly active, the schedule should include more opportunities for active outlets. Finally, the weather can also affect the schedule. When temperatures reach extremes, the schedule should be adapted to allow for more active indoor alternatives.

Transitions. One very important but often neglected aspect of the schedule is time between activities. It is helpful to think of transitions as part of the schedule: times that offer many learning opportunities for children. Think through the sequence of events as children go from one area to another, such as from the circle rug to the bathroom to the snack table, or from cleanup time to putting on coats to going outside. If transitions are not thought through, these times can result in chaos.

Children should always be aware of upcoming transitions. You might alert them through a regularly used cue or signal such as a song, chant, record, bell, or flick of the lights to announce that cleanup time, group time, or outdoor time is coming up. Even before announcing the end of an activity, however, give children a warning. This allows them to finish activities in which they are involved. Let them know that in a few minutes they will have to clean up.

Some transitions are used to limit the flow of children to the next activity. It is easier to let 4 children go to the bathroom at regular short intervals to wash hands than to send 20 children at one time. A familiar song or fingerplay can be used effectively to achieve this goal.

The daily schedule also contributes to children's behavior. When an appropriate schedule is established and followed, the children have the security of knowing what to expect. When the schedule allows ample time for children to pursue their own interests, they will more likely be constructively engaged in activities. When the schedule carefully considers the children's needs for activity, rest, and nourishment, they are more likely to function appropriately. When a developmentally appropriate schedule shows respect for the needs and interests of the children, they are more likely to meet the adult's expectations in return.

ADULTS' ACTIONS AND REACTIONS

A final aspect of the early childhood setting includes the adults who work with the children. Their actions and reactions also contribute to the children's behavior. Teachers who are knowledgeable about child development and early childhood education principles are better able to understand the children in their class and to meet their individual needs. In fact, research has found that the most competent early childhood teachers are those with specific training in the field. In addition, personal characteristics such as warmth, nurturance, and patience also contribute to the profile of an effective early childhood teacher.

Working with young children is a demanding job that requires energy, enthusiasm, creativity, and openness. Teachers who recognize the importance of their jobs, particularly their contribution to the formation of young children's personalities, are those who approach the job with care and foresight. Such teachers make decisions about children's behavior thoughtfully. They react to children with respect and consistency. They recognize that their decisions and actions can have a strong impact on the children, and they do not make decisions hastily or unthinkingly. These teachers recognize that children need and deserve the best, and thus these teachers give it.

CONCLUSION

One of the fundamental ways of encouraging appropriate behavior in young children is to set up a positive environment. As you have seen in this chapter, providing such an environment involves careful arrangement of physical space, concern for supplying appropriate materials and activities, good management of time, and the thoughtful actions and reactions of the adults in the setting. In fact, what adults might see as inappropriate behavior may, in actuality, be the result of an inappropriate environment or inappropriate expectations by the adults. A high-quality early childhood program, in its best sense, is preventive in nature. By paying close attention to these elements, challenging behaviors are often circumvented.

Biting • Throwing Objects at Others • Hitting Others • Using Inappropri
Calling • Nonsharing • Bribery • Stealing • Noncompliance • Disrupting
the Classroom • Running Aimlessly Around the Classroom • Shouting in th
Objects to Create Noise • Tearing Books • Breaking Toys • Flushing Objects
Wasting Paper • Destroying the Work of Others • Throwing Tantrums • Po
Talk • Thumb-Sucking • Pant-Wetting • Clinging • Seeking Attention • S
n Only One To • Infrequent Large Muscle Activity • Infrequent Dramatic
• Overea
Eating • Hording Food • Hitting • Biting • Throwing Objects at Others • Hi
ting • Nonsharing • Bribery • Stealing
ing Group Time • Leaving the Classroom • Running Aimlessly Around th
g in the Classroom • Dropping Objects to Create Noise • Tearing Books
ushing Objects Down the Toilet • Wasting Paper • Destroying the Work o
owing Tantrums • Pouting • Baby Talk • Thumb-Sucking • Pant-Wetting

chapter **3**

Why Children Exhibit Challenging Behaviors

A wide range of behaviors is present in any preschool classroom. Children, as individuals, develop unique ways of responding to what goes on around them. Most of these behaviors are appropriate and develop further when adults or peers show approval.

Some behaviors are more challenging. A preschool class may include a child who hits, one who disrupts the class, one who has difficulty interacting with other children, and one who has frequent toileting accidents. Such behaviors are by no means uncommon but should cause concern. This book provides practical guidelines for helping children learn appropriate behaviors to replace the challenging ones.

Sometimes, children's behaviors are prompted by a need or desire for attention. A child may have learned that the best way to capture an adult's attention is to do something the adult does not consider to be appropriate. For instance, Perry has learned that Teacher Ann will give him undivided attention if he hits one of the other children. If Perry has established a pattern of hitting other children to get attention, then the techniques suggested in this book may be the best way to change this behavior. Consider that human behavior is driven by the fact that there is a payoff. In Perry's case, Teacher Ann's attention is enough to maintain his hitting behavior. Why not, after all? Perry has found a great way to get the attention he desires! In the later chapters in which specific behavioral challenges are discussed, you will find frequent reference to what exactly is prompting the child's behavior.

On the other hand, children's challenging behaviors often are the result of factors in the environment that are beyond their control. It is, therefore, important for you, as the teacher, to consider possible external factors that might be causing challenging behavior. In fact, a careful consideration of possible causes of challenging behavior should always come before a decision is made to change the child somehow. If, in fact, a child's behavior is triggered by something beyond her control, it is important that you try to alleviate the environmental condition whenever appropriate. Of course, it is not always possible to change the circumstances that have triggered the behavior. For instance, as the teacher, you cannot make a severe allergy or a new baby sister go away, but you can acknowledge that the child is under stress and help her find alternative coping strategies. Some strategies will be suggested in the following chapters.

Following is a discussion of some external factors over which children have little or no control. These should always be given careful consideration when examining challenging behaviors.

ENVIRONMENTAL FACTORS THAT TEACHERS CAN DIRECTLY AFFECT

Sometimes, children's behavior is the result of a factor in the immediate early childhood environment. We will begin by looking at those aspects a teacher may well be able to change.

Physical Environment. The physical environment in which children function is very important. The environment itself can encourage or discourage certain behaviors. For example, a large classroom with few dividers to break up space invites running. Materials placed on high shelves require the child to be dependent on teachers. Traffic flow through an activity area may result in disruptive behavior and aggression.

Space is important. A close circle for story time, a line for waiting to get into the bathroom, or any other time when children are crowded can result in pushing or other aggressive behavior. Children's natural activity level combined with too little personal space will result in problems.

The activities and materials provided within the larger environment need to be carefully evaluated. There need to be enough materials so that there is not undue competition or nothing for some children to do. Activities and materials need to be developmentally appropriate and varied enough to provide for growth in all developmental areas.

Children's behaviors need to be continually assessed in terms of the environment. Often, it is not the child who needs to be changed but the physical environment.

Inappropriate Expectations for Children's Developmental Levels.
Adults who work with young children should be aware of the levels of development of the children in the classroom. Each stage of development has unique characteristics, needs, and behaviors. Children may act out because too much or too little is expected of them and, as a result, they are either frustrated or bored.

Adult expectations need to be in line with the abilities of each child. The room arrangement, materials, activities, and daily routine should be planned to fit the specific characteristics of the group, as discussed in Chapter 2. Challenging behaviors can easily occur if expectations or environment are not appropriate for the age of the child. Being familiar with child development helps the teacher plan for and react accordingly to the two-year-old who wants to play with a toy alone rather than share it, the three-year-old who can sit still for only 15 minutes of show-and-tell, and the four-year-old who experiments with new words that are sometimes inappropriate.

Inconsistent Messages.
Adults may tell children that a behavior is unacceptable on one occasion but react differently the next time the behavior occurs. When different expectations are conveyed at different times, a child is not given a clear idea of what is acceptable and what is not. Teachers are often not aware of such inconsistencies, and need to tune in more consciously to just what they are conveying to children. Similarly, there may be inconsistency between what is expected at home and what is expected at school. Communication with the families to discuss differences is important. If these differences continue, a child can be told, "It is okay to wrestle with your brother at home, but we cannot do this at school." Successful change of unacceptable behavior depends on consistent action in response to that behavior.

Oversensitivity to Stimulation.
A good preschool program is one that is busy, constructively active, and colorful. Most children thrive in an appropriately stimulating environment, but for some, the color, noise, activity level, and movement can be overwhelming. Sometimes, children who seem overly active, unable to settle down to any activity, unusually disruptive, or aggressive may find it difficult to concentrate or exercise self-control because the environment is just too stimulating. When this is the case, the children will often show subtle signs of distress; for instance, they may physically tense up when their ability to cope has been overtaxed.

Teachers can help such children in several ways. One is to provide at least one quiet area in the classroom where children can retreat if the environment becomes overwhelming. Such an area should be isolated, small, have subdued colors, and be simple in design and decor. Another strategy is to examine the classroom as a whole and determine if it could be altered to benefit all of the children. For instance, classroom furnishings and materials could be more effectively arranged to convey a very distinct sense of order. The noise level could be cut down through better room arrangement and use of soft materials such as carpeting and pillows. More muted or fewer colors could be used to cut down on the visual impact of the classroom. Also, see the section on alone time in Chapter 5 for further discussion of this issue.

ENVIRONMENTAL FACTORS THAT TEACHERS CANNOT CHANGE

There are some other external causes that affect children's behavior but that are generally not within the teacher's ability to change. We will examine several such factors.

Health Problems. A child's health can have a definite effect on behavior. A teacher might think about how she reacts when she is not feeling well, when her nose is stuffed up, when her head throbs, or when her stomach aches. Children have fewer resources than do adults to handle their behavior when they are not feeling well. They may not be verbal enough to tell the teacher how they feel; thus, they may act out because they are not feeling well. A sick child should not be in school, but some children have chronic health problems or continuous low-grade infections that keep them in school, though with a lower level of tolerance and functioning. A teacher needs to be sensitive to the child's health status and lower resistance to frustration.

Allergies. Some children's behavior may be affected by food or environmental allergies. As a result a child may be overactive, cranky, or have a short attention span. It is important to know the diagnosed allergies of the children in the class and what reactions they have. Some children also may be affected by medications they are taking.

Poor Nutrition. Children's behavior can be affected by what they do or do not eat. A child who comes to school hungry, for instance without breakfast, is vulnerable and likely to be irritable, tired, and cranky. A child whose diet is imbalanced or who lacks certain nutrients will not work to potential and may misbehave. Information on food intake and the eating schedule of children can help detect nutrition-related problems. If, for instance, children have a long traveling time to school, it may be wise to have a snack available when they arrive rather than an hour or two later.

Sensory Deficits. Behavior can also be affected by hearing or sight problems. A child whose vision is impaired may appear to be insecure, unwilling to try, clumsy, uncoordinated, unable to follow instructions, or even willfully destructive. Similarly, a child who is not hearing well may appear to be overly loud, easily distracted, inattentive, overactive, or disruptive. It is important to watch children carefully for signs of hearing or vision impairment before assuming that their challenging behaviors are in their control.

Lack of Attachment. One of the most important needs of children during infancy is formation of a secure attachment to a significant adult. Most children form such an attachment with their mothers. Unfortunately, the lifestyles of and demands on today's busy parents sometimes do not leave enough time for children. Some babies fail to develop a strong attachment, which later in childhood can translate into behavioral challenges. There is a strong research connection between insecure attachment during infancy and later behavioral difficulties.

Family Stress or Change. Children may exhibit unusual behaviors because the routine they are used to has changed and they do not understand what is happening. This may mean family discord such as parental separation or divorce, frequent arguments, or money problems. Or the change may involve unusual circumstances such as a new sibling, visiting grandparents, a move to a new house, mother or father temporarily out of town, or any number of other changes. It is, therefore, important to maintain frequent and open communications with parents to understand what is happening at home and to interpret or even anticipate children's behavioral reactions.

Stress of Modern Life. Today, many children lead lives that are hectic and busy. They are on the go, as their busy parents are, participating in various activities such as ballet or gymnastics, or traveling with their parents on vacations. Such experiences are enriching and enjoyable for children, but can fill their time so fully that there is little left for reflection and, often, play. In addition, many children experience more than one child care arrangement, and some as many as four or five on a regular basis. This "patchwork" of care is often a reflection of their parents' need for alternatives in care so they can meet their own busy schedules.

A side effect of being cared for by multiple adults may also be varied and inconsistent rules and expectations.

CONCLUSION

Children's challenging behaviors are not uncommon. There are many reasons why children behave as they do. Before an assumption is made that the behavior is in the child's control, it is important that other factors that might affect the child's behavior be carefully considered. If the behavior is in response to a situation that is beyond the child's control, then the teacher needs to try to remedy the situation if possible. If the root of the problem cannot be changed, as, for example, a chronic health disability or divorce, then the child can be helped to best cope with the situation through empathic and supportive help from the teacher.

You will find additional resources about children's behavior and causes of challenging behaviors in the CD-ROM at the back of this book.

Bitting • Throwing Objects at Others • Hurting Others • Using Inappropri Calling • Nonsharing • Bribery • Stealing • Noncompliance • Disrupting the Classroom • Running Aimlessly Around the Classroom • Shouting in t Objects to Books • Breaking Toys • Flushing Objects Wasting Paper • Destroying the Work of Others • Throwing Tantrums • Po Talk • Thumb-Sucking • Pant Wetting • Clinging • Seeking Attention • S in Social Play • Shyness at Only One Toy • Infrequent Large Muscle Activity • Infrequent Dramatic tion Span • Finicky Eating • Overeat ating • Hording Food • Hitting • Biting • Throwing Objects at Others • appropriate Language • Name-Calling • Nonsharing • Bribery • Stealing ping Group Time • Leaving the Classroom • Running Aimlessly Around th g in the Classroom • Dropping Objects to Create Noise • Tearing Books • ushing Objects Down the Toilet • Wasting Paper • Destroying the Work o owing Tantrums • Pouting • Baby Talk • Thumb-Sucking • Pant Wetting

chapter **4**

Children with Disabilities

Because of legislative mandates, as well as because it makes good sense, many programs for young children include youngsters with special needs. Inclusion of children with disabilities has benefits for all involved: the children with special needs, the nondisabled children, the parents of both groups, and the teachers. An inclusive program provides support for children with disabilities so they can become full participants in the social world of the early childhood program. It also provides modeling and support for those who do not have special needs so they develop empathy, tolerance for differences, nurturance, and helping skills. Parents, as do teachers, learn that all children, whatever their level of ability, have much in common with each other. In addition, teachers gain knowledge and skill in their field by learning from the children, parents, health and mental health professionals, and their own research.

Inclusion of children with disabilities, while it is beneficial and rewarding, is also challenging. Sometimes, behavioral challenges are an integral part of a child's disability. In some children, behavioral difficulties are the main challenge; in other instances, these are secondary. It should also be mentioned that often, children who have not been officially diagnosed as having a disability, especially an emotional or behavioral one, may have special needs similar to children who have been identified as having such. Teachers' tools in working with children with disabilities are vital to running an effective early childhood program that fully includes all children.

Also important is communication between teachers and parents. Parents are usually the best source of information about their own child's disability. Not only are they familiar with the general disability with which their child has been diagnosed, but they also have expertise as to how it affects their individual child. No two children are alike, and each child with a disability is unique in his symptoms, reactions, determination, abilities, and need for assistance. Parents should be the first and foremost resource for teachers who have a child with a disability in their care. Teachers should also recognize that parents with such a child have special needs themselves. Supportive and open communication is, therefore, especially vital.

The remainder of this chapter will discuss specific areas of disability. In addition to discussion of the areas of disability, each will be linked to potential behavior concerns.

AREAS OF DISABILITY

Emotional/Behavioral Challenges. Keep in mind that all children engage in challenging behaviors at times. It is those whose behavior is frequently out of control, especially those who are aggressive or disruptive, who are of concern. Such behaviors can stem from physiological malfunctions, although the vast majority are linked to social and environmental causes: poor attachment, inconsistent guidance, frequent physical punishment, abuse or neglect, and many other factors that can underlie emotional or behavioral deficits.

In recent years, more attention has been paid to autism spectrum disorder, which becomes evident in a child's earliest years. Autism is a neurological problem that is particularly noticeable because of difficulty in social interaction and communication. The severity and symptoms of this disorder vary widely, so treatment will also vary. If a child in your class has been diagnosed with autism spectrum disorder, ask the family to put you in touch with any therapists who are working with the child. A consistent approach at school and at home will be helpful in working with an autistic child.

If a child's behaviors are so disturbing that they constantly interfere with the functioning of the early childhood program, then that child most likely has a special need. Some children will have been diagnosed with an emotional or behavioral deficit; for those, help through publicly funded or private programs is available. For others, it may fall to the early childhood teacher to ask the parents to seek professional help.

Many of the strategies outlined in this book can be useful in working with children with emotional and behavioral deficits.

Physical Challenges. Physical disabilities can range from slight clumsiness to having almost no muscular control. Some children may be wheelchair-bound, may need help in carrying out many physical functions, may need some special orthopedic equipment, or may simply need a watchful eye as they negotiate their physical environment. Motor disabilities can be caused by genetics, by a brain dysfunction, by prenatal exposure to various toxic substances, or by an accident.

One of the more common physical disabilities is cerebral palsy—a condition that can vary from minimal to severe. Children with cerebral palsy often have difficulty in coordination. They may move their arms, legs, face, and neck in abnormal ways, but have no control over these movements. Cerebral palsy may be accompanied by mental retardation, but that is not always the case. It is important to get information from a child's therapists to ensure that you know how to work with the child in the most supportive way.

A child with a physical disability may also exhibit behavioral challenges, although these are secondary to the main disability. This can happen, for example, if the child feels frustrated about not being able to keep up with peers, participate successfully in an activity, or communicate needs. The teachers' sensitive planning and guidance, both of the child with the disability and of the other children, can help minimize situations that might result in behavioral challenges. Some of the strategies suggested in the topical chapters of this book can be of help to those working with children with motor disabilities.

Cognitive Challenges. Children whose intellectual functioning lags significantly behind their peers are classified as having special cognitive needs. Those who have milder involvement may simply lag behind age-mates in reaching developmental milestones and of may seem immature. More serious deficits indicate significantly lower IQ and less ability to function in expected ways. Memory and attention span are often notably deficient. Cognitive disabilities can stem from a wide variety of causes, including various genetic conditions, prenatal exposure to harmful substances, some illnesses, accidents, and, in extreme cases, abuse and neglect.

Some children with cognitive disabilities are quite passive and even-tempered. Children with Down syndrome, for example, generally tend to be affectionate and amiable. Other children with cognitive disabilities may exhibit behavioral challenges. These may stem from a sense of frustration, from not understanding expectations, from a lack of ability to communicate, or from general immaturity. The teachers' careful consideration of the child's abilities and limitations in planning activities and provision of gentle guidance can help minimize behavioral challenges. Some of the later chapters can be applied to children with cognitive deficits.

Learning Disabilities. Learning disabilities have become recognized as a medical problem in relatively recent times. They are somewhat difficult to recognize in young children because the symptoms can be caused by things such as boredom, disinterest, or normal activity level. Yet some children who seem to have problems with basic learning processes involved in listening, speaking, or thinking may have a learning disability. These problems tend to be more easily diagnosed in the early school years when children have difficulty mastering reading, writing, or math skills. Sometimes, problems with physical balance and coordination are included because children can have difficulty with space awareness.

One of the most common manifestations of a learning disability is attention deficit–hyperactivity disorder (ADHD), which should not be confused with busy children's normal activity level. Children with ADHD have very short attention spans, are constantly restless, have poor impulse control, cannot concentrate, and are very distractable. Such children need medical help and are generally placed on medication. The teachers' careful attention to such children's needs by arranging the room to minimize distractions, providing firm and consistent guidance, and facilitating concentration by planning interesting activities can help children with learning disabilities, especially ADHD, to function effectively in the classroom. Later chapters, especially Chapter 44, Short Attention Span, can provide some useful techniques for teachers of such children.

Prenatal Exposure to Drugs and Alcohol. Increasingly, early childhood teachers are seeing children who were exposed to various drugs while in the womb or who have been diagnosed with fetal alcohol syndrome (FAS) because their mothers consumed harmful amounts of alcohol during pregnancy. Some children, who are not as severely impacted by prenatal exposure to alcohol, are diagnosed as having fetal alcohol effect (FAE). There is considerable variety in how prenatal drug or alcohol exposure is manifested in young children. Some show minimal effects while others may be aggressive, impulsive, and unpredictable and may lack understanding of the consequences of their actions.

Many children who have been prenatally exposed to drugs and alcohol have the compounding factor of insecure home lives and lack of emotional support. Those who work with such children have found that responsive, nurturing teachers in a well-structured environment can be the best antidote to this deficit. Thus, such support for these children, as well as preventive measures to protect all children from potentially unpredictable outbursts, are important. Some of the ensuing chapters of this book provide strategies for meeting the needs of children suffering the effects of prenatal exposure to drugs or alcohol.

Sensory Challenges. Some children's special needs stem from a defect in hearing or vision. Such sensory deficits can range from mild to almost total loss of hearing or visual acuity. Hearing amplifiers or glasses can correct some problems. Sensory deficits can stem from many causes, both before and after birth.

Children with serious sensory deficits are usually diagnosed and treated early in life, but many children experience some loss of hearing or sight that goes undetected. Behavioral challenges may result when a child is mistakenly assumed to be deliberately making noise, knocking over items, or spilling things. The issue may be the inability to distinguish noise levels or to see well. Teacher alertness to potential sensory deficits as well as adaptation of the environment for children with diagnosed hearing and visual challenges is important for helping those children get the most out of the early childhood program. Ensuing chapters introduce some strategies that can help in this process.

Sensory Processing Disorder (SPD). *Sensory processing* refers to our ability to take in, organize, and interpret information through movement and our various senses—vision, hearing, touch, taste, smell. Some children are not able to respond appropriately to information they get through their senses because of the way their brains interpret the information that comes in and how they react to it. Some children with sensory processing disorder overreact to sensations, feeling overloaded with sensory information. Other children feel very little input and, as a result, constantly seek stimulation.

Children with SPD, because they get faulty information from their environment, often respond inappropriately. They are often labeled as "difficult" children because of their challenging behavior. Peers tend to avoid them, which contributes to low self-esteem. A child who has been diagnosed with SPD should receive appropriate therapy, coordinating home and school responses.

Speech and Language Challenges. Some children have difficulty communicating effectively because of a speech or language deficit. Such problems may be physiological in origin, may be a by-product of a cognitive defect, may be caused by lack of language stimulation in early life, or, as is often the case, may be of unknown origin. If a child is considerably more difficult to understand than his peers or if he rarely or never speaks (both at school and at home), there is a problem. If the child is seeing a speech therapist, coordination between the early childhood program and the therapist is important.

Children with speech or language problems may have difficulty participating in the early childhood program because they cannot adequately express their wishes and needs and, as a result, have trouble communicating with peers. Some children may find that physical "communication," such as hitting, is effective. Others may be withdrawn and may not participate in classroom activities. In either case, teachers' sensitive assistance to help the child become a full participant is important. Some of the following chapters suggest strategies that can be helpful in working with children with speech or language deficits.

Chronic Health Problems. Some children suffer from an ongoing health disability that may require special accommodation or may make functioning in the early childhood program difficult. Children with diabetes, asthma, cancer, cystic fibrosis, AIDS, and other long-term or terminal illnesses can be part of the early childhood program, although typically they miss school more than their peers. It is important to be aware of safeguards that need to be taken to protect others in the program from the child's infection. Parents and medical professionals can provide appropriate guidelines.

A child with a debilitating illness may be angry about her condition and may act out that anger against others. On the other hand, some such children may be withdrawn and may not participate in classroom activities. They may have limited energy or may feel depressed. Whatever the child's reaction, the teachers' assistance in helping the child feel comfortable, in making necessary accommodations to help the child become as full a participant in the class as possible, and in continuing to make her feel a part of the group, even if attendance is sporadic, are very important. Some of the following chapters will provide suggestions to help children with chronic illnesses.

CONCLUSION

Throughout the remainder of the text, in the chapters dealing with specific behavior challenges, there are references to children with disabilities and how a teacher might help them participate as fully as possible in the program. Look for the asterisk (*) in the following chapters designating that the information is relevant to children with special needs. Footnotes will also elaborate information where relevant.

You will find additional resources about children with disabilities and the potential for challenging behaviors in the CD-ROM at the back of this book.

• Biting • Throwing Objects at Others • Hurting Others • Using Inappropria Calling • Nonsharing • Bribery • Stealing • Noncompliance • Disrupting the Classroom • Running Aimlessly Around the Classroom • Shouting in t Objects to Create Noise • Tearing Books • Breaking Toys • Flushing Objects Wasting Paper • Destroying the Work of Others • Throwing Tantrums • Po Talk • Thumb-Sucking • Pant Wetting • Clinging • Seeking Attention • S bal to Social Play • Shyness at G t Only One Toy • Infrequent Large Muscle Activity • Infrequent Dramatic P n Span • Finicky Eating • Overeati Eating • Holding Food • tting • Biting • Throwing Objects at Others • H sp • Nonsharing • Bribery • Stealing ting Group Time • Leaving the Classroom • Running Aimlessly Around the g Objects to Create Noise • Tearing Books • A ushing Objects Down the Toilet • Wasting Paper • Destroying the Work of owing Tantrums • Pouting • Baby Talk • Thumb-Sucking • Pant Wetting

chapter **5**

Strategies for Dealing with Challenging Behaviors

Appropriate guidance of young children's behavior is vital. Children's self-concepts are strongly affected by how adults respond to them. Guidance approaches also have a direct impact on whether the class runs smoothly or with frequent disruptions. Some specific strategies help maintain positive behavior and eliminate challenging behavior. In this chapter, the strategies that are discussed in subsequent chapters of this book are reviewed, particularly in terms of their appropriateness to various situations.

REINFORCEMENT

The first and most important technique to use in dealing with children is positive reinforcement. It should be used often, but at appropriate times. Furthermore, it should *always* be paired with other approaches used to change a child's challenging behavior. Appropriate behavior is maintained when the child is told by adults that they appreciate that what the child is doing.

Keep in mind that verbal reinforcement needs to be meaningful and genuine; empty praise or perfunctory acknowledgment will *not* give the child a positive message. On the other hand, reinforcement does not have to be given verbally. Acceptance can be conveyed in many, often subtle, ways. A smile, a touch, eye contact, or a hug are just as potent as verbal affirmation in telling a child that her behavior is appreciated. In fact, there are times when the teacher does not want to interrupt children's activity but still show approval, and nonverbal reinforcement is the method to use.

It is particularly important to reinforce a child's actions when trying to change a negative behavior. Teachers should keep in mind that when a challenging behavior is being changed, something is being taken away from the child, specifically, the attention the child had previously been receiving for that behavior. In changing a negative behavior, it is most important to let the child know what is acceptable through reinforcement, not just to let the child know what is not acceptable. Every unacceptable behavior has an acceptable opposite, which should be encouraged and nurtured through positive reinforcement. If a child frequently hits, that child should be lavishly reinforced for interacting with peers in appropriate ways; if a child whines, that child should be praised for speaking appropriately; if a child tends to disrupt group activities, that child should be praised for participating appropriately.

Occasionally, very frequent reinforcement might be needed to help a child to learn an appropriate behavior quickly. In one example of this use of reinforcement, a three-year-old child's rate of hitting other children was changed from an average of 40 acts of aggression per hour to an average of 1. This child did not respond to any of the other strategies that were tried, and thus, a program of praise every half-minute was implemented. Within two days, the rate of hitting dropped dramatically. Over the subsequent weeks, continued though increasingly less frequent reinforcement eventually resulted in no hitting at all. Initially, it took a huge amount of the teachers' time to carry out this program of constant reinforcement but in the long run, it was a time-saver. Far less time had to be spent in comforting hurt children and dealing with this child.

IGNORING

Ignoring is a very effective strategy, but one that is very difficult to use. When a child repeatedly does something that is irritating to the teachers or disruptive to the class, ignoring is a good strategy to use. Ignoring should not be used, however, when children are hurting or potentially hurting themselves or others. Ignoring is especially effective if the child seeks adult attention before engaging in challenging behaviors. The child who looks to see who is watching before engaging in the behavior is overtly bidding for attention.

Total ignoring by all adults every time the behavior occurs is difficult but imperative if this strategy is to be effective. Raised eyebrows, sighs, and other nonverbal signs will be read easily by the child, conveying that the behavior is getting to the teachers, making the ignoring strategy ineffective. While this strategy is an important and powerful one to help eliminate irritating or disruptive behaviors, it is important to keep in mind that this removal of attention needs to be replaced by reinforcement of positive behaviors.

SELF-CONTROL TIME

There are times when it helps a child to have the opportunity to be away from the hub of activity and stimulation in the classroom to regain control over her responses and emotions. Self-control time differs from the more traditionally used time-out in that it allows the child more power over how it is implemented. It is not totally teacher-controlled. Whereas time-out often is used in a punitive way, self-control time allows the child to regain her composure and return to classroom activities when she has done so. The emphasis is on child rather than on teacher control over the situation.

Self-control time should be used sparingly and carefully. It should be used primarily when children hurt or potentially hurt others or themselves. Aggressive behavior needs to be stopped as quickly as possible, and self-control time is often, but not always, the best method for doing so. It should be used only when a child has repeated the aggressive behavior more than twice and after the teacher has discussed with the child that such behavior is not acceptable.

Before deciding to use self-control time, teachers need to agree to use this strategy consistently and in the same way. It is important that this be discussed by all involved teachers beforehand to agree on a definition of the behavior for which self-control time will be used, the place where it is to be carried out, and the actual approach they will use for self-control time.

This book suggests the following procedure for self-control time:
1. Quickly make sure that the child against whom the aggression was aimed is not hurt. If possible, another teacher should attend to the victim.
2. Calmly take the aggressive child by the hand to the self-control time area. Firmly but quietly say, "I cannot allow you to hurt other children. Please stay here until you are ready to join your friends again."
3. Move away and do not talk with or look at the child during self-control time. Verbal or visual contact may well serve as a reinforcer to the child for her behavior.

4. If another child approaches, quietly move this child away. Explain, "Jane needs to be by herself for a few minutes. You can talk to her when she joins the class again."

5. The child can rejoin classroom activities when she feels that she is ready to do so. Do not lecture. She knows the reason for the isolation. To channel the child into constructive behavior, you might suggest joining an ongoing activity. It is very important to reinforce the child as soon as possible for engaging in appropriate activity.

6. If the child rejoins the classroom before she is ready and again engages in the unacceptable behavior, say to her, "I guess you're not quite ready to join us," and take her back to the self-control area. Again allow her to determine when she is ready to rejoin the group.

Self-control time is not a punishment. Rather, it is a time for the child to calm down and regain control over herself. Sometimes, aggressive behavior is a reaction to a general feeling of anger or anxiety or unease, and time to get away from the stimulation of the class can help the child calm down.

ALONE TIME

Another approach that has been used successfully with some children is alone time. Some children may, at times, find themselves overwhelmed with the noise, activity level, and general stimulation of the classroom, and may need an opportunity to get away. Some children's neurological structure may be unable to handle such overstimulation; for instance, children who were born prematurely or children who were exposed prenatally to drugs and alcohol may benefit from such a strategy. A quiet, less stimulating area needs to be designated for this. Such an area can be inside or outside the classroom. If it is in the room, it needs to be secluded enough to give the child a sense of being away from the general activity and noise of the room.

A two-and-a-half-year-old boy who was extremely disruptive and aggressive in his class, and who had major tantrums four or five times every morning, did not respond at all to more conventional attempts to change or modify his behavior. One teacher noted that he almost visibly wound up before negative behaviors, and the staff began to discuss the possibility that the child could simply not deal with the stimulation level of the class at times. They worked out a new strategy.

The next day a teacher had a talk with him. She told him that she could "see" when he was beginning to feel upset and asked if he knew when he started to feel "mad." He indicated that he did. The teacher then told him that when he started to feel upset he could leave the room and go to a designated area, the office of another staff member. This room was equipped with a small table and chair and a few manipulative toys. He was required to let a teacher in the classroom know, however, anytime he left.

The change in the child was striking. Starting that same day, his unacceptable behaviors decreased dramatically although they did not disappear completely, and he left the room periodically to go to his designated out-of-the-classroom area. He never abused this opportunity to leave the room, did not go anywhere other than this room, and usually returned within 5 or 10 minutes. He left the classroom several times a day and continued to do this over a two-year period. The third year that he was at the child care center, he decreased his number of times away from the class but still maintained the option of leaving. By this time he was also able to verbalize that it made him feel better to be able to remove himself from the classroom when he started to feel upset.

When other methods of dealing with challenging behavior seem to fail, you might want to consider this alternative. Alone time should not be used indiscriminately, but reserved for children who seem to have a hard time handling a stimulating preschool class environment for long periods. The cause of the challenging behavior, in this case, is external, and this technique gives the child an opportunity to control the environment.

PREVENTION

Stopping a challenging behavior before it happens is an excellent strategy to use. Using prevention implies, however, that adults have carefully observed the child and have a pretty good idea of what triggers the behavior. If, for example, the teachers have noticed that a child gets frustrated easily when not successful in an activity and then turns on nearby friends, teachers should look for any occasion when the child might have difficulty in participating in an activity. This does not mean that they resolve all of the child's problems, but that they facilitate the acquisition of skills and problem-solving techniques. Prevention is especially effective with younger preschoolers, who do not yet have the self-control or ability to express themselves that older children have.

REDIRECTION

Another effective strategy to use with younger preschoolers, especially two-year-olds, is redirection. The teacher directs the child's attention to another activity or provides a duplicate or alternative toy. Two-year-olds do not yet have the social skills to handle the demands of school and sharing, and teachers need to help them gradually acquire such skills. Redirection should not be used routinely with older preschoolers, who need the guidance to solve social challenges in effective ways.

DISCUSSION

One strategy that works with many older preschoolers is discussion. Often, a child of four or five is quite willing to try to address behavioral challenges with the teacher. A misbehaving child does not feel good about himself. If the child is seriously interested in changing the behavior, you can discuss this with him and, in effect, become his partner.

It is important to find a quiet and private place to discuss such an approach with the child. If he puts forth effort to change, you need to be available to help him until he has mastered the positive behavior.

CREATIVE PROBLEM-SOLVING

Children need to learn to deal effectively with social conflicts, and one of the most effective ways is to help them engage in creative problem-solving. Teachers can facilitate skills of conflict resolution by encouraging children to identify and clarify the problem, brainstorm possible ways of dealing with the problem, evaluate these possibilities, select the one that best satisfies both parties, and find ways to implement the solution. The teacher needs to be a good listener, who can listen to, acknowledge without judging, and reiterate each child's position. The main feature of this approach is to avoid having one person, whether a child or an adult, impose his position on another person. Mutual respect, rather than power of one person over another person, is the key.

SPECIAL TIME

A very effective strategy to use with a child who engages in excessive attention-getting behavior is to set aside special time. Many families today, including those with a single parent or two working parents, are very stressed and busy, and often children do not get the attention they need. The result can be challenging behavior and acting out.

If you suspect that a child's challenging behavior is a cry for attention—any attention—you might consider special time. This means that the teacher sets aside a few minutes a day, every other day, or even twice a week, when he spends some time just with this child. This is not always easy with a full class of children, but some creative scheduling can help. Early mornings or late in the day before closing time could provide an opportunity. The beginning or end of nap or rest time might also be possibilities. Getting a volunteer into the class, asking the director to come in, or looking at the total staffing pattern could help find a few minutes here and there for special time with one or more children.

Special time should be the child alone with a teacher. The teacher can ask what the child would like to do for special time, then use this suggestion. It is amazing how a small time investment can pay off in greatly decreased acting-out behavior. In the long run, teachers will spend less time dealing with challenging behavior and will create a more positive classroom atmosphere.

STAR CHART

A star chart works particularly well if it helps the child to have a visible, tangible record of progress toward appropriate behavior. It is a visible reinforcer that, for some children and some circumstances, is quite effective. A star chart is not meant to be punitive, and it should never be used to reflect when the child does not engage in the appropriate behavior. It should be a record of successes, not failures.

Such a chart is simple to make, with days listed along the side and spaces for a star or other type of sticker when a child performs the appropriate behavior. Stars can be added each time a child performs a given behavior, or they can be put on the chart in time-related slots. Length of time will, of course, depend on the behavior.

CONCLUSION

The guidance strategies that a teacher uses are vital in shaping children's behavior. Nine approaches to changing children's challenging behavior were discussed in this chapter. Use of these strategies depends on the child as well as on the behavior, and subsequent chapters of this book suggest specific techniques or combinations of techniques for different behaviors.

Reinforcement is a very important strategy to use in guiding children and should be used routinely to let children know that what they are doing is appropriate, as well as in combination with any other strategies used to change a child's behavior. The opposite of reinforcement is ignoring, another very effective approach, though one that is difficult to implement. When ignoring a behavior, it is important at the same time to reinforce an opposite, appropriate behavior.

Self-control time should be used sparingly and only when children engage in aggressive or dangerous behaviors. It needs to be carefully planned and not considered as a punishment. A related strategy is alone time, where the child has the option of removing himself from the classroom when he feels his behavior about to go out of control.

Careful observation of children can give clues to what triggers some challenging behaviors. Prevention is an effective method that teaches the child alternatives by not allowing the behavior to occur. This is often effective with young preschoolers, as is redirection. Redirection can help a child whose self-control and language are not yet well developed find a way of dealing with potentially frustrating situations.

Older preschoolers who want to change an unsuitable behavior can participate in a discussion of that behavior with you. You are then in a position to become that child's partner in changing the behavior. Creative problem-solving is another effective method that teaches children to find socially appropriate ways of resolving conflicts. Special time works well with children whose inappropriate attention-seeking sends the message that they are desperately seeking attention. Finally, a star chart can be helpful by providing a tangible record of progress.

These various strategies are applied to different instances of challenging behavior in the following chapters. Their application is suggested based on general knowledge about children and their behaviors. You must use your judgment as to whether the suggested approach fits the child and situation for which you are seeking a resolution. Although we can apply some general principles, each child, each teacher, and each situation is unique.

 You will find additional resources for strategies to help children with challenging behaviors in the CD-ROM at the back of this book.

Biting • Throwing Objects at Others • Hurting Others • Using Inappropri
e-Calling • Nonsharing • Bribery • Stealing • Noncompliance • Disrupting
the Classroom • Running Aimlessly Around the Classroom • Shouting in th
Objects to Make Noise • Tearing Books • Breaking Toys • Flushing Objects
Wasting Paper • Destroying the Work of Others • Throwing Tantrums • Po
y Talk • Thumb-Sucking • Pant-Wetting • Clinging • Seeking Attention • S
pa... ...on in Social Play • Shyness at Gr
h Only One Toy • Infrequent Large Muscle Activity • Infrequent Dramatic P
...ort Attention Span • Finicky Eating • Overeati
eating • Hording Food • Hitting • Biting • Throwing Objects at Others • Hi
appropriate Language • Name-Calling • Nonsharing • Bribery • Stealing • N
...ting Group Time • Leaving the Classroom • Running Aimlessly Around th
g in the Classroom • Dropping Objects to Create Noise • Tearing Books •
ushing Objects Down the Toilet • Wasting Paper • Destroying the Work of
owing Tantrums • Pouting • Baby Talk • Thumb-Sucking • Pant-Wetting •

chapter **6**

Working with Families

Strategies for dealing with children's challenging behaviors are most effective if teachers and families work in partnership on finding solutions. In this chapter, we will examine some ways of making home–school cooperation more effective and rewarding for families, teachers, and children. We will include several pertinent topics in this discussion, including the foundation on which positive family–teacher interactions are built, dealing with issues as they arise, strategies for when families and teachers disagree, and some examples of communiqués that can be used when giving information to families.

THE FOUNDATION FOR POSITIVE FAMILY–TEACHER INTERACTIONS

Interactions between teachers and families must be built on a foundation of mutual trust and respect. These, of course, take time to establish. It should be mentioned at the start of this discussion that when a concern arises, it should *never* be the first time that a teacher speaks to a child's parent or other family members. Rather, teachers and families need to get to know each other gradually through a consistent series of positive interactions. Thus, if issues do arise, it will be much more fruitful to discuss these if there is already a trusting relationship between teacher and family. There are many ways to establish such a relationship and different contexts in which interactions can take place. We will examine several such opportunities, including the times when children are dropped off and picked up at school, special family events, individual family–teacher conferences, and written information.

Drop-off and Pick-up Times. The times when children are left at school at the start of the day and picked up at the end of the day provide excellent opportunities for establishing a respectful and constructive relationship. It is important to set aside time at the start and end of the school day to say a few affirming words to family members. Teachers consciously need to determine who will be available to talk with parents or other family members and who will oversee the children during times when parents are at the school. Even though drop-off and pick-up times are busy and often rushed, both for teachers and for families, spending even 15 seconds to make a friendly, positive comment to the child and family member is important in establishing this relationship.

Messages expressed during drop-off and pick-up times can convey a number of things. They tell the family that the child is welcomed to school, liked by her teacher, and valued as an individual rather than being viewed as just one of "the herd." They can also relay to the family the child's successes and triumphs at school. They communicate to the family that what happens in the child's life at school is as meaningful to the teacher as it is to the family and, therefore, is being shared. Such messages also convey the teacher's awareness of important occurrences in the life of the child and the family, whether this is an unexpected event, a loss, or a change. Following are a few examples of what a teacher might say to arriving or departing family members and children:

- "I'm so happy to see you, Alice! I made some play dough in new colors for today, and I know how much you enjoy working with play dough."
- "Jimmy, we've missed you and your mom! I hope your throat is feeling better and that you're ready to play with your friends."
- "Mr. Akers, how is the new baby? How is your wife doing? Rachel has been very excited and has told us all about her new little brother. We've put some additional baby props in the dramatic play area so that Rachel and the other children can play at school at being moms and dads with babies if they want to."
- "Carlos, I was so proud of you yesterday when you helped lead our group time. Did you tell your grandmother about that?"
- "Ms. Travino, I wanted to share with you these paper strips that Allen cut. He was really successful in holding the scissors and making them work. We were both excited!"

- "We had a great time splashing with the hose outside this afternoon when it got so hot. Sherry got her dress rather wet, so we changed her clothes so she'd be more comfortable. Her dress is in this plastic bag."
- "Hey, Rickie, your dad is here. Can you show him the picture we took of the rocket you built with the blocks? Mr. Lewandowski, you should have seen it! He built a magnificent structure and we took a photo of it so you could see it, too."

Such messages are positive, upbeat, and friendly. They convey your interest in and concern about the child and the family. Families will appreciate your information about the child's activities and achievements. Even if some family members always seem to be in a hurry, they may well begin to feel a sense of pride at their child's accomplishments and inclusion in the events of their child's day if you continue to convey the message that the child is valued and cherished at school. At times, you may also need to express a concern about the child's health; however, differentiate such a message from one that conveys something negative about the child such as a concern about challenging behavior. You might say, for example, "I wonder if Ariel is not feeling well. She had a hard time getting up from nap this afternoon and has been rather listless. Let me know if she seems to be coming down with something, would you please?"

Special Family Events. In addition to these very important informal communications between teachers and families when children are being dropped off or picked up at school, there are a number of more formal possibilities for teacher–family interactions. Many schools provide special events during which families and teachers can meet and talk. There are many possibilities for such events, some of which are listed below.

- Some schools find that meetings on specific topics are a very popular and a useful way to convey information to families. Provision of such group meetings, however, has to take into account the needs, interests, and availability of the parent or other family members. Busy families may find that one more event is more than they can muster energy for; thus, consider carefully whether such meetings would be the best way to communicate with families. Timing of the meeting is important, too, whether in the evening, on weekends, in the late afternoon, or at lunch time. Topics for such meetings can vary widely. One school finds that a spring meeting dealing with the transition to kindergarten or first grade is very popular with families of five-year-olds. Other topics that often interest families include dealing with behavioral challenges, the effects of television and how to limit its use, child health and nutrition, and emergent literacy skills.

- Another opportunity for families and teachers to interact is an open house. Such an event, especially early in the school year, provides an opportunity for families to visit the school, chat with the teachers, meet other families, and learn about the curriculum and activities in which the children participate.
- Food always provides a relaxing atmosphere around which people enjoy interacting. Thus, a lunch or dinner event, to which families and children are invited, provides yet another opportunity for families and teachers to meet. Holidays provide a good opportunity for such an event, but other times, for instance, ones associated with the curriculum, also offer good possibilities.
- Sometimes, a small group of family members and a teacher, interested in pursuing a specific topic, can meet for roundtable discussions. Such an event provides a more intimate setting for exchanging ideas and getting acquainted.
- Another popular way for families and teachers to interact is through workdays planned to improve some aspect of the school or classroom environment. Many good conversations between families and teachers can occur while they are hammering, sanding, painting, or washing down walls.

Group events such as these can be a good way for families and teachers to interact. Such events must be planned with care, and, if they involve a formal program, should also include some time for families and teachers to chat informally as well.

Family–Teacher Conferences. In addition, regularly scheduled conferences provide the opportunity for one-on-one interactions between individual family members and teachers. Such times provide opportunities for teachers and families to share insights and information about the child and to establish a positive relationship. Conferences, when families and teachers can meet privately without interruptions, are the best opportunity to discuss issues when they arise, which we will consider in more detail in the next section. Conferences, however, should not be focused on challenging behaviors; they should be an opportunity for families and teachers to share information about the child and all aspects of his development and functioning.

Written Communiqués. Written materials and bulletin board displays can also be very effective in communicating information to families about their children and the children's school environment and activities. A regular newsletter and information bulletins include information of interest to all the families. More detailed messages between a teacher and the family of a specific child can be used as a way of sharing information in addition to or, if necessary, as a substitute for, face-to-face interactions. One school, for instance, made a point of sending a "Happygram" home to each family at least once a week to share something significant from the child's school experience. Well-designed and uncluttered bulletin boards also provide a wonderful way of communicating with families, including information about the children's activities, abstracts of recent relevant research, or displays documenting the children's work. Some schools display documentation of the children's and teachers' work. Such documentation focuses on the process of learning, not only on the end product of classroom projects.

If some families in your program are not able to read or write English, you will need to find some alternative strategies for keeping in touch. Messages could be sent home on an audio tape or even a video cassette. Bulletin boards can be designed to convey the message through visual rather than through written means. If a number of families in the program speak primarily one language other than English, you may want to have a translated copy of group communiqués such as newsletters.

Electronic Communication. Many early childhood programs and many families have access to computer technology and the new means of communication it allows. E-mail, for instance, has provided an easy way for some teachers and families to share information. A list of e-mail address of all families allows teachers to provide general information in a quick, environmentally friendly manner. School Web sites, with a link for each classroom, are another way that many programs share information with participating and prospective families. In using such technology, however, teachers have to be sensitive to the fact that not all families are connected to the Internet or have computers. Alternative ways of sharing information with all families should always be available.

WHEN CHALLENGES ARISE

When teachers are concerned about a child's behavior, it is much easier to discuss this with the family if a friendly and positive relationship already exists between home and school. This is why we first discussed some of the ways in which a congenial relationship can be established. Concerns are best discussed when trust and mutual respect exist. It is inevitable that there will be concerns, expressed by families, teachers, or both, that need to be discussed. Most often, these revolve around children's behaviors. When families and teachers can work together to find ways to encourage appropriate behaviors, all parties, including the child, benefit. Following are some suggestions for discussing concerns with families when these arise.

- It is important to provide a private meeting place for discussion of behavioral challenges. Setting up a conference at which you and the family can meet without interruption is an important first step.

- If a family member raises concern about a behavioral issue, for instance, when the child is being dropped off or picked up, do not discuss it then and there. Instead, tell the family member that you would like to set up a meeting time as soon as possible when the issue can be discussed in private and with enough time to give it the consideration it needs.

- Be prepared for the meeting. Think through what you want to discuss, and have specific, factual information at hand. For instance, you may have observations related to the child's behavior that you can include as part of the discussion.

- Consider the child's behavioral challenge in the context of all of the child's undertakings. In other words, a child who hits other children most likely also engages in many other behaviors, including very constructive and social ones. Be prepared to provide the family with a good overview of the child's strengths, favorite activities, friendships, and accomplishments. In such a context, challenging behavior can be seen as just one of the child's activities rather than the main or only one.

- As the teacher, always approach a meeting with family members with the attitude that you have a common goal to discuss and that you must decide what is best for the child. Be positive and upbeat about the fact that you and the family will come to a resolution that will help change challenging behavior.

- Establish early in the meeting the context in which the behavior you are discussing with the family occurs. For instance, does it happen only at school, or at home and in other settings as well? If a challenging behavior happens both at home and at school, coming up with a consistent strategy that both family and teachers follow will be most effective in changing it. If, on the other hand, the behavior happens primarily at school, then the family can be kept informed and be supportive of the teacher's efforts.

- Never lay blame on the family. Approach the discussion with the intent of mutual problem-solving.
- Avoid analyzing and overinterpreting the child's behavior. Stay with factual information that describes what you have observed.
- Do not preach, lecture, or moralize to the family.
- Listen to the family members. You are not the "expert" on this child, the family is. Your task is to work in partnership with the family to find a resolution to the problem.
- You probably already have some ideas about how to deal with the challenging behavior, ideas that may well come from this book. Be prepared with these; however, do not approach the family as if you have already made up your mind about what to do and are merely informing the family rather than working together with them. Be open to many different ideas and talk these through to find the best approach.
- You may have already tried some ways of dealing with a challenging behavior in the classroom before you meet with the family. If this is the case, share these and ask whether they have tried similar or different methods at home.
- Above all, continue to see the meeting with the family as an opportunity to build positive links, work together, and find a way to deal with the child's troubling behavior to the benefit of all.

WHEN FAMILIES AND TEACHERS DISAGREE

The points on working together with families to deal with challenging behaviors presented above are predicated on a positive and trusting relationship in which both families and teachers agree on finding a mutually agreeable resolution. Not all family–teacher relationships are of this nature, however. There are times when families and teachers disagree, or when families display an attitude that makes it difficult to communicate effectively. Following are some ways of working more effectively with families in more difficult relationships.

- Always remember that a family's sense of who they are is closely tied to how other people view their children. Be sensitive to the fact that families who are told that their child displays some challenging behaviors at school may become defensive and closed.
- Families, in fact, may deny that there is a problem and tell you that it is the school, you, or the other children who are causing difficulties. Listen carefully to the family's point of view, for there may be truth in it. In addition, enlist the family's suggestions for dealing with the challenging behavior.

- Some families carry a great deal of anger and hostility, which may have nothing to do with you or their child. Be aware that you may be the unintended target of such anger and that there may well be more troubling issues that a family is facing. Your calm, empathetic understanding can help diffuse a family member's hostility.

- If the family disagrees with your assessment of their child, try to understand the family's point of view. Listen carefully and honestly to what they say. Use effective listening techniques to help ensure that you are correctly hearing the message that the family is conveying.

- There are some behaviors that you, as the teacher, should avoid to facilitate effective family–teacher communication. For instance, do not enter a conference expecting a specific outcome; approach each meeting with families with an open mind and an attitude that you will work together to facilitate a positive behavioral change. In addition, do not give the impression that you are an expert, superior to the family in knowledge and understanding. Remember, families know their children best. Also, avoid using technical wording; use everyday language instead. Avoid judging families, either openly or covertly; your attitude will show. It is certainly never helpful if you lose your temper and become angry, defensive, or hostile; try to stay calm and responsive.

- There may be occasional circumstances when it would be inadvisable to involve the family in a discussion of a child's challenging behavior. Some years ago, when I was director of an early childhood program, it became obvious that the mother of one of the children was very angry and negative. Several times she told the teachers, "If Trevor does something wrong, you tell me, and I'll wallop him good when we get home." During a teacher–family conference, she was asked, "Tell us what Trevor does well. What are his strengths?" She thought a moment, then said, "He doesn't have any." The staff decided that it would be best if challenging behaviors, which Trevor engaged in often, were handled by the teachers and not mentioned to the mother. Instead, the staff made a point of saying something very positive about Trevor to his mother every day when she picked him up. Over a two-year period, Trevor's mother became considerably more positive and began to talk more openly to the teachers.

Not all family–teacher interactions will be smooth and mutually supportive. There may be some family members you will not be able to reach because they are disinterested or occupied with other concerns.

Do not, however, jump to conclusions about the family's disinterest, which may be a reflection of being overwhelmed with problems. Apparent disinterest should never be mistaken for lack of caring. The points listed above are especially important to keep in mind when families disagree with you or are difficult to communicate with. It is in such difficult situations that your communication skills will be most needed.

SAMPLE COMMUNIQUÉS

Following are some examples of written notes that can be used to facilitate family–teacher communications. These prototypes can be used as needed.

Earlier, we mentioned that one school sent home "Happygrams" at least once a week as a way of establishing positive communications. These brief messages focused on a positive accomplishment of the child's day.

HAPPYGRAM

Date:

We want to share with you that today, your child (child's name)

_____

Next is an invitation to families to attend a group function. The wording will have to change to fit the event, of course.

WE NEED YOU! PLEASE HELP!

On (day and date), we are planning to renovate our playground and would love your help. We will sand and paint all wood surfaces, paint all metal structures, build a new playhouse, and do general cleanup outside. We will be here from 9 A.M. to 4 P.M., so come for some or all of that time. Lunch will be provided. Please sign up on the family bulletin board if you will come.

Thank you (from the teachers and your children!)

Sometimes, it is good to canvass families' input about group programs such as family meetings on a specific topic. Following is a sample survey.

FAMILY QUESTIONNAIRE

Dear Families:

In past years, we have held family get-togethers to discuss topics of interest to families. We would like to find out if you, as this year's group of families, would also like us to plan such events. Please take a few minutes to fill out this questionnaire and return it to the blue box outside your child's classroom. We'll get back to you soon.

What topic(s) would be of interest to you:

___guidance and discipline   ___moving to public school

___taming TV   ___prereading skills

___health and nutrition   ___good toys for children

Other ideas:

_____

_____

_____

What day(s) are best for you?

___M   ___T   ___W   ___Th   ___F   ___Sat

What time(s) of the day best fit your schedule?

___12 to 1   ___5 to 6   ___7 to 9

___Saturday morning   ___Saturday afternoon

Would you need child care in order to attend a meeting?

___YES   ___NO

Unless a block of time is set aside, as often is the case in public schools for family–teacher conferences, it may be best to plan to meet with a small number of families each week so your time is not overburdened. Notes to individual families a couple of weeks ahead of the scheduled time can help facilitate planning. Following is a sample of such a note.

IT'S CONFERENCE TIME!

Dear (names of family members):

Every year, I try to meet at least two times with the families of all the children in my class. This gives us the opportunity to exchange information and observations about your child. I meet with three or four families each week. Please let me know if the week of (date) would be convenient for you.

I can meet at any of the following times. Please let me know which of these would work for you:

___ 7 to 7:30 A.M.   ___ 5 to 5:30 P.M.

___ 1 to 1:30 P.M.   ___ 5:30 to 6 P.M.

(Your Signature)

I/we can meet on (date) ___ at (time) ___

Family Signature

Finally, you may want to set up a meeting with families about a special concern. If the above note is not appropriate because of timing, you can use the following format.

Dear (name of family members):

Sometimes I like to meet with the families of some of the children in my class more than the usual two times a year. I'd like the chance to get together with you soon. Would you be able to come to school to meet with me sometime in the next two weeks? Please let me know what time would work for you. I can be available any day before 8:00 A.M., between 1:00 and 3:00 P.M., or between 4:30 and 6:00 P.M. I look forward to seeing you soon.

(Signature)

Checklist for Family–Teacher Conferences

The following checklist provides some points that teachers should consider as they plan for a conference with a child's family, especially to discuss a challenging behavior that is of concern. It is important to maintain a positive and balanced attitude about the child, not one that is overly focused on a concern.

_____ Set a mutually agreeable time for the conference.

_____ Select a private place for the conference, one where you will not be interrupted.

_____ Be prepared to discuss the whole child, not simply a behavior that is challenging. In other words, be prepared to share information about the child's friendships, projects, skills, and accomplishments. You can bring examples or documentation of the child's work to share with the family.

_____ Enter the conference knowing that you and the family share common goals for the child.

_____ Be well prepared to discuss the challenging behavior that is of concern to you, bringing factual information, such as from observations, to back your words.

_____ Come prepared with questions that will help you understand the child better. Listen to what the family shares with you.

_____ Avoid overanalyzing the child's behavior, either before or during the conference. Your analyses and conclusions should be based on factual information.

_____ Do not approach the family as if you have already made up your mind about how to resolve your concern. Elicit and listen to the parents' ideas, which most likely come from personal experience, about what would work best.

_____ Before ending the conference, try to reach a mutual understanding about how the family and the teachers will work together toward resolving concerns.

 At the end of the section of the accompanying CD-ROM that includes practice scenarios, you will find an activity that encourages you to apply the principles in this checklist to preparing for a family–teacher conference related to those scenarios.

CONCLUSION

Working together with families is always important. After all, families and teachers are the adults with whom young children spend the majority of their time and, therefore, they are probably the most important people in their lives. A partnership between families and teachers, within which the important events in the child's life are shared and discussed, is to the benefit of the child. This is especially true when there is a concern about a child's behavior. When families and teachers exchange ideas and insight, this can help reach a resolution that is in the best interest of the child as well as the adults concerned.

SECTION 2

Aggressive

and **Antisocial**

Behaviors

• Nonsharing • Bribery • Stealing • Noncompliance • Disrupting Group Time • Leaving the Classro
nning Aimlessly Around the Classroom • Shouting in the Classroom • Dropping Objects to Create N
aring Books • Breaking Toys • Flushing Objects Down the Toilet • Wasting Paper • Destroying the W
thers • Throwing Tantrums • Pouting • Baby Talk • Thumb-Sucking • Pant-Wetting • Clinging • See
ntion • Nonparticipation in Activities • Nonparticipation in Social Play • Shyness at Group Tim
ng with Only One Toy • Infrequent Large Muscle Activity • Infrequent Dramatic-Play Participatio
ng Infrequently • Short Attention Span • Finicky Eating • Overeating • Messy Eating • Hording Foo
ng • Biting • Throwing Objects at Others • Hurting Others • Using Inappropriate Language • Na
ng • Nonsharing • Bribery • Stealing • Noncompliance • Disrupting Group Time • Leaving the Classro
nning Aimlessly Around the Classroom • Shouting in the Classroom • Dropping Objects to Create N
aring Books • Breaking Toys • Flushing Objects Down the Toilet • Wasting Paper • Destroying the V
thers • Throwing Tantrums • Pouting • Baby Talk • Thumb-Sucking • Pant-Wetting • Clinging • See
ntion • Whining • Self-Stimulation • Nonparticipation in Activities • Nonparticipation in Social Pl
ess at Group Time • Playing with Only One Toy • Infrequent Large Muscle Activity • Infrequ
matic-Play Participation • Talking Infrequently • Short Attention Span • Finicky Eating • Overeatin
sy Eating • Hording Food • Hitting • Biting • Throwing Objects at Others • Hurting Others • U
ropriate Language • Name-Calling • Nonsharing • Bribery • Stealing • Noncompliance • Disrup
up Time • Leaving the Classroom • Running Aimlessly Around the Classroom • Shouting in
sroom • Dropping Objects to Create Noise • Tearing Books • Breaking Toys • Flushing Objects D
Toilet • Wasting Paper • Destroying the Work of Others • Throwing Tantrums • Pouting • Baby T
mb-Sucking • Pant-Wetting • Whining • Self-Stimulation • Nonparticipation in Activitie
participation in Social Play • Shyness at Group Time • Playing with Only One Toy • Infrequent L
cle Activity • Infrequent Dramatic-Play Participation • Talking Infrequently • Short Attention Sp
cky Eating • Overeating • Messy Eating • Hording Food • Hitting • Biting • Throwing Objects at Ot
urting Others • Using Inappropriate Language • Name-Calling • Nonsharing • Bribery • Stealin
compliance • Disrupting Group Time • Leaving the Classroom • Running Aimlessly Around
sroom • Shouting in the Classroom • Dropping Objects to Create Noise • Tearing Books • Breaking
ushing Objects Down the Toilet • Wasting Paper • Destroying the Work of Others • Throwing Tantr
outing • Baby Talk • Thumb-Sucking • Pant-Wetting • Clinging • Seeking Attention • Whining •
ulation • Nonparticipation in Activities • Nonparticipation in Social Play • Shyness at Group Tir
equent Large Muscle Activity • Infrequent Dramatic-Play Participation • Talking Infrequently • S
ntion Span • Finicky Eating • Overeating • Messy Eating • Hording Food • Hitting • Biting • Thro
cts at Others • Hurting Others • Using Inappropriate Language • Name-Calling • Nonsharing • Br
ealing • Noncompliance • Disrupting Group Time • Leaving the Classroom • Running Aimlessly Arc
Classroom • Shouting in the Classroom • Dropping Objects to Create Noise • Tearing Books • Brea
s • Flushing Objects Down the Toilet • Wasting Paper • Destroying the Work of Others • Thro
rums • Pouting • Baby Talk • Thumb-Sucking • Pant-Wetting • Clinging • Seeking Attention • Wh
ng • Biting • Throwing Objects at Others • Hurting Others • Using Inappropriate Language • N

chapter 7

Hitting

Raymond, a four-year-old whose mother works full-time, has attended the Happy Hours Children's Center for almost two years. An outgoing, friendly, verbal child, Raymond enjoys all of the activities provided by his teachers. He is imaginative, and frequently engages in pretend play, building elaborate block structures that get incorporated into play scenarios, making props with construction toys, riding the trikes on the "freeway" in the play yard, and often in housekeeping and other dramatic play.

More often than not, Raymond appoints himself as the leader in group play, directing other children's actions and defining their roles. The other children generally go along with Raymond, but when they do not, Raymond hits. After he hits a child, he stalks off, saying, "No one likes me!" At this point, a teacher usually goes to Raymond, tells him that he has hurt the other child and ends up talking with Raymond for several minutes before he stops pouting and agrees to say "I'm sorry" to the child whom he has hit. The teacher continues to reassure Raymond that the other children like him but underscores that they do not like it when he hits them. Raymond generally protests vigorously but allows the teacher to convince him otherwise only after a period of time. Once the teacher leaves, Raymond quickly rejoins the group and reasserts his leadership role.

STATE THE BEHAVIOR

The child regularly hits other children.

OBSERVE THE BEHAVIOR

Spend some time observing and gathering information that can give you further insight into the behavior.

When does the child usually hit?
- At all times of the day
- At particular times, such as late in the day
- During specific activities or routines
- Indoors
- Outdoors
- When children are in close proximity, such as during group time
- During structured activities
- When children have free-choice activities
- During transitions

What seems to trigger the behavior?
- A classmate has something the child wants.
- A classmate takes something away from the child.
- A teacher says no to the child.
- The child is not able to accomplish a task.
- The child has an argument with another child.
- The child is pushed.
- The child is close to others.
- The child is tired.
- There is no observable provocation.
- The child cannot do what he wants.

Who is the victim?
- Usually the same child or a certain few children
- Anyone
- Only timid children
- Only assertive children
- Older or younger children
- Bigger or smaller children
- Boys
- Girls
- Adult(s)

What happens when the child hits?
- The child admits hitting.
- The child denies hitting.
- The child gets upset when the other child cries.
- The child gets hit back.
- The child looks to see if someone is watching before hitting.
- The child apologizes or tries to make the victim feel better.
- The child walks away from the child who was hit.
- The child stays nearby.
- The child laughs.

From this informal information gathering, you should have some idea of why and when the child hits. There is a difference between children who hit to defend property, children who hit out of frustration, and children who hit to get their own way. Hitting cannot be allowed for any reason, but you can help avert some causes for hitting by being observant and aware.

CONSULT WITH THE FAMILY

Once you have had the opportunity to observe the child's behavior, meet with the family to gain some insights into the child's behavior from their experiences and perspective. It is particularly important to discern whether hitting occurs primarily at school or whether it occurs in other settings as well. If the child does hit elsewhere, explore what happens at home or in other family settings. When, against whom, where, and how does the child engage in hitting? For instance, are siblings or other children involved? Share with the family what you have learned from your observations about the child's hitting at school, and discuss whether there are similarities in school and home incidents. Find out what strategies the family uses when the child hits. Brainstorm other options. Once you begin implementing strategies to decrease the child's incidents of hitting, keep the family informed, especially of successes.

CONSIDER THE IMPLICATIONS

When a child often hits others, it is easy for the teacher to react in self-defeating ways. Because injury to another child must be avoided if at all possible, a frequent response is to scold and lecture the hitter. The teacher may spend several minutes with the child each time hitting occurs, explaining what was done wrong and why others should not be hit. This attention may be negative, but it is attention nonetheless.

Almost invariably, the child who hits is very aware of having done something inappropriate. This awareness is often confirmed by the child who looks to see whether someone is watching before hitting or by quickly apologizing after the episode. Over a period of time, the teacher is reinforcing the child's feeling that an effective way to get attention is to hit another child.

EXPLORE ALTERNATIVES

From your informal observation, you might find an alternative remedy for hitting. Consider some of the following possibilities:

- If the child always hits one particular child, separating the two should be considered. Very possibly the victim is in some way provoking the other child to hit. Removing one of them from the scene may help. If one of the children can be placed in another classroom, this should be done. If this is not possible, then you should be alert at all times to where these two children are and make efforts to keep them separated. The hitter has no target if the other child is not sitting nearby or is playing in another area of the room.
- Crowded situations tend to provoke hitting in some children. It may help to decrease the times when crowding occurs. Eliminate lining-up times by using different group-management techniques to move children from one activity to another. For example, dismiss a few children at a time to go to the next area. Group times can be less crowded if children are asked to sit in a large circle or semicircle where everyone can see. You can sit next to or between certain children to further prevent potential problems. Say, "I'd really love to sit with you today," or "Will you sit next to me so you can be my special helper?"
- If a child tends to hit when frustrated, you should be more aware of situations in which this might happen. For instance, if a puzzle is difficult for a child, sit down with the child and help complete the puzzle or suggest a simpler one. This helps the child to achieve more success, which diminishes frustrations and subsequent hitting.
- Examine the classroom to be sure that available materials and activities are age-appropriate for the children in the group and that there are enough of these. If materials are too simple, too difficult, or scarce, boredom or frustration can lead to challenging behavior such as hitting.
- A very young preschooler may hit because he lacks the verbal skills to express his needs, is asserting his independence, or is

protecting what he perceives as his property. Two- and young three-year-olds need considerable help in learning socially acceptable ways to get what they want. For this reason, it is important to have a relatively low ratio of adults to children (one adult for every four to six young preschoolers). When the number of adults is appropriate, their combined vigilance can be used to gently guide children to getting their needs met by verbalizing for them, by prevention, or by offering a duplicate of or alternative to the item they want. For this reason, it is important to provide duplicates of most toys in a classroom of young preschoolers.

- If the child tends to hit late in the day or close to nap time, his behavior may be provoked by tiredness. If it is possible to have the child take an earlier nap, arrange such an alternative. Otherwise, keep a close watch on the child when you recognize that he is getting tired, and prevent situations that could lead to hitting.

- A child's hitting may be a reflection of insecure attachment. Often children who are not securely attached to a parent react with aggression toward others. This is a symptom of the need for attention, consistency, and reassurance. Children certainly develop an attachment to their teachers and caregivers, and a secure attachment at school can help a child develop a more stable sense of self.

- Some children may be experiencing undue stress, which may also result in aggressive behavior such as hitting. Providing a calm, consistent, and reassuring environment with nurturing teachers can, in the long run, help the child deal more effectively with stress.

If the solution to the problem does not lie in one of these suggestions, then you must follow a more detailed approach.

STATE THE GOAL

The goal is for the child not to hit other children.

APPROACH

The basic approach involves three simultaneous strategies:
- Try to prevent incidents of hitting.
- Praise the child for desired social behaviors.
- Use self-control time if the child does hit someone.

DEFINITION

Hitting is any instance of deliberate aggression in which a child strikes someone.

STARTING POINT

Before making changes, it is important to know how often the child hits another child in the classroom. This information provides a baseline against which improvements can be gauged. Whenever the child hits, take note of the incident by marking it on paper.

At the end of the day, add up the marks, and record the number on a Frequency Record-Keeping Graph. Keep track in this way for three consecutive days.

STRATEGIES

After you have kept track of incidents of hitting for three days, begin the following strategies. It is especially important that all teachers consistently follow the same approach.

Prevent Incidents of Hitting Whenever Possible.* From your informal observation, you should have some ideas of when to expect hitting. Be especially alert during such times. The old saying, "An ounce of prevention is worth a pound of cure" is very appropriate. Prevent hitting by looking for cues. For instance, if a child ends up hitting when playing with blocks, be in the block area when the child is there. Help the child deal with frustration if the blocks fall. Explain the need for sharing blocks, and provide the chance to work cooperatively with another child. Model appropriate behavior, and facilitate positive social interaction: "Look! Mary wants to play with us in the block area, too. Mary, we're building a barn. Would you help us find this size of blocks for the walls?" In other words, make a positive situation out of something that is potentially negative.

In this way the child eventually acquires the skills to deal with situations in ways other than hitting. As alternatives to hitting are

---

Prevention is especially important for children with disabilities. A child with a recognized emotional/behavioral disability, a child with a cognitive deficit, or a child who had been prenatally exposed to drugs or alcohol may need particular vigilance. It may take longer to help the child learn alternative ways of resolving conflicts.

learned, the hitting decreases. As hitting gradually disappears, you can trust the child's self-control more and decrease the constant vigilance.

Praise the Child for Desired Social Behaviors. At the same time that you are watching the child for potential hitting, observe positive behaviors. When the child handles a social situation well, say so. Let the child know how pleased you are. Remember, as hitting decreases, so does the negative attention—there are fewer chances to be scolded and lectured. But the child still needs and wants attention. Attention given for positive behavior helps ensure that the appropriate behaviors continue. If the child lacks social skills, it is especially important to reinforce behaviors close to the appropriate behavior.

If the Child Does Hit Someone, Use Self-Control Time. If a child hits another youngster, do the following:

1. Quickly make sure the child who was hit is all right. If possible, another teacher should attend to the victim.

2. Calmly take the aggressive child by the hand to the self-control time area. Firmly but quietly say, "I cannot allow you to hurt other children. Please stay here until you are ready to join your friends again."

3. Move away and do not talk with or look at the child during self-control time. Verbal or visual contact may well serve as a reinforcer to the child for his behavior.

4. If another child approaches the self-control time area, quietly move this child away. Explain, "Raymond needs to be by himself for a few minutes. You can talk to him when he joins the class again."

5. The child can rejoin classroom activities when he feels that he is ready. Do not lecture. He knows the reason for the isolation. To channel the child into constructive behavior, you might suggest joining an ongoing activity. It is very important to reinforce the child as soon as possible for engaging in appropriate activity.

6. If the child rejoins the classroom before he is ready and again engages in the unacceptable behavior, say to him, "I guess you're not quite ready to join us," and take him back to the self-control area. Again allow him to determine when he is ready to rejoin the group.

 Continue Keeping Track of the Behavior. To ensure that change is occurring, continue to record any hitting incidents on the graph. Progress will probably be gradual. By recording on the graph, you will be able to see change, even though it will be a while before the behavior will be completely eliminated. The decrease in hitting incidents should be encouraging because it means that the behavior is improving.

MAINTAINING THE CHANGES

Once hitting is eliminated, be sure to continue giving attention to appropriate social behavior. Let the child know how much you appreciate his willingness to replace the old inappropriate hitting behavior with new social skills.

The CD-ROM that accompanies this text contains several hypothetical scenarios designed for you to apply the guidance principles suggested in the various chapters of this book. Go to the Your Turn section of the CD to access these scenarios. The first two scenarios are particularly pertinent to this section of the text, Aggressive and Antisocial Behaviors.

chapter 8

Biting

Two-year-old Jenny has been in her school only two months. She comes three mornings a week while her mother takes classes at the university. Jenny is a little blonde who has not yet lost all of her baby fat. She loves coming to school, and joins all the activity with great enthusiasm. She is a very loving child who frequently hugs teachers and peers alike.

However, Jenny bites. If someone has a car, a puzzle, or a stuffed animal that Jenny wants, she simply bites the person who has the desired item. At other times, she walks up to a child, smilingly puts her arms around her friend, and sinks her teeth into the child's cheek. She has bitten her neighbor at snack time if the crackers did not reach her quickly enough and in the bathroom while waiting to wash her hands. A few days ago, she bit a child on the ankle when that child did not climb up on the climber quickly enough.

The teachers' response to Jenny's biting has always been to tell Jenny how much she has hurt the other child and to scold her for biting. She is reminded that she would not like it if one of the children bit her. Jenny is usually very contrite and apologizes readily to her victim. Her concern does not last long, however. She is back at play quickly. Sometimes she does not bite again for the remainder of the day, but at other times she finds a new victim within a few minutes.

STATE THE BEHAVIOR

The child frequently bites other children.

OBSERVE THE BEHAVIOR

Before taking any steps, observe the child for a few days to gain some insight into the behavior.

When does the child usually bite?
- At all times of the day
- During specific activities or routines
- Indoors
- Outdoors
- During group times when children are close together
- During teacher-directed activities
- During free-choice activities
- At nap time
- During transitions
- When the child is cranky

What seems to trigger the behavior?
- Someone takes something from the child.
- Someone else has something the child wants.
- The child is tired.
- It is close to mealtime.
- The child is not able to accomplish a task.
- The child is told no.
- The child sees another child hurt a peer.
- The child is in close proximity to others.
- The child is restless and not engaged in a specific activity.
- The child has to wait.

Who is the victim?
- Anyone
- Children of the same age or size
- Younger or smaller children
- Children who grab from the child
- Anyone close by

What happens when the child bites?
- The child looks to see if someone is watching before biting.
- The child apologizes or tries to make the victim feel better afterward.

- The child walks off as though nothing has happened.
- The child gets upset when the other child cries.

Other factors to observe:
- Whether the child bites herself
- Whether the child bites objects such as blocks and plastic rings
- Whether the child often puts clothing, toys, or fingers into her mouth

This preliminary observation should give you some idea about when, why, and how biting occurs. Most often the biter is a young preschooler, probably a two-year-old. Biting is a phase many young children go through, but it cannot be allowed because it is dangerous. Therefore, the more clues you have to help you deal with this behavior, the more you can work at preventing it.

CONSULT WITH THE FAMILY

Set up a meeting time with the family once you have had an opportunity to observe the child's biting for several days. Find out from the family if biting occurs in settings other than at school, for instance, at home. Discuss with family members what strategies they use when the child bites. Particularly if the child is a toddler or just moving out of the toddler phase, share with the family the fact that biting is quite common at this age, and that the behavior seems to disappear, even though biting should not be ignored or condoned. Brainstorm with family members what strategies they might have found effective. Be firm that you do not use punitive methods at school and that your aim is to help the child gain other skills to get what she wants. Once you have begun strategies to decrease biting, keep the family informed of successes.

CONSIDER THE IMPLICATIONS

Biting is a natural behavior for very young children. Many children, however, do not yet have the social awareness to control this behavior when it is directed against others. The two-year-old is still socially unsophisticated and not well attuned to the feelings of peers and to the finer points of social interaction. Furthermore, teething may be occurring, and like the baby who gums objects, the child may be trying to relieve the discomfort in one way or another.

The teacher must be aware that the two-year-old who bites is most likely going through a stage that will soon pass. The teacher cannot allow biting, but can be sensitive to the reason the child is biting and help prevent this behavior.

Whenever one child hurts another child, a teacher's natural reaction may be to consider the action as a misbehavior and to scold, lecture, or otherwise punish the biter. The child discovers that whenever she bites, she gets quite a bit of attention. Thus, the teacher's reaction reinforces biting as one way to get an adult to quickly attend. There is confusion for the child, who is held accountable for an act that to the child is not malicious. The child's self-concept suffers when adults get angry about behaviors that she cannot control yet.

EXPLORE THE ALTERNATIVES

Informal clues might give some ideas of environmental changes that can help the teacher deal with the young biter.

- Crowding may stimulate the two-year-old to bite; classes for this age should be kept small. Groups of 8 to 12 children, with two or three teachers, can help decrease this behavior.

- Two-year-olds need many sensory activities. The classroom should be set up to allow for a lot of touching, feeling, smelling, tasting, hearing, seeing, and manipulating. Because objects may be put into the child's mouth, they should be safe and hygienic. Allowing for tasting and biting of objects may help avert the impulse to bite people.

- The classroom environment should have age-appropriate materials and activities within the reach of the children. If materials are not geared for the needs and abilities of two-year-olds, children will experience frustration. Some children may express their frustration by biting their peers.

- The environment should also be arranged in such a way that all teachers can easily see all areas of the room and all the children. Careful supervision of very young preschoolers is especially important, and allows for more conscious preventive measures.

- A classroom for toddlers should have duplicates of most of the materials available to the children. Two-year-olds have not yet mastered the art of sharing. Thus, having access to more than one of their favorite play materials is reassuring and can prevent biting and other aggressive acts.

- Evaluate the timing of snacks and meals. A child may bite because of hunger, and providing food at frequent intervals may deter biting.

- There may be an alternative, physiological explanation when a child suddenly begins to bite other children when she has not done so before. For instance, the child may have an ear infection, and she seeks to relieve the discomfort by biting.

If the resolution to the concern does not lie in your earlier observations or one of these suggestions, then read the next section for a more systematic approach.

STATE THE GOAL

The goal is for the teachers to help the two-year-old find acceptable alternatives for biting and thus to decrease biting.

APPROACH

The approach presented here deals with biting by two-year-olds and relies basically on preventive measures by the teachers.

- Ensure that the classroom environment is as effective as possible.
- Prevent biting by being alert to potential situations in which biting may occur.
- Reinforce appropriate social behavior.
- If biting does occur, let the child know it is unacceptable.

Note that these steps are suggested for younger preschoolers. For an older child, use the strategies outlined in Chapter 5.

DEFINITION

Biting is any incident in which the child sinks her teeth into any part of another person's body.

STARTING POINT

To be able to effectively evaluate your actions and to recognize when the child begins to get over the biting stage, keep track of all incidents of biting. In a convenient place in the classroom, post a sheet of paper on which you can simply indicate with a checkmark each time the child bites. For three days, record the total number of bites on a Frequency Record-Keeping Graph.

STRATEGIES

After you have kept track of incidents of biting for three days, begin the following strategies. It is especially important that all teachers consistently follow the same approach.

Ensure that the Classroom Environment Is as Effective as Possible.
Continually check the classroom arrangement, materials, and schedule to ensure they meet the needs of two-year-olds. The more smoothly the

classroom runs, the less the potential frustrations and clashes between children. Two-year-olds tire easily, may need a snack between meals, have a short attention span, and desire immediate attention. They may play near rather than with other children and may have difficulty sharing. Take these characteristics into account both in your expectations and in how you plan and handle classroom routines.

Prevent Biting by Being Alert to Potential Situations in Which Biting May Occur. When you know that a child tends to bite under certain circumstances, you can take preventive steps. Stay near the child and carefully watch her. If she seems about to bite, pick her up and move her. If she fights you, gently restrain her until she stops struggling. If the child accepts being moved, immediately channel her attention to an activity. Do not lecture! Give the child something to bite on if she seems to need to bite.

Reinforce Acceptable Social Behavior. The two-year-old has much to learn about positive peer interaction, including the fact that biting is not an acceptable means of communication. Praise the child for appropriate social behaviors. Let her know that you like what she is doing, and help her verbalize her feelings to other children. The more the child learns positive alternatives to biting and other forms of aggression, the more her social interactions will be satisfactory to her and her peers.

If Biting Occurs, Let the Child Know It Is Unacceptable. Biting should be decreased through preventive measures, but occasionally a child will still bite. In such a case, do the following:

1. Say to the child who bit, "No! It hurts when you bite. See, Shonna is crying because it hurts."
2. Take the child who was bitten to wash the affected area and apply first aid as needed. Have the child who bit go along with you.
3. Involve the child who bit in the process of comforting and tending to the bitten child. Verbalize the process. Encourage the child to help by patting the child who was hurt, holding a bandage, or otherwise helping. This provides a model for empathy and positive social reaction.

Continue Keeping Track of the Behavior. Use the graph to keep daily track of the number of incidents of biting. If you find that there is still an excessive number, examine your preventive measures. These may need to be strengthened. With adequate vigilance by all adults in the room, biting should decrease considerably.

MAINTAINING THE CHANGES

When, over a period of time, the graph shows no more occurrences of biting, the child has probably passed through the biting phase. You can discontinue the deliberate preventive measures. Continue reinforcing acceptable social behavior, because socialization is a long-term learning process.

 The CD-ROM that accompanies this text contains several hypothetical scenarios designed for you to apply the guidance principles suggested in the various chapters of this book. Go to the Your Turn section of the CD to access these scenarios. The first two scenarios are particularly pertinent to this section of the text, Aggressive and Antisocial Behaviors.

Biting • Throwing Objects at Others • Hurting Others • Using Inappropriate Calling • Nonsharing • Bribery • Stealing • Noncompliance • Disrupting the Classroom • Running Aimlessly Around the Classroom • Shouting Objects to Create Noise • Books • Breaking Toys • Flushing Objects Wasting Paper • Destroying the Work of Others • Throwing Tantrums • Poking • Baby Talk • Thumb-Sucking • Pants-Wetting • Clinging • Seeking Attention • Short Only One Toy • Infrequent Use Music Activity • Infrequent Dramatic Attention Span • Finicky Eating • Overeating Eating • Hoarding • Biting • Hitting • Biting • Throwing Objects at Others • Inappropriate Language • Name-Calling • Nonsharing • Bribery • Stealing • Ruting Group Time • Leaving the Classroom • Running Aimlessly Around the in the Classroom • Dropping Objects to Create Noise • Tearing Books • Flushing Objects Down the Toilet • Wasting Paper • Destroying the Work of Calling Tantrums • Poking • Baby Talk • Thumb-Sucking • Pants-Wetting •

chapter 9

Throwing Objects at Others

Another crash! All the teachers quickly look around the room, all trying to see where Mark is.

They have become increasingly concerned because four-year-old Mark seems so easily provoked to anger. If Mark does not get his way, he loses his temper. In the past few weeks Mark has been getting angry over little things more frequently. When Mark gets angry, he picks up the nearest object and throws it at whoever provoked him. Mark has thrown blocks, puzzle pieces, brushes, trucks, dishes, shoes, stuffed animals, and even scissors and chairs. When he throws, he aims to hit, and often does. Luckily, no one has been seriously hurt, but Mark has caused several cuts and bruises.

The other children in the class have been actively expressing their fear and dislike of Mark, which also angers him. Recently, when Mark hit Marcie on the back with a block, Marcie's friend Ricky shouted, "I hate you, Mark! You hurt Marcie." In response, Mark picked another block and threw it at Ricky.

The teachers have scolded Mark, lectured him, tried to reason with him, and threatened to withhold privileges, but to no avail. Mark still throws objects when he gets angry.

STATE THE BEHAVIOR

The child regularly throws toys and other objects, deliberately aiming these at other children.

OBSERVE THE BEHAVIOR

A few days spent informally observing the child can give you a better idea of what is happening.

When does the child usually throw objects?
- Unpredictably, at any time of day
- During free-choice activities
- During structured activities
- Outdoors
- Indoors
- Early in the day
- Late in the day
- At mealtimes

What usually happens before the child throws an object?
- Another child angers him.
- Another child takes something away from him.
- Another child has something the child wants.
- The child argues with another.
- The child is hit by another child.
- The child is told no by another child or a teacher.
- The child looks to see if a teacher is watching.

Who is the victim?
- Usually the same child or a few children
- Anyone
- Anyone who provokes the child
- Only assertive children
- Only timid children
- Older and bigger children
- Smaller and younger children
- Boys
- Girls

What objects are usually thrown?
- Whatever is in the child's hand
- Any object within reach

- Only hard objects
- Only sharp objects
- Only soft objects
- Only small objects
- Only large objects
- One particular object or type of object

What happens after the child has thrown an object at another child?
- The object misses the target.
- The object hits the target.
- The child is angry if the object does not hit the target.
- The child admits throwing the object.
- The child denies throwing the object.
- The child retrieves the object.
- The child looks to see if an adult is watching.
- The child gets upset when the other child is hit.
- The child apologizes or tries to make the victim feel better.
- The child walks away.
- The child stays nearby.

These informal observations should give a more complete picture of when, how, and why the child throws objects. This information helps you to find a solution to the situation.

CONSULT WITH THE FAMILY

Once you have completed your observations, plan to meet as soon as possible with the family to discuss the child's behavior. Find out if the child throws objects at home or in other nonschool settings. If this is the case, ask the family under what circumstances the behavior seems to occur, why they think the child engages in the behavior, and what response they have found to be effective. Share with the family insights you have gleaned from your observations. Brainstorm with the family ideas for changing this behavior, and keep them informed of the child's successes once you begin to implement the strategies outlined below.

CONSIDER THE IMPLICATIONS

The child who throws objects at other children is a danger in the class-room. Another child could be seriously hurt from an airborne item, particularly if it is hard or sharp. The teacher may feel an urgent need to stop such potentially dangerous behavior. The teacher thus usually reacts quickly and emotionally to the child who has thrown by severely stating how dangerous the behavior is and what was done wrong. The teacher may even use some form of punishment because of the seriousness of the problem. In whatever way the teacher reacts, the following message is conveyed to the child: Throwing things gets quite a reaction out of adults. They get excited and pay particular attention when an object is thrown.

The child relieves anger or frustration by the act of throwing and then gets attention for the action.* Almost invariably, when a child aims and throws objects at someone else, it is done out of anger or frustration. Furthermore, it is often the case that such a youngster is not very verbal or has trouble expressing feelings. The child's inability or reluctance to use verbal expression leads to a physical expression of his anger or frustration. When the teacher scolds the child after he has thrown something, the child is given attention for negative behavior, but is not helped to deal with the problem.

EXPLORE ALTERNATIVES

Through observation you might find some clues to the behavior that will help you eliminate it fairly quickly.

- If the child throws only one particular object, remove that object from the classroom for a few weeks. If, for instance, the child throws only wooden unit blocks, take these away. After a week or two, you might try substituting larger hollow blocks, which would be difficult to throw; or lightweight plastic, cardboard, or homemade milk-carton blocks. After several weeks have passed, reintroduce the wooden unit blocks. Leave them in the classroom if the child has overcome the desire to throw the blocks.

- If one particular child is always the target, this child may provoke the aggression. If at all possible, separate the two children by putting them into different areas of the room. Guide them into separate activities, and keep a careful eye on their whereabouts. Removing the target may well remove the problem in this case.

- The child may benefit from activities in which throwing is a legitimate aim. For instance, set up a game in which the objective is to get small beanbags into a container or through a cut-out hole in a target.

*Usually one can recognize what triggers the frustration that leads to a reaction like throwing objects. In the case of some children who have been prenatally affected by drugs, there appears to be no precursor to an aggressive act. Behavior seems to be quite unpredictable. Vigilance is, therefore, especially important as a preventive measure.

If none of these suggestions provides a solution to the problem, then continue to the following, more detailed, approach.

STATE THE GOAL

The goal is for the child not to throw objects at other children and to learn appropriate ways of communicating anger or frustration.

APPROACH

The basic strategy will involve these simultaneous steps:
- Prevent as many incidents of throwing objects as possible.
- Systematically help the child learn appropriate alternatives to dealing with anger or frustration.
- Use self-control time if the child throws an object at someone.

DEFINITION

Throwing objects at others is any deliberate action in which a child attempts to hurt another child by aiming and throwing something at the child.

STARTING POINT

In order to know how often the behavior is occurring, spend three days keeping track of the frequency of object throwing. This must be done before you begin implementing any changes. Mark on a paper each time the child throws something at another child. At the end of each day, record this number on a Frequency Record-Keeping Graph to establish the base against which to gauge future improvements.

STRATEGIES

After gathering information on the frequency of throwing objects, begin the following strategies. All teachers must be aware of and cooperate in the approach in order for it to be effective.

Whenever Possible, Prevent the Child from Throwing an Object at Someone Else. Based on informal observation, you should have some idea of what provokes the child to throw objects and when to expect such behavior. Take careful note of any cues. For instance, the child might precede the behavior by clenching his fists or yelling. Or perhaps the only warning is a verbal or nonverbal disagreement between the child and a classmate.

Whatever the cues, however, it requires vigilance on the part of all the teachers to recognize these signs and then to prevent the behavior. When you recognize a cue, follow this approach:

1. Go to the child who throws things and place yourself in front of him. Block the other child from view by placing yourself between the two children.

2. Get to the child's level and gently but firmly place your hands on his upper arms to limit the freedom of his arms.

3. When you feel the tension going out of his body, release your hold, or change it to a hug.

4. At this time you are ready for the next step.

Systematically Help the Child Learn Appropriate Alternatives for Dealing with Anger and Frustration.

It is important to prevent the child from hurting others. But it is equally important to help the child gain skills in using acceptable alternatives to aggression. When the initial anger is gone, take a few moments to talk with the child about what has happened. At first, use the following approach:

1. Ask, "What's the problem?" If you have seen what preceded the anger, help the child verbalize the situation. "You are upset because Leslie has the truck you want." Even if you make the initial statement, make sure the child also verbalizes the problem in some way.

2. Once the problem has been stated, say, "I wonder what we can do about it?" Give the child the chance to come up with a suggestion. Praise the child if the suggestion is socially acceptable. If the idea is not acceptable, say, "What else could we try?"

3. If the child has no suggestions, state a way of handling the situation. For instance, say, "We could ask Leslie if you could play with her and the truck. You and Leslie could build a road with blocks for the truck to drive on."

4. Try role-playing: "Let's pretend I'm Leslie, and you want the truck I am playing with." Pretend you are playing with a truck. Ask, "What will you say to me?" Help the child to phrase an acceptable suggestion. Respond as if you were Leslie. Agree to share the truck.

5. When the role-playing is completed, praise the child and then help him find an activity to engage in.

6. It may take several weeks to reach this point, but remember that you are teaching the child a new response to feelings that previously aroused aggression.

When the child demonstrates an understanding of alternative ways of handling anger and frustration and responds naturally to role-playing, move to the next step:

1. Ask, "What's the problem?" By this time the child should have had enough practice to tell you why he is angry.

2. Once the problem has been stated, ask the child what he might do about it. Praise him for appropriate suggestions.

3. Now tell the child that you would like him to try his suggestion with the other child involved. For instance, say, "Let's go tell that to Leslie."

4. Go with the child and encourage a friendly solution to the situation. If necessary, use some subtle intervention to structure success. It is important for the child to recognize that the acceptable alternatives you have been teaching really work.

5. Praise both children involved for their cooperation.

As the child demonstrates increased competence in handling anger or frustration in acceptable ways, decrease your role gradually. The child should be able to assume increasing responsibility for his actions. Praise the child frequently; let the child know how happy you are with the new behavior. Also, at any time during the process of teaching new behavior, give lavish praise if the child handles a potential conflict situation in an acceptable way.

If the Child Does Throw an Object at Another Child, Use Self-Control Time. If the child throws an object at another youngster, whether he hits his target or not, do the following:

1. Quickly make sure that the child at whom the object was aimed was not hit. If the child was hit, make sure the child is all right. If possible, another teacher should attend to the victim.

2. Calmly take the aggressive child by the hand to the self-control time area. Firmly but quietly say, "I cannot allow you to hurt other children. Please stay here until you are ready to join your friends again."

3. Move away and do not talk with or look at the child during self-control time. Verbal or visual contact may well serve as a reinforcer to the child for his behavior.

4. If this has not been done already, pick up the object that was thrown and replace it in its appropriate place. Do not make an issue of having the child do this, because such a request can easily result in a power struggle. The point you want to make is that it is unacceptable to hurt or try to hurt others, not that objects have a proper place. The latter behavior, though an important one to convey to children, should be taught at another time in a different context.

5. If another child approaches, quietly move this child away. Explain, "Mark needs to be by himself for a few minutes. You can talk to him when he joins the class again."

6. The child can rejoin classroom activities when he feels that he is ready. Do not lecture. The child knows the reason for the isolation. To channel the child into constructive behavior, you might suggest joining an ongoing activity. It is very important to reinforce the child as soon as possible for engaging in appropriate activity.

7. If the child rejoins the classroom before he is ready and again throws an object at another child, say to him, "I guess you're not quite ready to join us," and take him back to the self-control area. Again allow him to determine when he is ready to rejoin the group.

Continue Keeping Track of the Behavior. It is important to continue to graph the number of object-throwing incidents that occur each day. By keeping track, you will be able to see at a glance whether change is occurring. You can also get an idea of when to move from one step to the next in your approach. For instance, before moving the child from role-playing with you to actually talking with another child, there should be a substantial decrease in object-throwing. Similarly, before you decrease your role in cuing the child's behavior, the object-throwing incidents should have decreased to zero or near zero. The graph tells you that the child is learning from your efforts.

MAINTAINING THE CHANGES

Once the child has stopped throwing objects at other children, be sure to continue praising the child for using appropriate alternatives to this behavior. What the child has learned has not eliminated situations that anger or frustrate him. These situations continue to occur. The child has learned some acceptable ways of handling these feelings and should feel satisfaction at having learned to control them. Continued support reinforces the new behavior.

The CD-ROM that accompanies this text contains several hypothetical scenarios designed for you to apply the guidance principles suggested in the various chapters of this book. Go to the Your Turn section of the CD to access these scenarios. The first two scenarios are particularly pertinent to this section of the text, Aggressive and Antisocial Behaviors.

chapter 10

Hurting Others

Teddy, who started at the nursery school three months ago, has earned the title of "most aggressive child" from the teachers. Teddy is quickly aroused to anger by other children, and then he attacks them in an uninhibited manner. He has no single way of hurting other children. He uses whatever means he can to get at them. He hits, bites, pulls hair, punches, slaps, pushes, pokes, knocks others down, and jumps on them.

From the beginning the other children in the class have not liked Teddy. When he engages in an activity, he generally plays alone. No one wants to be around him. Even so, Teddy finds ways to pick fights. Sometimes he goes to another child and grabs what the child is working with, saying, "I want that." If the other child resists, Teddy begins a fight. At other times he tries to join a group of children at play. If he is not accepted, he starts a fight. This behavior occurs three or four times every morning.

The teachers have talked to Teddy, expressed anger with him, and have tried to help the other children include him in their play. Teddy continues in his anger and aggression.

STATE THE BEHAVIOR

The child hurts other children in a variety of ways, such as hitting, kicking, biting, pinching, and wrestling. Several forms of aggression are used in unpredictable ways.

OBSERVE THE BEHAVIOR

Get as much information as you can through informal observation of the child.

When does the behavior occur?
- At all times of the day
- During specific activities, such as group times, discussion, or music
- When children are in close proximity
- During transitions from one activity to another
- During structured activities
- During free-choice activities
- At outdoor play times
- Indoors
- Around mealtime

What usually happens before the behavior occurs?
- Another child has something that the child wants.
- The child has a verbal argument with another child.
- The child is told no by a child or teacher.
- The child is close to others.
- The child is pushed.
- The child appears tired.
- The child is provoked by another child.
- The child is not able to accomplish a task.
- The child does not want to participate in class routines.
- There is no apparent provocation.

Who is usually the victim?
- The same child or a certain few children
- Anyone
- Anyone who argues with the child
- Only timid children
- Only assertive children
- Older or bigger children

- Younger or smaller children
- Boys
- Girls

What happens when the child hurts another youngster?
- The child looks around to see if an adult is watching.
- The child admits hurting the other child.
- The child denies hurting the other child.
- The other child hurts the offender in return.
- The child apologizes or tries to make the victim feel better.
- The child goes on to hurt other children.
- The child stays near the child who was hurt.
- The child tries to hurt the same child again.
- The child walks away.

How does the child hurt other children?
- There is a relation between what happened before the child hurt someone and how he hurts that child.
- There is a relation between whom the child hurts and how he hurts that child.
- There is a relation between where the child is at the time he hurts someone and how he hurts that child.
- There appears to be no relation between how the child hurts other children and what preceded the aggression, who the other child is, and where the incident takes place.

This informal observation period should provide clues to the problem, which will help you implement ways of eliminating such behavior.

CONSULT WITH THE FAMILY

As soon as possible, once you have completed your observations, meet with the family to discuss the child's behavior. Assure the family that you want to work together with them and learn from them what strategies they find to be effective. Determine if the behavior occurs in settings other than school, such as at home, church, or family gatherings. Ask the family about the circumstances under which the behavior occurs when the child is not at school. Share with them what you have learned from your observations. Discuss with the family possible reasons for the child's aggression against others. Also, emphasize that your goal is to help the child learn more productive ways of interacting with others. Keep in close contact with the family, and especially share with them decreases in the behavior once these begin to occur.

CONSIDER THE IMPLICATIONS

The child who hurts other children by using a variety of methods is unpredictable. Such a child is a serious problem in the preschool classroom. When an aggressive child uses hitting to hurt others, the teachers have some idea of how the aggression will be expressed. When the child shows no consistency in method, however, the teachers cannot be sure how an attack will occur. Furthermore, this situation presents more danger of serious injury, because often the child who reacts unpredictably has a quick temper and moves swiftly and recklessly. The child gets caught up in feelings of anger, resulting in uninhibited reactions. He may not be aware of how much he may be hurting another child. Admonishing, talking to, and punishing the child are the methods most often used by teachers to change the behavior. These methods, however, do not work. The child has to be told in no uncertain terms that such behavior is not to be tolerated. The child must also be helped to control his temper and reactions to situations that anger him.

EXPLORE ALTERNATIVES

There is probably no simple solution to dealing with the child who hurts others in varied and unpredictable ways. However, consider the following suggestions:

- If this behavior occurs only during specific activities or times of day, vary the routine. Young children often react negatively to crowding, waiting, or having to stop an activity. It may be such a situation that results in aggression. Crowding can be avoided: Designate a larger circle or semicircle at group times. Find alternatives to lining up: Have children go a few at a time to the bathroom or to get coats while the rest participate in singing songs or fingerplays. Young children are not able to wait very long. The program should be structured to minimize waits. If the teachers know that a particular child has difficulty waiting, structure the program to minimize such times until the child is able to wait for longer periods. It is also difficult for a young child to stop an activity in which he is engrossed. Unnecessary interruptions can be avoided. Plan sufficiently large time blocks for activities. Also, let the child know several minutes before the end of an activity that he will soon have to stop.
- If one child is usually the victim of aggression by the child who concerns you, separate the two. If possible, move one of the youngsters into a different classroom. If this cannot be done, keep the two children separated within the class. Encourage them to engage in different activities. Do not let them sit next to each other

at group times and mealtimes, and place them in different groups if the class is divided for small group activities. It may require considerable effort and vigilance, but the decreased aggression should be worth it.

• Often, an overly aggressive child is reacting to a situation in his own life over which he has little or no control. Be aware of what is happening in the child's life by talking to his family. You can then more easily convey understanding and empathy by letting the child know that you are aware that he feels hurt and confused. At the same time, the child can be provided with alternatives to striking out at others. For instance, you may tell the child, "When you feel sad or angry or upset, I will be here to give you a hug and talk with you about it." You will find more detailed examples of how to discuss feelings with the child later in this chapter.

In the case of the child who hurts other youngsters through a variety of means, these measures probably will not, of themselves, eliminate the problem. Such aggression is most likely triggered by more than classroom routine or the presence of a certain child. You may combine either of these suggestions with the following strategies.

STATE THE GOAL

The goal is for the child to stop hurting other children and to find acceptable alternatives for handling anger.

APPROACH

You will eliminate the child's behavior of hurting other children by using several simultaneous steps:

• Prevent instances of aggression whenever possible.
• Praise all positive interactions.
• Systematically help the child learn to control the impulse to hurt others.
• Use self-control time when the child does hurt someone.

DEFINITION

Hurting others through a variety of means includes all instances of aggression aimed at other children through use of different approaches such as hitting, kicking, biting, and punching. Teachers should agree on what constitutes aggressive behavior and list all forms of aggression that are noticed.

STARTING POINT

Before implementing any changes, take three days to count the number of times the child hurts others. Every time he hurts another child, mark the incident on paper. At the end of each day, transfer the total number onto a Frequency Record-Keeping Graph. This information provides a measure against which to evaluate later progress.

STRATEGIES

Once you have kept track of incidents in which the child hurts other children, you are ready to begin. It is important that all teachers cooperate and follow this approach consistently.

Prevent Aggressive Incidents Whenever Possible.* Informal observation should have given you some idea of when and under what circumstances the child is most likely to hurt others. Using such information, be on the lookout for any clues that indicate the child is about to hurt another child.

If the child's anger is already aroused, do one of two things, depending on the reactions of the child:

1. If the child is receptive to talking, discuss his anger with him.
2. If the child does not respond to talking and simply wants to hit someone, use physical restraint. Put your arms around the child in a way that conveys your concern for him as a person as well as your need to keep him from attacking another child. It is important not to reflect anger in the way you hold him. (If you find that you tend to show anger at the child in such circumstances, it would be better to let another teacher handle the situation. You cannot fight anger with more anger.) Hold the child in this way until you feel the tension leave him. Then give him a hug and tell him, "I'm glad you didn't hurt Luke." Help the child find an activity to engage in.

Preventing situations that might lead to anger and aggression is preferable to preventing aggression once anger has been aroused. Again, use the clues you found in your initial observations, and be alert to any potential problems. Consistency as to when, where, or under what circumstances the child usually hurts others alerts you to stay close by and be on the lookout for the behavior.

---

*Usually one can recognize a situation that leads to an aggressive reaction. In the case of some children who have been prenatally affected by drugs, there appears to be no precursor to an aggressive act. Behavior seems to be quite unpredictable. Vigilance is, therefore, especially important as a preventive measure.

Praise All Positive Social Interactions. The child needs to learn acceptable ways of dealing with peers. It is important to let the child know when his social behavior is appropriate. Praise positive interactions as often as possible:

- "Thank you for helping Luke. That was very nice of you."
- "I like the way you and Luke are working on the puzzle together."
- "It was really great of you to let Luke help you build that garage with the blocks. I know how much he likes to play with you."
- "Luke is pushing you on the swing. What fun! After you've had a turn, you can push him, right?" Avoid referring to the challenging behavior (e.g. "You're not hurting Luke. That's good.")

Systematically Help the Child Learn to Control the Impulse to Hurt Others.* It is important to convey to the child that feelings of anger are natural and alright, but that hurting other people in reaction to anger is not acceptable. Use every opportunity in which the child expresses any emotion to reinforce the point that emotions are normal and that they can be expressed in appropriate ways. In addition, set aside a special time each day to discuss feelings with the child and to work on acceptable ways of dealing with them. This special time should be one in which you can devote an undivided 5 to 10 minutes to the child. Be prepared to spend more time, however, if the child is really interested and responsive. Take the child out of the classroom if possible to avoid interruptions and distractions. Your discussions with the child should be suited to the child's responsiveness.

1. Begin by discussing situations that evoke different emotions. For instance, "Yesterday I got a new puppy and I was so excited and happy that I felt like dancing and singing. I really felt good inside! What makes you feel really happy?" If the child responds, ask for more details; if there is no response, name simple events that make you happy. Go on to discuss other feelings. "Sometimes I feel just the opposite. I get really sad. I had a very good friend, and she had to move away. That made me feel terrible. Do you feel sad sometimes?" Again, encourage response in whatever way you can. Discuss anger also. "You know, sometimes I get really angry. I know you must feel angry about things too at times. What makes you angry?" Share some examples of what angers you and help the child verbalize situations that anger him. It may take several days to identify situations that evoke various emotions.

*Discussion of emotions should be part of the early childhood curriculum, both in spontaneous ways and as part of activities. Helping children with emotional/behavioral deficits learn to express their emotions is an excellent way of helping them learn alternative methods of reacting.

2. Once the child has acknowledged that he feels differently in response to varied situations, focus your discussion on those feelings. "How does it make you feel inside when you are (happy, angry, sad, lonely)?" Help the child put into words the different inner responses to emotions. You should spend some time beforehand thinking about this because feelings are not easy to describe in words. This way you are prepared to help the child discuss them. Be careful, however, that it is the child who talks about the subject with help from you, not the other way around. Again, this step requires several days.

3. After the child has verbalized how he feels when he experiences different emotions, begin to talk about what the child does to express such feelings. Do not be critical about what he says. If the child tells you that he punches, hits, bites, or otherwise hurts someone who angers him, accept that for the present. Do not express dismay or lecture the child. Again, discuss various emotions in relation to how they are expressed in action.

4. The next step is to tell the child that you want to explore some different ways of reacting to emotions. If the child told you that when he is happy he smiles, ask how else he might express that happiness. Either of you might come up with ideas like clap hands, jump up and down, sing, hop around, or hug someone. In addition to other emotions, discuss alternative ways that the child can handle anger, such as:

   • talk to the person who angered him
   • find something else to do while waiting for the other child to finish with the toy he wants
   • pound on the floor or table instead of a child
   • talk to an adult to get help in handling angry feelings

5. Your discussions do not need to be strictly verbal. Use whatever props you want to help you. The use of puppets, clay, or blocks may be helpful in exploring feelings and emotions.

6. With each discussion step, look for opportunities during the day to illustrate what you and the child were talking about during the special time. At first, focus on what event evoked a particular emotion, then switch to discussing how it makes the child feel inside. Next, look for examples of external manifestations of the emotions. Finally, encourage the child to verbalize alternative ways of reacting. Prevention of aggressive incidents provides one opportunity for relating your daily discussions to the child's actual emotions. Do not limit this to negative incidents, however. Find examples of all kinds of emotions and feelings.

If the Child Does Hurt Someone, Use Self-Control Time. Take the following steps:

1. Quickly make sure that the child who was hurt is all right. If at all possible, another teacher should attend to the victim.

2. Calmly take the aggressive child by the hand to the self-control time area. Firmly but quietly say, "I cannot allow you to hurt other children. Please stay here until you are ready to join your friends again."

3. Move away and do not talk with or look at the child during self-control time. Verbal or visual contact may well serve as a reinforcer to the child for his behavior.

4. If another child approaches, quietly move the child away. Explain, "Teddy, needs to be by himself for a few minutes. You can talk to him when he joins the class again."

5. The child can rejoin classroom activities when he feels that he is ready. Do not lecture. The child knows the reason for the isolation. To channel the child into constructive behavior, you might suggest joining an ongoing activity. It is very important to reinforce the child as soon as possible for engaging in appropriate activity.

6. If the child rejoins the classroom before he is ready and again engages in the unacceptable behavior, say to him, "I guess you're not quite ready to join us," and take him back to the self-control area. Again allow him to determine when he is ready to rejoin the group.

Continue Keeping Track of the Behavior. As you work with the child on changing the aggressive behavior, continue keeping track of every time the child hurts someone. Record each day the total number of incidents of hurting other children by whatever means. It is quite possible that progress will be gradual. The graph will reflect even a small change; this will encourage you to continue these strategies.

MAINTAINING THE CHANGES

Once the child has stopped hurting others, continue praising positive social behaviors and acceptable responses to emotions like anger. Continue to encourage the newly learned behaviors. Remember, at one time the child reacted to anger by hurting others. Also, this aggressive behavior was reinforced while alternative behaviors were not praised.

Now that the situation is switched, reinforce the behavior that is valued and expected.

 The CD-ROM that accompanies this text contains several hypothetical scenarios designed for you to apply the guidance principles suggested in the various chapters of this book. Go to the Your Turn section of the CD to access these scenarios. The first two scenarios are particularly pertinent to this section of the text, Aggressive and Antisocial Behaviors.

chapter **11**

Using Inappropriate Language

Four-year-old Eileen has had considerable experience in child care. Her mother has worked since Eileen was one month old, leaving her first at the infant-toddler center and now at the adjacent child care center. Eileen is the youngest of five children, with two brothers in their teens, a sister in fourth grade, and a brother in second grade. Eileen is assertive and very talkative at school.

Recently she has added a variety of inappropriate words to her vocabulary, which is growing increasingly more colorful. When Eileen becomes upset, she uses a such words to express her feelings. At other times, she inserts them into normal conversation, usually smiling as she does so.

The teachers have conveyed their displeasure with Eileen's language, such as by saying, "Don't use that word, Eileen. It's not nice." This has not, however, affected her behavior. Eileen still uses inappropriate language, and some of the other children are now picking up some of her words. The teachers fear that they will soon be hearing complaints from other families.

STATE THE BEHAVIOR

The child uses inappropriate language regularly and frequently.

OBSERVE THE BEHAVIOR

It is important to gain an idea of when, where, why, and toward whom the behavior occurs. Spend some time observing the child.

When does the child usually use inappropriate language?
- Unpredictably, at any time of day
- During group activities such as story or discussion time
- During free-choice activities
- Early in the day
- Late in the day
- During outdoor play
- Indoors

What seems to trigger use of inappropriate language?
- The child is angry.
- The child is told no by a teacher or another child.
- The child is not able to accomplish a task.
- The child has a particular role in role-playing.
- The child is not engaged in an activity.
- The child has a leadership role in play with other children.
- The child is in the bathroom.
- The child is silly and giggly.

Toward whom does the child usually use such language?
- To anyone
- To one or a few children
- To all children
- To adults
- To good friends

What happens when the child uses such language?
- The child laughs.
- Other children laugh.
- Other children tell her that she shouldn't say such words.
- Other children repeat the word or words.
- The child looks to see if an adult has heard.
- A teacher tells the child not to say bad words.
- Adults react in a shocked manner.
- Adults laugh.

This preliminary observation should give you some idea of the context in which inappropriate language is used. Use this information in approaching a solution to the problem.

CONSULT WITH THE FAMILY

Children learn to use inappropriate language in many settings, often not at school. They may hear such words from peers at school, but they may also hear these at home, from older siblings, from family friends, from neighbors, or from television. Such behavior may be of concern to some families and not to others. When you meet with the family, let them know that your aim is to help the child use respectful and appropriate words when at school. If use of inappropriate words is not of concern to the family, tell them that you do not allow the use of such words at school and that you will work with the child to use appropriate language while at school. If, on the other hand, the behavior is a concern to the family, work with them to share insights and strategies to change the use of such language. Families may feel that their child has learned inappropriate words from peers at school; share with the family your observations and assure them that your rules for using respectful language apply to all the children. Keep family members informed of changes in the child's behavior.

CONSIDER THE IMPLICATIONS

Children acquire language by hearing it used around them, and in the same way they learn inappropriate words. When adults, peers, or siblings use such words, children are exposed to and learn them. For the most part, preschool children do not understand the literal meaning of these words, but they do soon come to realize that these words are somehow special. The child may observe that such words are usually said only under certain circumstances such as in anger, and that the words are given special emphasis through voice tone and inflection. Such words become even more special, however, when a child decides to use them.

When a child first says an inappropriate word, the reaction is clear. Adults who hear the word usually react in shock or with laughter, reflecting surprise at hearing such language from a little child. This initial reaction is then followed by a question about where the child learned such a word or by an admonition not to use it again. The child learns quickly that use of such words gets attention.

When a child uses unacceptable language in the preschool setting, teachers often react in this way. They do not consider such language to be appropriate for young children, and they try to eliminate it in whatever way possible. In the process, they usually call more attention to the problem. Since use of foul language evokes reinforcing responses, the language is difficult to eliminate. The situation is further compounded in the school setting by the fact that other children reinforce it by repeating the word, laughing, or otherwise paying attention to it.

EXPLORE THE ALTERNATIVES

There might be a relatively simple solution to the problem of inappropriate language. Examine the information from your informal observations, then see if one of the following suggestions might work.

- If the child does this only under certain circumstances, she might be doing so because of misinformation or lack of understanding. For instance, the child may use inappropriate language only when role-playing a certain person. Perhaps the only gas-station attendant the child knows swears all the time, and so she generalizes from this experience and believes that all gas-station attendants swear. Discuss this with the child, and try to correct the misconception. You may plan a visit to a gas station, or invite a gas-station attendant to visit the class.

- The child may engage in an attention-getting behavior like using unacceptable language because of boredom. Consider the information from your informal observations, particularly in relation to when such language occurs. If you find that inappropriate language happens often during planned or free-choice activities, it may be that the child feels unchallenged by the activity and chooses to create her own diversions. Carefully examine what is in the classroom, and provide more stimulating materials and activities, as appropriate. By providing alternative activities to engage and interest the child, you should soon note a decrease in the use of such words.

- Sometime during their fourth year, many children tend to go through a phase in which they enjoy making up and using *bathroom language*. Determine whether the child is imitating adult swearing or is using child-constructed words. The latter will sound like child's language (for example, *pee-pee, caca, poopoo, potty*). Because use of bathroom language is a phase, children naturally stop using it if you do not pay it undue attention. You might, however, find that the use of bathroom terms is getting out of hand. In that case, have a talk with the child or children most involved in using such words, and limit the words' usage in some way. You could, for instance, agree with the youngsters that such words may be used only in the bathroom and nowhere else.

- If the child who uses inappropriate language is a natural leader in the classroom, others may be following her example. It might be possible to enlist her aid in leading the class in a more appropriate behavior. Talk with the child, and let her know that you are unhappy that she is using inappropriate language and that others are beginning to use these words. Through discussion, try to come up with an alternative behavior that the child could help the other children learn. This might include using new art media, learning new songs, or playing new games. By reinforcing the child's leadership, it can be channeled into appropriate uses. Praise the child for her successes in teaching new skills to the other children.

If the solution to the problem does not lie in one of these suggestions, proceed with the following detailed strategies.

STATE THE GOAL

The goal is for the child to stop using inappropriate language.

APPROACH

To reach the goal, your strategy involves three simultaneous steps:
- Prevent use of inappropriate language whenever possible.
- Ignore use of inappropriate language when it does occur.
- Systematically reinforce periods during which no inappropriate words are used.

DEFINITION

Using inappropriate language is any use of words that is not suitable for a preschool child. This refers to adult swear words rather than to bathroom words made up by children. Make a list of the specific words you want to stop to ensure that all the teachers consider the same words to be inappropriate.

STARTING POINT

Before implementing changes, it is necessary to know how often inappropriate language occurs. For three days, mark every instance of swearing on paper. If it occurs five or six times an hour, collect information for the total day. If, however, it takes place more frequently, such as 20 or 30 times an hour, collect data for only one hour per day. Select an hour when this behavior usually occurs frequently. You should have a good idea of when this might be from your initial observations. At the end of the day, add up the marks, and record the total on a Frequency Record-Keeping Graph. This record provides a measure against which improvements can be gauged.

A meeting should be arranged with the child's family to discuss the problem. Unless the child picked up the use of inappropriate language from another child at school, the words were most likely learned from her home or neighborhood. The family may also have noted the child's language and may be concerned about it. Family and teachers need to discuss how the behavior has been learned and reinforced and how it can be eliminated. When there is a home–school partnership to change a child's behavior, the change is more effective.

After you have kept track of incidents of swearing for three days and talked with the family, begin the following approach. All teachers should consistently use the same strategies.

Let the Child Know Your Concern and How You Will Deal with Inappropriate Language in the Future. At a time when the child is not using such language, take her aside and have a friendly talk with her. Let the child know that you are concerned by her use of inappropriate words. Tell her how you will work with her to help her change this behavior. Be sure to tell the child why you consider use of such words unacceptable.

Ignore Inappropriate Language When It Occurs. Whenever the child engages in this behavior, whether it is out of anger or because the child wants your attention, ignore it. Do not respond by lecturing or admonishing or even by looking shocked. Such responses provide the attention the child desires. When a child uses such words, one of two things may happen in relation to the other children in the class.

1. If the other children do not react or take note of the language, do nothing. Simply ignore the inappropriate language by turning your back on the child as if nothing was said.
2. If the other children react by imitating, laughing, or talking about the word, divert the others as quickly as possible. Say, for instance, "Jane, Alice, Mike, and Todd, I want to show you a new game over here." Do not include the child who used the unacceptable words, and quickly lead the other children away. It is helpful if ahead of time you develop several ideas for such diversions. Do not talk about the fact that the child used an inappropriate word, and if one of the children brings it up, say simply, "Yes, I know," and drop the subject.

Prevent Incidents of Inappropriate Language Whenever Possible. From your informal observation you may have some clues as to when the behavior usually occurs. For instance, the child may use inappropriate language when she is angry or frustrated. If this is the case, be alert to any signs of confrontation with another child. Quickly move to the child and help her express what is bothering her in an acceptable manner. Praise the child for acceptable behavior. In other cases, the child may use such language, not as an outlet for feelings, but in a more matter-of-fact manner aimed directly at getting attention. In such a case, prevention is not as easy to implement, and ignoring the child is the better way to react.

Systematically Reinforce Time Periods during Which No Inappropriate Words Are Used. The following strategies will help the child eliminate this behavior:

1. From your baseline data, compute the average frequency of inappropriate language. If it occurs 6 times per hour, then the average frequency is 10 minutes (60 minutes ÷ 6). If it occurs 30 times per hour, then the average frequency is 2 minutes (60 minutes ÷ 30). This average represents not only how often the child uses such language, but also how long she goes without using it. Your aim is to increase the length of time without inappropriate words until the behavior completely disappears.

2. Make a chart to share with the child. Each vertical column represents a day, and each horizontal column represents a time block within that day. The spaces should be large enough for a star sticker. The chart looks like this:

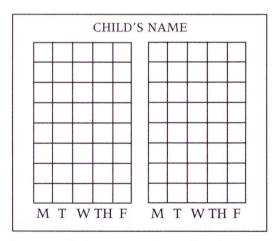

The number of squares within each day is determined by the interval of use of appropriate language. The shorter that interval is, the more squares are drawn on the chart. It might be impractical to keep such a chart all day. In that case, select a shorter period to fill in on the chart. Be sure the child is aware of when the chart is being used, and be especially alert to positive behaviors at other times so these can be verbally reinforced.

3. Carefully watch the clock and the child during times when the chart is being used. Each time the designated amount of time passes without unsuitable language, praise the child and tell her that she has earned a star. Give her the gummed star and let her paste it on the appropriate square on the chart.

4. At the end of the day, take the child to the chart again and praise her for the number of stars she has earned (even if she only earned one). Tell the child that you are sure she will earn even more stars the next day.

5. Over the next few days, the number of stars that the child earns should increase while incidents of inappropriate language use decrease. When the child has earned stars for at least half the squares on two consecutive days, begin to increase the intervals during which you expect appropriate language. This increase should be gradual and paced to ensure success. If at any time the behavior increases and the number of stars earned decreases considerably, shorten the time interval. You want to ensure that the child experiences success.

6. When use of inappropriate language has decreased to zero or near zero, tell the child how pleased you are with her changed behavior. Also tell her that you will discontinue using the star chart because you know she can continue to talk without swearing. Give her the chart to reinforce how well she has done. Most likely, by this time the novelty of using the chart will have worn off, and the child will not need the direct reinforcement it offered.

 Continue Keeping Track of the Behavior. Continue to count occurrences of unsuitable language each day to keep track of progress. If unsuitable language incidents were counted all day during baseline, continue to count for the full day. If a smaller time block was set, use the same period to collect data while implementing the above-listed strategies.

MAINTAINING THE CHANGES

Once you have eliminated inappropriate language use and stopped using the star chart, it is important to maintain the new behavior. Praise the child when she engages in desirable behaviors of all kinds. If the child occasionally uses an unsuitable word, ignore it. At a later time, tell her how pleased you are when she uses appropriate language.

 The CD-ROM that accompanies this text contains several hypothetical scenarios designed for you to apply the guidance principles suggested in the various chapters of this book. Go to the Your Turn section of the CD to access these scenarios. The first two scenarios are particularly pertinent to this section of the text, Aggressive and Antisocial Behaviors.

chapter 12

Name-Calling

"Penny is a crybaby! Penny is a crybaby!" Penny, as if on cue, begins to cry while five-year-old Erika smiles and walks away. Such incidents have been happening quite frequently at the Head Start Center, with Erika taunting other children through name-calling.

Though a bright and popular child, Erika has been upsetting more and more of the other children by giving them unflattering labels. What particularly bothers the teachers and the other children is that Erika's labels are often based to some extent on real behaviors. Penny does cry at times. Johnny has a speech deficit, which prompts, "Johnny is a funny talker!" Randy has a quick temper, so Erika calls him a bully. There are times when the names seem just spiteful, such as, "You stupid dummy!" or "You dirty dog!"

Repeatedly the teachers have told Erika that it is not nice to call names and upset other children, but Erika continues. After an incident, she seems unperturbed by a lecture from a teacher. When Erika is required to apologize, she does so cheerfully. As a rule, she acts as if nothing has happened, even though the other child may still be upset.

STATE THE BEHAVIOR

The child provokes and upsets other children by giving them unflattering names or labels.

OBSERVE THE BEHAVIOR

To gain some further insight into this name-calling behavior, spend some time observing the child to gather information.

When does the child call other children names?
- At any time of day
- Especially during free-choice activities
- During group activities
- During discussion times
- During outdoor play
- Indoors
- At mealtimes
- During toileting times
- At nap or rest time

What seems to trigger name-calling?
- Another child does something unusual.
- Another child does something of which the teachers do not approve.
- Another child angers her.
- Another child tells her no.
- Another child or group of children exclude her from play.
- No apparent reason.

Who is being called names?
- Any child in the class
- The same child or a few children
- Girls
- Boys
- Friends of the child
- Timid children
- Assertive children
- Younger children
- Older children

What happens when the child calls names?
- The child says the name loudly.
- The child repeats it once.
- The child repeats it many times.
- The child laughs or smiles when she is saying it.
- The child is upset when she says it.

- The child looks to see whether an adult has heard.
- The child looks to see whether other children have heard.
- The child tries to get other children to repeat what she said.
- The child apologizes.
- The child walks away from the other child.
- The child stays near the other child.

From informal observation you have gained some insight into the circumstances under which the name-calling takes place. Use this information to help find the best way to eliminate the behavior.

CONSULT WITH THE FAMILY

Once you have gathered your own information by observing the child, meet with the family to discuss the behavior. Find out if the child tends to use name-calling with siblings or friends outside school. Share your own observations about the behavior, and discuss the family's suggestions and insights. Keep the family informed about progress in changing the child's tendency to give other children inappropriate names.

CONSIDER THE IMPLICATIONS

Children like adults, want to feel good about themselves, so anything that does not reinforce a positive self-image is hurtful. The child who calls other children unpleasant names has found a way of hurting them. When the child first begins to put labels on others, there may be no intention of malice. As she notes the other children's reactions and then repeats the behavior to get a similar reaction, she becomes aware of an effective way to influence others.

A child's reaction to being called an unflattering name is usually strong. The victim of the name-calling may react in anger or hurt or by denial, crying, or some other means. In addition to this response, there is usually a reaction from adults as well.

Whether a teacher hears and intervenes or whether the other child calls the teacher's attention to the situation, an adult takes part in the action. Thus, the name-caller is reinforced in two ways. The victim responds very visibly, and an adult pays further attention by talking to the offender or otherwise conveying displeasure. The child has found a good way to get double attention and continues calling names as long as she is reinforced for it.

EXPLORE ALTERNATIVES

You may have some clues from your preliminary observations that can help you come to a relatively simple resolution of the problem. Consider the following suggestions:

- Does the child engage in name-calling only during a specific time of the day? It might be helpful to restructure the activity or routine during the time when name-calling occurs. A teacher should also stay near the child to help her remain constructively engaged in the activity planned for that time.
- If one child is always the target of the name-calling, separate the two youngsters. Move one child to a different classroom if possible, or keep the two children involved in different areas of the room. The less opportunity for name-calling, the less it occurs.
- If the child engages in name-calling as well as other challenging behaviors at school, she is probably not as much involved in classroom activities as she should be. Carefully check the materials and activities provided for the children for age-appropriateness. It is possible that the child's behavior stems from boredom or frustration. If materials and activities are too simple, too difficult, or insufficient in number or availability, the child may try to keep busy in other, less acceptable ways.

If none of these suggestions helps reduce the behavior, continue to the detailed strategies that follow.

STATE THE GOAL

The goal is for the child to stop calling other children unflattering names.

APPROACH

To stop the child's name-calling behavior, two steps should be carried out simultaneously:

- Reinforce as many positive behaviors as possible.
- Ignore all name-calling incidents in such a way that the child who is the target is also helped to ignore the behavior.

DEFINITION

Name-calling is any incident in which a child gives someone an unflattering label. Teachers should list the labels to be in agreement on what words or phrases fit the definition of name-calling.

Before any changes are implemented, it is important to know how often name-calling occurs. For three days, count the number of times the child calls another youngster by an unflattering name. Each time the child calls a name, mark it down on paper. At the end of each day, record the total on a Frequency Record-Keeping Graph.

STRATEGIES

After you have kept track of incidents of name-calling for three days, begin the following approach. It is important that all teachers use these strategies consistently.

Reinforce the Child for Positive Interactions with Other Children.*
Let the child know what behaviors are acceptable. Praise her for them. Whenever the child interacts positively with other children, let her know that you are pleased. Word your praise in such a way as to include the idea that it is nice to make other people feel good. For example, if the child is in the housekeeping area with some other children, say, "I like the way you're playing the mommy. Mommies make daddies and children feel good just like daddies and children make mommies feel nice." Or, if the child is working in the block area with another child, tell her, "You and Paul are building a wonderful tower! Doesn't it make you both feel great to be working so well together?"

When the Child Name–Calls, Ignore It and Help the Child Who Is the Target to Ignore It Also.
The child who name-calls is getting reinforcement for this behavior from the target child and an adult. It is relatively simple for the adult to ignore name-calling, but it is more difficult for a child not to react when given an unflattering label. Therefore, the adult needs to help other children to ignore incidents of name-calling or at least to minimize their reactions.

When you hear the child call someone a name, do the following:

1. As quickly as possible, get to the two children involved. Physically place yourself between them. Face the child who has been called the name and turn your back to the one who did the name-calling.

2. Put your arm around the child who was called the name (if the child reacts positively to physical contact from adults). Do this to reassure this child of your understanding. If possible, move away

*Children with emotional/behavioral deficits do not feel good about themselves and may try to inflict the same feeling of hurt on others through name-calling. The child's self-concept is boosted when alternative positive behaviors are acknowledged and she gets a very positive response from teachers for such behaviors.

from the name-caller, taking the victim with you. This should only take a few seconds.

3. As you move away with the child who was called a name, talk about something unrelated to the incident. Ask for help in an activity such as feeding the rabbit or mixing paint, or show the child something of interest.

4. If the child complains about the name-calling incident, say simply, "I know, it's not nice to be called such a name. We have to help Erika learn to give better names to her friends." Acknowledge that such labels are not pleasant, but at the same time enlist the victim's help in changing such behavior. Also establish that you do not want to create a disturbance over name-calling.

5. You may not be successful in decreasing the target child's reaction. Your aim in such a case is to get the victim away from the name-caller so the behavior will not be reinforced by the victim's reaction.

6. The child who has done the name-calling is given as little reinforcement as possible for this behavior. A few minutes after the incident, make a point of going to the name-caller and giving attention and praise for an appropriate behavior. Convey the message that it is the challenging behavior, not the child, that you disapprove of. Reinforce the fact that socially acceptable behavior gains your attention.

 Continue Keeping Track of the Behavior. Continue to count the number of name-calling incidents and record them on the graph. Your control over the victim's reaction to name-calling is not complete. You can only influence, but not dictate, how youngsters who are victims of name-calling react. Therefore, the name-caller's behavior will receive some reinforcement, and it may take a while before change is evident. Be persistent. Eventually you will be rewarded with a decrease in and the disappearance of this challenging behavior.

MAINTAINING THE CHANGES

Maintain interaction without name-calling by continued praise of appropriate social behaviors. Help the child recognize that it is more rewarding to be pleasant to others than to be negative. If an occasional name-calling incident occurs, treat it as you did while you were applying the strategies discussed earlier.

 The CD-ROM that accompanies this text contains several hypothetical scenarios designed for you to apply the guidance principles suggested in the various chapters of this book. Go to the Your Turn section of the CD to access these scenarios. The first two scenarios are particularly pertinent to this section of the text, Aggressive and Antisocial Behaviors.

chapter 13

Nonsharing

"These are mine! I had them first!" Mrs. Sing turns around to see four-year-old LaToya fiercely protecting some blocks she had been building with. LaToya puts her arms around as many blocks as she can reach. Carson stands by rather bewildered, then says, "I want to play, too." LaToya replies, "You can't! I need all of them, and you can't have any!" Mrs. Sing puts her arm around Carson and says in a low tone, "Come on now, LaToya. There are plenty of blocks. Let Carson play with some." "No!" Shouts LaToya. "They're mine!"

Carson decides to take matters into his own hands. He picks up several stray blocks that are out of LaToya's reach and starts to stack them. LaToya kicks over the blocks Carson just stacked, screaming, "You can't have any! They're mine!" Mrs. Sing becomes stern and lectures LaToya about sharing. A few minutes later, she forcibly takes some blocks from LaToya and moves these and Carson a few feet away. LaToya gets up and stamps away, crying, "I hate you! You took my blocks!" Mrs. Sing is unhappy with the outcome but does not know what else to do. LaToya is always unwilling to share.

STATE THE BEHAVIOR

The child refuses to share school or personal items with other children.

OBSERVE THE BEHAVIOR

Take a few days to observe the child to get an idea of the circumstances under which the child will not share.

When is nonsharing most likely to take place?
- Most times of the day
- Early in the day, soon after arriving
- Later in the day
- During show-and-tell
- During free-choice activities
- Around nap or rest times
- During transition times
- At cleanup times

What items does the child not want to share?
- Whatever the child is using
- Only personal items, such as toys from home
- Housekeeping area items, such as dolls, dishes, or clothes
- Blocks
- Art materials, such as paper, paint, or clay
- Manipulative materials, such as puzzles, tabletop blocks, or Legos®
- Sand-play or water-play implements
- Books
- Outdoor equipment and materials

With whom does the child refuse to share?
- Any other children
- Only one or a few children
- Boys
- Girls
- Older and bigger children
- Smaller and younger children

How does the child refuse to share?
- The child verbally tells other children that the items she is using belong to her and no one else.
- The child hits another child who asks for or tries to take an item.
- The child calls for a teacher to help.
- The child screams or cries out.
- The child hoards the items by putting her arms around them.
- The child moves to an isolated area where she is less likely to be disturbed.

- The child grabs other items if another child approaches.
- The child tells other children she does not want to play with them.
- The child refuses to take turns if the teacher suggests it.

How does the child react if another child does not share with her?
- The child becomes angry.
- The child cries.
- The child calls a teacher to help.
- The child forcibly takes or attempts to take what she wants from the other child.

Use these observations to gain insight into the behavior so you can best help the child change it.

CONSULT WITH THE FAMILY

Discuss with the family your concern about the child's unwillingness to share with other children as soon as you have gathered some preliminary observations. Discuss whether this behavior has always been the child's pattern or is a recently acquired behavior. For instance, a younger sibling who has recently become mobile could be compelling the child to feel protective of her possessions. Discuss with the family your thoughts on helping the child share more readily and find out what strategies they have found effective. Continue to exchange information with the family, particularly sharing successes as the child becomes more and more willing to share with others.

CONSIDER THE IMPLICATIONS

Before children can share with other people, they must feel secure with their own possessions, knowing that no matter who uses them, the items belong to them. It is only after children experience ownership from their own point of view that they can begin to understand someone else's right to ownership. Young children do not yet grasp the meanings of "mine" and "yours." They fiercely protect what is theirs and at the same time want what belongs to someone else. This is a normal stage in development, very typical of two-year-olds. The situation becomes more complex in a preschool setting, where few items are "yours" and most are "ours." Young preschoolers have to learn that they have the right to play with an item, but the other children have the right to play with it as well. Later, this simple rule becomes expanded when consideration is also expected.

Four- or five-year-olds must recognize the rights of others and must also at times be encouraged to give up or share their rights when another person wants to use an item they have. *Sharing* is a concept that needs a great deal of practice and the help of adults. Sharing means that children cannot always have exclusive use of whatever toys they want. Sometimes, they may not be able to use the toys they want, or they may be asked to give up a toy because other children have been waiting to use the toys. Sometimes, the children can use toys together in ways that often enhance rather than detract from play. Sharing requires a measure of social understanding and development. Children should learn the concept and use it at least part of the time. Preschoolers should exercise some sharing by three-and-a-half or four years of age.

EXPLORE ALTERNATIVES

Your expectations, understanding, and classroom arrangement can facilitate sharing by the children. One of the following suggestions may provide a way to work with this challenging behavior*:

- Remember that nonsharing is a stage most children go through. Do not expect sharing on the part of two-year-olds or some three-year-olds. Understand the child's need to develop a firm sense of "mineness" before they grasp the concept of "yourness." This understanding is necessary to set the stage for the later learning of sharing. One way a classroom of very young preschoolers can accommodate the nonsharing stage is in the materials available. It is better for a class of two-year-olds to have several of the same few items than many different toys. Thus, rather than having 40 distinct toys, it would be better to have 8 or 10 different items, but 4 or 5 exact copies of each. This way, if one child plays with a duck pull toy and another child wants that same toy, there will be a toy just like it to give to the second child. Such availability of duplicate items avoids the need to share.

- Preschoolers share school items much more readily than they do their own personal toys. It is not unusual and is quite natural for children to feel possessive about something that is theirs. If a child brings a treasured item to school and it is lost or broken, this situation does not help the child learn about sharing. It is, therefore, wise to establish and maintain some rules about personal belongings such as toys brought from home. Some suggested rules are as follows:
  1. There should be a special place where children can keep their belongings. A coat cubby or bin should suffice. If these are not available, somehow provide storage for special items from home. Separate home and school toys throughout the day.

A child with a cognitive deficit may be developmentally equal to a two-year-old, and nonsharing may be a reflection of developmental level rather than misbehavior.

2. Establish a specific daily or weekly period for sharing personal toys. Such a sharing time can be carefully supervised to ensure the safety of such items as well as the safety of the children. Remember that home toys are often not as durable as school items. Materials made specifically for the preschool are constructed to withstand considerably more wear and tear. Be alert to toys that seem especially fragile or brittle, and watch how they are handled. Put time limitations on the sharing period (a definite beginning and end), and have each child put away his or her own toys when the time is over.

3. Discuss bringing in objects from home with the children. With the children's help, establish some rules for handling personal belongings. Stress the need for respect of others' property. If the children are involved in setting guidelines and know the appropriate ways to share personal belongings, they will be much more inclined to follow such rules.

4. You may have experienced concerns when children bring in items from home. You may have found that items are broken or lost or children are unwilling to share. In this case you might consider not allowing children to bring such items to school for a time. Let the children and families know of this decision and why it was made. Then enforce the decision.

• If you have found that sharing school items is difficult for the children, examine your classroom to see if the difficulty arises from lack of availability of materials. If there are not enough materials for all of the children to be simultaneously involved, there will likely be issues with sharing. In a class of about 20 children, the basic classroom interest areas should be stocked so as to keep at least five or six children supplied at any given time. This includes areas such as blocks, dramatic play, manipulative toys, books, art, sensory play, cognitive games, and any other areas that are in your classroom. In addition, for any activities that you provide on a daily basis, there should be enough materials for all children who want to participate. Nonsharing can result if children feel that they have to compete for available materials. This does not mean, of course, that there has to be one of each item for each child. There should be enough materials for all the children to be constructively engaged at any given time. Situations will arise when more than one child wants a certain item. If these happen in an environment in which items are plentiful, sharing will be facilitated.

• Sometimes, children are attached to a very special item that gives them a feeling of security. A child should not be expected to share a security item such as a stuffed animal, doll, or blanket.

If necessary, the teacher should protect the child's right to the security item.

If none of these suggestions provides a solution to nonsharing, try the following detailed approach.

STATE THE GOAL

The goal is for the child to share school materials with other children at least two-thirds of the times that the child is asked to share. Two-thirds is a reasonable goal, since preschool children should not be expected to share all of the time but should share a reasonable amount of the time.

APPROACH

The basic strategy to eliminate nonsharing involves several steps:
- Make environmental changes to facilitate sharing.
- Provide systematic help to learn why and how to share.
- Reinforce spontaneous sharing.
- Deal with situations in which the child is not willing to share.

DEFINITION

Nonsharing means that the child is unwilling to allow other children to use materials the child is using or even materials that are simply nearby. For example, the child may be playing with only some of the blocks but tells others that they are all hers.

STARTING POINT

Before starting these strategies, gather information about how often the child does not share. Keep a pencil and paper handy in the classroom. Divide the paper into two columns. Title one column Sharing and the other Nonsharing. Carefully observe the child throughout the day. Whenever anyone asks the child to share, record the child's reaction in the appropriate column. Also, if the child voluntarily shares with another youngster, record this under Sharing. At the end of each day, compute the percentage of sharing opportunities in which the child actually shared. Use this formula:

$$\frac{\text{Sharing}}{\text{Sharing} + \text{Nonsharing}} \times 100 = \% \text{ of Sharing}$$

Thus, if the child had 20 opportunities to share, and your record shows five checks in the Sharing column and 15 in the Nonsharing column, your computation would be as follows:

$$\frac{5}{5 + 15} = \frac{5}{20} \times 100 = 25\%$$

Record the percentage on the Percentage Record-Keeping Graph. Your daily score tells you during what percentage of opportunities for sharing the child actually shared. The higher the percentage, the greater your progress.

STRATEGIES

After you have kept track of incidents of nonsharing for three days, you are ready to begin these strategies. It should be stressed that this approach is *not* intended for very young preschoolers, but for four- and five-year-olds.

Facilitate Sharing through the Environment. To help the child feel more positive about sharing with peers, provide as much help as possible through classroom setup, routines, and activities.

1. Classroom arrangement can facilitate sharing. As previously mentioned, the class should have ample materials so that children are not competing for the few available materials. There should also be duplicates of popular materials, especially in a class of younger children. Examine the space provided in each interest area. There should be enough room for several children to work comfortably together or independently without getting in each other's way. Be sure, too, that the various interest areas are set off from each other, with boundaries defined by furniture, storage, or other dividers. Sharing is easier for children if they are not constantly in each other's way and thus feel they must defend their space and materials.

2. Teacher supervision is a controllable factor that can facilitate sharing. Challenges in sharing will be less likely in activities for which each child has his or her own item, such as a book. When several children are building with blocks or making collages from a central supply of materials, concerns related to sharing are more likely to occur. These activities need careful teacher involvement.

3. Specific projects for activity times may be planned to encourage sharing. There should be ample supplies for all the children for art activities. Materials such as paint, glue, or glitter should be

provided in several small containers rather than in one large one so the children have fairly quick access to what they want. Cooking activities should be selected to allow each child who participates to have some active involvement in the process. Another way to avoid concerns about sharing is to consider whether certain activities should be limited to a specific number of children. If, for instance, the cooking activity involves adding and stirring six ingredients, allow no more than six children to participate at a time. The activity can be repeated with groups of six until all the children who want to cook have a turn.

4. A school usually has a few items for which there is more demand than supply. Swings are an example. Often there are more children wanting to swing than there are available swings. In such a case sharing has to take place or there will be some unhappy children.

   There are some techniques you can use to encourage sharing if the children are reluctant to let someone else have a turn. A definite time limit, agreed on by the children, can be used. You can either have a timer on hand or refer to a clock or watch. When the specified time is up, it is the next child's turn. Another way of handling the use of swings (or any other equipment that lends itself to being timed) is to specify a number of times the child can swing back and forth. After the child reaches that number, it is the next child's turn. The child on the swing, the children waiting, and the teacher can count together to add another dimension to this activity.

Systematically Help the Child Learn to Share. Use this step if the child rarely or never shares. The other steps should suffice for a child who shares at least sometimes (at least 20% of the time, according to the baseline data).

Implement the following sequence of steps. Because of the nature of this strategy, it may be helpful if only one teacher works with the child.

1. Begin by structuring situations for the child to experience sharing. At least once a day, find a cooperative and even-tempered child who is involved in an activity that is suitable for sharing. Go to the child who has difficulty in sharing at a time when that child is not overly involved in an activity (for example, soon after a child-selected activity time begins). Take the child by the hand and go to the other child and ask, "Can we play with you? We'd like to share the toy you're using." Stay with the two children. Make several comments about sharing and how nice it makes one feel. Stress the positive value of sharing. Continue this step daily for one to two

weeks, until you feel the child who has difficulty sharing has begun to understand your message.

2. The next step requires that the child be the one who shares. At least once a day find a situation in which the child you are concerned about is involved in an activity that lends itself to sharing. Go to the child and say something like, "Can I play with you? I'd like to share the toys you're using." Choose your approach carefully to encourage the child to answer "Yes." Join in the activity and let the child know how much you appreciate his or her sharing with you. If the child answers "No," simply say, "All right. Maybe we can work together later." Leave the child alone. Do not lecture or scold. Convey that sharing is a positive experience, not something one is forced into.

   This step may take a few days or weeks. Allow enough time for the child to understand what you are conveying by setting up these situations. Once the child is sharing with you and enjoying the experience on a regular basis, move on to the next step.

3. When you feel the child is ready to share with someone other than adults, shift the focus to children. At least once a day, when you see the child engaged in an activity that lends itself to sharing, find another child who is not involved in an activity at the time, and invite that child to share with you. Go to the child whose sharing difficulties you are concerned about and say, "Carson and I would like to share with you. Will you share with us?" If the child says "Yes," then join in the play. Be involved only to the extent that is necessary. Let the two children take the major role in the play. Verbalize how nice it was of the child to share her activity with a friend.

   If the child says "No," don't make an issue of the matter. Tell her that perhaps another time she will feel like sharing.

   When the child is sharing with another child on a regular basis, after at least two weeks move on to the next step.

4. This step is similar to Step 3, except that the teacher's role is lessened. Approach the child with another youngster, and say, "Carson would like to share the blocks with you." Allow the children to work out the details of the play. Retreat once the two have agreed to work together. Periodically reinforce them by your attention and praise.

5. When the child consistently shares at least two-thirds of the times that you approach her with another child, begin to withdraw your involvement further. Use Step 4 every other day, then every third day, and so on until it has been phased out. At the same time, the child should be sharing spontaneously and increasingly more often. This will be reflected in the graph.

Reinforce Spontaneous Sharing When It Occurs. The strategies described gradually help the child share more freely. Be on the lookout throughout the day for situations in which the child shares. At such times be lavish in your praise. It is important to let the child know that you value this behavior. When you first begin this approach, offer praise every time the child shares. Later, when sharing takes place more frequently, decrease your rate of reinforcement gradually. Eventually you should only have to give reinforcement intermittently, at about the same rate as you reinforce the other children in the class.

Help the Child Handle Situations in Which She Is Not Willing to Share.* There will be times, at first quite frequently, when the child is unwilling to share with other youngsters. Your handling of such situations will have a considerable effect on the child's future attitude toward sharing. Sharing has to originate from inside the person who shares; it cannot be forced. Therefore, it is important to present sharing as a positive experience.

Whenever a situation arises in which the child is refusing to share, do the following:

1. Go to where the two children are as soon as you notice a concern or a potential concern related to sharing. Be sure that your manner is calm and quiet at all times.

2. Ask the children what is happening. Restate what they verbalize as the issue. For instance, "Carson, you would like some of the cookie cutters to use with the clay. LaToya, you had the cookie cutters first and want to keep them. Is that right? What can we do here?"

3. If the children are not too upset by the situation, encourage them to suggest some alternatives. Especially, urge the child who is unwilling to share to come up with suggestions. If an idea is brought up that makes both children happy, implement that idea, and praise the children for sharing so well. Point out the merits of working together and helping each other.

4. If one or both children are overly upset by the situation and are unwilling to compromise, do not make a fuss over the situation. Say simply, "Carson, LaToya is not ready to share right now. Why don't you come with me, and we'll see if we can find something else for you to use with the clay." Look for an alternative acceptable to the other child. Also reassure this child that you will see that he gets a turn with the desired object soon.

By helping a child with emotional/behavioral problems learn how to handle her negative feelings, whether in relation to sharing or to any other behavior, you will provide a valuable learning opportunity that, over time, will help diminish her challenging behaviors.

5. Once the child has refused to share under any conditions, move away from her. You do not want to make an undue fuss over her attitude; you also do not want to give more attention than necessary. Above all, do not lecture and scold. That will not change the mind of a chronic nonsharer but will only reinforce the behavior.

6. Such nonsharing situations provide good timing for creating a sharing experience. If possible, set up a structured sharing situation within 5 or 10 minutes. The type of experience you provide depends on which step is currently being used. By doing this, you provide a positive experience in sharing as a contrast to the nonsharing that was just taking place.

Continue Keeping Track of the Behavior. As you implement this approach, continue to keep track of sharing and nonsharing on the graph. This provides information on progress and shows when the goal is reached.

MAINTAINING THE CHANGES

When the child consistently shares at least two-thirds of the time, you can discontinue implementing these strategies and record-keeping. However, do give periodic praise for sharing. Once the child realizes that sharing is a positive experience that has its own rewards, the child will continue to share on her own. Do keep in mind that preschool children still have much to learn about social behaviors. Your help and guidance in sharing situations continues to be needed.

The CD-ROM that accompanies this text contains several hypothetical scenarios designed for you to apply the guidance principles suggested in the various chapters of this book. Go to the Your Turn section of the CD to access these scenarios. The first two scenarios are particularly pertinent to this section of the text, Aggressive and Antisocial Behaviors.

chapter 14

Bribery

"Hey, Terry, I'll give you some of my Halloween candy if you let me have your Tonka® cars," whispers Francisco, age four. Terry, who brought his Tonka collection for show-and-tell, replies, "No way!" "Yeah, but you got three red ones! You don't need that many," counters Francisco. When Terry again tells him no, Francisco alternatively asks for an accounting of what Terry got for Halloween, a listing of all the tempting goodies he has gotten, and a continued request for at least one of Terry's cars. Ultimately, a teacher puts a stop to the bartering by mentioning that show-and-tell items are not to be traded or given away and puts Terry's car collection in the director's office for safekeeping.

At lunch that day, Francisco notices that Sherrie has a peanut butter sandwich in her lunch box. "I'll give you my tuna sandwich for your peanut butter sandwich," says Francisco. Sherrie shakes her head, takes a determined bite of her lunch, and turns to the child sitting at her other side.

Later still, Francisco tells Brent and Candy, "I have some money in my coat. I'll give it to you if you let me play." Both children say, "I don't want to play with you," and move elsewhere to continue their game.

The teachers have noted that when Francisco wants something from another child, he invariably offers some kind of bribe to get it. He is usually unsuccessful. The other children react negatively to his approach. There are times, however, when he has a taker to his offers and "buys" friendship, food, and other items in this way.

115

STATE THE BEHAVIOR

The child frequently uses bribery to win friendship or favors from other children.

OBSERVE THE BEHAVIOR

Spend a few days observing the behavior to gain further insight into how it takes place.

When is the child most likely to use bribery?
- During free-choice activities
- During sharing times when children have brought personal toys from home to school
- During outdoor play
- During mealtimes
- Usually early in the day
- At any time of the day

What does the child try to gain through bribery?
- Friendship
- The right to join in the play of another child or group of children
- A turn with a toy that another child brought from home
- A chance to take a personal toy home
- The gift of another child's personal toy
- A turn with a school toy
- Part or all of another child's meal
- A piece of gum or candy from another child

What does the child offer in exchange for the favor requested?
- To play with the other child
- Food
- Money
- A toy
- The chance to cut ahead in line for something children are taking turns for
- Friendship
- An outlandish offer ("I'll give you a million dollars")

To whom does the child offer bribes?
- Any other child
- Only certain children
- Girls

- Boys
- Younger and smaller children
- Older and bigger children
- Outgoing children
- Quiet children

What happens when the child bribes another youngster?
- The other child accepts the offer.
- The other child does not accept the offer.
- The other child discusses the request.
- The other child ignores the briber and walks away.
- The other child gets upset.
- The other child calls a teacher.

Does the child fulfill the offer in exchange for the favor?

Use the information from these observations to help you deal more effectively with the concern.

CONSULT WITH THE FAMILY

After gathering observational information about when, why, and to whom the child offers bribes, meet with the family to discuss the behavior. General conversation about the family's usual form of guidance may also give insight into whether family members often give the child a treat, toy, or special activity in exchange for a promise from the child to carry out an expected task, such as putting away his toys or staying in bed at night. In such a case, you might gently suggest some other techniques for the family to get the child's cooperation in everyday events. On the other hand, if this behavior is of concern to the family, find out if it occurs in settings other than school. Brainstorm with the family about ways that the behavior could be handled. Once you have begun your strategies for decreasing this behavior, keep the family informed of progress.

CONSIDER THE IMPLICATIONS

Children, like adults, develop a variety of techniques to get something they want from another person. Most of these are based on a socially acceptable system of give and take. It is quite common for children to offer something in return for what they ask. It is a concern when this method is the only one used by a child. The child who consistently uses bribery has a limited repertoire of social techniques. There are several concerns about such behavior. First, the child is not developing to full social potential. Appropriate social development should mean that the child acquires many techniques for obtaining what he wants. Second, other children and adults have a negative response to a child who uses frequent bribery. Ultimately, the child's self-concept suffers because others respond negatively. Such a child needs help to learn a range of ways to get what is wanted or needed from other people. Otherwise, the child will continue to try using bribery to get things. In the long run, the child has unsatisfactory social relations, at the expense of self-image.

EXPLORE ALTERNATIVES

Consider whether one of the following suggestions might provide an answer to the situation:

- Be sure that what you consider to be a problem is indeed a problem. All children, at one time or another, use the trade-off technique to gain what they want. In a preschool class you may often hear, "If you _____, then I'll _____." If a child occasionally uses such a format, this is acceptable. It is only when the child uses it exclusively that you should be concerned. Watch and listen. If the child uses other means to get things, do not be too concerned. To decrease bribery (especially of material and unrealistic objects), make a point of reinforcing other ways of asking for what the child wants.

- A child may feel a need to use bribery because there is undue competition for available items in the classroom. Examine the facilities. There should be an ample supply and variety of materials to constructively engage all children at all times. If there are a few popular items of limited quantity, work out a method for sharing so that everyone may have a turn.

- When items that are not normally a part of the classroom are present, problems may result. This can happen when a child brings a highly popular or unique toy from home or when a child has candy, gum, or other treats that are not a part of the school's usual menu. Such items may cause a child to try bribery to gain the favor of the child with the treats. If this situation is the root of the concern, set up some rules to control it. You may want to ban food items other than what is part of the normal menu unless there are enough treats so everyone can have one or because they do not meet your school's nutritional standards. You may need to set up regulations to convey how toys from home are to be handled (see Chapter 13 for suggestions).

- If a child's bribes are often unrealistic, you can help the child see how outlandish the offers are. Point out that the child does not have "a million dollars" or whatever was promised. Suggest alternatives. Be sure that when you interfere in such a situation, the children are not engaged in a humorous conversation or "tall tales" contest, but that the bribe is being made in earnest.

If none of these suggestions helps deal with the issue, move on to the following detailed approach.

STATE THE GOAL

The goal is for the child to use a variety of ways of getting what is needed and wanted from others instead of using bribery.

APPROACH

The basic method for eliminating overuse of bribery involves these steps:
- Develop a systematic strategy to help the child acquire other techniques for getting things.
- Reinforce the use of other techniques.
- Ignore bribery when it occurs.

DEFINITION

Bribery is a situation in which a child tries to win friendship, favors, or material objects from others by promising something in return. To be defined as a problem, bribery should occur at least 50% of the time that the child wants something from someone else.

STARTING POINT

Spend three days gathering information about how often the child uses bribery. This information will be used as a basis for assessing later progress. Select a one-hour period or two half-hour periods per day during activities when you expect bribery to occur, according to your earlier informal observations. Draw a line down the middle of a piece of paper and label the columns Bribery and Other. For the period of observation, make a mark in the Bribery column each time the child clearly uses bribery. Make a mark in the Other column when the child uses another technique to get something. The following is a list of techniques other than bribery that a child might use to get something from other children.
- *Asking* for the desired item. This means that the child goes to another youngster and simply states that he wants something the other child has. The child might say, "Let me try!" "Can I have a piece of gum, too?" "Can I play with that?"

- *Sharing* the desired thing with another child. Here the child expresses his desire to have or use something but he suggests that he and the other child share. The child might say, "Can I have a turn now?" "Let's do that together, okay?" "Can I help you?"
- *Offering* something in the hope that the other child will share or offer the desired thing. In this case, the child does not come out and express his desire, but tries to gain it more subtly by offering something that he thinks will induce the other child to share or give up the desired item. Here the child might say, "Would you like to play with this?" "I'll give you a piece of my candy." "I've got the doll buggy. Do you want to use it for your baby?"
- *Waiting* for an invitation to use or share the desired thing. This means that the child stands by passively, neither asking for the desired item nor offering something in exchange, in the hope of being given a turn or being asked to share the desired item. The initiative may be taken by the other child or by a teacher who is standing nearby.
- *Substituting* the desired item with something else. In this instance, the child decides to find a substitute for the desired item. He may decide to play with a similar toy, join another child in play, or in some other way be satisfied with something else.
- *Forgoing* the desired item. Rather than trying to gain the desired thing, either actively or passively, the child decides to get along without it.

Not all of these techniques are apparent to the observer. For instance, the decision to forgo or substitute may occur in the child's mind, without your knowledge. Therefore, count only those techniques that are readily recognizable.

When using bribery, the child may combine a number of techniques. For example, the child might say, "I'll give you the cookies from my lunch if you let me play with your doll." "Can I play with you? You can drive my truck on the blocks." "If you give me your candy bar, I'll bring you a million dollars tomorrow."

At the end of each day, total the marks in the two columns. Then compute a percentage of bribes in relation to total techniques, as follows:

$$\frac{\text{Bribes}}{\text{Bribes + Other Techniques}} \times 100 = \% \text{ of Bribes}$$

Record this percentage on the Percentage Record-Keeping Graph.

STRATEGIES

After you have kept track of the percentage of bribery in relation to other means of getting desired objects for three days, you are ready to begin the approach. All teachers should be aware of it and implement it as appropriate.

This approach is for a child who uses bribery to the exclusion of other techniques for getting what he wants. If the child uses bribery occasionally but also uses other methods, do not worry.

Implement a Systematic Strategy to Help the Child Acquire Other Techniques for Getting What Is Desired. Use the information gathered from informal observation to determine when bribes are most likely to be offered. Then be on the lookout for such situations to implement your approach.

1. At least five times a day, try to stop the child before he offers a bribe. Look for signs of wanting an object, a playmate, or a favor. Such signs might include the child stopping what he is doing, looking around the room, or looking at a specific object or person.

2. Go to the child and say, "What would you like?" Encourage an answer. If you are fairly sure what the child wants and he does not tell you, ask specifically: "Would you like the blocks?"

3. Now suggest that you and the child try to get what he wants. Recommend a very specific approach, using the techniques previously mentioned. The following are examples of what you might say:

   - *Asking:* "You want to play with the new blocks? Let's ask Nancy if you can use them now." "You'd like to run Tracy's truck. We'll ask him to let you use it, okay?"

   - *Sharing:* "Since you want a turn on the swing, we'll see if you can push Christine for awhile, and then she can push you." "You really want to play with Claude and Tiffany, right? Let's ask them if you can join their tea party."

   - *Offering:* "It would be fun to be a firefighter with them. Let's find a hose and see if they'd like you to join them." "You can take this sifter to the sandbox. Maybe Rachel will let you use the funnel when she sees it."

   - *Waiting:* "Let's stand by the table and watch. Maybe they'll ask you to play bingo when they've finished this game."

If, for some reason, these techniques are not appropriate or do not get the desired response, suggest that the child find a similar alternative or that he forgo the thing he wants. Use these techniques only if the others are not possible.

4. If the first techniques work for the child, state this success verbally. Say for instance, "See, you got to use the blocks by asking!" or "Suggesting that you share the swing and push each other worked! You got to swing."

5. Continue using this strategy as often as possible, at least five times per day. When you begin to see a decrease on the graph in the percentage of bribes used (indicating an increase of other techniques), you know the approach is working. Gradually cut back on the number of times you lead the child through this process. If you note a slowdown or reversal in the rate of improvement, you may be withdrawing your support too quickly. By the time you have reached the objective, you should be helping the child use other techniques only periodically.

Reinforce the Use of Other Techniques When These Are Used Spontaneously. Throughout the day, watch for times when the child receives things by spontaneously using alternative techniques. Whenever you see this, go to the child and give reinforcement. You may do this by praising the child, by simply being there, or by commenting on his success. It is important to let the child know that you approve of such acts. Once the child uses these techniques fairly frequently, gradually cut back on the rate of reinforcement. Eventually you should be reinforcing these techniques no more frequently than you do with other children.

Ignore Bribery When It Occurs. Offering something in exchange for a desired item is a legitimate means of getting that item. Because the child already has this well-developed technique in his repertoire of behaviors, there is no need to reinforce it. Simply pay no attention when the child uses this technique to get what he wants. As you expect other techniques to increase, this one will automatically decrease. By ignoring it, you will help this process.

Continue Keeping Track of the Behavior. Keep daily track of bribes and other techniques. Compute the percentage, and record it on the graph each day. As you implement this approach, count only spontaneous use of other techniques. Do not count the situations in which you help the child gain what he wants through alternative techniques. You may decide not to use the systematic approach during the hour that you are counting behaviors. The graph reflects progress and tells when to decrease the systematic teaching of alternatives and when to cut back on reinforcement of spontaneous use of these alternatives.

MAINTAINING THE CHANGES

Once the child has learned and freely uses various ways of getting what he wants, continue to give periodic reinforcement for the alternative methods. The child should gain intrinsic satisfaction from use of these different methods as other children respond more positively. As a result, the child gets what he wants more frequently without constantly using bribery.

 The CD-ROM that accompanies this text contains several hypothetical scenarios designed for you to apply the guidance principles suggested in the various chapters of this book. Go to the Your Turn section of the CD to access these scenarios. The first two scenarios are particularly pertinent to this section of the text, Aggressive and Antisocial Behaviors.

chapter 15

Stealing

"Marissa took my ball!" yells Fanny. Marissa digs her hands deeper into her pockets and says, "Did not!" when questioned by Mrs. Lyle. "Let me see what you've got in your sweater pocket, Marissa," she coaxes. Marissa resists and begins to cry when Mrs. Lyle forces her hand out of her pocket. Marissa pulls out a small red ball. "That's my ball," states Fanny. "No, it isn't. It's mine," cries Marissa. Mrs. Lyle gives the ball to Fanny, while Marissa continues to insist tearfully that the ball is hers.

Mrs. Lyle sighs and again talks to Marissa about taking things that are not hers. Almost daily, incidents occur in which Marissa has taken a toy that belongs to another child and claimed it to be her own. In addition, lately there have been mysterious disappearances of small classroom items. No one has seen Marissa take these items, but the teachers strongly suspect that she did. They are at a loss about what to do because Marissa always denies stealing, even when confronted with the evidence.

STATE THE BEHAVIOR

The child takes items that belong to someone else or to the school.

OBSERVE THE BEHAVIOR

For a few days observe the behavior to gain further insight. Because stealing is usually done surreptitiously, this requires very careful observation.

When does the child steal?

- Unpredictably, at any time
- During planned activities
- During free-choice activities
- During group times
- When children are getting or putting away coats or other belongings in their cubbies
- During cleanup times
- During transitions
- During lunch or snack times
- At nap time

What precedes stealing?

- The child talks about liking a particular toy.
- The child plays with a particular toy.
- The child keeps coming back to the admired item.
- The child asks if she can keep the item.
- The child is not allowed to handle or play with the item by the child to whom it belongs.
- The child stays near the child to whom the item belongs.

What happens when the child steals?

- The child looks around to see if someone is watching.
- The child puts the item in her pocket.
- The child holds the item in her hand.
- The child hides the item somewhere in the classroom.
- The child takes it to her cubby.
- The child denies taking the item if asked.
- The child insists the item belongs to her.
- The child gets upset when she is found to have the item.
- The child claims she has the item by accident.
- The child returns the item to its rightful owner.
- The child refuses to return the item.

What does the child steal?

- Small items that fit into a pocket
- Larger items

- Toys that other children bring from home
- School toys or materials
- Parts of larger items (such as a puzzle piece)
- Any type of item
- One specific item or type of item
- Food

Use these informal observations to gain greater understanding of when and how stealing takes place. This information will be used in implementing the approach to eliminate the behavior.

CONSULT WITH THE FAMILY

Discuss with the family your concerns about the child's stealing behavior, and share your observations. Find out if the child has engaged in stealing in other settings, for instance, from the market or from children outside the school setting. If the child engages in this behavior at other times, find out from the family what strategies they have used. Work together with the family to try to come up with some possible reasons for this behavior, and some possible ways of preventing and stopping the behavior. Keep the family informed about progress toward eliminating stealing.

CONSIDER THE IMPLICATIONS

When a young child takes something that does not belong to her, she usually does this simply because she wants the item in question. A preschooler is still developing a sense of ownership, which eventually becomes part of a broader sense of ethics and morals. Property rights are still unclear. Sometimes the desire for something appealing, combined with the child's natural impulsiveness, becomes more important. So, the child takes the item.

The child needs to learn that it is wrong to take something that does not belong to her. She learns this, along with what other behaviors are socially acceptable or unacceptable, through the long-term process of socialization. When the child is taught through gentle guidance what ownership means and why it has to be respected, she adopts values that include consideration for others' belongings. If, however, the child is made to feel shame and guilt when she takes something that does not belong to her, she becomes resentful.

Everyone has some desires that are out of reach. Young children have to be helped to understand such desires and alternative ways of dealing with them. Stealing cannot be allowed in the preschool, but it can be handled in a way that does not make the child feel bad about herself.

EXPLORE ALTERNATIVES

Some relatively simple steps may help minimize the opportunity for stealing. Consider whether one of the following suggestions might work.

- When children bring toys or other belongings from home to share at school, issues can arise. The owner of a desirable item gains a certain amount of power, because the owner can say who may or may not play with the toy. If another child is prevented by the owner from using the item, the rejected child may become very resentful. At the same time, the item becomes even more desirable because she cannot have it. Such a situation may invite stealing. Consider these alternatives to allowing children to bring toys from home to school.

    1. Items from home can be completely banned. If you decide to do this, write a letter to all families explaining that home toys are creating a variety of issues. Enlist the families' help in enforcing the new rule. If a child still brings something from home, stop the child from taking the item into the classroom right at the beginning of the day. After admiring the object, remind the child of the new rule and ask the parent to take it back to the car. If this is not feasible, tell the child you will take the item to the office and will return it when the child goes home.

    2. Limit the time for sharing items from home at school. You might designate one day of the week as "sharing day." Or you may set aside a limited time each day when children can share home items. Provide a place where toys from home can be kept safe at other times of the day.

    3. Set some rules on how personal toys are to be shared. Children can help in deciding on appropriate rules. They may decide, for example, that everyone is given at least one turn with the toy.

- Another way to discourage children from taking items is by keeping the classroom neat and well organized. When school materials are stored in a haphazard way, no one quite knows what is in the classroom or where it belongs. When everything in the room has its place and is clearly visible, the message is that all items in the room are important and contribute to the class. It is not as easy to take a toy that clearly belongs in a specific place as it is to take a toy that has no particular place.

- If the child takes only one specific item or type of item from the classroom, you can do one of two things. You may remove the item from the room for two or three weeks, if such a move would not be too limiting to the functioning of the class. Or you can keep a close watch on this item to prevent the child from taking it.

If none of these suggestions serves as a way to handle the concern, then continue to the following strategies.

STATE THE GOAL

The goal is for the child to stop taking items that do not belong to her.

APPROACH

To eliminate stealing, the basic strategy involves these steps:
- Reinforce appropriate handling of classroom materials or items belonging to peers.
- Make environmental changes.
- Prevent stealing.

DEFINITION

Stealing involves any incident in which a child deliberately takes and keeps an item that does not belong to her, whether the item belongs to the school or to another child. It is a problem if such behavior occurs regularly. All teachers should discuss and agree on what behaviors will be considered as stealing (such as putting an item into her pocket or placing an item in her cubby).

STARTING POINT

To compare later progress, it is important to know how often the child steals before starting the strategies to eliminate stealing. For three days, count the number of stealing incidents that occur. It will require considerable vigilance to collect this information because the child probably does not steal openly. This information may not be as precise as it could be, but try to be as accurate as possible. Because of your added vigilance, incidents of stealing may decrease. Mark on paper each time the child steals something and transfer the total to the Frequency Record-Keeping Graph at the end of each day.

Keep track of incidents of stealing for three days, and begin the approach to change this behavior. Follow the strategies consistently.

Reinforce Appropriate Handling of Classroom Materials or Items Belonging to Peers. If the child is still learning respect for property that is not hers, she needs to be told what she is doing well. Therefore, whenever the child appropriately handles classroom materials or items belonging to peers, she should be verbally reinforced:

> "I like the way you are holding Paula's doll carefully. Thank you for helping her take good care of it."

> "I'm so glad that you put all the pieces back in the box. If everyone helps take care of them like you do, we won't lose any."

> "You remembered to put the tricycle in the shed! Here it won't rust, so everyone can enjoy riding it when they want to."

Discourage Stealing through Appropriate Changes in the Environment or the Routine. Examine the organization of the classroom in relation to stealing. It is not as easy to take an item off a shelf that is neatly arranged, with the item displayed clearly. It is much easier to take something that is part of a haphazard jumble. Convey your respect for classroom materials, as well as an awareness of what is in the room, through careful arrangement and storage.

Consider whether children should be allowed to bring items from home to school. Set specific rules and limitations on when, how, and under what circumstances personal items are to be shared. Such guidelines should also discourage stealing.

Prevent Stealing without Shaming the Child.* The following is an approach to help prevent children from taking home items that do not belong to them. It is done through a *pocket hunt*. Follow these steps:

1. Explain to the children in a group time that classroom items and children's belongings have been disappearing. Acknowledge that it is easy to put a toy in one's pocket accidentally. Enlist everyone's help in preventing such losses in the future.

2. Just before the children leave school, conduct a pocket hunt to find items that belong to the school or to children. It is important

---

*A child with severe cognitive limitations may not understand the concept of ownership. A child who had been prenatally exposed to drugs may not be able to understand the consequences of her actions. In both cases, prevention may mean keeping a watchful eye on the child to avoid her taking objects belonging to someone else.

that no one child be singled out. Everyone must participate, including the teachers. Provide a box into which items are deposited. Have everyone put anything that does not belong to them into the box. An adult might contribute a crayon or other small item to the box to avoid placing a stigma on children who do have things in their pockets. Whatever is in the box should be returned to its rightful place or owner. Handle this hunt as a game, not an inquisition. Minimize reactions and conduct the activity in a matter-of-fact manner. Never shame a child or accuse her of stealing. Simply point out that items need to be replaced in their proper locations or returned to their owners.

3. The timing of the pocket hunt is important. If all the children leave at the same time, as in a preschool or in a program in which the youngsters board a bus together, the hunt can be carried out just before everyone leaves. If the school is a child care program for which children leave at different times, however, a different arrangement needs to be worked out. Plan the pocket hunt for a few minutes before the child about whom you are concerned leaves. In this way you minimize the recurrence of stealing in the time between the pocket hunt and the time the child leaves, while still involving a group of children in the process.

4. If the items stolen are primarily the personal belongings of other children, keep closer track of ownership of such toys. At the beginning of each day, as you greet youngsters, ask them if they brought something special to school. If they did, record the item and its owner on a list. In this way you can double-check that all children have their own belongings after the pocket hunt at the end of the day.

Continue Keeping Track of the Behavior. The conditions under which you kept track of stealing during your initial three days of measurement will differ slightly from your measurements during implementation of the outlined strategies. Continue counting items the child has that do not belong to her and record them on the graph. This can be done more easily during the pocket hunt. Record the number of items the child empties from her pockets that do not belong to her. The pocket hunt itself should decrease stealing, so expect a fairly rapid drop once you begin.

MAINTAINING THE CHANGES

Continue the pocket hunt even after the child no longer takes objects that do not belong to her. After an additional two weeks, begin to decrease the hunts gradually to every other day, then to every third day, then to once a week. Discontinue the hunts when you see no recurrence of stealing. However, continue praising the child periodically for handling materials with care. Similarly, keep evaluating the environment so that it discourages stealing by the way it is arranged.

The CD-ROM that accompanies this text contains several hypothetical scenarios designed for you to apply the guidance principles suggested in the various chapters of this book. Go to the Your Turn section of the CD to access these scenarios. The first two scenarios are particularly pertinent to this section of the text, Aggressive and Antisocial Behaviors.

chapter 16

Noncompliance

Teacher Jessica rings the bell, which signals the end of outdoor playtime. Children begin putting away tricycles and sand toys, stacking the large blocks, and walking toward the classroom door. Within a few minutes, the outdoor play area is cleaned up and almost all of the children have returned to the classroom.

"Spunky, please get off the swing. It's time to come inside now," says Teacher Jessica. Five-year-old Spunky ignores his teacher and pumps harder and higher on the swing. "Everyone else is already inside, Spunky. You're the last one on the playground." No response. "Spunky! Now!" Spunky continues to swing. Finally, Teacher Jessica goes to the swing, forcibly stops it, and takes Spunky's arm. Spunky pulls away, yelling, "I don't want to go inside," and runs to the other side of the play area. It takes several more minutes before Teacher Jessica finally catches up with Spunky and forcibly brings him in.

Later that morning, Spunky refuses to put away the blocks after activity time, refuses to join the others for story time, refuses to wash his hands before snack, refuses to sit at the table for snack, and refuses to get up from the table after his belated snack. The teachers are all very frustrated with Spunky's noncompliance. No matter what they ask, Spunky answers with a verbal or nonverbal "No!"

STATE THE BEHAVIOR

The child frequently and consistently refuses to comply with reasonable demands.

OBSERVE THE BEHAVIOR

Spend a few days observing the child informally so that you can gain some insight into when noncompliance is most likely to occur.

When is the child most likely to be noncompliant?
- At all times of the day
- Early in the day, soon after arriving
- Late in the day, just before it is time to go home
- At transitional times, when children end one activity and move on to another one
- At cleanup times
- During self-selected activities
- During teacher-directed activities
- During group activities
- During indoor activities
- During outdoor activities
- At toileting times
- At mealtimes
- At nap times

What is the child doing when he is noncompliant?
- The child is involved in an activity by himself.
- The child is involved in an activity with other children.
- The child is not involved in an activity.
- The child has been asked by an adult to do something different from what he is currently doing.
- The child is upset.
- The child is involved in block play (or dramatic play, sensory activities, book reading, large motor activity, and the like).

What happens when the child is noncompliant?
- Teachers usually talk to and coax him.
- Teachers often let him continue what he is doing.
- Teachers try to coax him, and if this does not work, they allow him to continue what he was doing rather than what was requested.
- Teachers forcibly make him do what they have requested.

- The child remains with the activity as long as he can.
- The child often switches to another activity, but not the one teachers asked for.
- Other children call attention to the child's noncompliance.

Use the insights you gain from these observations to help you eliminate noncompliance.

CONSULT WITH THE FAMILY

Noncompliance is not an unusual behavior in young children, and it is likely that the child who often refuses to comply with the teachers' reasonable requests also fails to do so with the family's requests. If this is the case, meet with the family as soon as you have observed the behavior in some depth to find out what strategies they have used and found successful. Brainstorm with the family ways that could help change this behavior, and try to find techniques that could be carried out and reinforced both at home and at school. Continue to communicate success with the family once you begin to see decreases in the behavior so that family and teachers can encourage each other.

CONSIDER THE IMPLICATIONS

Noncompliance frequently comes about when family members and other adults are inconsistent in following through on what they request of children. Children are often asked to comply with requests that are not necessarily pleasant ("It's time to go to bed now." "Put away your toys and come to dinner." "You have to get dressed now to go to school."). Resistance to such directives is not unusual. If, however, adults do not actually require compliance, children are given the message that, if they resist long enough, they will not have to obey.

The child who is frequently noncompliant engages in power struggles with adults. When an adult asks the child to do something, the child refuses, not because the request is unreasonable, but because he does not want to obey. Such power struggles lead to resentment and anger by both the adult and the child, and often result in entrenching both more firmly. The adult's position is, "I am the adult, the one in charge here, and he *will* do what I ask." The child's stance, on the other hand, is, "I will do what I want, not what someone else tells me to do."

Repeated, consistent noncompliance can become a habit with serious consequences later in the child's life. If the child persistently defies authorities, he will continue having issues with adults in increasingly wider spheres. Thus, it is important to help the young child be more responsive to reasonable requests from significant adults in his life.

EXPLORE ALTERNATIVES

Consider whether one of the following suggestions might help you deal with the issue of noncompliance.

- Young children, as they become secure in their own sense of independence, need to have many opportunities to make decisions. If a child is not allowed many choices in his day-to-day life, he may respond by defying the choices others make for him. Examine the environment and expectations to determine whether the child receives appropriate opportunities to make his own decisions.

- In early childhood programs, children generally follow classroom rules that spell out your expectations. Rules should be simply stated, logical, and few in number. Examine your expectations. Make sure that all the children understand the rules and the reasons for them. In fact, children can be involved in setting up the rules. When children take part in the rule-making process, they are more invested in the rules and are more likely to comply with them.

- While adults expect general compliance from children, their requests should always be reasonable. Carefully examine what it is that you ask of the children. Are your requests logical? Do they make sense from the perspective of the children? Do the children understand why they should comply with your requests? Children are much more likely to conform to expectations if you explain the reasons for these. Whatever the reasons, they should never be arbitrary or capricious.

- It is also important not to overburden children with an undue number of requests for conformity. Children generally are willing to comply with reasonable rules but will become either defiant or passive if too many demands are made on them. Examine your environment to ensure that it reinforces your expectations whenever possible. For instance, if running inside the classroom can pose a safety hazard, arrange the room to discourage running rather than frequently saying to children, "You may not run inside."

- It is also important to keep in mind that compliance is not necessarily a positive attribute. While we expect children to obey logical and reasonable rules, children should not be expected to follow every directive just because it comes from an adult. In fact, healthy assertiveness involves a measure of independent decision-making that, at times, will go against the requests of others. Thus, the aim of any approach to deal with noncompliance should be to decrease unreasonable noncompliance, not to foster blind compliance with any and all requests.

If none of these suggestions helps alleviate the concern about noncompliance, continue on to the following approach.

STATE THE GOAL

The goal is for the child to comply with reasonable requests.

APPROACH

The basic strategy to eliminate unreasonable noncompliance involves the following steps:

- Ensure that the environment supports compliance with reasonable rules.
- Whenever possible, avoid situations that might result in noncompliance.
- Provide many opportunities for the child to make decisions.
- Reinforce compliance.
- Use self-control time when the child is noncompliant.

DEFINITION

Noncompliance involves the child's failure to follow reasonable requests.

STARTING POINT

Before you begin these strategies, take three days to get a more precise idea of how often the child fails to comply with reasonable requests. Every time the child fails to do so, mark this down on paper. At the end of each day, transfer the total number to the Frequency Record-Keeping Graph. This initial count will give a base against which to compare later progress.

STRATEGIES

Start using the following approach after the initial three-day count. All teachers must follow these strategies at all times to provide the needed consistency to change the behavior.

Ensure That the Environment Supports Compliance with Reasonable Rules.* Carefully examine all aspects of the environment to evaluate whether unspoken rules are tacitly reinforced. The following are some suggestions:

1. Review room arrangement. The room should clearly define the purpose of various areas. Its arrangement should convey how many children can comfortably participate in various activities.

2. If classroom materials are clearly labeled and stored, children are more likely to return them when they have finished using them. Also, materials, equipment, and activities that are developmentally appropriate generally convey reasonable guidelines for their use.

3. Also examine the daily schedule. The child may feel that he does not have enough time to adequately participate in favorite activities. Ensure that time blocks, especially for both indoor and outside self-selected activities, are long enough to allow children to select, participate in, and finish one or more endeavors.

4. Consider whether there is a good balance between self-selected and teacher-directed activities. The bulk of the day should allow for child-selected activities. When a child has many opportunities to make his own decisions, he will be less inclined to refuse to comply with adult requests.

5. Also, examine the balance between active and quiet times. Children should not become overtired from extended activity or restless because of too much time spent passively sitting.

Whenever Possible, Avoid Situations That Might Result in Noncompliance.† Together with all the teachers who interact with the child, discuss and carefully think through what you ask the child to do. The fewer the requests for compliance, the fewer the opportunities for noncompliance.

1. Whenever possible, minimize requests for the child to follow instructions. Ask only what absolutely has to be carried out. Later,

---

*A child who has been diagnosed with attention deficit–hyperactivity disorder (ADHD) may often seem noncompliant because of restlessness and inability to focus. Careful thought to how the environment is set up and ensuring that it reinforces expectations can be especially helpful for a child with ADHD. The classroom arrangement, for instance, can provide areas that minimize distractions to facilitate concentration. Times of change in the daily schedule—for instance, during transitions—can be especially difficult for the child with ADHD. Added support, structure, and encouragement will help.

†A child with an emotional/behavioral problem is often an angry child. Such a child may well engage in frequent power struggles with adults. Careful forethought to expectations and how they are stated can help diffuse many power struggles, resulting in a more pleasant and positive environment for all.

as the child's rate of noncompliance decreases, add other reasonable requests so that, gradually, requests for compliance are similar for all of the children.

2. Use nonverbal rather than verbal requests. For instance, after giving a warning that outdoor play will end in a few minutes, go to where the child is playing, take him by the hand, and move inside without undue discussion. If the child resists, use the self-control time strategy described below.

3. Provide choices whenever this is appropriate. Rather than saying, "Put the Legos® back in the box," try asking, "Would you like to start putting the red or the blue Legos away first?"

4. Avoid giving direct orders to the child. The way you word requests conveys your respect for the child. "I would appreciate it if you would _____" is much more pleasant than "You have to _____."

5. If there is a task about which the child has no choice, be careful with the wording you use. You can make a game of such a situation. Rather than saying, "Go to the table to sit down for snack now," try, "Let's fly like butterflies to the table for a snack."

Provide Many Opportunities for the Child to Make Decisions. As often as possible during the school day, offer opportunities for the child to make independent decisions about the activities in which he participates and how he engages in them. Provide choices whenever possible, for which the child can genuinely say "yes" or "no" to what is suggested. There should be absolutely no negative consequences when the child does not wish to participate in a suggested option. Keep in mind, however, that you should not give the child a choice if you are not willing or able to accept "no" as an answer.

Reinforce Compliance. Whenever you ask the child to do something and he complies with your request, praise him. Let him know that you are pleased with such behavior and that you value it. You might say, "Thank you! I really appreciate it when you help with cleanup when I ask you!" or "What a lovely smile! That's the way I like to see my helpers!" The child will feel good because of such a response and will also realize that you feel good. Given time, the child will recognize that there is nothing to be gained from noncompliance, but that there is a reward for positive action.

Use Self-Control Time When the Child Is Noncompliant. The environmental changes, increased opportunities for decision-making, and reinforcement described above should decrease incidents of noncompliance. Also, your decisions to minimize requests for compliance should ensure that what you ask the child to do is reasonable and necessary.

Thus, when noncompliance occurs, do not engage in an argument that will lead to a clash of wills. Instead, use the following self-control time strategy:

1. When a child refuses to comply with a request, take the child by the hand and lead him to the designated self-control time area. Firmly but quietly say, "I cannot allow you to _____ (for instance, stay outside alone). Please stay here until you are ready to join your friends again."

2. Move away and do not talk with or look at the child during the self-control time.

3. If another child approaches the self-control time area, quietly move this child away. Explain, "Spunky needs to be by himself for a few minutes. You can talk to him when he joins the class again."

4. The child can rejoin classroom activities when he feels that he is ready. Do not lecture. He knows the reason for the isolation. To channel the child into constructive behavior, you might suggest joining an ongoing activity. It is very important to reinforce the child as soon as possible for engaging in appropriate activity.

5. If the child rejoins the classroom before he is ready and again is noncompliant, say to him, "I guess you're not quite ready to join us," and take him back to the self-control area. Again allow him to determine when he is ready to rejoin the group.

 Continue Keeping Track of the Behavior. Continue recording the number of incidents of noncompliance that occur each day on the graph. This graph will illustrate progress as you replace noncompliance with more positive behavior.

MAINTAINING THE CHANGES

Once noncompliance with reasonable requests has been eliminated, decrease the amount of reinforcement you provide so that you praise the child at about the same rate as you do the other children in the class. Continue to evaluate the environment and the reasonableness of requests, and provide many choices and opportunities for decision-making for all the children.

 The CD-ROM that accompanies this text contains several hypothetical scenarios designed for you to apply the guidance principles suggested in the various chapters of this book. Go to the Your Turn section of the CD to access these scenarios. The first two scenarios are particularly pertinent to this section of the text, Aggressive and Antisocial Behaviors.

• Nonsharing • Bribery • Stealing • Noncompliance • Disrupting Group Time • Leaving the Classr
nning Aimlessly Around the Classroom • Shouting in the Classroom • Dropping Objects to Create N
aring Books • Breaking Toys • Flushing Objects Down the Toilet • Wasting Paper • Destroying the W
thers • Throwing Tantrums • Pouting • Baby Talk • Thumb-Sucking • Pant-Wetting • Clinging • See
ntion • • Nonparticipation in Activities • Nonparticipation in Social Play • Shyness at Group Tir
ing with Only One Toy • Infrequent Large Muscle Activity • Infrequent Dramatic-Play Participatio
ng Infrequently • Short Attention Span • Finicky Eating • Overeating • Messy Eating • Hording Fo
ng • Biting • Throwing Objects at Others • Hurting Others • Using Inappropriate Language • Na
ng • Nonsharing • Bribery • Stealing • Noncompliance • Disrupting Group Time • Leaving the Classr
nning Aimlessly Around the Classroom • Shouting in the Classroom • Dropping Objects to Create N
aring Books • Breaking Toys • Flushing Objects Down the Toilet • Wasting Paper • Destroying the V
thers • Throwing Tantrums • Pouting • Baby Talk • Thumb-Sucking • Pant-Wetting • Clinging • See
ntion • Whining • Self-Stimulation • Nonparticipation in Activities • Nonparticipation in Social Pl
ness at Group Time • Playing with Only One Toy • Infrequent Large Muscle Activity • Infreq
matic-Play Participation • Talking Infrequently • Short Attention Span • Finicky Eating • Overeati
sy Eating • Hording Food • Hitting • Biting • Throwing Objects at Others • Hurting Others • U
propriate Language • Name-Calling • Nonsharing • Bribery • Stealing • Noncompliance • Disrup
up Time • Leaving the Classroom • Running Aimlessly Around the Classroom • Shouting in
sroom • Dropping Objects to Create Noise • Tearing Books • Breaking Toys • Flushing Objects D
Toilet • Wasting Paper • Destroying the Work of Others • Throwing Tantrums • Pouting • Baby T
mb-Sucking • Pant-Wetting • Whining • Self-Stimulation • Nonparticipation in Activitie
participation in Social Play • Shyness at Group Time • Playing with Only One Toy • Infrequent L
cle Activity • Infrequent Dramatic-Play Participation • Talking Infrequently • Short Attention Sp
cky Eating • Overeating • Messy Eating • Hording Food • Hitting • Biting • Throwing Objects at Ot
urting Others • Using Inappropriate Language • Name-Calling • Nonsharing • Bribery • Stealin
compliance • Disrupting Group Time • Leaving the Classroom • Running Aimlessly Around
sroom • Shouting in the Classroom • Dropping Objects to Create Noise • Tearing Books • Breaking
ushing Objects Down the Toilet • Wasting Paper • Destroying the Work of Others • Throwing Tantr
outing • Baby Talk • Thumb-Sucking • Pant-Wetting • Clinging • Seeking Attention • Whining •
ulation • Nonparticipation in Activities • Nonparticipation in Social Play • Shyness at Group Tir
equent Large Muscle Activity • Infrequent Dramatic-Play Participation • Talking Infrequently • S
ntion Span • Finicky Eating • Overeating • Messy Eating • Hording Food • Hitting • Biting • Thro
ects at Others • Hurting Others • Using Inappropriate Language • Name-Calling • Nonsharing • Bri
ealing • Noncompliance • Disrupting Group Time • Leaving the Classroom • Running Aimlessly Arc
Classroom • Shouting in the Classroom • Dropping Objects to Create Noise • Tearing Books • Brea
s • Flushing Objects Down the Toilet • Wasting Paper • Destroying the Work of Others • Thro
rums • Pouting • Baby Talk • Thumb-Sucking • Pant-Wetting • Clinging • Seeking Attention • Wh
ng • Biting • Throwing Objects at Others • Hurting Others • Using Inappropriate Language •

SECTION 3
Disruptive Behaviors

• Nonsharing • Bribery • Stealing • Noncompliance • Disrupting Group Time • Leaving the Classro
nning Aimlessly Around the Classroom • Shouting in the Classroom • Dropping Objects to Create N
aring Books • Breaking Toys • Flushing Objects Down the Toilet • Wasting Paper • Destroying the W
thers • Throwing Tantrums • Pouting • Baby Talk • Thumb-Sucking • Pant-Wetting • Clinging • See
ntion • • Nonparticipation in Activities • Nonparticipation in Social Play • Shyness at Group Tim
ing with Only One Toy • Infrequent Large Muscle Activity • Infrequent Dramatic-Play Participatio
ng Infrequently • Short Attention Span • Finicky Eating • Overeating • Messy Eating • Hording Fo
ng • Biting • Throwing Objects at Others • Hurting Others • Using Inappropriate Language • Na
ng • Nonsharing • Bribery • Stealing • Noncompliance • Disrupting Group Time • Leaving the Classro
nning Aimlessly Around the Classroom • Shouting in the Classroom • Dropping Objects to Create N
aring Books • Breaking Toys • Flushing Objects Down the Toilet • Wasting Paper • Destroying the v
thers • Throwing Tantrums • Pouting • Baby Talk • Thumb-Sucking • Pant-Wetting • Clinging • See
ntion • Whining • Self-Stimulation • Nonparticipation in Activities • Nonparticipation in Social Pl
ness at Group Time • Playing with Only One Toy • Infrequent Large Muscle Activity • Infrequ
matic-Play Participation • Talking Infrequently • Short Attention Span • Finicky Eating • Overeati
sy Eating • Hording Food • Hitting • Biting • Throwing Objects at Others • Hurting Others • L
ppropriate Language • Name-Calling • Nonsharing • Bribery • Stealing • Noncompliance • Disrup
up Time • Leaving the Classroom • Running Aimlessly Around the Classroom • Shouting in
sroom • Dropping Objects to Create Noise • Tearing Books • Breaking Toys • Flushing Objects D
Toilet • Wasting Paper • Destroying the Work of Others • Throwing Tantrums • Pouting • Baby T
mb-Sucking • Pant-Wetting • Whining • Self-Stimulation • Nonparticipation in Activitie
participation in Social Play • Shyness at Group Time • Playing with Only One Toy • Infrequent L
cle Activity • Infrequent Dramatic-Play Participation • Talking Infrequently • Short Attention Sp
cky Eating • Overeating • Messy Eating • Hording Food • Hitting • Biting • Throwing Objects at Ot
urting Others • Using Inappropriate Language • Name-Calling • Nonsharing • Bribery • Stealin
compliance • Disrupting Group Time • Leaving the Classroom • Running Aimlessly Around
sroom • Shouting in the Classroom • Dropping Objects to Create Noise • Tearing Books • Breaking
ushing Objects Down the Toilet • Wasting Paper • Destroying the Work of Others • Throwing Tantr
outing • Baby Talk • Thumb-Sucking • Pant-Wetting • Clinging • Seeking Attention • Whining •
ulation • Nonparticipation in Activities • Nonparticipation in Social Play • Shyness at Group Tin
equent Large Muscle Activity • Infrequent Dramatic-Play Participation • Talking Infrequently • S
ntion Span • Finicky Eating • Overeating • Messy Eating • Hording Food • Hitting • Biting • Throw
ects at Others • Hurting Others • Using Inappropriate Language • Name-Calling • Nonsharing • Bri
ealing • Noncompliance • Disrupting Group Time • Leaving the Classroom • Running Aimlessly Arc
Classroom • Shouting in the Classroom • Dropping Objects to Create Noise • Tearing Books • Brea
• Flushing Objects Down the Toilet • Wasting Paper • Destroying the Work of Others • Throw
rums • Pouting • Baby Talk • Thumb-Sucking • Pant-Wetting • Clinging • Seeking Attention • Whi
ng • Biting • Throwing Objects at Others • Hurting Others • Using Inappropriate Language • Na

chapter 17

Disrupting Group Time

"Today I want to read a story about a very special little train," says Miss Slater as she opens the reading selection for today's group time. The children quiet down, and 16 expectant faces turn toward the teacher from around the circle. Halfway through the second sentence of the story, Miss Slater is interrupted by a thud. She pauses for just a second, then resumes reading, but several children turn toward the noise. As Miss Slater turns to the second page, there is a giggle from the same part of the circle, followed by some whispering. Miss Slater stops reading. "Brian, you need to sit quietly and listen now."

Brian, aged three and a half, wiggles back into place, smiles sweetly at Miss Slater, and sits quietly with his hands folded in his lap. The story is continued. Thirty seconds later a loud, "Ouch! Brian kicked me!" is heard from Brian's neighbor. "Brian, let's keep our feet to ourselves, please!" Again, Brian smiles.

The story resumes. Almost immediately, Brian starts wiggling, then gets up and moves to another area of the circle, right in front of one of the block shelves. He squeezes himself between two children who have to move slightly to give him enough room to sit. Miss Slater continues reading, though she throws Brian an annoyed look.

Brian reaches slowly behind him and pulls out a unit block. He examines it carefully, then turns to Cindy next to him and declares loudly, "Look what I got." A nearby teacher says, "Shhh!" Brian reaches for another block and begins

143

banging the two blocks together. Several children laugh, and most turn to look toward him. Miss Slater tells Brian to put the blocks away immediately, but Brian continues banging them together.

One of the other teachers gets up, goes to Brian, and tries to take the blocks away. Brian resists, crying, "They're mine! They're mine!" A struggle ensues. All the children watch this interchange at first, but soon some begin talking and a few get up and go elsewhere. Miss Slater closes the book and announces the end of group time. The teachers feel discouraged because Brian disrupts group times in this way more and more often.

STATE THE BEHAVIOR

The child frequently disrupts group activities such as story time, music, dance, or movement.

OBSERVE THE BEHAVIOR

Take a few days to observe the child's disruptions and gain greater insight into this behavior.

How does the child disrupt group activities?
- The child talks or whispers to other children.
- The child giggles.
- The child talks or whispers to no one in particular.
- The child pushes or shoves other children.
- The child brings toys to the group and plays with them noisily.
- The child moves from place to place in the circle.
- The child gets up and walks away from the group.
- The child plays noisily with other objects elsewhere in the classroom.

With whom does the child disrupt the group?
- The child acts alone.
- The child is disruptive only when sitting next to a particular child or a few children.
- The child tries to involve other children in disruptive activities.

What activity is under way when the child disrupts?
- Music
- Creative movement
- Discussion
- Story time

What happens before the child disrupts group activities?

- The child pays attention to the activity.
- The child is distracted from the activity.
- The child squirms and wiggles.
- Another child distracts the child.
- The child sits near an adult.
- The child sits away from adults.
- The child sits by a friend or friends.
- The child looks to see if adults are watching before he disrupts the activity.

What happens after the child is disruptive?

- Other children look toward him.
- Other children laugh.
- Other children join in.
- The child continues disruptive activity when asked to stop.
- The child quiets down when asked.
- The child gets upset when asked to quiet down.
- The child engages in increasingly more disruptive activities as the group time proceeds.
- The child denies being disruptive.

Use the information from these informal observations to help you deal with the situation.

CONSULT WITH THE FAMILY

Because disruption of group time is a behavior that occurs primarily in the school setting, you may want to work on eliminating this behavior without unduly worrying the family. If you do meet with the family, you can mention your concern, but also indicate that you and the other teachers are working on changing the behavior. In this case, let the family know that your strategies have been successful once the behavior begins to decrease and eventually disappears.

CONSIDER THE IMPLICATIONS

Group activities are planned into the curriculum for several reasons. There is usually a concept or skill that is being conveyed. Group time may serve to reinforce or strengthen a concept presented to the children during another part of the curriculum. Group activities also foster enjoyment of music, literature, and dance. Finally, group times provide practice in group social behaviors such as sitting quietly, listening, waiting a turn, and consideration for others in the group. These behaviors are learned gradually, but by the time children leave preschool, they have acquired some of the skills required in kindergarten or elementary school.

With very young children, group time lasts only a few minutes. As children get older, these periods are expanded. Whatever its length, however, group time must be stimulating and exciting enough to hold the interest of all the children in the group.

Because teachers carefully plan group time to fulfill a variety of objectives, it is dismaying when one child disrupts the activity. This affects not only the child who is disruptive, but also the other children who miss the lessons planned for the group. Adults feel frustrated and angry as well. The child learns that being disruptive gains considerable attention. Adults talk to him, sit by him, and otherwise pay attention only to him every time he talks, pushes, or makes distracting noises. The child finds the individual reactions he is getting from adults, even if these are negative, much more enjoyable than what is happening during group time. Unfortunately, all the teachers' attempts to stop the behavior only serve to reinforce it. The more the child disrupts, the more the teachers react, and the more the child realizes that disruption is a behavior that gets attention.

EXPLORE ALTERNATIVES

Examine the information from your informal observation to see if there are some clues for a simple resolution to the problem.

- Group activities, because they are directed at a relatively large number of children at one time, are not easy to plan. The youngsters in a group have a range of interests, abilities, and attention spans. Consider whether group activities are stimulating enough for all the children, or if one or more youngsters are disruptive because the planned activities bore them. Try a change of pace. Introduce new activities, provide new types of activities, or shorten the length of group time. If the usual pattern for group time is to do two fingerplays and then read a story, change the pattern. Try to tell rather than read a story, use flannelboard props instead of a book, or let the children act out a familiar story. Listen to music, dance, have a round-robin story, or let the children tell a story while you write it down. There are many ideas for group time available in resource books. With age-appropriate activities, the right balance of repetition and novelty of activities, and an appropriate length for activity time, you can hold the interest of the group.

- It is difficult to plan group time if children have a wide variety of attention spans and interests. Break the class into two or three homogeneous, smaller groups, with one teacher for each. In this way, group time is geared more directly to the youngsters in each group.

- If a child is disruptive in group time only when sitting next to a particular child or children, separate these youngsters. You might assign places for all the children in the group. For instance, write everyone's name on a large card, place the cards in a circle, then let the children find their places. If there are two children you want to separate, say, "I'd like to sit with you two today. How about making a little space between you where I can sit?"

- Examine the area in which group time is held. Are there distracting items within close reach? If so, consider moving either the items or the location of the group activity.

- Examine the timing of the group activity. If it is preceded by quiet or structured activities or a period when the children are required to sit, they may not be able to sit quietly for yet another activity. Restructure your daily schedule so that quiet and active times are alternated.

- Some children have a difficult time sitting still and attending because they do not have the needed attention span to handle quiet activities that require more than a few minutes of their concentration. It is important, therefore, to make sure that the child's disruptive behavior is caused by the reinforcement he gets from adults and other children, rather than by an inability to sit quietly and attend. If you suspect that the child may be disrupting group activities because he has a particularly short attention span, turn to Chapter 44, rather than continuing with this chapter.*

If none of these suggestions provides a way for decreasing the child's disruption of group activities, continue on to the following strategies.

STATE THE GOAL

The goal is for the child to stop disrupting group activities.

*Some children with special needs may have difficulty during group activities. For instance, children with cognitive deficits or attention deficit–hyperactivity disorder (ADHD) may lack the ability of the other children to attend. Providing an alternative for these children, modifying the activity to meet their needs, or breaking into two or three smaller groups can help. Children with vision or hearing disabilities may lose interest in the activity because they are not able to perceive important visual and oral cues the other children receive. Teachers have to be aware of these children's abilities and limitations, and make necessary adjustments.

APPROACH

The basic approach to eliminate disrupting group times involves three steps:

- Evaluate and restructure group times to maximize interest by the children.
- Reinforce appropriate group behavior.
- Remove the child from the group, after one warning, if the child is disruptive again.

DEFINITION

Disrupting group time includes any deliberate actions, such as making noise or causing other interruptions that upset group activities. The teachers, as a group, need to identify specific actions that they consider disruptive so as to agree on a definition of the behavior.

STARTING POINT

Before beginning to try to eliminate the behavior, it is important to establish how often and how quickly the behavior occurs. Your aim is to eliminate disruptions during group times. Work toward achieving this goal by trying to increase the time between disruptions, with the ultimate goal of eliminating disruptions altogether. To provide a measurement tool that will be consistent during your initial count as well as later during implementation of the strategies, add the number of disruptions up to two only. Thus, your count will be zero, one, or two. (The reason for this limit will become evident later.)

In addition, time the period that elapses before the child makes the first interruption after group time begins. Define the beginning of group time as when the lead teacher begins the first group activity. If appropriate, also time the period that elapses from when the teacher resumes the group activity after the first disruption, to the second disruption.

Consider each group time as an individual event, and record the information for each time separately on the Limited Frequency Record-Keeping Graph, which includes only frequencies of zero, one, and two. In addition, record the duration of time before the first and second disruptions on two Duration Record-Keeping Graphs, using separate graphs for each incident. This information should be gathered over a minimum of two days. Include only those group times in which the child is regularly disruptive.

STRATEGIES

After you have kept track of incidents of disrupted group times for a minimum of two days, you are ready to begin implementing your approach. It is important that all teachers follow these strategies consistently.

Evaluate and Restructure Group Times to Maximize the Children's Interest. Examine group activities carefully. Watch all the children's reactions to determine whether they show enjoyment, interest, boredom, or distraction. If a number of children are not involved in the activities you provide, it is time for a change. Make any necessary changes in the activities, types of activities, and/or length of group times.

Reinforce Appropriate Group Behavior. During implementation of this approach, it is important that you sit next to the disruptive child during all group activities. This is most important to the success of this approach. At the same time, another teacher should conduct the group activities so that you can be relatively free to attend to the child as needed. Reinforce the child as unobtrusively as possible when he is sitting quietly and attentively. Turn and give him a smile. Whisper in his ear, "You can really hear all of the story when you sit so still. It's a neat story." Give him a squeeze if you have an arm around him. Let him know you are pleased with his behavior.

When you begin this approach, provide reinforcement frequently. From your informal observations and baseline data, you should have some idea of how often the child has been disrupting the group. If the behavior occurs on an average of every two minutes, reinforce good behavior about every minute. If it occurs every 10 minutes, reinforce every five minutes. Praise the child before he has the chance to disrupt group time.

As disruptive behaviors decrease, gradually decrease reinforcement. This individual reinforcement can be completely eliminated once the disruptions have stopped. Continue praising appropriate behavior in the entire group. You might say, "My, you are all listening so carefully today!"

If the Child Is Disruptive, Give One Warning and Then Remove the Child from the Group.* Disruptive behavior occasionally occurs during group activities. On the first day when you implement these

---

*Ensure that your expectations that the child attends and participates during group activities are appropriate. A child with a cognitive deficit or ADHD may not be able to attend, and alternative activities or arrangements should be devised. Expectations need to be developmentally appropriate for each child.

strategies, before the first group time, have a friendly talk with the child. Tell him that you are concerned about his behavior during group time and why it bothers you. Then tell the child what will happen in the future if he does disrupt. Let him know that he will get a warning the first time and will be required to leave the group if he disrupts a second time. You may want to provide a specific cue that you and the child agree on, for instance, holding up your hand and looking at him. Emphasize, however, your positive expectations and that you will help him stop disruptive behavior at group time. During group times, sit by the child to give intermittent reinforcement. If the child is disruptive, do the following:

1. When the first disruption of group time occurs, say to the child in a quiet tone, "You may not [specify the behavior]. The next time you interrupt, you will have to leave the room."

2. If the child stops, praise him within 30 seconds for being attentive to the activity.

3. If a second disruption takes place, get up, have the child get up, and leave the room with him as quietly and quickly as possible. Outside the room, in a quiet area, seat the child on a chair you have placed there for that purpose. Say, "You will have to stay here until group time is over." Stay nearby, but do not pay attention to the child. You might have some reading materials on hand to occupy you while you wait. If the child is within view of another responsible adult, go back into the classroom. This other adult must be briefed beforehand, however, about the situation and what is to be done and not done.

4. As soon as group time is over, have the child return to the class. Do not lecture or scold. Simply say, "You may go back in now."

Continue Keeping Track of the Behavior. As you follow through with this approach, continue counting and timing the duration of disruptive incidents as you did during the initial two days. Because the child is removed from the classroom after the second disruption, you can only count up to two. You will know that the warning procedure is effective when you find that you are consistently recording only one disruption on the graph. You will know that the strategies were effective when the count reaches and stays at zero. Much improvement can be reflected in the measure between two and one and between one and zero; therefore, record the length of time that elapses between disruptions. Increases in this duration indicate that you are on the right track.

Measure behavior only during the same group times that you included in the initial information-gathering period. The Limited Frequency Record-Keeping Graph and the two Duration Record-Keeping Graphs will give enough information to evaluate the success of the approach. The first improvements should be reflected in the time measurement. Later changes and final success will be evident in the information on both types of graphs.

MAINTAINING THE CHANGES

Tell the child periodically that you appreciate how well he behaves in group activities. Continue to evaluate group times to ensure that they are appropriate for and interesting to all the children in the class. The child may on occasion disrupt group time again. In this case, remind him gently that he is disturbing the class and that he will have to leave if he does it again.

The CD-ROM that accompanies this text contains several hypothetical scenarios designed for you to apply the guidance principles suggested in the various chapters of this book. Go to the Your Turn section of the CD to access these scenarios. Scenarios 3 and 4 are particularly pertinent to this section of the text, Disruptive Behaviors.

chapter **18**

Leaving the Classroom

"Where is Cosgrove? Has anyone seen Cosgrove?" All the teachers take a quick count and by unspoken signal, Mr. Turner goes out the door and down the hall. There he finds four-year-old Cosgrove sitting in his coat cubby, looking glum. Mr. Turner gets down to Cosgrove's eye level and says, "Hey, Cosgrove, we missed you. Where have you been?" No answer.

"Cosgrove, you know what? We're going to be taking out the new puzzles that came in the mail yesterday. Do you want to try one of them?" No answer. "There's one with a fire engine and one with a polar bear and another with Sesame Street characters and several others. Which would you like to try?" Still no answer.

"Come on, Cosgrove. Let's go back inside. Take my hand." Cosgrove sits on his hands. After several more minutes of coaxing, Mr. Turner and Cosgrove go back into the classroom. A half-hour later, Cosgrove is gone again.

This pattern of frequently leaving the classroom has been going on for several months. The teachers have tried patient coaxing, have expressed their frustration, and have talked with Cosgrove, but to no avail. When Cosgrove first began leaving the room, he treated such occurrences as a silly game, laughing and teasing and running from the teachers as they tried to get him back. After a while, however, the teachers became angry with this repeated behavior, and Cosgrove's reactions changed to the pouting he displayed with Mr. Turner. The adults feel at a total loss as to what to do with Cosgrove.

152

STATE THE BEHAVIOR

The child frequently leaves the classroom without a legitimate reason.

OBSERVE THE BEHAVIOR

To get a better idea of when and why the child leaves the classroom at inappropriate times, spend some time observing this behavior informally.

When does the child leave the room?
- Unpredictably, at any time of day
- When the child first arrives at school
- Later in the day
- Before a specific activity or routine
- During activity times
- During free-choice time
- During transitions

What happens before the child leaves the room?
- The child is not engaged in an activity.
- The child is engaged in isolated play.
- The child is playing with another child or group of children.
- The child verbally expresses a dislike for an activity.
- The child is told no by a teacher or another child.
- The child is wandering aimlessly around the room.
- The child has an argument with another child.
- The child is not able to accomplish a task.
- The child cries and asks for his family.

What does the child do when he leaves the room?
- The child looks to see if an adult is watching before leaving.
- The child announces that he is leaving.
- The child leaves quietly.
- The child encourages other children to accompany him.
- The child gets upset when asked to return to the class.
- The child laughs when asked to return.
- The child plays "hard to get" when an adult tries to bring him back.
- The child returns to the class by himself.

Where does the child go when he leaves the room?
- The child stays right outside the door.
- The child stays within fairly close range of the classroom.

- The child goes to the school kitchen.
- The child goes to the playground.
- The child leaves the school building.
- The child goes into the street.
- The child walks toward home.
- The child heads in a specific direction (such as a nearby park or store).

Use these observations to help you work on eliminating this behavior.

CONSULT WITH THE FAMILY

A child who leaves the classroom should be of concern to the family since there is the frightening possibility that the child could wander away from the school altogether. Thus, a prompt discussion with the family about your concern, especially once you have had the opportunity to gather some more information from observation, should take place. Find out if the child has the habit of wandering off in other settings and, if so, how the family deals with this behavior. If this seems to be a behavior specific to school, brainstorm with the family about why the child might be leaving the class and what strategies might help eliminate this behavior. Once you have begun working on decreasing this behavior, keep the family informed frequently about progress toward your goal of having the child stay in the classroom without wandering off.

CONSIDER THE IMPLICATIONS

The child who walks out of the classroom may do so for one of two reasons. The child may genuinely want to be somewhere else or the child may be seeking attention. If the child really wants to be somewhere else, it is important to work on remedying his unhappiness with the situation. It is the latter case, attention-seeking, that is the focus of this chapter. As with any attention-seeking behavior, the child has learned that adults pay attention when he leaves the classroom.

Teachers of preschoolers are given the responsibility of caring for the children in the absence of the family. Any time a child is out of sight, there is a danger that something unexpected can happen. Therefore, adults react very quickly when a child leaves the classroom. The child is followed and brought back into the classroom as soon as possible. It is this very act that reinforces the behavior. Every time the child seeks attention by leaving the class, a teacher obliges by giving that attention by following, chasing, talking to, coaxing, and bringing the child back. A vicious cycle is created that does not eliminate the behavior but only reinforces it.

EXPLORE ALTERNATIVES

Before deciding to change the child's behavior, think about whether some simpler changes might not resolve the concern. Carefully consider the following suggestions:

- A child may walk out a door simply because the door is open. Perhaps keeping the classroom door closed will take care of the situation.

- A child may want to leave the classroom because he does not want to be there. If this is the case, the child will show signs of distress at other times. For instance, a child to whom the school experience is new may not want to be at school. Knowing that his family went out the door, he may try to leave the same way.

- If school is not offering activities and materials that are challenging enough for a child, he may decide to find a better way of keeping busy. Leaving the room may represent an adventure or more exciting things to do. Carefully examine the classroom's arrangement and contents to be sure they are appropriate for the child's abilities and interests. Introduce some new, more stimulating activities into the curriculum. If the child finds enough of interest in the classroom, he may not need to seek challenge elsewhere.

- If coats and personal belongings are kept outside the classroom, such as in a hall or entryway, a child may be leaving the room for this reason. A coat, sweater, blanket, or other item in his cubby may be the reason the child frequently leaves, particularly if that child feels insecure without the item. In such a case, let the child keep the security item with him in the classroom. Once he no longer needs its security, the item can go back into the cubby.

- A child may leave the classroom because of curiosity. He may indicate this by asking questions. Plan a tour through the school building and its surroundings. Such a tour should provide satisfaction for the child's curiosity as well as the possibility for a wealth of related activities.

If none of these suggestions presents a way to change the behavior, continue to the detailed approach.

STATE THE GOAL

The goal is for the child to stop leaving the classroom at inappropriate times.

APPROACH

To change this behavior, the basic strategy involves the following simultaneous steps:

- Arrange the classroom and its contents and plan activities to encourage staying in the room.

- Prevent the child from leaving the room whenever possible.
- Praise the child for engaging in activities in the room.
- Provide opportunities for the child to leave the room legitimately.
- Ignore inappropriate departures, if at all possible.

DEFINITION

Leaving the classroom includes any occasion when the child goes out of the classroom without legitimate reason. Such behavior occurs on a repeated and frequent basis.

STARTING POINT

It is important to know how often the child leaves the classroom to be able to recognize progress when the child begins to decrease this behavior. For three days, count the number of times he leaves the room inappropriately. Each time he leaves, mark this down on paper. At the end of each day, record the total number on the Frequency Record-Keeping Graph.

STRATEGIES

Begin implementing the approach. It is important that all teachers follow it consistently.

Arrange the Room and the Program to Encourage the Child to Stay in the Class. Provide the child with good reasons to stay in the class. It is easier to remain in the room if it provides interest, challenge, and stimulation. Consider the following ideas:

1. Rearrange classroom furnishings to provide renewed interest in the class. If possible, provide a new area, or convert an old area to a new purpose. You might add a science table, a cooking area, a music center, or a sensory area. Similarly, you could convert the housekeeping area into a pretend airport, store, or restaurant.

   As you rearrange the room, take into account preventive measures. Arrange the room in such a way that a teacher can be stationed near the door. The activity area that is nearest the door should be one that generates a good deal of interest. An alternative idea would be to have a table near the door and provide activities there.

2. Be sure that the materials stored in the classroom are of high interest to the children. Introduce some new materials if your school is

equipped to rotate items. Materials in the room should be appropriate for the abilities of the children and available in ample amounts for everyone. Also examine storage spaces. Classroom items should be attractively displayed, uncluttered, and easily accessible to the children.

3. It may also be time to plan some different activities. It is easy to become unimaginative in relation to curriculum planning. For new ideas, scan some of the many preschool activity books available. Both the teachers and the children will feel a renewed interest in school with some new ideas.

4. The daily schedule might also be due for a change. Rearrange the order of events. Lengthen or shorten time blocks. Add or subtract activities. Take into consideration that the children have changed since school began. They are older and have learned and experienced many things.

These suggestions should be discussed by the entire staff. They are not meant for a classroom that has only been in session a few weeks. They are intended to provide a possible change of pace where the room arrangement, materials, curriculum, and schedule have been the same for two or three months or more. Periodic change can be stimulating, but change that occurs too often and too quickly can be confusing.

Prevent the Child from Leaving the Room Whenever Possible.
Several things can be done to make preventive measures effective. With vigilance, it is possible to prevent the child from inappropriately leaving the classroom altogether.

1. Keep the classroom door closed. In this way, you are placing an obstacle between the classroom and the outside that will take extra time for the child to overcome.

2. Provide an added cue for yourself to inform you if the child does try to leave. Fasten a bell or other signaling device toward the top of the door. Whenever anyone opens the door, the bell will ring. If you hear the bell at a time when the door should be closed, it is easy to quickly check.*

3. An adult should be near the door during structured and unstructured activities. This teacher will have a dual role. The teacher will be involved in an activity that is ongoing in the class and will be on the lookout for the child who frequently leaves the class.

---

*A child with a cognitive disability may not understand the safety rules of the classroom. An aural cue such as a bell can be particularly helpful in the case of such a child.

4. From your informal observation you should have an idea of when the child leaves the classroom and what he usually does before this happens. Be on the lookout for such cues. If the child usually wanders aimlessly around the room before he exits, help him become involved in an activity. If he walks out after he becomes angry or frustrated, help him deal with those feelings more effectively.

5. If the child is already at the door and about to walk out, stop him. Put your arm around him, close the door, and turn back to the class. Tell the child that you want him to choose an activity. Help him become involved in one. If he struggles, keep a gentle but firm hold on him until he calms down. Do not discuss the situation at length; simply say, "You may not go out."

6. If the child usually leaves during group activities, you will need a different approach. One teacher should be seated with the child during group times. The child can either sit on the teacher's lap or next to the teacher. If the child tries to leave, the adult should restrain him by gently but firmly holding on to him until he stops struggling. (See Chapter 17 if the situation is one in which the child regularly disrupts group time.)

Praise the Child for Engaging in Activities in the Classroom. The aim of these strategies is to get the child to remain in the classroom and to constructively engage in activities. Let the child know that you are pleased when he does so. Make a point of reinforcing him frequently through verbal praise, a smile, a pat, or a hug. Once the child decreases the attempts to leave the class, gradually cut down on the reinforcement until you are praising him at about the same rate as you do the other children in the group.

Provide Opportunities for the Child to Leave the Class Legitimately. Let the child know that there are appropriate reasons to leave the class, but these have to be approved by a teacher. The child may be sent on errands to the office or to another classroom. The responsibility of conveying a message helps the child feel important and trusted. The child should not be sent on an errand for at least an hour after he has tried to leave the room. Such a responsibility should be given on a day when he has stayed in the room and has been constructively involved.

Being able to send children on errands depends on the facility. Examine your building and surroundings to be sure such activity is suitable and safe. Take into account the age of the child in your class. Two-year-olds and young three-year-olds should not be sent out of the room alone. Older preschoolers enjoy such responsibilities and may be trusted.

Another way of legitimately leaving the room is through planned class activities. You might visit other classes, walk around the building, or visit the kitchen periodically.

Ignore Inappropriate Departures, If at All Possible. Your preventive measures should eliminate or considerably reduce the behavior. On occasion, however, the child may still leave the room. You have one of the following two options, depending on your facility:

1. If at all possible, ignore the child's behavior. The child is seeking the attention that usually follows his exits. The less attention given, the better. To ignore such behavior, prepare some safety precautions beforehand. The child should not be able to leave the school premises. Other adults in the building should be able to keep an eye on him once he is out of the class. Teachers in other classes, office personnel, and the kitchen staff should be alerted to the situation, asked not to give attention to the child, and requested to watch him carefully. Eventually the child will return to the class. At this point say nothing about the fact that he was gone. Tell him what activities are available, then praise him a few minutes later for being involved.

2. If, for safety reasons, you cannot let the child leave the room, redouble your preventive efforts. If on occasion the child does leave the room, follow him. With a minimum of fuss and attention return the child to the class. Do not even give the child eye contact as you walk back with him. Once you are in the room, tell him, "You may not leave the classroom because it is not safe for you to be outside alone." Hold the child gently but firmly until he stops struggling if this is the case. Help the child find an activity to engage in and give him praise once he is involved.

Continue Keeping Track of the Behavior. Each day, keep track of the number of times the child actually leaves the room as well as the number of times he tries to leave. Define what indicates an attempt to leave so that all the teachers agree on what this means. An example might be that the child attempts to open the door. Because preventive measures should eliminate or nearly eliminate actual exits, it is necessary to include attempted departures in the daily count. You will not achieve your goal until the child voluntarily remains in the room. Recording only incidents in which the child actually leaves the room may not give an accurate picture of the behavior. Draw a vertical line after the initial count and record each day's count as follows:

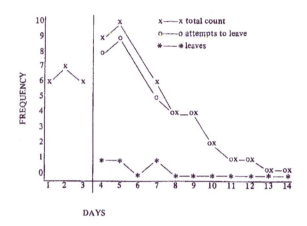

There should be few incidents of actual departures from the class. If there are many, examine the preventive measures. When the total is at zero for several days, this approach may be considered successful and can be discontinued.

MAINTAINING THE CHANGES

Continue praising the child for involvement in classroom activities. Also continue to examine all aspects of the environment to ensure that it is as stimulating as possible to the children. Once you interest the child in school, he should feel no need to leave the room.

The CD-ROM that accompanies this text contains several hypo-thetical scenarios designed for you to apply the guidance principles suggested in the various chapters of this book. Go to the Your Turn section of the CD to access these scenarios. Scenarios 3 and 4 are particularly pertinent to this section of the text, Disruptive Behaviors.

chapter **19**

Running Aimlessly around the Classroom

It is activity time. The teachers have prepared and introduced several activities for the children. The children have selected the area in which they want to work. Three-year-old Sylvia chooses to go to the easel. She picks up a brush saturated with paint and makes a quick line down the center of the paper. She repeats with another such line, allowing the paint to drip down the paper and onto the floor. Sylvia returns the brush to the paint jar, flings off her paint smock, and shouts, "I'm done, teacher!"

She walks to the block area, watches a few seconds, then goes to the manipulative table where several children are working. She takes out a puzzle, empties the pieces, then walks away. After a quick look around the room, Sylvia runs to the bathroom. She quickly dashes out and darts back to the art area. Within a few seconds, Sylvia is running around the room, distracting children, interrupting play, and knocking over the block tower that Jimmy carefully built.

Mrs. Anderson sighs. This is a typical day with Sylvia running aimlessly around the classroom. Mrs. Anderson catches Sylvia and says, "Stop running around, Sylvia. You need to find something to do." Sylvia smiles and walks over to the block area. Within half a minute she starts running around again. Again Mrs. Anderson asks Sylvia to stop but succeeds in only a few more seconds of calm.

The third time, Mr. Gomez restrains Sylvia by holding her arms, saying, "Come on, Sylvia, let's find something for you to do." He takes the child by the hand and leads her to the sand table. Mr. Gomez collects several implements, stands by Sylvia for a couple of minutes, and talks with her while watching her play. He then walks away from the sand table area. A minute later, Sylvia is again on the run. The teachers feel exasperated. Sylvia's behavior continues in spite of their efforts.

STATE THE BEHAVIOR

The child runs around the classroom aimlessly rather than engaging in planned activities.

OBSERVE THE BEHAVIOR

Observe the child for a few days to gain insight into the behavior.

When does the behavior occur?
- During planned activity times
- During free-choice activities
- During group times such as story, discussion, or music
- At cleanup times
- During transitions

What seems to trigger the behavior?
- The child finishes an activity.
- The child plays with a particular child or a few children.
- Another child or several children exclude her from joining them in play.
- The child is not able to complete a task.
- The child is asked by a teacher to do something.
- The child expresses dislike for the planned activities.
- A teacher does not attend to the child when she asks for help or attention.

What happens when the child engages in the behavior?
- The child looks to see whether an adult is watching.
- The child runs right by one or more adults as she goes around the room.
- The child tries to get other children to join her.
- The child runs randomly through the various areas in the classroom or follows a specific route.
- The child makes noise as she runs around the room.
- The child runs around the room quietly.
- The child responds to a teacher trying to interest her in an activity.

These preliminary observations should give you an idea of when and under what circumstances the child runs aimlessly around the classroom. Use this information to implement your plan.

CONSULT WITH THE FAMILY

A child who runs around the classroom aimlessly, disrupting ongoing activity, may be of more concern to teachers than to the family since this behavior occurs primarily in the school setting. You may try to deal with the behavior without unduly concerning the family. If you are meeting with the family for a regularly scheduled conference, you can mention that this is a behavior you have been working on decreasing so that the child can engage more fully in school activities. In that case, keep the family informed of progress toward that goal.

CONSIDER THE IMPLICATIONS

Disruptive behavior is usually motivated by a need for attention. The child who engages in a disruption such as running aimlessly through the classroom is saying, "Hey! Look at me!" For one reason or another, the child has found that she does not get adult attention as often as she needs it. She probably does not get enough reinforcement for appropriate behavior. The child also finds that adults pay attention to her when she is disruptive. As soon as she runs around the room, a teacher talks to her, attempts to stop her, scolds her, and tries to interest her in an activity. Running around the room results in adult attention. If this attention is not given quickly enough, the child increases the behavior to get a reaction from an adult. A teacher may provide the expected reinforcement and thus cause a self-defeating pattern to emerge. The more a teacher tries to stop the child's aimless running about the room, the more the child is reinforced for engaging in this activity. Your informal observations may lead you to another conclusion: that the child has a very short attention span and therefore is unable to stay with an activity for any length of time. If this is the case, turn to Chapter 44. The current chapter focuses on aimless running around the classroom used as an attention-seeking behavior.

EXPLORE ALTERNATIVES

Disruptive behaviors are often a response to the classroom environment. Examine the school carefully for potential problems before attempting to change the child's behavior.

- Take a critical look at the classroom arrangement. The arrangement depends on the shape and size of the room and on the furnishings and equipment available. The arrangement should be related to the ages, total number, interests, and special needs of the children. Examine the placement of furniture, storage spaces, and equipment. Open spaces invite running. Poorly defined interest areas are not conducive to engagement in defined activities and can lead to frequent interruptions. All staff members should be involved in discussion and arrangement of the classroom.

- Another cause of disruptive behavior such as running about the classroom can be lack of availability of activities and materials. A child may become frustrated if activities are too difficult. She may become bored if activities are too simple or frustrated if there are not enough materials for everyone. She may create her own diversions through disruptions. Carefully examine what is in the room in relation to the child's developmental level, needs, and interests. If only one child is reacting disruptively within the environment, consider whether another classroom might be more appropriate for her.*

If aspects of the classroom environment do not seem to be the cause of the concern, continue on to the following approach.

STATE THE GOAL

The goal is for the child to stop running aimlessly around the classroom and to engage instead in the activities planned for that time.

APPROACH

The basic strategy to eliminate aimless running around the room involves three simultaneous steps:

- Arrange the classroom environment to discourage such behavior as much as possible.
- Reinforce all occasions when the child is constructively engaged in activities.
- Ignore any running that may take place.

DEFINITION

Running aimlessly around the classroom includes any incident in which the child runs about the room with no evident purpose, instead of taking part in a game or activity.

Whenever a child whose developmental level is different from the other children's is integrated into the classroom, it is important to ensure that there are activities and materials that will engage the child's interest at her developmental level.

STARTING POINT

To know how often, on the average, the child runs around the room aimlessly, count the number of such incidents over a three-day period. If this behavior occurs only at specific times, rather than throughout the day, decide on a specific time block to do the counting. Consistently use that same time period for all future counts. Mark down on paper each incident of aimless running when it occurs. At the end of each day, record the number on the Frequency Record-Keeping Graph. These three days of counting before you implement any changes will provide a basis against which progress can be compared once you begin the suggested strategies.

STRATEGIES

Start using the following approach after the initial three-day count. All teachers must follow these strategies at all times to provide the needed consistency to produce a change.

Rearrange the Classroom to Discourage Running. All teachers should participate in a brainstorming session to arrange the classroom more effectively. The aim is to discourage running by eliminating any straight, empty stretches that exist in the room. Do not block exits or place small obstacles in the direct path of traffic, but use furniture and materials as effective dividers and definers of space.

The two illustrations on next page show the same furnishings arranged differently in the same room. In Room A, the length of the room is open to running. Although furnishings are grouped by interest areas, the spaces surrounding these are not well defined. Children playing in different areas can easily get in one another's way. These problems are resolved in Room B. Much of the running space is eliminated because the furniture arrangement uses all of the space in the room, not just the edges. Interest areas are defined. Each group of furnishings defines its own, contained space. Children can work without outside interference.

If a child in the classroom spends too much time running aimlessly around the room rather than engaging in constructive activities, carefully examine the room first. Rearrange it to best facilitate the behavior you want. Once you have made room changes, continue to evaluate the classroom and make appropriate changes. There is no one right way of arranging a classroom, but some arrangements are better than others.

ROOM A

ROOM B

Reinforce the Child for Being Constructively Engaged in Activities.

You want the child to replace aimless running around the room with constructive participation in planned or self-selected activities. Reinforce this behavior when it occurs. Whenever the child is constructively engaged, tell her you are pleased. Praise her socialization, her work, her

technique, her product, or whatever else is appropriate. Time such reinforcement to maximize its effect:

1. At first, praise the child every time you see her engaged in constructive activity. If she stays with an activity, reinforce her about
   every two minutes.
2. As the child decreases aimless running and increases activity
   involvement, gradually decrease the frequency of praise.
3. Finally, once the child's behavior has reached the goal, cut back
   reinforcement. Praise this child with about the same frequency as
   you praise the other children in the class.

If the Child Does Run around the Room, Ignore the Behavior.
It is difficult to ignore the child when she is running around the room
because such behavior is very disruptive to classroom functioning.
However, it is important that all teachers completely ignore this
behavior when it occurs. For the first few days, this behavior may be
more intense than usual. The child may await the customary adult
reactions. Once the child realizes that there is no reinforcement
forthcoming for such aimless running, the behavior should quickly
disappear.

Continue Keeping Track of the Behavior. Continue recording
the number of running incidents that occur each day on the graph.
Collect this information during the same period in which the initial
three days of observations were made. This graph provides information you need to decide when to decrease reinforcement for positive
behavior.

MAINTAINING THE CHANGES

Continue reassessing the room arrangement in relation to the behavior
of all the children, even after concerns about running have been
resolved. Continue letting all the children know periodically that you
appreciate appropriate behavior. These measures should prevent further incidents of aimless running. The child will realize that there is no
attention forthcoming for such behavior.

The CD-ROM that accompanies this text contains several hypothetical scenarios designed for you to apply the guidance principles
suggested in the various chapters of this book. Go to the Your Turn
section of the CD to access these scenarios. Scenarios 3 and 4 are
particularly pertinent to this section of the text, Disruptive Behaviors.

chapter 20

Shouting in the Classroom

A piercing whoop interrupts the normal noise level of the class of four-year-olds. "Stop that, Charles!" says one of the teachers, while the other two turn toward the source of the noise and grimace. Charles gives them each an engaging smile, then continues with his play. A few minutes later, Charles gives an extended Tarzan call, and soon thereafter he shrieks with an ear-splitting intensity.

Statements like, "Stop it, Charles!" and "Charles, you're really bothering everybody!" are accompanied by sighs, ear-covering motions, and scathing looks from the adults. Charles, who is physically small for his age but bright and verbal, has been making noisy interruptions since school began two months ago. They occur primarily indoors and during activity times, story times, singing, and group discussions. The teachers are bothered by Charles's disruptions, which interfere with the smooth functioning of the class.

STATE THE BEHAVIOR

The child makes unnecessarily loud noises in school at inappropriate times.

OBSERVE THE BEHAVIOR

Take some time to observe the child informally to gain insight into the behavior.

When does the behavior occur?
- At any time of day
- At times when children are expected to remain relatively quiet
- During outdoor play
- Indoors
- During self-selected activities
- During activity times
- During group activities such as music, story, dance, or discussion
- At nap or rest times
- During transitions

What seems to precipitate the behavior?
- There is general quiet in the classroom.
- There is an overall high noise level in the classroom.
- The child is engaged in solitary play or activity.
- The child is involved in social play.
- The child is involved in spontaneous role-playing activity.
- Others talk during group activities.
- The child plays with a particular child or group of children.
- The child is asked to do a particular task, such as help with cleanup time.

What happens when the child shouts?
- The child looks around to see if an adult is going to react.
- The child repeats the noise one or more times.
- The child seems upset.
- The child smiles.
- The child tries to get other children to join in the noise.
- The child becomes upset when reprimanded by an adult.
- The child seems unconcerned about adult reactions.

You should now have an idea of the circumstances under which the child makes unnecessary noise in the classroom. Use such information to find a way to change the behavior.

CONSULT WITH THE FAMILY

Loud outcries and noises may be of as much concern to the family at home as they are to teachers at school. Once you have had the opportunity to observe the child's behavior more carefully, meet with the family to discuss your concerns. Stress that your goal is for the child to engage more fully in the school's activities. If the child also makes unpredictable and unnecessarily loud noises at home, find out from the family under what circumstances they have noted the behavior. Discuss with the family how they deal with the behavior and share with them your ideas about eliminating it. Once you have begun to implement an approach to change the behavior, continue to communicate with the family to keep them informed of progress.

CONSIDER THE IMPLICATIONS

Probably at some point in the past, the child found that adults react very quickly to loud noises. The louder and more piercing the noise made by the child, the greater the reaction. Such response from adults only reinforces the behavior. The child shouts, and an adult reacts. The next time the child wants adult reaction he shouts and an adult reacts, and thus the cycle perpetuates itself. Because loud noise above the normal volume in the classroom is disruptive, teachers feel compelled to react quickly when it happens. Teachers reinforce shouting, and the behavior continues as long as adults pay attention to it.

EXPLORE ALTERNATIVES

There might be a simple resolution for working with the child who shouts unnecessarily. Carefully consider the following suggestions:

- Examine your expectations for the children to be sure that they are appropriate for the age and developmental level of the class. Young children should not be expected to remain very quiet. They are exuberant and enjoy making noises appropriate to their play. An active and productive preschool classroom is not always a quiet place.
- It is possible that a child whose voice level is slightly louder than that of the other children has been repeatedly asked to "keep it down." The child concludes that making noise is a good way to get attention. In such a case, faulty adult expectations have led to this behavior. Work on eliminating shouting, but keep in mind that the child normally speaks loudly.
- A child who is frequently loud may have a hearing problem. Young children are susceptible to ear infections, which sometimes cause blockages and result in hearing loss. Also consider fluid in the ears and wax buildup as possible reasons for impaired hearing. Consider such possibilities carefully. The child may be loud or make loud noises simply to reassure himself that he can be heard.

If you suspect a hearing problem, try a crude test. Make various noises behind the child and watch for reactions. If the test confirms your suspicion, ask the family to have the child's hearing tested.*

- Examine your schedule to see whether it is too restrictive for the children. The youngsters may react to an overly structured situation by disruptive means such as shouting. You may be expecting the children to listen, engage in activities for which they are given no choices, or sit quietly for periods that are too long. If this is the case, rearrange your daily schedule. Alternate quiet and active times. Alternate teacher-directed and child-selected activities. Decrease the length of group times as appropriate.

- Also examine adult behavior. Do teachers shout instructions or other declarations to the children in a loud voice? Do teachers call across the room to talk to a child instead of moving to the child? The example set by the teacher can be an important factor in children's behavior. Ensure that the teachers model appropriate voice level. At the end of activity time, for instance, it is more effective for the teachers to move from group to group and say in a normal tone of voice, "it's time to clean up now," rather than to make a megaphone announcement to the entire class.

- Be sure that the child who shouts understands your expectations. Tell him that he may shout outside as much as he wants, but that indoors his voice level needs to be kept down. If the child cannot abide by such a rule, then move to the following strategies.

STATE THE GOAL

The goal is for the child to keep his voice at an appropriate level in the classroom.

APPROACH

Essentially, the strategy to eliminate disruptive shouting involves these steps:

- Give attention to appropriate classroom behaviors.
- Provide for a "noisy time."
- Ignore incidents of shouting.

*Many children, often because of repeated ear infections, have some hearing loss. Be sensitive to this possibility.

DEFINITION

Shouting includes all instances in which the child raises his voice well above what is acceptable in the classroom. In addition to shouting, this may include yelling, shrieking, whooping, and other annoying loud noises.

STARTING POINT

Before working on changing the behavior, take three days to count the number of daily shouts. This will provide information against which you compare improvements. If a child makes unnecessary noise mostly during a specific period, use only this period in which to count shouts. Specify an hour to use consistently every day to gather information. Keep a pencil and paper handy for marking down each time the child shouts. At the end of each day record the total on the Frequency Record-Keeping Graph.

STRATEGIES

Once you have kept track of incidents of shouting for three days, you are ready to begin. It is very important that all teachers follow this approach consistently.

Reinforce Appropriate Classroom Behaviors. Whenever you try to eliminate a behavior, it is also important to let the child know what behaviors you expect and value. Therefore, make a point of praising the child frequently for appropriate behaviors. This should include keeping voice level down, as well as engaging in activities and social play and contributing to discussions. At first, reinforce such behaviors as often as possible. Later, as the frequency of shouting decreases, gradually decrease such praise. Give praise for such behaviors at about the same rate as you give it to other children in the class.

Provide for a Daily "Noisy Time." Make a clear distinction between appropriate and inappropriate places in which one can make noise. Tell all the children in the class that there will be a noisy time when they go outside. Encourage them to "save" noises for this occasion. Design the noisy time to what you are comfortable with. You might, for instance, let all the children together make as much noise as possible for a few seconds. (You may have to forewarn people who work or live nearby.) Another approach is to have the children take turns making different noises.

The reason for the noisy time is to provide a legitimate outlet of the urge to make noise and to designate appropriate and inappropriate times and places to make noise. As with any novelty, the children will probably enjoy this for a while. When their interest wanes, you can discontinue this activity. By that time, the child who was making inappropriate noise in the classroom should have substantially decreased or completely stopped the behavior.

Ignore Incidents of Shouting When They Do Occur. Whenever the child shouts, do not react in any way. It is important that all adults in the classroom act consistently in this matter. The child receives considerable reinforcement through the reactions of adults whenever he shouts. Therefore, when all attention is withdrawn, expect the behavior to increase. You will probably have to tolerate quite a bit of noise for the first day or two of ignoring. Once the child realizes that no one is paying attention, he will quickly decrease, then stop, the behavior. Other youngsters may call your attention to the noise. Simply say, "I know," then go on to talk about something else. Use any opportunity to praise the child for appropriate behaviors. Make your message as clear as possible. The child gets attention for acceptable behaviors, but is ignored for shouting.

Continue Keeping Track of the Behavior. As you implement these strategies, continue to count and record behaviors on the Frequency Record-Keeping Graph. Record the total count each day. Most likely, the count will increase on the first day or two. It should drop quickly to zero if these steps are consistently followed.

MAINTAINING THE CHANGES

After the rate of shouting is at zero for a few days, consider the approach successful. Continue praising desired behaviors periodically, as you do with all the children. If, on occasion, the child does revert to shouting, ignore it completely.

The CD-ROM that accompanies this text contains several hypothetical scenarios designed for you to apply the guidance principles suggested in the various chapters of this book. Go to the Your Turn section of the CD to access these scenarios. Scenarios 3 and 4 are particularly pertinent to this section of the text, Disruptive Behaviors.

Biting • Throwing Objects at Others • Hitting Others • Using Inappropr e-Calling • Nonsharing • Bribery • Stealing • Noncompliance • Disrupting he Classroom • Running Aimlessly Around the Classroom • Shouting in bjects to Create Noise • Breaking Toys • Flushing Objects Wasting Paper • Destroying the Work of Others • Throwing Tantrums • Po y Talk • Thumb-Sucking • Pant-Wetting • Clinging • Seeking Attention • h Only One Toy • Inadequate Muscle Activity • Irregular Dramat Finicky Eating • Overeat Eating • Hording Food • Hitting • Biting • Throwing Objects at Others • ppropriate Language • Name-Calling • Nonsharing • Bribery • Stealing ting Group Time • Leaving the Classroom • Running Aimlessly Around th g in the Classroom • Dropping Objects to Create Noise • Tearing Books • lushing Objects Down the Toilet • Wasting Paper • Destroying the Work owing Tantrums • Pouting • Baby Talk • Thumb-Sucking • Pant-Wettin

chapter **21**

Dropping Objects to Create Noise

Crash! The adults and children look toward the source of the noise. Five-year-old George is standing next to the overturned wooden refrigerator in the housekeeping area. It is apparent that he dropped the refrigerator simply to make noise. Earlier in the day, George collected a number of blocks, placed them on a shelf, then climbed on the shelf to drop the blocks, one by one, onto the linoleum below. Two teachers ran toward George. One teacher lifted him off the shelf and put him on the floor. The other rescued the blocks. Both adults conveyed their displeasure about the incident to George. During all this time, George's face reflected pleasure about the event. He nodded when asked if he would please not do that again. George put away the blocks and righted the refrigerator in response to a teacher's request. The teachers feel frustrated because they know, from past history, that George will again drop objects for the sake of making noise.

STATE THE BEHAVIOR

The child deliberately drops objects onto the floor or another surface for the purpose of making noise.

OBSERVE THE BEHAVIOR

Observe the child for a couple of days to gain an understanding of the circumstances under which deliberate dropping of objects takes place.

When does the behavior usually occur?
- At any time of day
- During free-choice periods
- During activity times
- During structured activities
- During activities when children are required to listen, such as story or music times
- At quiet times like rest or nap times
- During cleanup time
- During transitions

What happens before the child drops an object?
- The child is involved in play with other children.
- The child is involved in solitary play.
- The child looks around to see where adults are.
- The child collects objects.
- Another child or a teacher says no to him.
- The child cannot complete a task.
- The child is asked to keep quiet.

What happens when the child drops an object?
- The child tries to make it look like an accident.
- The child makes a point of showing that it was a deliberate act.
- The child voluntarily picks up and replaces the object.
- The child picks up the object when asked to by a teacher.
- The child refuses to pick up the object.
- The child gets upset by a teacher's reaction.
- The child shows no concern.

What objects does the child drop?
- Anything
- Usually the same object or same type of object
- Large items
- Small items
- Wooden, metal, plastic, or cardboard items
- Breakable items

- Nonbreakable items
- Items that make noise on impact

Where does the child drop objects?
- Anywhere
- On cement
- On wood
- On tile
- On linoleum
- On carpeting
- On tables or shelves

This preliminary observation should give you some clues about the behavior. Use these clues when you implement the strategies discussed below to eliminate the dropping of objects.

CONSULT WITH THE FAMILY

Once you have had the opportunity to observe the child's behavior more carefully, set up a meeting with the family and discuss your concerns, stressing the potential safety hazard to the child and others in the classroom. Find out from the family if the child tends to drop or knock over objects at home as well. If, at home, the child also drops objects for the sake of making noise, ask the family what strategies they have tried and found helpful for eliminating this behavior and share your ideas. Once you have decided on an approach and the behavior starts to decrease, keep the family informed of the child's successes.

CONSIDER THE IMPLICATIONS

Children who engage in being disruptive do so because they enjoy the attention such behavior brings. The child who deliberately drops objects for the sake of the noise this creates is no different. Such behavior quickly brings adults to the spot for several reasons.

First, the noise from the dropped object is irritating. Second, although preschool materials are made to be sturdy, rough handling through deliberate dropping can result in damage. Finally, this behavior is potentially dangerous because someone could be inadvertently hurt. For these reasons, adults respond swiftly and give considerable attention to the child who has deliberately dropped something. Not only do teachers lecture and scold the child for such behavior, but they also insist that the child pick up what has been dropped. At this point the child may well prolong the attention by changing the issue. He may refuse to clean up. The resulting power struggle between the teacher who says, "Yes, you will pick up these items" and the child who responds, "No, I won't" can ensure several more minutes of attention. Consequently, the child receives satisfaction by dropping objects for the sake of making noise. Meanwhile, the adults are frustrated. Their reactions reinforce rather than eliminate the behavior.

EXPLORE ALTERNATIVES

Consider the following ideas carefully. One may provide a resolution to the behavior.

- The child may have a hearing problem. A child who has trouble hearing may be trying to reassure himself that he can be heard by making deliberate noises. Conduct a crude test by making various noises behind the child and checking for reactions. If this test confirms your concern, talk to the family, and recommend that they have the child's hearing checked.*

- The child may drop objects because of a physical disability. A visual disability may cause the child to bump into and knock over objects frequently. Similarly, poorly developed eye–hand coordination can result in objects being dropped more often than normal accidents would warrant. If you suspect such a problem, recommend further medical testing to the family.†

- The room environment may invite such behavior. For instance, interest areas in which play is usually noisy should be carpeted. The block area must contain some kind of soft floor covering. The housekeeping area might also benefit from carpeting, if it is available. When hard objects are placed on hard flooring, noise occurs naturally. This may well present the original idea for disruptive behavior to a child. Noise that results from dropping a hard object on a hard floor gets adult attention. This behavior may become a repeated one.

- If the child's behavior is focused on turning over large items, such as housekeeping furniture, rearrange these. You might place these items against a wall so the child cannot get behind and push. You could back the items against the rear of another piece of furniture, such as shelves or storage units.

*Many children, often because of repeated ear infections, have some hearing loss. Be sensitive to this possibility.
†A child with cerebral palsy may have poor muscle control and, as a result, frequently drop objects in his hand. Similarly, the child who frequently bumps into objects may have decreased visual acuity or poor peripheral vision. A child with a learning disability may have difficulty in coordination—for instance, eye–hand coordination—and inadvertently bump into or drop objects. Be sure to eliminate possible physiological causes for the behavior.

- If the child drops only one particular object or type of object, consider removing it temporarily from the classroom. If, for instance, the child repeatedly drops dishes from the housekeeping areas on the floor, remove the dishes for a while. You might convert the area into a store by replacing the dishes with empty food cartons, a cash register, and paper bags. After two or three weeks, try replacing the removed items.

- Be sure that the child understands the purpose of the various materials and equipment in the classroom. Systematic help in learning how to use them may stop the disruptive behavior of dropping things. A child will respect the equipment more if he understands it.

If none of these suggestions helps in providing a resolution to the problem, continue to the following approach.

STATE THE GOAL

The goal is for this child to stop dropping objects for the purpose of making noise.

APPROACH

To reach this goal, your basic strategy will involve three simultaneous steps:
- Prevent the dropping of objects whenever possible.
- Reinforce appropriate use of materials and equipment.
- Ignore the behavior when it occurs.

DEFINITION

Dropping objects to create noise includes any incident in which the child deliberately drops an object on the floor or other surface for the purpose of making noise. Objects may be dropped or thrust downward from any height onto the floor or other surface.

STARTING POINT

Before you begin to implement changes, take three days to gather some initial information about the behavior. Mark on paper every time the child deliberately drops something. At the end of each day, transfer the total number to the Frequency Record-Keeping Graph. The information from these three days gives a count against which to compare later change.

Now begin the following approach. It must be followed by all the teachers in the class consistently.

Prevent the Dropping of Objects Whenever Possible. From your informal observation, you should have some clues about what precedes the behavior. Use these clues to prevent the child from carrying out his intention. For example, if the child usually collects objects before dropping them, watch for such behavior. When you see him collecting items, go to the child and engage him in a situation in which these items will be used appropriately. Say, "I see that you've gathered some puzzle pieces together. Let's put them into the puzzle frames where they belong." Or, you might have noted that the child looks around for a few seconds to find an object to drop. If you see this, go to the child and direct his interest elsewhere.

It is possible that dropping of objects occurs whenever the child plays with certain other youngsters, with a particular toy, or in a particular interest area. When you see the child in a situation that often precedes dropping objects, stay nearby and guide the situation to avoid such behavior.

Reinforce Appropriate Use of Materials.* Because dropping objects is an inappropriate way of handling classroom materials and equipment, let the child know that you are pleased when he uses objects properly. Convey to the child the need for respect of the items through your reinforcement. Say, for instance, "You are really using the paints carefully." "I like the way you're turning the pages of that book so they won't tear." "Thank you! You certainly stacked those pots and pans neatly." "What a great way to use those blocks! First you built a road, and now you're using the small blocks as cars."

At first, reinforce appropriate use of materials as often as possible. When the child's rate of object-dropping decreases, cut back gradually on the amount of praise you give. Eventually, reinforce the child's careful handling of materials as often as you would praise such behavior in the other children.

Ignore the Dropping of Objects If It Does Occur. The child is reinforced by teacher attention when he drops objects. Withdraw that attention to stop the behavior. It is difficult at first to ignore dropping of

---

Some materials in the classroom may be developmentally inappropriate for a child with a cognitive disability. Ensure that there are plenty of materials he can use and also help that child learn how to use all materials respectfully.

objects since the behavior will probably increase before it decreases. But once the child gets the message that no one will pay attention to the behavior, he will stop it. If the child does drop an object, none of the adults in the classroom should react in any way. Act as if nothing has happened. If another child calls your attention to the noise, simply say, "I know," and change the subject. Do not make an issue of forcing the child to pick up the dropped item. If it does not present a safety hazard, leave it where it is. If someone might stumble over it, wait a minute, and then quietly move it out of the way. If an object was broken and presents a danger, sweep up the pieces without saying anything about the incident to the child. When cleanup time comes, treat the dropped object like all the other items that need to be put away.

It may seem natural to insist that the child pick up and put away the dropped item. Ask him only once, in a matter-of-fact manner, to pick it up. If he does, praise him. If he does not, turn away. Such a situation can easily lead to a confrontation, which, in turn, provides attention from you. Use other opportunities to teach the need to clean up.

Continue Keeping Track of the Behavior. Each day that you follow these strategies, continue counting incidents of deliberate object-dropping. Record the data on the graph. It is likely that once the child realizes there is no attention forthcoming for dropping objects, the behavior will quickly decrease and then disappear.

MAINTAINING THE CHANGES

To ensure that object-dropping will not happen again, continue giving periodic reinforcement for proper use of materials and equipment. If the behavior recurs, ignore it the same way you did earlier.

The CD-ROM that accompanies this text contains several hypothetical scenarios designed for you to apply the guidance principles suggested in the various chapters of this book. Go to the Your Turn section of the CD to access these scenarios. Scenarios 3 and 4 are particularly pertinent to this section of the text, Disruptive Behaviors.

SECTION 4

Destructive Behaviors

• Nonsharing • Bribery • Stealing • Noncompliance • Disrupting Group Time • Leaving the Classroom
Running Aimlessly Around the Classroom • Shouting in the Classroom • Dropping Objects to Create Noise
Tearing Books • Breaking Toys • Flushing Objects Down the Toilet • Wasting Paper • Destroying the Work of
Others • Throwing Tantrums • Pouting • Baby Talk • Thumb-Sucking • Pant-Wetting • Clinging • Seeking
Attention • Whining • Nonparticipation in Activities • Nonparticipation in Social Play • Shyness at Group Time
Playing with Only One Toy • Infrequent Large Muscle Activity • Infrequent Dramatic-Play Participation
Talking Infrequently • Short Attention Span • Finicky Eating • Overeating • Messy Eating • Hording Food
Hitting • Biting • Throwing Objects at Others • Hurting Others • Using Inappropriate Language • Name-Calling
Nonsharing • Bribery • Stealing • Noncompliance • Disrupting Group Time • Leaving the Classroom
Running Aimlessly Around the Classroom • Shouting in the Classroom • Dropping Objects to Create Noise
Tearing Books • Breaking Toys • Flushing Objects Down the Toilet • Wasting Paper • Destroying the Work of
Others • Throwing Tantrums • Pouting • Baby Talk • Thumb-Sucking • Pant-Wetting • Clinging • Seeking
Attention • Whining • Self-Stimulation • Nonparticipation in Activities • Nonparticipation in Social Play
Shyness at Group Time • Playing with Only One Toy • Infrequent Large Muscle Activity • Infrequent
Dramatic-Play Participation • Talking Infrequently • Short Attention Span • Finicky Eating • Overeating
Messy Eating • Hording Food • Hitting • Biting • Throwing Objects at Others • Hurting Others • Using
Inappropriate Language • Name-Calling • Nonsharing • Bribery • Stealing • Noncompliance • Disrupting
Group Time • Leaving the Classroom • Running Aimlessly Around the Classroom • Shouting in the
Classroom • Dropping Objects to Create Noise • Tearing Books • Breaking Toys • Flushing Objects Down the
Toilet • Wasting Paper • Destroying the Work of Others • Throwing Tantrums • Pouting • Baby Talk
Thumb-Sucking • Pant-Wetting • Whining • Self-Stimulation • Nonparticipation in Activities
Nonparticipation in Social Play • Shyness at Group Time • Playing with Only One Toy • Infrequent Large
Muscle Activity • Infrequent Dramatic-Play Participation • Talking Infrequently • Short Attention Span
Finicky Eating • Overeating • Messy Eating • Hording Food • Hitting • Biting • Throwing Objects at Others
Hurting Others • Using Inappropriate Language • Name-Calling • Nonsharing • Bribery • Stealing
Noncompliance • Disrupting Group Time • Leaving the Classroom • Running Aimlessly Around the
Classroom • Shouting in the Classroom • Dropping Objects to Create Noise • Tearing Books • Breaking Toys
Flushing Objects Down the Toilet • Wasting Paper • Destroying the Work of Others • Throwing Tantrums
Pouting • Baby Talk • Thumb-Sucking • Pant-Wetting • Clinging • Seeking Attention • Whining • Self-
Stimulation • Nonparticipation in Activities • Nonparticipation in Social Play • Shyness at Group Time
Infrequent Large Muscle Activity • Infrequent Dramatic-Play Participation • Talking Infrequently • Short
Attention Span • Finicky Eating • Overeating • Messy Eating • Hording Food • Hitting • Biting • Throwing
Objects at Others • Hurting Others • Using Inappropriate Language • Name-Calling • Nonsharing • Bribery
Stealing • Noncompliance • Disrupting Group Time • Leaving the Classroom • Running Aimlessly Around the
Classroom • Shouting in the Classroom • Dropping Objects to Create Noise • Tearing Books • Breaking
Toys • Flushing Objects Down the Toilet • Wasting Paper • Destroying the Work of Others • Throwing
Tantrums • Pouting • Baby Talk • Thumb-Sucking • Pant-Wetting • Clinging • Seeking Attention • Whining
Biting • Throwing Objects at Others • Hurting Others • Using Inappropriate Language • Name-Calling

chapter 22

Tearing Books

A soft sound catches Ms. Larkin's attention. She turns to find Jamie with the ripped page of a book in her hand. The three-year-old recently began attending the child care center and is still discovering the do's and don'ts of school. "Oh, no, Jamie! That's a library book!" Ms. Larkin rushes to Jamie, takes the book from her, and looks in dismay at the ripped page. She sits down by Jamie, tells her that she may not tear books, and explains why. Jamie listens and nods when asked if she will not do that again.

Ms. Larkin is not hopeful because this is the third book Jamie ripped today. Over the past two weeks, Jamie has damaged several books. The teachers talk to Jamie and have her help repair the books with tape. Last week, the director talked to Jamie's parents to tell them they had to assume the cost of replacement of library books. Jamie's father told Ms. Larkin that Jamie got a good paddling for what she did. Jamie has continued to tear books.

STATE THE BEHAVIOR

The child regularly and frequently tears the pages of books deliberately.

OBSERVE THE BEHAVIOR

To gain more information about the behavior, spend a few days observing the child.

When does the behavior occur?

- During free-choice activities
- During planned activity times
- During group times when a teacher reads books
- After story time
- At cleanup time
- During transitions
- During nap time

What happens before the child tears a book?

- The child looks through a book.
- The child plays alone.
- The child plays with another child or group of children.
- The child is excluded from play by a group of children.
- The child is frustrated with a task.
- A teacher or a peer tells the child no.
- The child wanders aimlessly around the room.

What does the child do when she tears a book?

- The child looks to see whether an adult is watching just before she tears a page.
- The child looks to see whether a teacher heard or saw just after tearing.
- The child continues tearing pages.
- The child puts the book back on a shelf.
- The child leaves the book lying on the floor or on a table.
- The child walks away from the torn book.
- The child calls attention to the torn book.
- The child laughs about what has happened.
- The child gets upset because the book is torn.
- The child apologizes for the damage.

Such observations should give you some idea of the circumstances under which the child tears books. Use this information to help eliminate the behavior.

CONSULT WITH THE FAMILY

After you have the opportunity to observe the circumstances under which the child tears books, set up a meeting with the family to discuss your concerns. For one thing, find out if the child engages in this behavior at home as well as at school. If this is the case, then work together with the family to eliminate this behavior. If, on the other hand, the child tears books at school only, enlist the family's help and ideas for changing the behavior, and then keep them informed of progress.

CONSIDER THE IMPLICATIONS

Acquiring respect for material objects is one of the things children learn during the preschool years. The equipment, games, toys, and other items in the school need to be treated with care so they can be enjoyed and used by others. Most preschool materials are made to be very sturdy, but some items, like books, are more fragile. Children who have been around books usually understand that they need to be handled carefully. Occasionally, however, a child treats books disrespectfully, damaging them in the process.

The reason for such behavior may vary. The child may, for instance, damage books because she has never been taught that books need special care. Or the child may lack the physical coordination to turn the pages without tearing them. Finally, the child may have learned that damaging a book brings attention from the teachers, and therefore continues to do it.

Whenever the child rips the page of a book, adults get very excited, talk to her about her behavior, and may even engage her in helping to fix the book. There is a great deal of adult attention for the child who tears a book, and she may tear pages more often to earn this attention. When a child repeatedly tears pages of books, she is telling you that she has found a definite way of gaining teacher attention.

EXPLORE ALTERNATIVES

There may be some environmental changes that can help you eliminate the tearing of books. Carefully consider the following suggestions before moving on to the approach outlined below for changing the child's behavior.

- The concern a teacher has for the items in a classroom is conveyed through the way they are arranged in the room. If books are haphazardly strewn around the class, it is an unspoken message that books are not really very important. Examine the way books are stored. They should be arranged attractively in a quiet area of the class. If possible, the book area should be somewhat enclosed to discourage unnecessary traffic. A few carefully displayed books are more attractive than many cluttered books on a shelf. Consider arranging 5 to 10 books so that the fronts of the books face out, rather than having 40 books packed into the shelf with only the spines showing. Rotate the books frequently to introduce new ones as the children are ready for them.

- If the child who tears books is in a class of very young children, the books you provide may not be age-appropriate. Very young pre-schoolers are just beginning to learn how to handle books carefully. Furthermore, their small motor control may not be developed enough to turn thin paper pages properly without tearing them. For a class of primarily two-year-olds, provide toddler books. Such books are made of more durable materials such as cardboard or cloth. They are also designed for very young children by portraying common objects, using simple designs, showing bold colors, and telling a simple story. As two-year-olds graduate to older classrooms, they become more adept at handling books.*

- A young child may tear books because she enjoys the experience of tearing. Supply paper for this purpose in the art area. Invite the child to engage in a tearing activity by providing different colored papers and old magazines. The products of the tearing activity may be used for a collage.

If none of these suggestions is appropriate for resolving the problem, continue to the following strategies.

STATE THE GOAL

The goal is for the child to stop tearing books, while learning to use them appropriately.

APPROACH

The basic strategy to eliminate tearing of books involves several simultaneous steps:

- Prevent the child from tearing books.
- Make any necessary environmental changes.
- Reinforce the child for appropriate behavior.
- Ignore the inappropriate behavior.

A child with a motor disability may have difficulty in turning book pages. Similarly, a child with a cognitive disability may not have the maturity to understand the respectful use of books. Provide developmentally appropriate books geared for the child's physical skill level, or be available to help the child successfully use more fragile books.

DEFINITION

Tearing books is defined as any deliberate ripping of the pages of books that happens on a regular basis.

STARTING POINT

Before starting on these strategies to change this behavior, gather some initial information. For three days, count the number of times the child tears a page of a book. Record each incident by marking it down on paper. For consistency in counting, consider each page ripped as a separate incident. If the child takes a book and systematically tears four pages, record four marks. If, however, two or three pages are torn together in one ripping motion, count this as only one incident. At the end of each day, transfer the total number on to the Frequency Record-Keeping Graph.

STRATEGIES

Once you have kept track of incidents of book-tearing for three days, implement the following approach. It is important that all teachers follow these strategies consistently.

Prevent the Tearing of Books Whenever Possible. From your informal observation, you should have some clues as to when book-tearing incidents occur and what precedes them. Use these clues to help prevent such behavior. If, for example, you find that the behavior happens only when the child is playing by herself and never when she is engaged with a group of children, be more alert to potential book-tearing when she is alone. Stay near the child, and keep an eye on any moves toward the book area. Or you might have found that the behavior occurs primarily during cleanup time. In such a case, focus your attention on the child at the time. Use cues from your initial observations to help you pinpoint when and how preventive efforts should be used.

Facilitate Prevention of Book–Tearing Incidents through Environmental Changes. The arrangement of the classroom may help teachers prevent incidents of book-tearing. The following are some suggestions to help implement such changes.

1. Make the book area more appealing and cozy to encourage reading rather than destructiveness. If necessary, rearrange the entire classroom to find a good spot for the book area. Display only a few books in an attractive manner. Provide one or two simple activities to supplement the books. Set out a few seashells if you

have books about shells or oceans. Include a matching game on animals and their homes if you put out books on houses. A warm carpet, pillows, or beanbag chairs also serve to make this area appealing.

2. Be sure that the book area is visible from most parts of the room. If teachers are to prevent the tearing of books they should be able to see the area at a glance. The area should retain its coziness and air of seclusion and at the same time remain visible to teachers from other areas.

3. Another approach might be to incorporate the book area more firmly into the curriculum and activities of the class. For instance, the book and dramatic play areas might be combined to become a library. Children can role-play as librarians and customers. Books can be checked out, shelved, and returned. A reading area can be arranged next to the checkout desk. By making the book area a more active part of the room in this way, a teacher can supervise the activity and carry out preventive measures to avert the tearing of books.

Reinforce Appropriate Behaviors. The child needs to know what behaviors are expected, as well as what is considered inappropriate. When you begin this approach, let the child know what behaviors you appreciate and what you do not like in relation to her handling of classroom materials. Do this at a time when the child has not torn pages of a book, and speak to the child in a friendly and relaxed manner. Say, for instance, "I really appreciate it when you stack the blocks carefully and put the shoes neatly on the shelf. That is the way we should take care of everything in our classroom. I get very upset, though, when you tear books. Other children can't enjoy the books once they have been ruined." Be alert to instances when the child handles materials carefully, and frequently give praise for these actions. Reinforce expected behaviors to focus attention on what is appropriate. Eventually the child will find that it is more rewarding to handle classroom materials respectfully rather than to mishandle them. When the frequency of book-tearing decreases by about half, start to decrease the frequency of praise for appropriate behaviors. When the child completely stops tearing books, gradually decrease praise. Praise the child as often as you do the other children for taking care of classroom items.

Ignore Book-Tearing When It Occurs. If the child does tear a book in spite of your preventive efforts, take the following steps:

1. Go quickly to the child. Take the book away from her and say, "No! You may not tear the book."

2. Move away from the child, and pay her no further attention for two minutes.

3. If you think she may tear another one (based on her behavior during your initial observation), remove her from the area. Take the child by the hand, or pick her up if she resists, and move her across the room. Say nothing while you move her, and avoid eye contact. Give her no attention for the next two minutes.

4. After two minutes, go to the child and try to involve her in another activity. Do not lecture or discuss the incident.

It may be difficult for you to ignore book-tearing incidents because such behavior is destructive and should be dealt with. Remember, however, that your reactions, no matter how negative, still provide attention to the child for the behavior. Ignoring simply removes the attention. These steps should help eliminate book-tearing with time.

Continue Keeping Track of the Behavior. As you implement these strategies, continue counting the number of book-tearing incidents. Continue to record the daily count on the graph as you did the initial counts. Keeping the graph helps you see progress and indicates when you have reached your goal.

MAINTAINING THE CHANGES

When the child stops deliberately tearing books, reinforce this behavior by continuing praise for handling classroom materials with care. Assess the arrangement of the room to ensure it conveys your respect for books. If the child tears a book again, ignore the incident. Let the child know that you are very disappointed with such behavior.

The CD-ROM that accompanies this text contains several hypothetical scenarios designed for you to apply the guidance principles suggested in the various chapters of this book. Go to the Your Turn section of the CD to access these scenarios. Scenarios 5 and 6 are particularly pertinent to this section of the text, Destructive Behaviors.

chapter 23

Breaking Toys

The class of four-year-olds at the child care center is busy today. Children are involved in a variety of activities. A sudden loud crunching noise is heard above the normal sounds of the room. All three teachers look around simultaneously to notice Louie with his foot on a plastic train car. Two of the teachers run toward Louie, who gives the broken toy a kick and says, "I hate that thing!" One teacher takes Louie's hand and walks him away. Another examines the broken train car. "We might as well throw it away," she says in disgust. She searches the floor for broken splinters. Meanwhile, Louie throws down one of the small plastic people that fit into the train, that he has been holding in his hand. Louie starts to walk away.

"Wait a minute, Louie. You broke another toy. Why did you do that?" Louie yells, "That dumb piece wouldn't go in. That thing doesn't work anyway. I'm glad it's broken!" The teachers do not know what to do. This is the third toy that Louie has broken this week. Louie has damaged or destroyed other materials before this week.

STATE THE BEHAVIOR

The child deliberately and regularly breaks toys and other materials in the classroom.

190

OBSERVE THE BEHAVIOR

Spend a few days informally observing the child to gain further insight into the behavior.

When does the child usually break toys?
- Unpredictably, at any time of day
- Early in the day
- Late in the day
- During planned activity times
- During free-choice activities
- During outdoor play
- Indoors
- During cleanup time
- During transitions
- Around nap time

What happens before the child breaks a toy?
- The child is angry.
- The child is frustrated with a task.
- Another child or a teacher tells him no.
- The child is excluded from play by another child or by other children.
- The child is prevented from engaging in an activity.
- The child is not productively engaged in an activity.
- An activity ends.

What does the child do when he breaks a toy?
- The child looks around to see if an adult is watching.
- The child calls a teacher's attention to the broken toy.
- The child tries to hide the broken parts.
- The child gets upset because the toy is broken.
- The child appears unconcerned.
- The child walks away from the broken pieces.
- The child stays nearby.
- The child continues to play with the broken toy.
- The child denies breaking it, if asked.
- The child admits breaking it.
- The child offers an explanation for why the toy broke.

What kinds of toys are usually broken?
- Any kind
- Large

- Small
- Wooden
- Plastic
- Cardboard
- Metal
- Fabric
- Toys with moving parts
- Items from a particular interest area, such as art or housekeeping

How does the child usually break toys?

- The child throws items to the floor with force.
- The child tears them.
- The child steps on them.
- The child rips or pulls apart the toys.
- The child forcibly breaks or snaps off parts.
- The child pounds the toy with another item.
- The child takes out screws or other fasteners.

This initial observation should help you gain some idea of when and under what circumstances the child breaks toys.

CONSULT WITH THE FAMILY

A child who deliberately breaks toys and other objects poses a hazard to himself and others. Once you have had the opportunity to conduct a more focused observation of the child's behavior, meet with the family to enlist their help in eliminating this behavior. Discuss with them whether the child breaks objects at home as well, or if this behavior seems to occur mainly at school. Brainstorm with the family in considering why the child may break objects and what strategies can help to eliminate the behavior. Once you have begun working on eliminating such destructive actions, keep the family informed about the child's progress.

CONSIDER THE IMPLICATIONS

A child who deliberately breaks toys poses a potential safety hazard to the classroom. Broken or jagged edges on toys, if not removed or repaired immediately, can seriously hurt another child or the child who broke the toy. Furthermore, when toys are damaged, there is cost and time involved in replacement or repair. For these reasons, this behavior needs to be eliminated quickly.

It is not always easy to stop a child who engages in such behavior. The child who habitually destroys toys has found a way of gaining immediate attention from adults. Whenever the child breaks a toy, an adult quickly and noticeably responds. Such responses may be verbal (talking, scolding), emotional (show of anger, dismay, frustration), or physical (picking up the broken pieces, throwing them away, repairing them). More than one adult is involved if the teacher who originally responds consults with other teachers or the director of the school. The child gets a great deal of attention when he destroys a toy.

Breaking toys may serve as a way of expressing anger for the child. The typical reactions of adults provide attention, but do not help the child cope with feelings such as anger. This attention does not help eliminate the behavior; it only reinforces it.

EXPLORE ALTERNATIVES

There may be a relatively simple resolution for the concern about the child who habitually breaks toys. Consider the following suggestions:

- The child's toy-breaking behavior may not be deliberate. Examine all materials in the classroom to see whether they are as durable as preschool materials should be. It is possible that a number of items in the class are fragile and the child plays rather roughly with them. In this case, the breaking of toys may not be deliberate.

- Examine the materials in the classroom for age-appropriateness. If children feel either frustrated or unchallenged by items in the room, they may use them in unacceptable ways. Toys may be broken as a result. If toys in the room are not appropriate for the children, change the materials quickly. This may require exchanging materials with other classes in the school, bringing items out of storage, or gradually buying or making new toys.

- A child may break toys because of curiosity. If a child frequently ruins a toy by taking it apart, he may simply be trying to find out what makes the toys work. In such a case, talk to the child about the inappropriateness of his behavior. Provide him with items that he can legitimately take apart. These may include old watches, alarm clocks, and other mechanical devices that no longer work. Furnish screwdrivers, blunt tweezers, and other tools for tinkering, and supervise such activities to ensure safety.

- Toys may get broken inadvertently because the child has a visual or perceptual problem. A child who does not see well or whose perception of what he sees is distorted may unintentionally break toys because he miscalculates their location or position. Such a problem, however, will manifest itself in other ways as well. If you suspect a visual or perceptual problem, discuss it with the family and encourage them to consult with their doctor.*

If none of these suggestions helps to resolve the concern about frequently broken toys, then continue with the following approach.

STATE THE GOAL

The goal is for this child to stop the deliberate breaking of toys.

APPROACH

The basic strategy to eliminate breaking of toys involves four simultaneous steps:

- Prevent toy-breaking incidents whenever possible.
- Praise careful handling of classroom materials.
- Systematically help the child learn to control his impulse to break toys.
- Use self-control time if the child does break a toy.

DEFINITION

Breaking toys involves any instance in which the child deliberately destroys classroom materials or equipment. Do not include unsuccessful attempts to inflict damage.

STARTING POINT

Spend three days to find out how often the child breaks toys. Such information provides a basis with which to compare later improvement. Mark on paper each time the child breaks a toy. At the end of each day, record the total on the Frequency Record-Keeping Graph. If the behavior is not a daily occurrence, recall how many times per week, over the past three weeks, toys were broken, and make the count on a weekly basis.

STRATEGIES

After collecting baseline data, begin to implement the following approach. It is important that all teachers follow these steps consistently.

An untreated visual disability can be the cause of inappropriate behavior. Encouraging the family to seek medical help is important to help the child see as well as possible and to feel successful in the activities he undertakes.

Prevent Toy–Breaking Incidents Whenever Possible. Your informal information-gathering should provide some clues about when and under what circumstances the child breaks toys. Use this information to help you prevent the behavior as often as possible. If the child consistently engages in this destructive behavior during a particular time of the day, be particularly vigilant at such times. Also, watch for behaviors that tend to precede toy-breaking. If the child usually breaks things when he is playing alone, then stay nearby and help him avoid toy-breaking incidents. If such behavior occurs when the child feels upset because he is unable to complete a task, be alert to signs of frustration. Help him handle the task. The more clues you have as to how and when toy-breaking takes place, the better you will be able to prevent it.

Praise Careful Handling of Classroom Materials. As you work on eliminating a negative behavior, let the child know what behaviors are acceptable in lieu of the inappropriate ones. Look for and reinforce occasions when the child handles classroom materials with care. Praise him for using items correctly, for putting materials back on the shelf when he finishes using them, and for any other signs of respect for classroom equipment. At first, praise such behaviors every time you see them take place. As toy-breaking incidents decrease gradually, also decrease the amount of praise you give. By the time the negative behavior has stopped, reinforcement should be given at about the same rate as it is given to the other children in the class.

Systematically Help the Child Learn to Control Impulses to Break Toys.* Anger or frustration may be the emotion the child feels before breaking a toy. Such a destructive reaction is usually expressed impulsively, before the child thinks through what he is doing. The child needs to learn alternative ways of handling such feelings. He must also learn that it is his reaction, not the emotion itself, that is unacceptable. Set aside a special time each day to talk with the child about feelings. Plan to devote 5 to 10 minutes of undivided attention, though you may need more time if the child is especially responsive. The cooperation of the other teachers will be important for carrying out this time. The following sequence is suggested.

1. Begin by discussing situations that evoke different emotions. For instance, "Yesterday I got a new puppy, and I was so excited and happy that I felt like dancing and singing. Boy! I really felt good inside! What makes you feel really happy?" If the child responds, ask for more details. If the child does not respond, name more

---

*A child with an emotional/behavioral disability may exhibit anger by attacking classroom materials. Systematic help to find alternative ways of expressing anger and articulating emotions can provide a powerful tool for this child.

things that make you happy. Go on to discuss other feelings. "Sometimes I feel just the opposite. I get really sad. I had a very good friend, and she had to move away. That made me feel terrible. Do you feel sad sometimes?" Also discuss anger. "You know, sometimes I get really angry. I know you must feel angry about things, too, at times. What makes you angry?" Share some examples of what angers you, and help the child to verbalize situations that anger him. It may take several days to identify situations that evoke various emotions.

2. Once the child acknowledges that he feels differently in response to varied situations, focus your discussion on those feelings. "How does it make you feel inside when you are (happy, angry, sad, lonely)?" Help the child put into words the different inner responses to emotions. Beforehand, think about how to verbalize emotions, because feelings are not easy to describe in words. This way you will be better prepared to help the child discuss them. Be careful, however, that it is the child who talks about the subject with help from you, and not the other way around. This step may require several days.

3. When the child has verbalized how he feels inside when he experiences different emotions, begin to talk about what he does to express such feelings. Do not be critical of what he says. If the child tells you that he feels like breaking things when he gets upset, accept that for now. Discuss various emotions in relation to how they are expressed in action.

4. The next step is to tell the child that you want to explore some different ways of reacting to emotions. If the child tells you that when he is happy, he smiles, ask how else he might express that happiness. Either of you might come up with ideas like clapping hands, jumping up and down, singing, hopping around, and hugging someone. Discuss ways of handling anger and frustration. You might suggest that the child talk to an adult to get help in handling angry feelings, ask for help in finishing a task that seems impossible, or pound on the floor or a table instead of on a toy.

5. Your discussions need not be strictly verbal. Use whatever props you want to help you. Puppets, clay, or blocks might provide a good medium for exploring feelings and emotions.

6. With each step, look for opportunities during the day that illustrate what you and the child have talked about. At first, focus on the event that has evoked a particular emotion. Switch to how it makes you feel inside. Next, look for examples of how the emotion may be expressed. Finally, encourage the child to verbalize alternative ways of reacting. Be sure to use examples of all kinds of emotions and feelings.

If the Child Does Break a Toy, Use Self–Control Time. Because breaking toys is a potential safety and health hazard, it needs to be stopped as quickly as possible. Therefore, use self-control time whenever this behavior occurs. If the child breaks a toy, do the following:

1. Quickly make sure that the broken toy presents no immediate hazard. If a cleanup is necessary, another teacher should attend to it.

2. Calmly take the child who broke the toy to the self-control time area. Firmly but quietly say, "I cannot allow you to break toys. You will have to sit here until you are ready to join your friends again."

3. Move away and do not talk with or look at the child during self-control time. Verbal or visual contact may well serve as a reinforcer to the child for his behavior.

4. If another child approaches, quietly move this child away. Explain, "Louie needs to be by himself for a few minutes. You can talk to him when he joins the class again."

5. The child can rejoin classroom activities when he feels that he is ready. Do not lecture. He knows the reason for the isolation. To channel the child into constructive behavior, you might suggest joining an ongoing activity. It is very important to reinforce the child as soon as possible for engaging in appropriate activity.

6. If the child rejoins the classroom before he is ready and again breaks a toy, say to him, "I guess you're not quite ready to join us," and take him back to the self-control area. Again allow him to determine when he is ready to rejoin the group.

Continue Keeping Track of the Behavior. Continue counting the number of toy-breaking incidents, and record the total on the graph. The graph shows progress toward the goal and informs you when you have reached it. Your timing of changes in reinforcement for appropriate behaviors depends on accurate record-keeping.

MAINTAINING THE CHANGES

When the child no longer breaks toys, continue to let him know what behaviors you value. As he handles classroom materials with care, let him know periodically that you are pleased. Continue to help the child verbalize his feelings.

The CD-ROM that accompanies this text contains several hypothetical scenarios designed for you to apply the guidance principles suggested in the various chapters of this book. Go to the Your Turn section of the CD to access these scenarios. Scenarios 5 and 6 are particularly pertinent to this section of the text, Destructive Behaviors.

chapter **24**

Flushing Objects Down the Toilet

"Teacher, I'm going potty," says three-year-old Becky, walking past an adult stationed near the swings, "Okay, Becky," she is told. Becky goes inside and is out of sight. Mrs. Connor pushes children on the swings for several minutes. When Becky does not return, Mrs. Connor decides to check on her.

She finds Becky flushing an overflowing toilet. A small plastic piece from a Noah's Ark game is circling round and round with the water. Becky turns to Mrs. Connor and exclaims, "It's stuck!" The water reaches the rim and trickles begin to flow over onto the floor. "Becky! What did you put in the toilet?" Becky's eyes open wide innocently, and she shakes her head, saying, "Nothing." "I can see something in there, Becky." With this, Mrs. Connor fishes out the object floating in the water. She hands it to Becky and says, "No one else is in the bathroom. You must have done it. Now, go to the sink and wash this."

Becky rinses the plastic carefully, then dries it and her hands. She then goes back to the toilet and watches Mrs. Connor, whose arm is immersed in water as she tries to find a blockage. "There's more water coming out on the floor, teacher," says Becky helpfully. A moment later, Mrs. Connor angrily drags out three more plastic animals.

Becky watches with interest, and willingly helps wash the retrieved objects and wipe water off the floor. Unfortunately, this is not the first time Becky has flushed objects down the toilet. The teachers are upset and baffled by Becky's behavior.

STATE THE BEHAVIOR

The child frequently and regularly throws small objects into the toilet and flushes them down.

OBSERVE THE BEHAVIOR

Observe the child for a few days to gain some more information about this behavior.

When does the child flush items down the toilet?
- Unpredictably, at any time of day
- During washup and toileting times
- During free-choice activities
- During planned activity times
- During cleanup times
- During transitions
- During outdoor play

What does the child do before this behavior occurs?
- The child goes to the toilet.
- The child goes to the bathroom to wash her hands.
- The child plays with a game that contains small parts.
- The child plays in the housekeeping area.
- The child engages in activity alone.
- The child plays with another child or a few children.
- The child does not engage in any activity.
- The child does not succeed in gaining a teacher's attention.

What does the child do when she flushes something down the toilet?
- The child looks to see whether an adult is watching.
- The child secretly takes one item or more into the bathroom.
- The child openly takes one item or more into the bathroom.
- The child plays with the object in the toilet before flushing.
- The child calls a teacher's attention to the object in the toilet.
- The child calls a teacher's attention after flushing.
- The child flushes the toilet more than once.
- The child denies flushing objects down the toilet.
- The child gets upset when asked if she flushed something down the toilet.
- The child walks away as if nothing has happened.
- The child talks about what she has done.

What objects does the child flush down the toilet?

- Any small object
- Puzzle pieces
- Parts of manipulative materials
- Paper or cardboard items
- Paintbrushes
- Toothbrushes
- Soap
- Doll clothes
- Small blocks

These observations should provide you with some idea of when, what, and how the child flushes items down the toilet.

CONSULT WITH THE FAMILY

In casual conversation with the child's family, find out if the family has noted that the child has a great fascination with water. If family members indicate that this is, indeed, the case, ask further if the child sometimes flushes objects down the toilet at home. Once you have established that this might be a common issue between home and school, share with the family concerns and ideas about the causes and solutions for flushing objects down the toilet. A common strategy, used by both family and teachers, will reinforce the approach that is implemented to eliminate this behavior. Continue to communicate successes with the family. If, on the other hand, family members say that the child does not flush objects down the toilet at home, let them know that you will work on eliminating this behavior at school and will keep them informed of how things are going.

CONSIDER THE IMPLICATIONS

Most likely, the child who flushes objects down the toilet has a fascination with water and/or the mechanical operation of a toilet. This absorption is fairly common with very young children. They enjoy and are soothed by the sound, motion, and feel of flowing water. Some enterprising youngsters may take this fascination further to include experimentation. There is, after all, considerable scientific inquiry involved in finding out what floats and sinks, what blocks the toilet, and what disappears or reappears.

When a child flushes an object down the toilet, adults may react strongly. They explain and scold and try to regain the lost object or unclog the toilet. A plumber may even be called in to help. All this activity reinforces the behavior rather than stops it. The child derives pleasure from flushing objects down the toilet and then receives considerable attention for doing so.

EXPLORE ALTERNATIVES

There might be a relatively simple resolution to working with the child who flushes objects down the toilet. Consider the following suggestions:

- Very young children enjoy and need many activities that provide varied tactile experiences. If such sensory stimulation is not provided in the class program, children may create their own. Water play is an important sensory activity that should be provided frequently in a class for young children. If you do not often allow time for water play and have children who create their own (such as in the toilet), increase water-play activities. Provide a water table or plastic bin with plain water, soapy water, or colored water. Add various implements such as funnels, plastic bottles, pieces of hose, sieves, and straws. You may find that as your curriculum satisfies the sensory needs of the children, behaviors like flushing items down the toilet disappear.*

- Examine the program provided for the children. It is possible that a child does not find enough activities or materials of interest. Therefore, the child creates her own diversion through activities such as flushing objects or other objects down the toilet. Be sure that what you are providing is age-appropriate. Activities and materials should be challenging but not frustrating. A child will cease behavior like flushing objects if there are enough stimulating and interesting things to do in the classroom.

- The teacher of two-year-olds should not be surprised by behavior such as flushing objects down the toilet. This behavior is quite normal. If it occurs in a class of very young children, it is best to take a preventive approach. When a child goes into the bathroom, you should follow. In a matter-of-fact manner, stop the child from tossing items into the toilet. Do not make a fuss over the incident. Be sure that you provide many alternative sensory activities, including water play. The child will outgrow this behavior. Until then, simply be extra vigilant and patient.

If none of these suggestions provides a resolution to the concern, continue to the following approach.

Some children with cognitive disabilities may be in a developmental stage in which they seek frequent sensory stimulation. Also, children with sensory impairments may need additional sensory stimulation. Provide many such activities, including water play.

STATE THE GOAL

The goal is for the child to stop throwing objects and other items into the toilet and flushing them down.

APPROACH

The basic strategy to stop the child from flushing items down the toilet involves three simultaneous steps:

- Prevent the behavior.
- Provide alternative activities.
- Decrease attention to the behavior when it does occur.

DEFINITION

Flushing objects down the toilet includes any incident in which the child throws an item (other than a reasonable amount of toilet paper) into the toilet and flushes it.

STARTING POINT

It is important to know how often this behavior occurs. For three days, count all instances of flushing items down the toilet. Mark on a paper each time the child does this. At the end of each day, record the total on the Frequency Record-Keeping Graph. Keep track in this way for three consecutive days. Because it may not always be evident when the child flushes an object down the toilet, be particularly vigilant to get an accurate estimate.

STRATEGIES

After you have kept track of incidents of object-flushing for three days, begin the following approach. It is important that all teachers follow it consistently.

As Often as Possible, Prevent the Child from Flushing Objects Down the Toilet. You are in a good position to prevent this behavior because of the limited area that needs to be carefully watched. The access to the bathroom may be observed in conjunction with other duties. A teacher should stay near the door or entry to the bathroom. If necessary, rearrange the classroom so there is an activity center near the bathroom. If the child who flushes objects down the toilet approaches the bathroom door, the adult supervising the activities area should follow.

1. Go immediately to the child before she enters the bathroom, and intercept her.

2. Make a fast visual check for obvious or hidden items that can be flushed down the toilet.

3. If the child is not carrying anything, smile, and allow her to go on to the bathroom.

4. If you are not sure whether she is concealing an item to flush down the toilet, smile, and walk into the bathroom with her. Stay there until she is finished. If she tries to toss something into the toilet, simply take the item away. Say, "No, you may not throw things into the toilet," and then walk out.

5. If the child has a object with her, take it away and say, "I'll keep this here for you until you are finished in the bathroom." The child may change her mind about going into the bathroom. In this case, you need to make sure she moves elsewhere before you return the object to her.

6. Whatever course you take, do not make a fuss. The objective is to eliminate as much attention for this behavior as possible.

Provide Alternative Activities to Satisfy the Need for Water Play. Assume that the child who flushes objects down the toilet simply enjoys playing with water. Therefore, plan to provide water play as an activity option more frequently. If the weather is nice, a water table or bins of water can be set up outdoors. Water play can also be accommodated inside with a sheet of plastic or old newspapers protecting nearby surfaces. If you find the child headed for the bathroom with an object to drop in the toilet, guide her toward the water activity instead. Suggest that the child use the item she is holding at the water table. If the item is not appropriate for water play, provide an alternative object.

Minimize Attention When the Child Does Flush an Object Down the Toilet. Your preventive measures will eliminate most instances of the behavior. If on occasion it does occur, do not overreact. It is important that you say little and show as little reaction as possible. Keep these points in mind:

1. If you notice an item has been dropped in the toilet, say nothing and remove it. Wash the object and walk away from the child. Do not provide attention for the behavior.

2. If the child comes and tells you she has flushed something down the toilet, say, "Oh, really?" and continue about your business. Later, when the child is not nearby, check the toilet to see if it is clogged. If it is, close it off to further use and make alternative arrangements until it can be repaired. Be particularly vigilant to prevent further incidents from occurring.

3. If another child tells you a object has been flushed down the toilet, say "Thank you," and check out the situation as unobtrusively as possible. Again, minimize your reactions to the child who flushed the object.

Continue Keeping Track of the Behavior. The strategies suggested should work together to eliminate the behavior. Preventive measures should keep such incidents to a minimum. Alternative activities should satisfy the need for enjoyment of water play. Ignoring object-flushing incidents should eliminate the reinforcement that normally follows the behavior.

At this point, graph the behavior by counting items thrown into the toilet, as well as items taken to the bathroom and confiscated there. Count each item separately. Record the total on the graph.

MAINTAINING THE CHANGES

When the child no longer takes items to the bathroom, you can discontinue the close watch you kept on the child. Continue to provide opportunity for water play. It is probable that the child who flushes objects down the toilet is a very young preschooler. By the time you complete this approach, she may have outgrown the urge to engage in this behavior.

The CD-ROM that accompanies this text contains several hypothetical scenarios designed for you to apply the guidance principles suggested in the various chapters of this book. Go to the Your Turn section of the CD to access these scenarios. Scenarios 5 and 6 are particularly pertinent to this section of the text, Destructive Behaviors.

chapter 25

Wasting Paper

Three-year-old Tony washes his hands and pulls out a paper towel to dry them. He wipes the towel over one hand and drops it in the wastebasket. He pulls out another towel, again merely pats a hand, and discards the towel. Tony repeats this procedure seven more times. "Tony!" exclaims a teacher. "You don't need so many towels!" Tony says, "My hands aren't dry yet," and quickly pulls out two more towels. "That's enough now," says the teacher, but Tony yanks out another paper towel. The teacher moves Tony away from the towel dispenser and explains at length why paper towels should not be wasted. Tony fidgets. He has heard this lecture several times before.

A little while later, Tony is at the easel. He takes a brush saturated with paint and dabs it on the large sheet of paper fastened to the easel. "I'm done," he exclaims. "Can I have more paper, please?" A teacher takes down Tony's creation and secures another sheet of paper. Tony again makes a quick swipe at the paper and exclaims that he is finished. In this way, he uses five sheets of paper in as many minutes. "That's enough now, Tony," the teacher tells him.

Tony goes to the stack of cut papers, picks up a handful, and drips paint on several before the teacher notices. "Tony, no one else will be able to paint if you use all the paper. That's not fair, is it?" Tony protests that he wants to make more pictures. The teacher talks to him, pleads with him, and finally coaxes him into playing in the block area. The teachers know that soon Tony will again waste paper. He has been doing it for a long time.

STATE THE BEHAVIOR

The child regularly, frequently, and deliberately wastes paper.

OBSERVE THE BEHAVIOR

Informally observe the child for a few days to gain some insight into when, where, how, and why the child wastes paper.

When does the child waste paper?
- During art activities
- During free-choice times
- During toileting times
- During mealtimes
- During transitions
- Whenever paper is available

How does the child waste paper?
- The child flushes it down the toilet.
- The child throws it in the trash can.
- The child tears it.
- The child makes only a line or scribble on the paper when painting or crayoning and quickly declares the picture finished.
- The child deliberately spills liquids and then uses many napkins or paper towels to clean up.

What happens before the child wastes paper?
- The child engages in an art activity.
- The child stays near the art area but does not participate.
- The child goes to the bathroom.
- The child washes his hands.
- The child plays with water.
- The child eats lunch or a snack.

What does the child do when he wastes paper?
- The child announces that he is using a lot of paper.
- The child moves away from adults who might be watching.
- The child looks to see whether an adult is watching.

- The child gets upset when asked to use less paper.
- The child shows no concern for requests to use less paper.
- The child uses less when an adult is there to monitor.

Use this information to help you understand the behavior better so you can deal with it effectively.

CONSULT WITH THE FAMILY

Wasting paper may not be of major concern to the family, so this may be a behavior that you, as the teacher, can deal with at school. At a regularly scheduled meeting, you could mention to the family that the child seems deliberately to use undue amounts of paper and that you have successfully worked on making him more aware of moderating his paper use.

CONSIDER THE IMPLICATIONS

Supplies in the preschool classroom are usually abundant so that children can explore and express their creativity. Paper for painting, drawing, cutting, pasting, and folding is usually readily available. To foster self-help skills, children have ready access to toilet paper, paper towels, and napkins. However, with an increasing awareness of ecological concerns and with rising costs of paper, teachers often remind children to use paper products sparingly. A child might realize that the teacher gives extra attention when he pulls out three paper towels instead of one or he paints 10 sketchy pictures instead of 2 or 3 complete ones. The teacher may talk to the child about not wasting paper, and spend time explaining, reminding, or scolding. If the behavior occurs often enough, the child can gain considerable attention from adults. Efforts to talk the child out of wasting paper will only serve to reinforce the behavior.

EXPLORE ALTERNATIVES

Consider whether any of the following suggestions might help provide a fairly simple resolution to the concern.

- If the child uses a great deal of paper in the art area, be careful about assuming that the child is deliberately wasting paper. Many young children go through a stage in which they are impressed by the volume of artwork they produce and thus try to finish as many pictures as they can. Another explanation for abundant artwork may lie in the development of children's graphic art. Children's art evolves in identifiable stages. Scribbles develop into various shapes and eventually into recognizable objects. At any of these stages, the child may consider the picture complete, though only a small part of the paper is used. The relationship of the picture to the background may be important to the child. A picture may be placed only in the middle, by a side, or in a corner of the paper. You can suggest that the child use other parts of the paper. Do not insist, however, if the child thinks that the picture is complete.

- The child may be handling large amounts of paper because of the sensory experience paper offers. If you suspect this is so, provide a variety of sensory activities for the children. Include a bin of shredded newspaper to run fingers through. Plan papier-mâché projects in which children can handle, tear, soak, and manipulate paper to create shapes.

If these suggestions do not provide an answer to the concern, continue to the following approach.

STATE THE GOAL

The goal is for the child to stop deliberately wasting paper.

APPROACH

To eliminate wasting paper, the basic strategy involves four simultaneous steps:

- Provide activities in which paper can be handled and used.
- Take preventive measures to avoid the behavior.
- Praise appropriate use of paper.
- Ignore wasting paper if it does occur.

DEFINITION

Wasting paper involves any deliberate overuse of any kind of paper in which the child intends to throw paper away or prevent someone else from using it. All the teachers should discuss and agree on how many papers have to be used to be considered wasteful. For example, using more than two paper towels for drying hands may be considered wasteful.

STARTING POINT

Determine exactly how often the child wastes paper. For three days, count the number of papers wasted, according to your definition. You will need to keep a close watch on the child to gather this information.

Each time he wastes paper, note the number of papers wasted. At the end of each day, add up the total number and record it on the Frequency Record-Keeping Graph, on which you will keep track of quantity of paper wasted. At the same time, also note the number of paper-wasting incidents, and record these on another Frequency Record-Keeping Graph. These graphs indicate how much paper is wasted and how often this happens. The numbers on the vertical axes of these two graphs will be different. On the first one, you may need to number by increments of 5 or 10 if the child uses large quantities of paper.

STRATEGIES

After you have kept track of incidents of paper-wasting for three days, begin the following steps. It is important that all teachers follow them consistently.

Provide Activities in Which Paper Can Be Handled and Used.
The child's behavior may be prompted by an enjoyment of the feel of paper. In addition to the normal art activities, provide activities that use paper in different ways. Set out paper and scissors for cutting or tearing. Provide papers of various textures to feel, match, and compare. Prepare texture bins with shredded papers of different weights, softness, and textures for the children to run their hands through. Arrange collage activities that use various kinds of paper. Encourage the child who wastes paper to engage in these activities, and convey your approval of his participation in them.*

Prevent the Wasting of Paper Whenever Possible. Vigilance on the part of all the teachers will help prevent wasting paper. The areas in the room where there is paper are limited. Therefore, it is easy to watch the areas. Preventive measures depend on where and what kind of paper the child wastes.

1. *Paper towels in the bathroom.* When the child finishes washing his hands, guide his hands on the paper towel holder. Stand in front of the holder after the child has taken one towel. Tell him, "Good! See how nicely you dried your hands with that towel?" Leave the bathroom after the child does.

2. *Toilet paper in the bathroom.* When the child is going to the bathroom, allow him to pull a reasonable amount of toilet paper off the roll. (Your definition should tell you how much is not too much.) Put your hand on the roll to stop more paper from being pulled off.

Children with cognitive or sensory disabilities may both need and enjoy sensory activities. It is important to offer many such opportunities for sensory experiences for these as well as all the other children.

Tell the child, "That's just the right amount of paper to use. Good!" If the child wants to flush excessive amounts of toilet paper or pull out paper towels for no reason, stop him. Say, "You may not waste paper." Direct him to an ongoing activity, preferably one for which paper is being used.

3. *Art activities*. If the child is engaged in an art activity, intervene only if you are sure that he is deliberately wasting paper. If this is the case, limit the number of pictures he can make. When the child first enters the art area, let him know you are pleased that he wants to participate, but tell him there is a limit on the number of pictures he can make. This can be worded positively: "You'll be able to paint five pictures today! Here's your first paper. You can help me count when you're ready for more paper." If the child asks for more after five pictures are done, tell him he has used up all his papers for today. Help the child count the papers again and suggest that he might want to do some more painting on the five pictures he already made. Point out where there is more room on the papers.

4. *Spills*. If you suspect that the child is spilling liquids so he can use papers to clean up, provide different cleanup props. The child can be given sponges or a mop.

Praise Appropriate Use of Paper. Whenever the child uses paper in a way you expect, praise him. Say, for instance, "I like the way you used the paint on all parts of the paper." (Do not criticize, however, if the child does not cover the entire paper. Your objective is not to shape his art preferences but to prevent wasting paper.) "Thank you for using only one paper towel to dry your hands. We have to be sure there is enough for everyone." "Say, you're really getting good at tearing off just the right amount of toilet paper!" Give the child attention for engaging in the paper-related activities you have provided. At first, reinforce the child often for using paper appropriately. Later, as wasting paper decreases, decrease the reinforcement also. Once the child no longer wastes paper, you can eliminate such praise. Continue to give attention when he engages in other desired activities, as you do with all the children in the class.

Ignore the Wasting of Paper If It Does Occur. You should decrease incidents of wasting paper through preventive steps. If the child does waste paper, however, ignore this behavior as much as possible. Do the following:

1. Go to the child. Take away the paint brush or other materials he is holding.

2. Say, "No! You may not waste paper." Do not explain or go into a lengthy discussion.

3. Move the child away from the area.
4. Turn away from the child, and pay no attention. Involve yourself with another child or activity.
5. After about two minutes, go to the child and give reinforcement for any constructive activity or interaction in which he is engaged. If the child has not become involved in an activity, help him find one.

 Continue Keeping Track of the Behavior. Continue counting and graphing the amount of paper wasted and the number of paper-wasting incidents. Because of your preventive measures, the amount of paper wasted should immediately decrease. If the child shows signs of wasting paper (such as reaching for more towels or art paper) but is prevented from doing so, count these as incidents. The number of papers wasted indicates whether your preventive measures are effective. The number of paper-wasting incidents recorded indicates if the entire approach to stop this behavior is effective.

MAINTAINING THE CHANGES

Continue to intermittently praise appropriate activity. Also, provide sensory activities in the curriculum that involve paper. If the child does waste paper on occasion, give as little reinforcement as possible, as you did when you were working on eliminating this behavior.

 The CD-ROM that accompanies this text contains several hypothetical scenarios designed for you to apply the guidance principles suggested in the various chapters of this book. Go to the Your Turn section of the CD to access these scenarios. Scenarios 5 and 6 are particularly pertinent to this section of the text, Destructive Behaviors.

chapter 26

Destroying the Work of Others

Arlene has been carefully laying out game cards on the table. Five-year-old Pam walks by and scatters the cards on the floor with a swipe of her hand. Arlene shrieks, and a teacher comes to the rescue, saying, "Oh no, Pam! Why did you do that? Arlene has been working so carefully on her game, and now you have ruined it. Pick those cards up right now!" Pam stands by without making a move. "Pam, I asked you to pick up the cards you spilled." Pam again makes no move but then bends down and picks up one card. "That's better," says the teacher, turning to Arlene to soothe her. Pam watches this, then walks away.

A little while later, Pam goes to the art area where Chad is putting the finishing touches on a picture. A teacher looks at Chad's work and says "You did a beautiful job, Chad. I really like the way you've made the flowers and trees." Pam goes to the shelf for a piece of paper and crayons and sits down by Chad. She begins making a picture but suddenly reaches to Chad's paper with her crayon and scribbles several lines through the middle. Chad yells and then punches Pam. The teacher rushes to the scene, tells Chad he should not hit, and tries to calm the crying Pam.

Later that day, Pam knocks down some blocks, tears two paintings, and pulls all the shoes off the dress-up shelf that Susie is arranging. The teachers feel dismayed because Pam is increasingly destroying more of what other children make, and nothing is helping to stop the behavior.

STATE THE BEHAVIOR

The child deliberately destroys the work of other children.

OBSERVE THE BEHAVIOR

Spend a few days observing the behavior to gain further insight into when and under what circumstances it occurs.

When does the child destroy other children's work?
- Unpredictably, at any time
- During free-choice activities
- During planned activity times
- During cleanup times
- During transitions
- When children are getting ready to go home

What is the child doing before she ruins the work of other children?
- The child works by the child whose work she ruins.
- The child works elsewhere in the classroom.
- The child is not engaged in any activity.
- The child plays with a particular child or children.
- The child has difficulty completing a task.
- The child expresses a dislike for an ongoing activity.
- The child is rebuffed by the child whose work she destroys.

What does the child do when she destroys another child's work?
- The child looks around to see whether an adult is watching.
- The child waits for the other child to look away before attacking the other's work.
- The child walks away as if nothing happened.
- The child gets upset.
- The child admits to destroying the other child's work when confronted by a teacher.
- The child denies it.
- The child apologizes on her own.
- The child apologizes when asked to do so by a teacher.
- The child offers to make amends.

Who is usually the victim of the behavior?
- Anyone
- Friends
- Boys

- Girls
- Younger or smaller children
- Older or bigger children
- Children with whom the child has had a conflict
- Children for whom the child has expressed a dislike

How does the child destroy work?

- The child knocks over block constructions.
- The child knocks over structure made of various construction materials.
- The child tears or throws away artwork.
- The child crumples artwork or spills water over it.
- The child scribbles over artwork with paint, crayons, or other media.
- The child knocks props off a table or other surface in the housekeeping area.
- The child undresses dolls.
- The child messes up another child's arrangement.
- The child empties puzzle pieces out of the frame.
- The child crushes clay sculptures.

Use the clues you gain from these informal observations to help you eliminate the problem.

CONSULT WITH THE FAMILY

Acts that destroy the projects that other children have been working on need to be stopped as soon as possible. Once you have had the chance to carefully observe when, against whom, and how the child destroys the works of others, meet with the family to enlist their help in changing the behavior. Discuss with the family why they think the child may be ruining the works of other children in the class and solicit their suggestions for eliminating such behaviors. Once you have begun to work on changing such destructive acts, keep the family informed of successes.

CONSIDER THE IMPLICATIONS

Preschool programs are designed to foster creativity. In almost every area of the preschool class, children have the opportunity to express themselves in their own unique ways. Most preschool materials are designed to be used in whatever way each child likes. There is not a right or wrong way to use them. In addition to encouraging creativity, preschool materials also allow for independence and foster good self-concept. Young children are proud of their work. It is, therefore, unfortunate when another child destroys something they have made. The child who deliberately ruins another youngster's work may be doing so out of anger, dislike, frustration, or mischief. Whatever the reason, such destructiveness cannot be tolerated.

Teachers are anxious to stop this behavior. They may try reasoning, lecturing, showing anger, expressing disappointment, or insisting on apologies. Their concern is particularly urgent because the children whose work has been ruined also express a variety of reactions. When a child destroys another youngster's work, she is getting doubly reinforced for her actions. On the one hand, she has hurt another child, and the child is probably reacting loudly and visibly. On the other hand, a teacher also reacts strongly and spends time letting the child know what she has done wrong. Therefore, a child who repeatedly destroys another child's work gains considerable attention for such behavior. Though this attention is meant to stop the behavior, it only serves to reinforce it.

EXPLORE ALTERNATIVES

Consider whether the following suggestions might provide a relatively simple resolution to the problem.

- Examine the classroom to ensure that there are enough materials for all the children who want to use them. A child may be reacting destructively toward others because she is not able to participate in an activity because of a lack of materials. In such a case, provide more materials so everyone who wants to has a chance to take part in any given activity.
- An undue number of destructive incidents may be occurring because of room arrangement. If blocks are frequently getting knocked over, check to see whether the block area is isolated enough. It may be that block structures are being destroyed because the area lies in a major traffic path in the room. Perhaps paintings are being ruined because easels are too close to each other and children inadvertently bump into each other's pictures. Examine the area where problems are occurring and consider whether a different room arrangement might alleviate the problem.
- Inspect your system of storing children's finished products such as artwork. There needs to be a fairly secluded area where wet paintings or glued products can dry. Each child should have a special place to keep the day's work until it can be taken home.

This storage should not be messy or cluttered, since such conditions convey lack of respect for the child's work and leave items vulnerable to damage. How you handle and store creative work lets the child know how much you value it.

- If the child destroys the work of only one particular child, consider separating the two children. The victim may provoke the other's destructiveness. If possible, place one of the children in another class. If you cannot do this, then make an effort to keep the two children separated during periods when destructive acts occur.

If none of these suggestions helps with the problem of the child who destroys the work of others, then move on to the following approach.

STATE THE GOAL

The goal is for the child to stop destroying the work of other children.

APPROACH

The basic strategy to eliminate this behavior involves four simultaneous steps:

- Encourage the child to engage in creative activities, and reinforce such efforts.
- Reinforce appropriate social behaviors.
- Prevent destructive behaviors whenever possible.
- Use Self-Control Time if the child does ruin another child's work.

DEFINITION

Destroying the work of others includes any deliberate act to ruin the work of another child. This involves tearing, cutting, spilling on, scribbling over, knocking down, disarranging, or in any other way interfering with the product as the other child created it.

STARTING POINT

For three days, count all incidents of destroying the work of others to provide a basis against which later progress can be compared. Mark on paper each time the behavior occurs. At the end of each day, add and record the total on the Frequency Record-Keeping Graph.

STRATEGIES

Now that you have kept track of incidents of destroying the work of others for three days, begin implementing the following approach. It is important that all teachers follow it consistently.

Encourage and Reinforce Creative Activities by the Child. For the child to recognize and respect the value of other children's creative efforts, she first has to be aware of this value in relation to her own work. Provide a variety of creative activities, and encourage the child to participate in them. Be attentive to the child when she participates in these activities; comment on her work in ways that indicate your interest in and appreciation of her creative efforts. You might comment on the use of color, shape, and design, or on the process and amount of work expended on the work. Such uncritical acknowledgment that does not judge but recognizes the child's effort is more effective than well-intentioned praise. For instance, "That's a great picture" can stifle creativity because it imposes a value judgment or becomes meaningless if it is repeated to every child.

At first, attend to the child as often as possible. Later, as destruction of others' work decreases and finally stops, cut back attention gradually until you are giving it about as often as you do to all the children in the class.

Keep in mind also that creative work includes not only art activities but a much wider range of involvement. Creativity is present with blocks, other construction materials, the housekeeping area, sand play and water play, music, dance, and language activities.

Reinforce Appropriate Social Behaviors. While you are conveying to the child your displeasure with destructive behavior, you also have to let her know what behaviors you value. Reinforce the child when she engages in appropriate social behaviors. Convey to her that you and the other children appreciate it when she plays cooperatively, shares, has fun, and otherwise enjoys positive social interactions. In this way you are letting the child know what you want, not just what you do not want.*

Prevent Destructive Behavior Whenever You Can. From your informal observation, you should have some idea of what happens when the child acts destructively. Use such clues to help you prevent destructiveness whenever possible. For instance, if you found that the child paints

217

Chapter 26 Destroying the Work of Others

A child with an emotional/behavioral disability who destroys the work of others out of anger will benefit from the reinforcement of appropriate behaviors.

on other children's pictures when she is at the easel, prevent this by turning the easels to different angles and then keeping careful watch. Or if you found that the child tears other children's pictures once they are finished, find a more inaccessible storage area.*

Whatever your clues, use them to anticipate and prevent the behavior. Be especially vigilant during activities in which the child has previously shown destructiveness. If you see clues signaling potential attack on another child's work, block the child by placing yourself between her and the work. Try to redirect her into another activity.

Use Self-Control Time If the Child Does Ruin Another Youngster's Work.
If the child destroys the work of another youngster, do the following:

1. Prearrange for another teacher to deal with the child whose work was ruined. This adult should make any repairs possible or help the child reconstruct what was destroyed.

2. Calmly take the child who had destroyed the other child's work to the self-control area. Firmly but quietly say, "I cannot allow you to ruin what other children have made. You will have to sit here until you are ready to join your friends again."

3. Move away and do not talk with or look at the child during self-control time. Verbal or visual contact may well serve as a reinforcer to the child for his behavior.

4. If another child approaches, quietly move this child away. Explain, "Pam needs to be by herself for a few minutes. You can talk to her when she joins the class again."

5. The child can rejoin classroom activities when she feels that she is ready. Do not lecture. She knows the reason for the isolation. To channel the child into constructive behavior, you might suggest joining an ongoing activity. It is very important to reinforce the child as soon as possible for engaging in appropriate activity.

6. If the child rejoins the classroom before she is ready and again ruins another child's word say to her, "I guess you're not quite ready to join us," and take her back to the self-control area. Again allow her to determine when she is ready to rejoin the group.

Continue Keeping Track of the Behavior.
Continue counting the number of times the child destroys the work of others, and record this information on the Frequency Record-Keeping Graph. The graph helps you know at what pace to decrease the amount of praise you give the child for engaging in creative activities and positive social interaction.

In a child who was exposed to drugs or alcohol prenatally, ruining the work of others may be an impulsive reaction. Prevention is the best strategy.

MAINTAINING THE CHANGES

When the child no longer destroys other children's work, you have reached your goal. Continue periodic reinforcement of creative efforts, and encourage positive social interaction with other children. If, on occasion, the child does ruin another's work, use self-control time.

The CD-ROM that accompanies this text contains several hypothetical scenarios designed for you to apply the guidance principles suggested in the various chapters of this book. Go to the Your Turn section of the CD to access these scenarios. Scenarios 5 and 6 are particularly pertinent to this section of the text, Destructive Behaviors.

• Nonsharing • Bribery • Stealing • Noncompliance • Disrupting Group Time • Leaving the Classroom • Running Aimlessly Around the Classroom • Shouting in the Classroom • Dropping Objects to Create Noise • Tearing Books • Breaking Toys • Flushing Objects Down the Toilet • Wasting Paper • Destroying the Work of Others • Throwing Tantrums • Pouting • Baby Talk • Thumb-Sucking • Pant-Wetting • Clinging • Seeking Attention • Nonparticipation in Activities • Nonparticipation in Social Play • Shyness at Group Time • Playing with Only One Toy • Infrequent Large Muscle Activity • Infrequent Dramatic-Play Participation • Talking Infrequently • Short Attention Span • Finicky Eating • Overeating • Messy Eating • Hording Food • Hitting • Biting • Throwing Objects at Others • Hurting Others • Using Inappropriate Language • Name-Calling • Nonsharing • Bribery • Stealing • Noncompliance • Disrupting Group Time • Leaving the Classroom • Running Aimlessly Around the Classroom • Shouting in the Classroom • Dropping Objects to Create Noise • Tearing Books • Breaking Toys • Flushing Objects Down the Toilet • Wasting Paper • Destroying the Work of Others • Throwing Tantrums • Pouting • Baby Talk • Thumb-Sucking • Pant-Wetting • Clinging • Seeking Attention • Whining • Self-Stimulation • Nonparticipation in Activities • Nonparticipation in Social Play • Shyness at Group Time • Playing with Only One Toy • Infrequent Large Muscle Activity • Infrequent Dramatic-Play Participation • Talking Infrequently • Short Attention Span • Finicky Eating • Overeating • Messy Eating • Hording Food • Hitting • Biting • Throwing Objects at Others • Hurting Others • Using Inappropriate Language • Name-Calling • Nonsharing • Bribery • Stealing • Noncompliance • Disrupting Group Time • Leaving the Classroom • Running Aimlessly Around the Classroom • Shouting in the Classroom • Dropping Objects to Create Noise • Tearing Books • Breaking Toys • Flushing Objects Down the Toilet • Wasting Paper • Destroying the Work of Others • Throwing Tantrums • Pouting • Baby Talk • Thumb-Sucking • Pant-Wetting • Whining • Self-Stimulation • Nonparticipation in Activities • Nonparticipation in Social Play • Shyness at Group Time • Playing with Only One Toy • Infrequent Large Muscle Activity • Infrequent Dramatic-Play Participation • Talking Infrequently • Short Attention Span • Finicky Eating • Overeating • Messy Eating • Hording Food • Hitting • Biting • Throwing Objects at Others • Hurting Others • Using Inappropriate Language • Name-Calling • Nonsharing • Bribery • Stealing • Noncompliance • Disrupting Group Time • Leaving the Classroom • Running Aimlessly Around the Classroom • Shouting in the Classroom • Dropping Objects to Create Noise • Tearing Books • Breaking Toys • Flushing Objects Down the Toilet • Wasting Paper • Destroying the Work of Others • Throwing Tantrums • Pouting • Baby Talk • Thumb-Sucking • Pant-Wetting • Clinging • Seeking Attention • Whining • Self-Stimulation • Nonparticipation in Activities • Nonparticipation in Social Play • Shyness at Group Time • Infrequent Large Muscle Activity • Infrequent Dramatic-Play Participation • Talking Infrequently • Short Attention Span • Finicky Eating • Overeating • Messy Eating • Hording Food • Hitting • Biting • Throwing Objects at Others • Hurting Others • Using Inappropriate Language • Name-Calling • Nonsharing • Bribery • Stealing • Noncompliance • Disrupting Group Time • Leaving the Classroom • Running Aimlessly Around the Classroom • Shouting in the Classroom • Dropping Objects to Create Noise • Tearing Books • Breaking Toys • Flushing Objects Down the Toilet • Wasting Paper • Destroying the Work of Others • Throwing Tantrums • Pouting • Baby Talk • Thumb-Sucking • Pant-Wetting • Clinging • Seeking Attention • Whining • Self-Stimulation • Nonparticipation in Activities • Nonparticipation in Social Play • Shyness at Group Time • Infrequent Large Muscle Activity • Infrequent Dramatic-Play Participation • Talking Infrequently • Short Attention Span • Finicky Eating • Overeating • Messy Eating • Hording Food • Hitting • Biting • Throwing Objects at Others • Hurting Others • Using Inappropriate Language • Name-Calling

SECTION 5

Emotional

and **Dependent**

Behaviors

• Nonsharing • Bribery • Stealing • Noncompliance • Disrupting Group Time • Leaving the Classroom • Running Aimlessly Around the Classroom • Shouting in the Classroom • Dropping Objects to Create Noise • Tearing Books • Breaking Toys • Flushing Objects Down the Toilet • Wasting Paper • Destroying the Work of Others • Throwing Tantrums • Pouting • Baby Talk • Thumb-Sucking • Pant-Wetting • Clinging • Seeking Attention • Nonparticipation in Activities • Nonparticipation in Social Play • Shyness at Group Time • Playing with Only One Toy • Infrequent Large Muscle Activity • Infrequent Dramatic-Play Participation • Talking Infrequently • Short Attention Span • Finicky Eating • Overeating • Messy Eating • Hording Food • Biting • Throwing Objects at Others • Hurting Others • Using Inappropriate Language • Name-Calling • Nonsharing • Bribery • Stealing • Noncompliance • Disrupting Group Time • Leaving the Classroom • Running Aimlessly Around the Classroom • Shouting in the Classroom • Dropping Objects to Create Noise • Tearing Books • Breaking Toys • Flushing Objects Down the Toilet • Wasting Paper • Destroying the Work of Others • Throwing Tantrums • Pouting • Baby Talk • Thumb-Sucking • Pant-Wetting • Clinging • Seeking Attention • Whining • Self-Stimulation • Nonparticipation in Activities • Nonparticipation in Social Play • Shyness at Group Time • Playing with Only One Toy • Infrequent Large Muscle Activity • Infrequent Dramatic-Play Participation • Talking Infrequently • Short Attention Span • Finicky Eating • Overeating • Messy Eating • Hording Food • Hitting • Biting • Throwing Objects at Others • Hurting Others • Using Inappropriate Language • Name-Calling • Nonsharing • Bribery • Stealing • Noncompliance • Disrupting Group Time • Leaving the Classroom • Running Aimlessly Around the Classroom • Shouting in the Classroom • Dropping Objects to Create Noise • Tearing Books • Breaking Toys • Flushing Objects Down the Toilet • Wasting Paper • Destroying the Work of Others • Throwing Tantrums • Pouting • Baby Talk • Thumb-Sucking • Pant-Wetting • Whining • Self-Stimulation • Nonparticipation in Activities • Nonparticipation in Social Play • Shyness at Group Time • Playing with Only One Toy • Infrequent Large Muscle Activity • Infrequent Dramatic-Play Participation • Talking Infrequently • Short Attention Span • Finicky Eating • Overeating • Messy Eating • Hording Food • Hitting • Biting • Throwing Objects at Others • Hurting Others • Using Inappropriate Language • Name-Calling • Nonsharing • Bribery • Stealing • Noncompliance • Disrupting Group Time • Leaving the Classroom • Running Aimlessly Around the Classroom • Shouting in the Classroom • Dropping Objects to Create Noise • Tearing Books • Breaking Toys • Flushing Objects Down the Toilet • Wasting Paper • Destroying the Work of Others • Throwing Tantrums • Pouting • Baby Talk • Thumb-Sucking • Pant-Wetting • Clinging • Seeking Attention • Whining • Self-Stimulation • Nonparticipation in Activities • Nonparticipation in Social Play • Shyness at Group Time • Infrequent Large Muscle Activity • Infrequent Dramatic-Play Participation • Talking Infrequently • Short Attention Span • Finicky Eating • Overeating • Messy Eating • Hording Food • Hitting • Biting • Throwing Objects at Others • Hurting Others • Using Inappropriate Language • Name-Calling • Nonsharing • Bribery • Stealing • Noncompliance • Disrupting Group Time • Leaving the Classroom • Running Aimlessly Around the Classroom • Shouting in the Classroom • Dropping Objects to Create Noise • Tearing Books • Breaking Toys • Flushing Objects Down the Toilet • Wasting Paper • Destroying the Work of Others • Throwing Tantrums • Pouting • Baby Talk • Thumb-Sucking • Pant-Wetting • Clinging • Seeking Attention • Whining • Biting • Throwing Objects at Others • Hurting Others • Using Inappropriate Language • Name-Calling

chapter 27

Crying

"Teacher!" calls four-year-old Steven. Ms. Courtney turns to Steven, but then is distracted by two children about to topple a block tower behind her. A moment later, Steven bursts into tears. After salvaging the tower, Ms. Courtney moves to Steven. She puts an arm about him and asks why he is crying. He continues to cry, and after some coaxing finally gulps, "I need more paper." "That's no problem," says Ms. Courtney, releasing Steven and placing another piece of paper on the easel for him. Steven continues to cry and does not resume painting for several minutes, during which Ms. Courtney continues to comfort and talk to him.

Later that morning, Steven cries several times: when he is not able to sit next to Rhonda at story time, when Jimmy calls him a crybaby, when all the swings are occupied by the time he gets to them, when there are no more blocks for the structure he is building, and when the snack is passed to the right instead of to the left by his right-hand neighbor. The teachers have dried many tears for Steven during the four months he has been in school.

STATE THE BEHAVIOR

The child frequently cries although there is little or no provocation.

OBSERVE THE BEHAVIOR

Spend some time observing the child to gain further insight into the child's crying behavior.

When does the child cry?
- Unpredictably, at any time of day
- Early in the day, soon after arriving at school
- Later in the day, when it is time to go home
- Near nap time
- Near mealtimes
- During structured or teacher-directed activities
- During free-choice activities
- During outside play
- At cleanup time
- When activities are ending
- During transitions
- At toileting times

What happens before the child starts to cry?
- Another child has something the child wants.
- Another child takes something away from him.
- Another child or several children will not let him join in their play.
- The child has a verbal or physical fight with another child.
- A teacher does not answer the child.
- The child is told no by a teacher.
- The child's mother or father has just left.
- The child is unable to complete an activity.
- The child is not allowed to engage in an activity.
- The child does not want to participate in an activity.
- The child complains of an injury or other pain.
- The child falls or stumbles and hurts himself.
- There is no apparent provocation.

What does the child do when he cries?
- The child stops crying when the problem is remedied (such as getting the toy he wants).
- The child continues crying even after he is given what he wants.
- The child stops crying when picked up and comforted by a teacher.
- The child stops crying only after a teacher has held him a while.
- The child resists the attempts of adults to hold or comfort him.

- The child talks about why he is crying (such as, "I want my Mommy!").
- The child says nothing; he only sobs.
- The child responds when a teacher talks reasonably to him.
- The child does not listen to reason.
- The child cries all the harder when someone talks to him.

Use these observations to help you find the best way of dealing with the child to eliminate unnecessary crying.

CONSULT WITH THE FAMILY

After carefully observing the child's behavior, set up a meeting with the family to discuss the child's frequent crying. Find out from the family if there have been some recent changes in the child's life that might cause anxiety or fear. Also ask the family if the child has always responded to frustration and problems by crying for an adult to help him. Explore possible reasons for this behavior. Discuss with the family whether they have tried some ways of eliminating this behavior and whether these have been successful. If crying seems to occur primarily at school but not at home, consider with the family what might be causing the behavior. Tell the family that you will continue to try to discover its reasons. Once you have begun strategies to decrease undue crying, keep communicating with the family to let them know how the child's behavior is changing.

CONSIDER THE IMPLICATIONS

Crying is a way of communication during early life. As the child grows, he learns to have increasingly more control and discovers other ways of conveying his needs. Language is the most important substitute for crying that the young child learns. However, crying continues to be a means of communication for most people. In early childhood, it is used quite frequently to express hurt, anger, fear, frustration, sadness, and other emotions.

Sometimes, however, a child overuses crying. This can develop if the child has been frustrated in getting attention in more acceptable ways. The child finds that crying brings attention from family members and other people. It is easy for a pattern to emerge from such a circumstance. The child wants attention and tries to get it by talking but is ignored. The child then cries and gets attention, and is thus reinforced for crying. If this happens often enough, crying may become a primary means of communication.

In the preschool setting, children often cry. Some children have valid reasons for crying, but others cry because they find it to be an effective attention-getting device. It is important to differentiate between the two reasons for crying. If children cry because they are scared, lonely, hurt, or otherwise upset, it is important to remedy the problem or help them deal with it. If, on the other hand, the child cries for attention, a different approach is needed. If teachers continue to reinforce with attention, crying will continue.

EXPLORE ALTERNATIVES

Because crying is not always used to get attention, it is important to recognize the reason for crying and to deal with the underlying issue. If a child does not cry very often, then there probably is a good reason when he does cry. Even if a child cries quite often, you cannot assume that this behavior is motivated solely by a need for attention. Consider the following situations:

- A child's entry into school may be a traumatic experience. Some children cry for some time after they first begin school. It is important to help the child overcome this distress so he feels comfortable while at school and can gain as much as possible from the experience. A family member may stay with the child when he first enters preschool or child care until he gets to know the new environment and teachers a little better. Children who are new to school also need to be reassured that they have not been abandoned and that after school they will return home. Such reassurance may need to be repeated many times.*

- A child who cries for part of the day when he first starts school is genuinely distressed. Do not ignore this kind of crying. Soothe and comfort the child by talking to him, attending to him, and holding him. Help the child know that he has not been abandoned. A young child in the process of overcoming his anxiety may form an attachment to you as a substitute for the parent(s) he misses. This attachment may be necessary for a short time but should be discouraged once the child feels comfortable with school. In most cases, the need to cling to the teacher decreases as enjoyment of school activities and peer interaction increase.

- If a child's frequent crying is a relatively recent behavior, examine whether some change in his life has caused this. A new baby, a

A child with an emotional/behavioral disability may be excessively shy and unable to adapt to new situations. Gentle and supportive response from the teachers is particularly important in such a case.

death in the family, a divorce, or any other source of stress might be unsettling. This makes the child more vulnerable to emotional upsets and results in frequent crying. Talk with the family to see how you can work together to help the child deal with whatever is bothering him. In such an instance, the child needs your support and attention.

- Some children have an excessive number of accidents, which result in crying. It is possible that a child has intentional accidents for the sake of the attention these bring. Carefully observe the child to help discriminate between real and staged accidents. Be alert to motor or perceptual problems, which could cause an undue number of accidents.*
- If a child cries frequently because he is hurt in social situations, work to improve his social acceptability rather than work on decreasing crying. Consult Chapter 38 or one of the chapters related to aggression if the child's nonacceptance results from aggressive behavior. Once you eliminate the cause of the crying, the behavior should decrease.†
- A child who has difficulty in verbal communication may use crying as an alternative means of letting others know what he needs.§

If none of these situations describes the conditions under which the child cries frequently and you conclude that the crying is really an attention-seeking ploy, continue to the following strategies.

STATE THE GOAL

The goal is for the child to decrease crying so that he cries only when the situation warrants it, not as a means of gaining attention.

APPROACH

To eliminate attention-seeking crying, use the following steps:
- Ignore the child when he is crying.
- Give attention and reinforcement when the child is not crying.

---

*Be alert to potential motor or sensory disabilities in children who have frequent accidents.
†Challenging behavior of a child with an emotional/behavioral disability can compound the disability. It is important to help such a child learn alternative, socially acceptable behavior.
§A child with a language disability may find crying a much more effective means of getting attention than attempts at communication. It is important that teachers are as attentive as possible in understanding what the child is trying to convey.

DEFINITION

Crying is a behavior in which the child weeps, sobs, and the like. This behavior is of concern when it is used excessively as a way of getting attention from adults, rather than as a response to pain, anger, frustration, sadness, or other emotion.

STARTING POINT

Spend three days collecting some initial information. Mark on paper each time the child cries. At the end of each day, total and record that number on the Frequency Record-Keeping Graph. This will provide you with information with which to measure progress.

STRATEGIES

Once you have gathered information on the number of incidents of crying for three days, you are ready to begin. For this approach to be effective, all teachers must follow it consistently.

Ignore Crying. Once you determine that crying is one of the child's ways of gaining attention, you can change this behavior by eliminating the attention. Crying continues because it is reinforced through adult attention. A reversal of this pattern is possible if the attention is completely removed. When the child cries, do the following:

1. Take a quick look at the child to make sure that he is not hurt. If you are unsure of the cause of the crying, go to the child for a closer look, and ask him what the problem is.

2. If you decide there is a real cause for the crying, take care of the problem, and comfort the child. You may find this is not often the case if the child habitually cries for attention.

3. If you conclude that the child is crying for the attention it will bring him, tell him, "I can't understand you when you cry." If he continues, move away. Do not look at him or indicate through your facial expressions or posture that he has gained your attention. Continue ignoring the child for as long as he cries.

4. Crying can be disruptive in the classroom. If the child cries during nonstructured, child-selected activities, leave him where he is. If other children seem concerned and remind you that the child is crying, tell them that you are aware of it and the child is not hurt.

     If crying occurs during story time, music, or another group activity, you may have to remove the child from the room. If he is disruptive to the point at which the other children cannot pay attention to the activity, then prearrange an area to which the child can be removed. Make sure that he is not given attention. When you remove the child from the room, say, "We cannot hear the story when you are crying like this. I'm going to take you out of the classroom. When you've stopped crying you may come back."

5. Be aware that the child will probably cry for longer and more loudly than usual the first few times his behavior is ignored. This is to be expected, since the child continues to try to get your attention by crying. Be persistent. After the first few times of being completely ignored during his crying incidents, the child will quickly decrease the behavior. It is important, however, that he is totally ignored throughout the time he cries. If *any* attention is paid, it reinforces the child's belief that crying is effective for getting attention.

6. Listen to the child, but do not watch him, to be alert to when he stops crying. Go to the child immediately when he stops crying. Give him your full attention at this time. You might say, "There! Now we can see what activity you can do. I'll come and sit with you for a while." Direct the child toward an activity and spend time working with him.

7. The child may begin to cry again when you approach him after he has stopped. Tell him, "I can't talk with you when you're crying." If he stops again, involve him in an activity. If he continues to cry, move away, and ignore him until he stops. (On your daily total, count this as one incident.)

Reinforce the Child When He Does Not Cry. Convey to the child that you will not give him attention when he cries. Let him know what behaviors you expect and value. Be ready to give the child frequent attention when he participates in school routines in expected ways. Tell him often how pleased you are when he engages in activities, joins in constructive play, follows instructions, helps in cleanup, or participates in peer interaction. Give him praise, attention, hugs, or any other appropriate reinforcers. The combination of reinforcing expected behaviors and ignoring crying should result in a fairly rapid change in the child's overall behavior.

 Continue Keeping Track of the Behavior. Count the number of instances of crying that occur every day. Continue recording the total for each day on the graph. Remember, the first few days may reflect an increase in totals as the child tries harder to get attention by crying. Once the child realizes that he can gain attention in ways other than crying, the total should quickly decrease.

MAINTAINING THE CHANGES

When unnecessary crying stops, continue reinforcing desired behaviors intermittently. Your aim is to let the child know that he should continue acceptable behaviors and that you will reinforce him for these. If crying for attention occurs again, ignore it as you did earlier. Ignoring the behavior should again eliminate it.

The CD-ROM that accompanies this text contains several hypothetical scenarios designed for you to apply the guidance principles suggested in the various chapters of this book. Go to the Your Turn section of the CD to access these scenarios. Scenarios 7 and 8 are particularly pertinent to this section of the text, Emotional and Dependent Behaviors.

ing • Throwing Objects at Others • Hurting Others • Using Inappropriate
lling • Nonsharing • Bribery • Stealing • Noncompliance • Disrupting Gro
Classroom • Running Aimlessly Around the Classroom • Shouting in the
cts to Create Noise • Tearing Books • Objects D
ting Paper • Destroying the Work of Others • Throwing Tantrums • Pout
k • Thumb-Sucking • Pant-Wetting • Clinging • Seeking Attention • Stim
ticipation in Group • Short Attention Span • Picky Eating • Overeating
ly One Toy • Infrequent Large Muscle Activity • Infrequent Dramatic Play
alking Infrequently • Short Attention Span • Flaicky Eating • Overeating
ng • Hording Food • Hitting • Biting • Throwing Objects at Others • Hurti
opriate Language • Name-Calling • Nonsharing • Bribery • Stealing • Non
g Group Time • Leaving the Classroom • Running Aimlessly Around the C
the Classroom • Dropping Objects to Create Noise • Tearing Books • Bre
ng Objects Down the Toilet • Wasting Paper • Destroying the Work of O
ng Tantrums • Pouting • Baby Talk • Thumb Sucking • Pant-Wetting • Cl

chapter 28

Throwing Tantrums

"Caroline, come on! Get up. This is ridiculous. Now get up, please!" Three-year-old Caroline continues to lie on the floor, kicking, flailing her arms, and crying. Teacher Sally tries to lift Caroline off the floor and succeeds only after she has been kicked in the shin. Caroline stiffens her body and resists being held, all the time continuing to scream and strike out with arms and legs. Teacher Sally loses her grasp and lets Caroline go. Caroline gets up and runs a few feet away. There she throws herself on the floor again and resumes her tantrum.

By this time, several children are watching the performance and another adult has joined in the act. The other teacher says sternly, "Caroline, get up right now! Stop this nonsense!" Caroline continues to wail and kick. Finally, after the two teachers have struggled for several more minutes, Caroline decreases her crying. She eventually sits up and lets herself be consoled.

The teachers sigh in relief but know that the calm is only temporary. Caroline will, undoubtedly, throw another tantrum soon.

STATE THE BEHAVIOR

The child frequently has tantrums when she does not get what she wants.

OBSERVE THE BEHAVIOR

Spend some time observing the child to see what triggers tantrums and what happens after the child has had a tantrum.

When do tantrums occur most often?

- Unpredictably, at any time of day
- During structured times when the children are expected to follow specific guidelines
- During free-choice activities
- During outdoor play periods
- During cleanup times
- During transitions
- When it is time to go home
- Early in the day, soon after arriving
- At nap time
- At mealtimes

With whom do tantrums occur?

- One particular teacher
- Any adult
- The child's parent(s)
- Certain children

What happens to the child just before she throws a tantrum?

- The child does not get something she asks for.
- The child is hit by another child.
- Something is taken away from her.
- The child wants a toy that another child is playing with.
- The child is prevented by another child or children from joining in play.
- The child is told no by another child or a teacher.
- The child does not want to join an activity.
- The child does not want to finish an activity at the end of the activity period.

What does the child do when she throws a tantrum?

- The child looks around to see whether an adult is watching.
- The child increases the intensity of noise and/or motion when an adult is nearby.
- The child increases the tantrum when an adult tries to talk to her.
- The child decreases the tantrum when an adult tries to talk to her.

- The child reacts to the presence or comments of other children.
- The child stops the tantrum if she is picked up by an adult.
- The child increases the tantrum if she is picked up by an adult.
- The child hurts herself often while having a tantrum.
- The child tries to hurt others, such as by kicking or biting.

Use the insight you have gained from these informal observations to help you plan an approach to eliminating tantrums.

CONSULT WITH THE FAMILY

Tantrums are not unusual occurrences for young preschoolers, and if they happen at school, they probably happen at home as well. If the child engages in an unusual number of tantrums, discuss this with the family once you have had the chance to carefully observe the behavior. Share insights with the family about why, when, and after what provocation tantrums seem to take place. Brainstorm with the family to come up with ideas for decreasing tantrums and their intensity. Once you have begun your strategies to eliminate tantrums, keep the family informed of progress.

CONSIDER THE IMPLICATIONS

The child who throws tantrums has found that such behavior is an effective attention-getting device. Some children, from earliest infancy, show a tendency to be excitable and react strongly to what goes on in their environment. It is such a child, more than the one who was a placid and calm baby, who is likely to throw tantrums as a preschooler. The tendency to react strongly is particularly noticeable during the toddler and early preschool period, when the child is striving for autonomy. This is often a time when wills clash as the child wants to exercise her newfound freedom and adults try to rein her in.

The young child is still immature and does not understand socially acceptable ways of reacting to something she does not like. She may decide to show how she feels in a very dramatic way. The child may throw herself on the ground, kick her feet, pound with her fists, contort her face, scream, and cry. Such a tantrum is definitely an attention-getter.

Adults often react by trying to stop the behavior, but often find that trying to reason with the child and coax her to stop the tantrum is ineffective. They may give in to what the child wanted in the first place. The child gets her way and gets considerable attention in the process.

Once the child learns that throwing tantrums is effective, she repeats the behavior more often. Adults may continue to try to reason with the child, or they may lose their patience and revert to anger and spanking as a way of dealing with tantrums. Both reactions result in added attention. A child who starts preschool with a history of getting her way through tantrums often tries to use this behavior at school also. Teachers should be aware of this tendency and must be careful not to reinforce it further with their attention.

EXPLORE ALTERNATIVES

The child who resorts to tantrums needs special guidance to overcome this behavior. The following considerations may help you understand and avert unnecessary tantrums:

- Preschool children develop increasing independence and need to be given opportunities to exercise that autonomy. A child is less likely to react with a tantrum when she is given chances to do things by herself and for herself. The classroom and curriculum should be designed to encourage independence as much as possible. For example, the arrangement of the classroom should help children easily reach materials, hang up their coats, and reach the toilets and sinks. The curriculum should allow for choices, so that children may learn to make decisions. This is one way of expressing independence.

- Very young preschoolers are the children most likely to have tantrums. Because they are not yet adept at some of the more acceptable ways of expressing their wishes, they often react in physical ways, such as tantrums. Recognize the social, emotional, and language abilities and limitations of two-year-olds, and keep these in mind as you deal with their tantrums. It is best to ignore tantrums when they occur and to reinforce more acceptable behavior. The main concern with two-year-olds is that having tantrums does not become a habitual behavior. You should discourage the behavior by ignoring it right from the beginning.*

If neither of these situations describes the conditions under which the child throws a tantrum and you conclude that the tantrum is really an attention-seeking ploy, continue to the following strategies.

*A child who is developmentally at a younger age level, for instance one with a cognitive disability, may resort to tantrums similar to those of a toddler. A child with a language impairment may find that tantrums are an effective alternative means of communication. Ignoring the tantrum but allowing the child to exercise her growing autonomy will be helpful.

STATE THE GOAL

The goal is for the child to stop throwing tantrums and to learn appropriate ways to express her wishes.

APPROACH

To eliminate tantrums, the basic strategy involves three simultaneous steps:

- Ignore tantrums when they occur.
- Frequently reinforce appropriate behaviors.
- Help the child deal with emotional reactions in acceptable ways.

DEFINITION

Throwing tantrums is a collection of behaviors including the child throwing herself bodily on the floor, kicking, pounding fists, crying, screaming, and other dramatic actions carried out in reaction to an upsetting event.

STARTING POINT

Take three days to collect some initial information on how often the child has tantrums. Mark on paper each time she throws a tantrum, and keep a record of how long each tantrum lasts. At first, the child may not decrease the frequency of tantrums but may decrease their duration. Have a clock or watch with a second hand available. When the child has a tantrum, time it and write down how long it lasts. At the end of each day, record the total number of tantrums on the Frequency Record-Keeping Graph and the average duration of all tantrums for that day on the Duration Record-Keeping Graph. Compute the average duration by adding the length of time of all the tantrums and dividing by the number of tantrums:

$$\frac{\text{Total Minutes of All Tantrums}}{\text{Total Number of Tantrums}} = \text{Average Duration}$$

STRATEGIES

Once you have kept track of the number and duration of tantrums for three days, continue to the following approach. It is very important that all teachers follow these steps consistently.

Ignore Tantrums When They Occur. When the child throws a tantrum, completely ignore it. In the past, the child was given considerable attention for this challenging behavior. The child expects that attention to continue. The duration, the intensity, and the total number of tantrums may increase when you first begin ignoring them. Once the child realizes that she receives no attention, no matter how hard, how long, or how often she throws tantrums, she should quickly decrease and stop this behavior. When the child has a tantrum, do the following:

1. Do not give any reinforcement whatsoever. Ignore all behavior associated with the tantrum. Do not approach the child, talk to her, reason with or explain to her, or even look at her. Act as though she is not in the room. Do not let your facial expression or bodily posture convey that you are in any way concerned with the child's behavior. Even in the midst of a tantrum, a child picks up cues from you that express your concern, your frustration, or your anger with the situation. You must feel, as well as act, your detachment from the child's behavior.

2. Leave the child where she is, if possible. Continue the classroom routine around the tantrum. If the child's tantrum is so disruptive that you cannot continue planned activities, you have one of two choices. You can move the child out of the room to continue her tantrum elsewhere, or you can change the schedule. If you do the former, be sure the child is placed in a spot where an adult can watch her without paying her any attention. It is important that ignoring be carried out wherever the child is. If you decide to change the schedule, be sure you do this only if it is not overly disruptive. For instance, if your plans call for reading a story followed by outside play, simply reverse the order. The child may continue her tantrum where she is while the other children go outside.

3. If another child calls your attention to the tantrum, say that you are aware of it and that you want the other child to stop the tantrum on her own. Convey that you will give the child attention once the tantrum has stopped, but not before.

4. Keep your ear tuned to the child. If you hear that the tantrum has stopped, go to the child. Sit by her if she needs a few moments to calm down, but do not talk about the tantrum. When she is ready, help her select and join an activity. If the child has been outside the room, tell her she may return.

5. If the child resumes her tantrum after you go to her, walk away. Ignore the behavior until she stops. Do not attend to the child during the tantrum.

Frequently Reinforce Appropriate Behaviors. At the same time as you are ignoring tantrums, let the child know what behaviors you value. Be alert to the child's appropriate behaviors and reinforce them frequently. Look for times when the child is engaged in activities, interacting with other children, helping with cleanup, or in any other way participating as expected. Use your informal observations for clues to what might trigger tantrums. If you see a potential problem situation that the child has handled in an acceptable way, give lavish praise and attention.

Help the Child Find Acceptable Alternatives to Handling Emotional Reactions. The child may react consistently with a tantrum to situations in which she feels angry, frustrated, or in some way upset. She must learn to use more acceptable reactions. Carefully watch for situations to which the child might react with a tantrum. If you see a potential tantrum situation, do the following*:

1. Go to the child quickly, and take any immediate measures that may need to be taken (such as preventing an aggressive act or preventing a toy from being grabbed from someone).
2. Get down to the level of the child and put your arm around her. Verbally acknowledge the emotion that the situation has aroused. Say, for instance, "I know. It really makes you feel angry when you can't have the toy you want." "It hurt when Terry and Arnold told you they didn't want to play with you." "Boy! When you want to keep working on that wood sculpture but it's time to clean up, it really upsets you."
3. Encourage the child to express her feelings either by agreeing with you, elaborating on your statement, or explaining a different feeling.
4. Now say, "What can we do about it?" Quickly explore a few alternatives for handling the situation with the child.
5. If appropriate, help the child carry out a resolution to the situation.
6. Provide praise for her handling of the situation. If the child begins to throw a tantrum at any point, move away. Ignore such a tantrum in the way discussed earlier.

 Continue Keeping Track of the Behavior. As the approach to eliminate tantrums progresses, continue to count and time the tantrums each day, and record these figures on the appropriate graphs. Expect an increase on the duration graph and a possible increase on the frequency graph for the first few days. This increase should soon level off and then quickly decrease as the child realizes that she is not going to get attention for tantrums.

*Tantrums may be an effective way for a child with an emotional/behavioral deficit to express herself. When a teacher helps the child find acceptable alternatives to communicating her emotions, the teacher is helping the child deal with more than just tantrums.

MAINTAINING THE CHANGES

Continue to give praise for appropriate behaviors, particularly for acceptable ways of dealing with difficult situations. Give such praise at the same rate as you do for the other children in the class. If the child throws a tantrum again, simply ignore it.

The CD-ROM that accompanies this text contains several hypothetical scenarios designed for you to apply the guidance principles suggested in the various chapters of this book. Go to the Your Turn section of the CD to access these scenarios. Scenarios 7 and 8 are particularly pertinent to this section of the text, Emotional and Dependent Behaviors.

Iting • Throwing Objects at Others • Hurting Others • Using Inappropriate
alling • Nonsharing • Bribery • Stealing • Noncompliance • Disrupting Gr
• Classroom • Running Aimlessly Around the Classroom • Shouting in the
cts to Create Noise • Tearing Books • Flushing Objects D Objects D
sting Paper • Destroying the Work of Others • Throwing Tantrums • Pout
lk • Thumb-Sucking • Pant-Wetting • Clinging • Seeking Attention • Stim
ticipation in Activities • Nonparticipation in S aung
nly One Toy • Infrequent Large Muscle Activity • Infrequent Dramatic Play
Talking Infrequently • Short Attention Span • Finicky Eating • Overeating
ng • Hoarding Food • Hitting • Biting • Throwing Objects at Others • Hurti
opriate Language • Name-Calling • Nonsharing • Bribery • Stealing • Nor
g Group Time • Leaving the Classroom • Running Aimlessly Around the c
the Classroom • Dropping Objects to Create Noise • Tearing Books • Fl
ng Objects Down the Toilet • Wasting Paper • Destroying the Work of Ot
ng Tantrums • Pouting • Baby Talk • Thumb-Sucking • Pant-Wetting • Cl

chapter **29**

Pouting

"All right, children, it's time to put everything away now. Your parents will be coming to pick you up soon." This statement is made several minutes after the teacher warned that cleanup time was coming. Children start putting away toys and materials.

Three-year-old Tessa, however, continues with the matching game she is using. A teacher walks up to her and says, "Come on, Tessa. You have to put things away now. It's almost time to go home." Tessa lays out more cards and ignores the teacher. "Tessa, that's enough now!" says the teacher, beginning to pick up some of the cards. Tessa takes the cards she holds in her hand, slams them on the table, crosses her arms in front of her, and pouts. "Come on, Tessa. Help me put these cards back in the box." Tessa mumbles, "I don't want to," and continues to pout. "You know you're supposed to clean up what you use, Tessa." Tessa refuses to help, pouting the whole time.

The teacher finally puts the game away and Tessa is in a foul mood when her mother arrives to take her home. The teachers are concerned because Tessa frequently refuses to do what is expected of her and shows her displeasure by pouting.

STATE THE BEHAVIOR

The child pouts frequently to express displeasure.

239

OBSERVE THE BEHAVIOR

Take several days to observe the child's behavior closely. Such observation should give you some clues about when and under what circumstances the child pouts.

When does the child seem to pout most?
- Any time of day
- Early in the day
- Late in the day
- Around nap time
- Around mealtimes
- During free-choice activities
- During structured activities
- At cleanup times
- During transitions
- During outdoor play periods
- When an adult is nearby
- When other children are nearby

What seems to trigger the pouting?
- The child is told no by a teacher or another child.
- The child is prevented from doing something.
- The child does not want to do something she is asked to do.
- The child is prevented from joining in play by other children.

What happens when the child pouts?
- An adult tells her to stop pouting.
- The child gets what she wants as a result of pouting.
- The pouting changes to crying.
- The child verbally expresses what is bothering her.
- The child does not talk about what is bothering her.

Use these observations to help you determine how to prevent and then stop the child's pouting behavior.

CONSULT WITH THE FAMILY

A child who pouts at school most likely is continuing a longstanding behavior. Pouting usually evolves as a way of reaction over time, and the family is, quite likely, as frustrated with the behavior as the teachers are. Once you have had the opportunity to observe the circumstances under which pouting occurs most often, set up a meeting with the family to discuss your concerns about this behavior. Find out from the family how long the child has used pouting as a way of conveying her displeasure and what strategies they have tried to deal with the pouting. Share your observations and ideas about decreasing this behavior. Once you have begun to work on eliminating pouting, keep in frequent communication with the family to let them know of progress.

CONSIDER THE IMPLICATIONS

When a child pouts, she uses a nonverbal means of expressing her displeasure. Her face screws up, her mouth and forehead pucker, and her body may stiffen, with her arms crossed in front. Pouting often signals that the child is going to stand firm to what she wants. It underlines the child's struggle for power with an adult. The child is conveying that she does not want to do what someone has asked her to do or that she is upset because someone will not let her do what she wants to do. Often in this kind of situation, the adult continues to insist and the child continues to refuse.

At some point, the child learned that she could get her own way by standing firm against the adult's wishes and pouting. Later, pouting and stubbornness became standard behaviors for the child. When such a child enters preschool, she expects to continue getting her way. She uses pouting to convey that she wants to do something other than what has been asked of her and to display her feelings if she is not allowed to do what she wants. If teachers give attention to the child when she pouts, they reinforce the behavior.

EXPLORE ALTERNATIVES

Consider whether one of the following suggestions will help you deal with the child who pouts:

- The child may have noticed another youngster pouting and may be imitating this child. Children learn by assuming different roles. A child may simply be trying out an expression she has seen on another child or even an adult. Unless the pouting is accompanied by marked stubbornness, ignore it and do not worry about it.
- Be careful to avoid situations that put you in direct confrontation with the child. Provide many choices in the program. The child should have a chance to select what she wants to do. Take care to word requests so they do not result in a stubborn reaction. For instance, say, "Let's get these beads back in the box. I'll start picking up the red ones. Which color do you want to pick up first?" rather than, "You're going to have to pick up all these beads you dumped

out." The opportunity to make choices and some tactful wording by teachers may help avert stubbornness and pouting.

If neither of these suggestions provides help for the child who pouts, move on to the following approach.

STATE THE GOAL

The goal is for the child to stop pouting by discontinuing the stubborn clashes of wills with adults.

APPROACH

The basic strategy involves three simultaneous steps:

- Avoid situations that might result in pouting and stubbornness.
- Reinforce compliance.
- Ignore pouting when it does occur.

DEFINITION

Pouting involves a child's physical reactions, such as puckering the mouth and forehead, which reflect the child's unwillingness to comply with what she is asked to do or not to do.

STARTING POINT

Before continuing, spend three days gathering initial information. Every time the child pouts, mark it down on paper. At the end of each day, total the frequency marks, and transfer the total to the Frequency Record-Keeping Graph. These three days provide you with information with which you can compare later progress.

STRATEGIES

Follow this approach once you have collected information for three days on how often the child pouts. It is important that all teachers follow these steps consistently.

Avoid Situations That Might Result in Pouting and Stubbornness.
Examine the information from your informal observation for clues as to what triggers pouting and when it is most likely to occur. Avoid potential pouting situations as often as possible, as they result in the child having negative feelings about herself. If she gets her own way, she is still aware

of the adult's displeasure or anger with her. If she does not get her way, she gets neither satisfaction nor the adult's approval. It is important, therefore, to avoid potential problem situations to protect the child's sense of self-worth. Following are some suggestions that will serve as preventive measures:

1. Avoid giving direct orders to the child. Word requests to the child in a way that reflects your respect for her as a person. Children are much more likely to comply if you say, "I would appreciate it if you would _____" than if you say, "You have to _____ ." Children deserve consideration and courtesy as much as adults do.

2. Give the child choices. There is less likely to be a clash of wills if you ask a child, "Would you like to put the napkins on the table, or would you rather pour the juice?" than if you say, "You have to put the napkins on the table." The child who is given a choice by the teacher does not feel trapped in a black-and-white situation of "Do it, and please me" or "Don't do it, and risk displeasing me."

3. Give the child the chance to say no if a choice is really hers to make. If you say, "Would you like to work at the woodworking table?" and the child answers "No," there should be no negative reactions from you. In such a case simply say, "Fine. You must want to paint at the easel or build in the block area." If you ask the child a question to which she can answer yes or no, be sure to accept either answer.

4. If there is a task about which the child has no choice, be careful with the wording you use. You might make a game of such a situation. Rather than say, "You have to go to the rug and sit down for story time now," try, "Let's pretend we're bunnies and we're hopping over to the rug for story time."

5. If the child wants to do something that you cannot allow, stop the child in an understanding way. Let her know that you understand there is something she would really like to do. Explain why you cannot let her do it. Provide an alternative. For example, say, "I know you really want to paint now, but we have to get ready for lunch. After nap time I'll bring out the paints again, and then you can have a chance to paint if you'd like. Is there a special color of paint you'd like me to prepare?"

Reinforce Compliance. When you ask the child to do something and she complies with your request, praise her. Let the child know you are pleased with such behavior and that you value it. You might say, "Thank you! I really appreciate it when you help with cleanup when I ask you!" or "What a lovely smile! That's the way I like to see my helpers!" The child will feel good from such a response and will also realize that you feel good. Given time, the child will recognize that there is nothing to be gained from resisting and pouting, but that there is reward for positive reaction.

If the child wants to do something that you cannot allow and she stops when asked, praise her. Help her find an alternative activity.

Ignore Pouting When It Occurs. Pouting is a habit the child has acquired over time. When you make a request and the child reacts by pouting, do the following:

1. Immediately stop what you are saying when the child starts to pout. Pause for a few seconds, and look at the child.
2. Say to her, "I cannot talk to you when you are pouting."
3. Wait a few more moments. If the child continues to pout, walk away. Say, "I'll talk to you when you stop pouting."
4. If the child makes an effort to stop pouting when you ask her to, praise her and continue talking to her.
5. If you have asked the child to do something that she refuses to do, do not make an issue of the matter. You are only reinforcing her pouting if you insist or argue with her. Simply walk away. Do not engage in a clash of wills.
6. If the child wants to do something that you cannot allow, walk away. If the child persists in the activity, particularly if it poses a safety hazard or is disruptive, remove her from it. Take the child to a chair in a quiet corner of the room or outside the class and ask her to stay there for a few minutes. Then move away and pay the child no attention. After about three minutes, tell her she may return. Remember that your aim is to minimize attention for pouting. Place the child in a chair, or remove her from the room only as a last resort.

With time, these steps should help the child realize that there are more effective ways of reacting to requests than pouting.

Continue Keeping Track of the Behavior. Each day of implementing these strategies, count the number of times the child pouts. Record the total on the graph. Progress will probably be slow because you are trying to eliminate a habitual response. You should see a steady decline on the graph over time. Be persistent until you reach your goal.

MAINTAINING THE CHANGES

When the child has stopped pouting, remember that part of the change is due to your change in response, as well. Therefore, continue communicating with the child in ways that reflect your concern for her interests, your understanding, and your respect. Give appropriate choices whenever possible. Also, continue giving reinforcement for desired behaviors. If the child occasionally responds by pouting, ignore it as you did when you were implementing the earlier-discussed strategies.

 The CD-ROM that accompanies this text contains several hypothetical scenarios designed for you to apply the guidance principles suggested in the various chapters of this book. Go to the Your Turn section of the CD to access these scenarios. Scenarios 7 and 8 are particularly pertinent to this section of the text, Emotional and Dependent Behaviors.

"Baby want cwacker." "What do you want?" "Cwacker," answers four-year-old Arnold. "Come on, Arnold, stop the baby talk. What do you need?" Miss Arden begins to feel exasperated, and her voice reflects this. "Me want cwacker. Me want eat cwacker," responds Arnold. "Oh! You want a cracker. Well, we'll be having snack in a few minutes." Arnold smiles, and as Miss Arden walks away, says, "Goo-goo!"

Later that day, Arnold engages in a similar conversation with Mrs. Rochester when he wants to swing. "Baby wanna swing." After several minutes of tolerant explanations about all the swings being occupied, which Arnold knows, a swing becomes vacant and Arnold gets into it. Arnold sits with his thumb in his mouth until Mrs. Rochester asks, "Why aren't you swinging, Arnold?" "Baby no know how swing." Mrs. Rochester sighs and pushes Arnold several times. She knows he is quite capable of swinging himself.

Throughout the rest of the day, Arnold continues using baby talk and acting like a baby, much to the concern of his teachers. His use of appropriate speech for his age is becoming more and more rare.

STATE THE BEHAVIOR

The child uses baby talk, speaking in a manner not characteristic of his age.

OBSERVE THE BEHAVIOR

Take some time to observe the child informally so you can gain some insight into this behavior.

When is the child most likely to use baby talk?

- Early in the day, soon after arriving
- Any time of the day
- Late in the day
- Near nap or rest time
- Around mealtimes
- During teacher-directed activities
- During group activities
- During child-selected activities
- At toileting times
- During transitions
- At cleanup times

What is the child doing when he uses baby talk?

- The child is talking with an adult.
- The child is asking a question.
- The child is requesting a toy or material.
- The child is seeking the teacher's attention.
- The child is playing alone.
- The child is playing with other children.
- The child is upset.
- The child has been asked not to do something.
- The child has hurt himself.
- The child has been hurt by another child.
- The child is not engaged in any activity.
- The child is asking for help in carrying out an activity.
- The child is playing in the housekeeping area.
- The child often assumes the role of the baby in the housekeeping area.
- The child often engages in activities such as crawling or sucking his thumb.

What happens when the child uses baby talk?

- Teachers usually pay attention.
- Teachers ignore such talk.
- Teachers ask the child not to talk like a baby.
- Other children take note of the child.

- Other children laugh.
- Other children pay no attention.
- Other children fall into play with the child, assuming he will take on the role of baby.

What does the child talk about when he uses baby talk?

Use the insight you gain from these observations to eliminate baby talk.

CONSULT WITH THE FAMILY

Work with the family to determine whether there is a change in the child's life that might be at the root of the baby talk, especially if the behavior has become evident only recently. Share with the family your observations and find out if the child engages in similar behaviors at home. Ask the family about the circumstances under which they have noted this behavior. If the child uses baby talk both at home and at school, work together with the family to come up with a strategy to use consistently in both settings. Stay in frequent touch with the family to share progress.

CONSIDER THE IMPLICATIONS

The child who uses baby talk deliberately, not because of a speech impediment, is probably doing so because this behavior brings him attention. It is possible that as the child was growing up, he found that the use of appropriate speech did not gain the attention he desired and needed. Somehow, he discovered the use of baby talk as a way of getting attention. He may have made some statements in a style recognizably below his ability and age level and found that adults listened, laughed, and commented as a result. The child may also revert to baby talk if his status changes from only child to older brother. A child may try to regain the singular position he enjoyed before the new baby came by imitating that baby in the hope that his parents will attend to him more and treat him like that baby. Once the child finds that baby talk gains him attention, whether indulgent or critical, he may decide to continue to use it.

When a child in preschool uses baby talk to a considerable extent, the teachers may unintentionally reinforce the behavior. Reactions like, "Aren't you a cute baby!" or "Stop it, now. You're too old to talk like that!" only serve to reinforce the behavior. A more systematic approach is necessary to eliminate baby talk.

EXPLORE ALTERNATIVES

Consider whether one of the following suggestions might help you work with the child who uses baby talk:

- A child's immature speech may be due to a speech defect of some kind. A hearing problem or developmental delay could cause the child to use language that is not age-appropriate. If the child constantly uses baby talk and you note other signs of immaturity or poor hearing, recommend to the family that medical testing be done.

- The child who uses baby talk may be doing this for a relatively short period after a new brother or sister has entered his life. Such a reaction is fairly common and can be handled in a way that respects the child's response to this major change in his life. The child who talks like a baby is expressing some confusion and concern about his new status. As a teacher, you can help the child deal with the situation by being understanding, clarifying his feelings, and answering questions. Follow the strategies outlined in this chapter to discourage baby talk. At the same time, spend time with the child talking about his new brother or sister and what has happened to him as a result.

- Children enjoy role-playing and engage in this activity frequently. Most children prefer taking on the role of adults rather than of younger children when they have this choice. Some children, either by their own choice or by peers, are cast into the role of the baby during dramatic play and enter such a role wholeheartedly. Do not confuse the child's assumption of the baby role during role-playing with baby talk as defined in this chapter. It is only when talking like a baby is not appropriate (at the wrong time, wrong place, or wrong occasion) that it may present a concern.

- Be sure that your expectations of the child are appropriate. There is a wide range in the abilities and development of young children. Some two-year-old children have large vocabularies and are very expressive in their use of language. Others are barely beginning to talk, using single words or two-word combinations to communicate. Both are common among two-year-olds and should not give cause for concern. By age three, however, children should have a fairly good command of the language. If a child is not talking in sentences and has a very limited vocabulary, then developmental, speech, or hearing tests may be needed to pinpoint the cause of the language delay.*

*Always be sensitive to possible underlying physiological causes for a child's behavior. If a speech defect, hearing problem, cognitive deficit, or developmental delay underlies a problem, your approach needs to involve medical, not behavioral, intervention.

- A child's baby talk may reflect a lack of self-confidence. He may, for example, have had experiences in which adults have put him down or failed to acknowledge his accomplishments. Giving the child responsibilities to help in the classroom, along with frequent appropriate praise, may help.

If none of the previous suggestions serve to answer the concern, continue on to the following approach.

STATE THE GOAL

The goal is for the child to stop using baby talk when this is not appropriate and to speak in a manner characteristic of his age.

APPROACH

The basic approach to eliminating baby talk involves two simultaneous steps:
- Ignore it when it occurs.
- Reinforce appropriate use of language.

DEFINITION

Baby talk means that the child speaks in a way that reflects less than his ability. It may include use of incomplete sentences, single words, gurgles and coos, mispronunciation of words, or elimination of certain consonants.

STARTING POINT

Spend three days collecting initial information. Carefully listen to the child, and record each time he uses baby talk by making a mark on a piece of paper. Consider each incident in which the child uses only baby talk as one count; this may include just a word or two, or it may involve an entire conversation of several minutes. If the flow of baby talk is broken by normal speech and then resumed, count this as two incidents. At the end of each day, add all the marks and record the total on the Frequency Record-Keeping Graph.

STRATEGIES

After gathering baseline data, you are ready to begin. It is important that all teachers follow the steps at all times.

Ignore Baby Talk When It Occurs. Baby talk is easy to reinforce if you give it attention. Whether your reaction is tolerant and amused or it conveys that you are displeased with the baby talk, the fact that you are reacting is reinforcing this behavior. It is important, therefore, to ignore baby talk whenever it occurs. Use the following steps:

1. If you hear the child using baby talk, do not turn toward him, look at him, speak to him, or otherwise convey that you are paying attention to this behavior. Your actions should say that you are not even aware of it.

2. If you are talking to the child and he uses baby talk, stop what you intended to say and tell him instead, "I cannot talk to you when you use baby talk." Wait a few seconds. If the child talks normally, resume your conversation. If he continues to use baby talk, turn your back to him and walk away. It is important when you do this to give him attention for appropriate speech as soon thereafter as possible.

3. The child may want physical attention (to be hugged, to sit on your lap, to be picked up) and may convey this through baby talk. He may connect affectionate responses with being baby-like. Let him know that a show of affection is not reserved for babies. Tell him, "I'll be glad to pick you up when you tell me in *your* voice." If the child drops the baby talk, give him the response he asked for. If he continues the baby talk, walk away. As soon thereafter as possible, however, give him a hug or a squeeze when he uses appropriate speech.

4. If the child uses baby talk during a group activity, ignore it as well. When you call on the child to answer a question or make a comment, if he answers in baby talk, first look away from him. Then say, "Can someone else tell me _____?" Call on another child then. Do not comment on the baby talk or in any way call attention to it. Your reaction should not be punitive, merely neutral. Do not let your facial expression show displeasure or annoyance. Such a reaction would only convey that the child did annoy you by using baby talk.

5. If another child calls your attention to the fact that the child is using baby talk, simply say, "I know." Try to redirect this child's interest into an activity. It will be helpful to decrease peer attention as well as your own reaction as much as possible.

6. Provide opportunities for role-taking in the housekeeping or dramatic play area. If the child takes on the role of the baby, respond as appropriate, but clarify that being a pretend baby is fine when it is part of a play scenario in which a group of children are engaged.

Reinforce Appropriate Use of Language. As you ignore the child's baby talk, let the child know what behavior you expect and value by reinforcing it when it occurs. Be alert to the use of appropriate language by the child. Pay attention to him when he speaks properly. You can reinforce proper speech by being attentive and responsive when he uses it. Periodically tell him, "I really like the way you are talking," or "It's great to hear you talk so clearly!" If the child uses baby talk a great deal, it is especially important to reinforce him when he speaks properly. Listen for appropriate language, and praise it or attend to it immediately. Once the rate of baby talk decreases considerably, you can reinforce less often. Be sure you still reinforce appropriate speech or the child may revert to baby talk.

Continue Keeping Track of the Behavior. Each day, continue to keep a record on the graph of the number of incidents of baby talk in the same way as you did initially. A decline in incidents of baby talk tells you when to cut back on the frequency of reinforcement given for appropriate language use.

MAINTAINING THE CHANGES

After baby talk has been eliminated, continue to attend to appropriate speech. If the child talks to you normally, give him your attention and the courtesy he deserves. If he occasionally uses baby talk, simply ignore it.

The CD-ROM that accompanies this text contains several hypothetical scenarios designed for you to apply the guidance principles suggested in the various chapters of this book. Go to the Your Turn section of the CD to access these scenarios. Scenarios 7 and 8 are particularly pertinent to this section of the text, Emotional and Dependent Behaviors.

chapter 31

Thumb-Sucking

Corey has been in the child care center for two years, since he was two years old. As a two-year-old, his thumb-sucking was tolerated because it was not unusual for his age. Now that he is four, his teachers worry because Corey spends so much time with his thumb in his mouth, doing nothing else. They have tried pulling his thumb from his mouth, coaxing him to remove it, and telling him that he is too old to suck his thumb. Corey is happier when he has his thumb in his mouth. The teachers feel frustrated but are resigned to his behavior. They wish they could get Corey more actively involved in classroom activities. They feel he is missing too much.

STATE THE BEHAVIOR

The child frequently keeps a thumb (or fingers) in his mouth.

OBSERVE THE BEHAVIOR

Observe the child for a few days to gain some insight into his behavior.

When is the child most likely to suck his thumb?
- Throughout the day
- Early in the day

- Toward the end of the day
- Near nap time
- Around mealtimes
- During group times
- When children are required to listen
- During self-selected activities
- During transitions

What is the child doing just before he puts his thumb in his mouth?

- The child is not engaged in an activity.
- The child takes a brief break while participating in an activity to suck his thumb.
- The child plays alone.
- The child plays with other children.
- The child engages in an activity that does not require him to use both hands.
- The child sits by a teacher.
- The child sits alone.
- The child talks to an adult or another child.
- The child seems tired.
- The child is unable to complete a task.
- The child becomes upset.
- The child holds a favorite blanket or other security object.

Does the child engage in activities while he sucks his thumb?

What happens when the child stops sucking his thumb?

How long does the child usually suck his thumb?

CONSULT WITH THE FAMILY

A child who sucks his thumb much of the time at school most likely also engages in this behavior in other settings, including home. Consult with the family to see if they are concerned with the behavior. Share with them your concern that the child is spending much of his time with his thumb in his mouth and, therefore, is not participating as much as he might in school activities. Work together with the family to share ideas and come up with some strategies to decrease the behavior. Indicate to the family that changing the behavior may be a long-term process, but reassure them that it will help if you reinforce each other in the home and school settings. Keep in close touch about progress because it may not be overly evident at first. Your continued careful record-keeping will help make progress more visible.

CONSIDER THE IMPLICATIONS

Thumb-sucking is usually a long-standing habit that starts in early infancy. In fact, babies suck their thumbs even before they are born, in utero. For some children, thumb-sucking partly satisfies the need for sucking, which all infants have. It assumes the function of providing security as the child gets older.

When a preschooler frequently sucks his thumb, he does so not only because it is a long-standing habit but also because it has become a way of reacting to unknown or even everyday events. By the time the child reaches the preschool years, it may be difficult to eliminate thumb-sucking. Usually some form of social pressure makes the child change this habit, often at the cost of his feelings of self-worth. Such a child is frequently told that what he is doing is "baby stuff." He may be ridiculed, laughed at, and even punished.

Family members are usually quite concerned about thumb-sucking. This behavior can affect tooth development, which may result in costly orthodontic work later. Also, it does not seem appropriate for a child no longer in infancy. Family and teachers can help the child stop sucking his thumb. This is a long-range goal that must be achieved in such a way that it does not compromise the child's self-esteem and self-confidence.

EXPLORE ALTERNATIVES

If a child habitually sucks his thumb, this behavior is easy to identify. Usually children who suck their thumbs do so more often under conditions of stress. This section explores some causes of thumb-sucking and possible ways of reducing the behavior.

- Examine the activities and curriculum provided for the children. These must be appropriate for the children enrolled. They should neither be above their level, causing frustration, nor be below their ability, causing boredom. Children may react to a program that does not really meet their needs by exhibiting behaviors such as thumb-sucking. Change activities as needed if you decide that the children's needs are not being met. When children are involved in and enjoy what they are doing, they are less likely to feel the need for thumb-sucking.

- Thumb-sucking may provide sensory stimulation. Consider children's indirectly expressed need for activities that provide such stimuli. Include these in your program. Plan more water play, sand play, mud play, cooking projects, and smell- and taste-discrimination activities. Set out bins that contain objects with a variety of textures. Provide a variety of activities to help satisfy the enjoyment of sensory stimulation.

- Examine the interaction between teachers and the child. A child may react with thumb-sucking if he perceives the adults as overly directive, overpowering, or domineering. Children generally respond more openly to gentle and quiet guidance. Observe adult–child interactions in the classroom. If one or more of the teachers seem to upset the child, consider making some changes. Discuss the concern with all the teachers in a group meeting. Look for ways to make interaction with adults less stressful for the child.
- A child whose hands are busy with activities will not be as likely to put a thumb in his mouth. Provide a well-balanced schedule of activities and options so the child has numerous opportunities to use his hands and does not find himself with nothing to do.
- Thumb-sucking is not unusual among young preschoolers. A two- or young three-year-old may suck his thumb at times when he feels a need for comfort. Most young children who suck their thumbs gradually stop doing so on their own. If the child about whom you are concerned is very young, do not concern yourself too much about his thumb-sucking. Chances are that it will decrease as the child gets a bit older. Provide a developmentally appropriate environment with a rich variety of activities, including sensory ones, to help the child use his hands in many ways.

Consider these suggestions and incorporate any that are appropriate into the following approach.

STATE THE GOAL

The goal is for the child to decrease thumb-sucking while at school. It is probably unrealistic to expect the child to completely stop this behavior. A decrease will help the child to eliminate it eventually.

APPROACH

The basic strategy for eliminating thumb-sucking involves three simultaneous steps:

- Provide a chart for the child to keep track of his progress.
- Provide activities that are alternatives to thumb-sucking.
- Frequently reinforce the child for not sucking his thumb.

DEFINITION

Thumb-sucking is a behavior in which the child keeps a thumb or other finger in his mouth and often does not participate in activities while he is doing so.

STARTING POINT

Spend three days gathering some basic information. About every 15 minutes throughout the day, look at the child. Do not include nap time. If the child has his thumb in his mouth, make a mark on paper. At the end of the day, transfer the total number to the Frequency Record-Keeping Graph. The maximum number of marks will be determined by the length of your program day. If the child is enrolled for three hours, then the maximum possible number of marks is 12. (One mark every 15 minutes equals 4 marks per hour, times three hours, equals 12.) If the child is enrolled for 10 hours per day, then the maximum number of marks may be 32 or 34. (Exclude one and one-half to two hours for a nap.) Set up the following chart for collecting the daily counts:

Date	9:00	9:15	9:30	9:45	10:00	10:15	10:30	10:45

This kind of information-gathering tells you not only how often the child sucks his thumb but also when the behavior is most likely to occur. A pattern may emerge to help you focus your approach on times when the behavior happens most often.

STRATEGIES

After gathering this initial information, start on the following strategies. It will be best if one teacher consistently implements the first step (charting) of the approach. The other two steps should be carried out by all the teachers.

Make the Child Aware of Your Goal and Keep Track with Him on a Chart. Thumb-sucking is not maintained by adult attention and reinforcement. The child receives intrinsic satisfaction when he sucks his thumb. Ignoring the behavior will not eliminate it. Tell the child the goal and your reasons for it. Actively involve the child in reaching that goal.

1. Before you begin, have a talk with the child about thumb-sucking. Tell him that you realize he enjoys sucking his thumb; do not deny the pleasure and reassurance he derives from it. However, convey to the child that the behavior concerns you. Tell the child that you really would like him to take part in and enjoy all activities but that you know he cannot do so when his thumb is in his mouth. If you think the child can understand, talk to him about the long-range effects thumb-sucking can have on his teeth.

2. Tell the child that you want to work with him to decrease some of the thumb-sucking. Say, "Let's see if the two of us together can cut down your thumb-sucking. We'll make it a game that we can play. I'll put up this chart [described below], and you'll get to put a special star on it every time you don't suck your thumb for 10 minutes [or less time, if the child sucks his thumb constantly]." Speak enthusiastically, and let the child know that you fully expect him to succeed.

3. Purchase a box of gummed stars and make the chart on which the child will keep track. This is not the same as the chart on which you keep track of daily thumb-sucking. Use the child's chart for about one hour per day. Select an hour during which various activity choices are available to the child. The chart can be decorated to make it more appealing, but basically it should look as shown here. Each horizontal row represents one day.

CHILD'S NAME						
Date	10:00	10:10	10:20	10:30	10:40	10:50

4. At the beginning of the hour during which you will be checking the behavior, tell the child that it is time to begin the game. Tell him, "Remember, you'll get a star for your chart if you don't suck your thumb for 10 minutes. I'll watch you, and you watch yourself. Ready? Begin!"

5. Encourage the child frequently. Tell him how well he is doing and how proud you are of him. Do not wait until the end of the 10 minutes to give praise.

6. If the child finishes the 10 minutes without sucking this thumb, be lavish and enthusiastic in your verbal praise. Give the child a star, and let him paste it in the appropriate space on the chart. Tell the other teachers that the child earned a star so they can also reinforce him.

7. If the child does not go the full 10 minutes, do not make a fuss. Simply say, "Let's try again." If the child consistently cannot last 10 minutes without putting a thumb in his mouth, decrease the time interval to 5 or even fewer minutes. Arrange the situation so that the child can experience success.

8. At the end of the hour, tell the child that the "game" is over for today, but he can play it again tomorrow. Remind him not to suck his thumb during the rest of the day.

9. Share the chart with the child's family at the end of the day. Do this when the child is present.

Provide Many Activities That Offer Alternatives to Thumb-Sucking.
As indicated before, when the child's hands are busy, he is less likely to suck his thumb. As you plan the curriculum, keep the following considerations in mind:

1. Be sure most activities involve action by the children. During story time, the children may pantomime parts of the story with their hands and arms. There should be no activities in which the child is required to merely watch an adult do something. Young children learn by doing, not by passively watching.

2. Provide activity choices. There should be times during the school day when children can select what they want to do. If a given activity does not interest a child, there should be other activities from which to choose. Not only does this provide for varied interests within the group, but it also encourages conscious decision-making by the children.

3. There should be a variety of sensory activities planned into the curriculum. Children respond well to media that provide different types of tactile and other sensory stimulation. Water, sand, mud, clay, finger paint, glue, rice, beans, Styrofoam, cornstarch, and liquid soap all have unique textures. Each helps to satisfy the need for varied sensory stimulation.

4. If the activities begin to seem stale because you have done them so often, plan some changes to rekindle the children's interest. A child may suck his thumb because he is bored. Plan changes through new activities, new interest centers in the classroom, and rearrangement of the daily schedule. Look for activity ideas in some of the many preschool activity books that are on the market. Add new interest centers such as a music area, a science table,

or a beauty shop. Rearrange the classroom to accommodate a new center. Change the schedule to add new types of activities, eliminate old ones, rearrange the order of daily events, or adjust some time blocks. Periodic novelty revitalizes the children's, and your, interest in the program.

Frequently Reinforce the Child for Not Sucking His Thumb. At all times of the day, look for occasions when the child does not have his thumb in his mouth. Reinforce what he is doing by your presence or by praise, a pat, or a hug. Periodically tell the child you are proud of him because he is sucking his thumb less and less. Let him know that you are aware of the effort he is making to change his behavior and that you appreciate it.

Continue Keeping Track of the Behavior. Throughout each day that you implement these strategies, continue to check the child about every 15 minutes and mark whether he is sucking his thumb. Record the total each day on the graph. Because thumb-sucking is a long-standing habit, progress may be slow. Expect the change to take some time; you will see a gradual decline on the graph.

MAINTAINING THE CHANGES

Discontinue the chart when the child loses interest or reaches the goal. Continue to provide a well-rounded program. Give the child periodic reinforcement for participation, as you do with all the children. The child may again suck his thumb at times when he is tired, does not feel well, or feels stressed. This is to be expected and should be accepted by adults.

The CD-ROM that accompanies this text contains several hypothetical scenarios designed for you to apply the guidance principles suggested in the various chapters of this book. Go to the Your Turn section of the CD to access these scenarios. Scenarios 7 and 8 are particularly pertinent to this section of the text, Emotional and Dependent Behaviors.

chapter 32

Pant-Wetting

This is the beginning of Cheryl's second year in the Head Start Center. Since she began in the program, the teachers have watched her blossom from a shy and reluctant child into one who eagerly engages in school activities and enjoys the friendship of other children. During her first year at the center, the teachers spent much time and effort getting Cheryl to be a fully participating member of the group. Now Cheryl is one of the veterans.

About a month after this school year began, Cheryl came up to one of the teachers and whispered, "Miss Lopez, I went potty in my pants." Miss Lopez took Cheryl to the bathroom, took off her wet clothes, and found some dry things for her to wear. About a week later, the incident was repeated. It happened twice more that same week. For the past three weeks, Cheryl has had two to three accidents every day. The teachers are concerned because this behavior never happened last year. They have tried to shame Cheryl into stopping by telling her, "Big girls don't do that."

STATE THE BEHAVIOR

The child frequently wets her pants.

OBSERVE THE BEHAVIOR

It is very important to get as many clues as possible about the child who wets her pants. Your informal observation will be helpful.

When does the child usually wet her pants?
- At unpredictable times; there seems to be no pattern
- Within an hour of meals and snacks
- During nap
- During outside play
- During indoor activities
- Soon after arriving at school

What usually precedes pant-wetting?
- The child is in the bathroom.
- The child sees another child urinate.
- The child undresses to go to the bathroom.
- The child has gotten up from the toilet.
- The child washes her hands.
- The child is engaged in water play.
- The child drinks water or juice.
- The child sits on a teacher's lap.
- The child is unable to complete a task.
- The child is told no by a teacher or another child.
- The child is tired.
- The child is engrossed in an activity.

What does the child do after she wets her pants?
- The child announces the accident to anyone nearby.
- The child quietly tells one teacher.
- The child tells no one.
- The child prefers to remain in the wet clothes.
- The child wants to undress and put on fresh clothes by herself.
- The child asks the teacher to change her.

This preliminary observation should give you some ideas about what might trigger pant-wetting, when it occurs, and how the child feels about it. Such information is very useful in trying to end this behavior.

CONSULT WITH THE FAMILY

Pant-wetting in a child who has already mastered toileting can be frustrating for teachers and families alike. Consult with the family as soon as you have gathered some information through observation about your concern. Find out if the child wets her pants at home, either while sleeping or at other times. Discuss with the family whether there has been a change in the child's life that might be worrying her. If you have any clues that pant-wetting stems from a potential physical cause such as a bladder infection, suggest to the family that they take the child to the doctor. If complicated clothing seems to be part of the issue, you can suggest simpler, alternative clothing such as pants with elastic at the waist. If, after brainstorming possible causes, you and the family decide that toilet accidents seem to be a bid for attention, share with the family possible strategies and try to implement these consistently both at home and at school. Keep the family informed frequently of successes in changing the behavior.

CONSIDER THE IMPLICATIONS

It is important for the preschool teacher to keep in mind the relatively short time the young child has been toilet-trained. Many young preschoolers have accidents because they are not yet completely trained. The excitement of the moment can easily become more important than the urge to urinate. Suddenly the child can wait no longer and wets her pants. It takes time and practice for the young child to master the timing and to recognize the bodily cues that accompany toileting. Preschoolers three years old and younger can be expected to have occasional accidents.

If the child has already mastered toilet training but still has frequent accidents, it may be a bid for attention. If the teacher reacts by providing this attention through lecturing, changing the child's pants, or punishment, the child's notion that pant-wetting is a way to get attention is reinforced. At the same time, the child is given the message that what she has done is not fitting for a child her age. This causes the child to feel shame and question her self-worth.

EXPLORE ALTERNATIVES

There are many factors besides behavioral ones that can cause a child to wet her pants. Carefully consider whether one of the following might be the root of the issue.

- Young children are susceptible to urinary-tract and kidney infections. A medical problem may cause pant-wetting. Be alert to complaints or indications of pain, burning, or itching by the child. Even if you do not notice such cues, discuss the behavior with the family. You may recommend they take the child to a doctor for a checkup.*

Be well informed about the various ways that chronic health problems are manifested. Difficulty with bladder or bowel control may be a side effect of a child's illness.

- A child's level of maturity is also an important factor in dealing with pant-wetting. It should be expected that young preschoolers will have accidents. When accidents occur, they should be handled in a matter-of-fact way. Children who have recently become toilet-trained should be praised when they urinate in the toilet. At the same time, teachers of two- and three-year-olds should build frequent toileting times into the daily schedule and should be alert to cues such as a child holding herself. With young children, toileting is still a learning process rather than an accomplished skill and should be treated as such.*

- Sometimes, children have accidents because they cannot undo their clothing quickly enough. Overalls, small buttons, belts with complicated buckles, tight snaps, and other gadgets can prove to be obstacles to getting undressed. Look at the children's clothes and watch how the youngsters handle them in the bathroom. If complicated fasteners keep the child from getting his clothing off easily, talk with the family and suggest some alternatives or simple alterations.

- An unusual occurrence or stress in the child's life may also cause her to start to wet her pants. If something is amiss, take time to talk with the child and reassure her as much as possible. Understanding the unknown may relieve the problem if the child is worried about something that no one has explained.

- Accidents can also be averted by careful scheduling. Teachers should give a reminder and provide time for going to the bathroom before nap, before going outside, and before leaving on a field trip. This is especially important if the children are going to be spending some time in a place where a bathroom is not readily available.

If none of these suggestions resolves pant-wetting, try the more detailed approach that follows.

STATE THE GOAL

The goal is for the child to stop wetting her pants.

APPROACH

This approach is intended for an older preschooler who has been thoroughly toilet-trained for at least half a year but who unexpectedly begins having regular toileting accidents. A medical cause for incontinence

---

Developmental maturity may be delayed in a child with special needs; for instance, a child with a cognitive deficit. Full bladder and bowel control often take longer to achieve.

must be ruled out before proceeding. The basic strategy includes these steps:

- Frequently remind the child to go to the bathroom.
- Praise the child for going to the bathroom by herself.
- When an accident does occur, ignore it.

DEFINITION

Pant-wetting is any time when the child does not urinate into the toilet but instead urinates in her clothes. This is considered a problem if it happens frequently and regularly.

STARTING POINT

Before starting any changes, keep track for three days of how often pant-wetting occurs. Jot down the time of each accident. Mark on paper each time the child has an accident. At the end of each day, record the total number on the Frequency Record-Keeping Graph. This information provides a base against which you can measure success once you implement the strategies discussed below.

STRATEGIES

After gathering initial information, begin the following strategies. All adults should use these steps consistently.

Frequently Remind the Child to Go to the Bathroom. Your initial count should give you an idea of how often toileting accidents occur. Compute an average time and use it as a guide for timing reminders. For instance, if accidents occur every hour on the average, remind the child every 30 minutes to go to the bathroom.

1. Tell the child it is time to go to the bathroom. Take the child by the hand and lead her to the bathroom.
2. Ask the child to pull down her pants to urinate. If she objects, tell her she must try. Be firm.
3. If she urinates in the toilet, praise the child.
4. If the child is unable to urinate after two minutes, let her leave the bathroom.

If after three to five days the child is urinating regularly in the toilet and if the number of accidents has decreased, begin to lengthen the time between reminders. Gradually eliminate the reminders when the child's pant-wetting decreases substantially.

Praise the Child for Going to the Bathroom by Herself. If the child goes to the bathroom without a reminder, or if she tells you she has to go to the bathroom and then does so, praise her. Let her know how much you appreciate her behavior when she does not wet her pants. If the child is not embarrassed about her accidents, let other teachers and children know in her presence that she went to the bathroom without a reminder and that you are proud of her. Do not do this if it embarrasses the child.

When an Accident Does Occur, Ignore It. If the child comes to you and tells you she had an accident, do the following:

1. Do not comment on it. In an unconcerned manner say, "I guess you'll have to change clothes."
2. Be prepared ahead of time. Keep a change of clothes and a plastic bag for the wet clothes to give to the child. Do not spend time with the child hunting for a change of clothes because this gives the child attention.
3. As soon as you give the child the clothes, leave. Do not stay nearby. Go elsewhere and let the child take as long as she needs to change. Withdraw the attention that usually follows an accident.
4. When the child has changed, let her put away the wet clothes and rejoin the group. Make no comments about the accident. If she tries to talk about it, do not respond.

Continue Keeping Track of the Behavior. At the end of each day of implementing these strategies, record the number of pant-wetting incidents on the graph. This record shows the progress and indicates when to decrease the number of reminders to go to the bathroom.

MAINTAINING THE CHANGES

When pant-wetting has ceased to occur for several days, you can assume the behavior has been changed. Discontinue reminders to go to the bathroom, and gradually discontinue praise for going to the bathroom without a reminder. Remember, however, that the child began the behavior in an effort to gain attention. Continue to give her praise and reinforcement for appropriate behaviors just as you do with the other children in the class.

The CD-ROM that accompanies this text contains several hypothetical scenarios designed for you to apply the guidance principles suggested in the various chapters of this book. Go to the Your Turn section of the CD to access these scenarios. Scenarios 7 and 8 are particularly pertinent to this section of the text, Emotional and Dependent Behaviors.

chapter 33

Clinging

Mrs. Estes returns to the classroom after a break. Rusty rushes toward her and flings his arms around her legs. Three-year-old Rusty had been standing near the door, neither participating in activities nor talking to anyone, since Mrs. Estes left 10 minutes earlier. Mrs. Estes smiles and ruffles Rusty's hair, then moves across the room. Rusty releases his hold on her legs, but hangs onto her skirt and follows her around the room.

Mrs. Estes often talks to, smiles at, and touches Rusty. "Rusty, I need to get some more red paint." Mrs. Estes tells him. She tries to release the child's hold on her skirt. Rusty, however, hangs on. "Well, all right. Why don't you come with me and help me?" Rusty happily leaves the class with Mrs. Estes. An hour later, Rusty is still hanging onto her. Mrs. Estes and the other teachers are concerned. Her mobility is hampered and she is not able to give as much attention to the other children as she would like. Rusty has been clinging to Mrs. Estes since school began almost three months ago. Lately, however, this behavior is more pronounced.

STATE THE BEHAVIOR

The child clings to the teacher. The child does not engage in appropriate class activities, and the teacher's time is tied up in dealing with the child.

OBSERVE THE BEHAVIOR

Gain further insight into this behavior by informally observing the child for a few days.

When does the child usually cling to a teacher?

- Throughout the day
- Soon after he arrives at school
- Toward the end of the school day
- Around rest or nap times
- At mealtimes
- During outdoor play
- During free-choice activities
- During group times
- During teacher-planned activities
- During structured activity times
- During transitions
- At cleanup times
- When the child is required to use self-help skills (putting on a coat or undressing for the bathroom)

How does the child cling to a teacher?

- The child physically holds onto a part of the teacher or the teacher's clothing.
- The child frequently asks to be picked up.
- The child climbs onto the teacher's lap whenever the teacher is seated.
- The child puts his arms around the teacher.
- The child stays close to, but does not necessarily touch, the teacher.

To whom does the child cling?

- Any adult
- One specific teacher
- Whichever teacher first greets him in the morning

What does the child do when the teacher to whom he clings is not available (out of the room, absent for the day, or busy elsewhere)?

- The child cries.
- The child finds another teacher to cling to.
- The child does not participate in activities.
- The child joins classroom activities more than when the teacher is present.

What are the child's relations to other people?

- The child clings to his parents.
- The child parts from his parents with difficulty when brought to school.
- The child leaves school with difficulty when picked up at the end of the day.
- The child interacts with teachers other than the one to whom he clings (if he clings to only one teacher).
- The child interacts with the children at school.

These informal observations should provide you with some information about the behavior to use as you work on eliminating it.

CONSULT WITH THE FAMILY

In your observations of the child's clinging behavior, note how the child behaves around the family. If clinging seems to occur with the family member who brings the child into school and then is transferred to a teacher once the family member is finally able to leave, the family most likely is also concerned about this behavior. Thoroughly discuss with the family whether there is some circumstance in the child's life that is making him feel insecure and in need of frequent reassurance. Help the family brainstorm some ways of relieving such stressors if at all possible. Work together with the family to come up with strategies to decrease clinging. Once you have begun an approach to change the behavior, keep the family informed of progress.

CONSIDER THE IMPLICATIONS

The child who persistently clings to a teacher probably began this behavior in response to a need for assurance and security. A child may feel such needs when he first starts school, when his usual routine is changed, or when a traumatic event disrupts his life. At such times, the child needs to be given whatever reassurance he seeks to deal with the situation that has caused the insecurity. Once the child feels comfortable with his life, clinging should decrease and stop. Clinging is stopped by the child himself, through subtle withdrawal by the teacher, or through a combination of the child's and teacher's actions. Sometimes, however, such dependent behavior continues beyond the child's need for special reassurance. The child learns that when he clings to the teacher, he gets considerable attention.

It is also likely that if clinging persists over an extended period, the teacher begins reacting negatively to it. The teacher may be paying attention to the child, but the attention is paid in a way the reflects the teacher's annoyance, exasperation, or even anger. The child's message is, "I'll take attention in whatever way I can get." The teacher's message is, "If you force me to pay attention to you, I'll let you know indirectly how annoyed you make me feel." As a result, the child feels that he is not worth positive attention from the teacher. He feels insecure because his relations with the teacher result in a negative reaction. Therefore, the child clings all the more because he wants assurance that he is worthwhile. Clinging can lead to a self-defeating cycle in which neither child nor teacher is happy but which neither is able to break.

EXPLORE ALTERNATIVES

Consider the following suggestions for a resolution to the problem of the child who clings to the teacher:

- Carefully examine possible reasons for the child's behavior. There may be a real need that causes the child to feel insecure. If clinging began recently, check with the family to determine whether something unusual is upsetting the child. Talk with the child to ask what is bothering him. If you can pinpoint the reason for the behavior, you can help the child understand the situation better and find appropriate ways to deal with it.*

- If the child clings to only one adult but is a functioning member of the class when that adult is absent, you may find the cause of the issue outside the child. This teacher may behave in a way that invites clinging by the child. When this is the case, the teacher should examine such behavior and how it affects the way the child acts. The effect this teacher causes should be discussed in a helpful and nonthreatening manner. It would be helpful if such a discussion is based on objective observations made by another teacher or the director of the school.

- To record such observations, an adult should write down as clearly as possible everything that was verbally and nonverbally conveyed at a time when the child was clinging to the teacher. (Direct quotes, gestures, and facial expressions should be noted.) The observations should contain no interpretations by the writer but

*A child who has a history of neglect or abuse will have special needs, including a need for much positive attention. If you know that the child's background includes abusive or neglectful experiences, your role as a nurturing adult in the child's life and the attention you give him are very important. Also, a child with a serious visual deficit may feel the need to cling to an adult because he is afraid to move around the room on his own. In such a case, the child needs to be helped to learn the parameters of the room by having an adult take him on a systematic "tour" of the classroom and pointing out, verbally and by feel, where key features are. At the same time, the room needs to be kept free of unexpected stumbling blocks.

should be based on what visibly happened. Objective observations can be recorded in a 10- to 15-minute period. You need only a few of these for valuable information on what actually happens to cause the child's clinging behavior. By pinpointing the cause, the behavior can be more easily changed.

- The child may cling because he feels uncomfortable in the class. Perhaps the child has been placed in a class where the children are older and larger than he is or are beyond his developmental level. He may feel justifiably insecure in this setting and therefore clings to the teacher. If this is the case, move the child to a more appropriate class, if possible.

If none of these suggestions helps deal with the concern, then continue to the following steps.

STATE THE GOAL

The goal is for the child not to cling to a teacher but to engage constructively in the ongoing activities of the class.

APPROACH

The basic approach to stop clinging behavior involves four steps:

- Tell the child what is expected of him.
- Move away from the child when he starts to cling.
- Give reinforcement when the child engages in desired activities.
- Set aside time for special attention, depending on whether or not the child clings.

DEFINITION

Clinging behavior involves all actions that keep the child close to the teacher, such as following, hugging, grabbing, or holding onto clothing. The teachers, as a group, should list all behaviors they consider to be clinging so they agree on a definition.

STARTING POINT

Ascertain how much of the time the child clings before continuing. For three days establish what percentage of time the child spends clinging to the teacher. Decide on one particular hour during which you expect considerable clinging to occur. Time how much of that hour the child clings to the teacher. The total number of minutes the child clings can then be converted into a percentage.

$$\frac{\text{Number of Minutes of Clinging}}{60 \text{ Minutes}} \times 100 = \% \text{ of Clinging}$$

For instance, if the child clings 45 minutes out of the hour, compute as follows:

$$\frac{45}{60} = 0.75 \text{ or } 75\%$$

Transfer this percentage to the Percentage Record-Keeping Graph. These three days of baseline provide a basis for comparing later progress.

STRATEGIES

After establishing a baseline, begin the following approach. It is important that it be followed consistently by those to whom the child clings and supported by all other adults in the classroom.

Let the Child Know Your Expectations. Tell the child what behaviors you expect from him in place of clinging. Tell him that you do not appreciate his clinging because it prevents him from participating in planned classroom activities, prevents you from doing your job, and deprives other children of your attention. Explaining these reasons will help you convey why you often feel annoyed when he clings. Be sure to express your feelings honestly. Be careful to assure the child that it is his behavior, and not him, that upsets you.

Emphasize the behaviors that you appreciate and will reinforce. Tell the child that from now on you will ignore clinging but will pay attention to him when he behaves in appropriate ways. Explain how he can earn special attention from you by not clinging.

Move Away from the Child When He Starts to Cling. Whenever the child starts clinging to you, move away. If you are seated, stand up. If you are standing, walk elsewhere. If you are not busy, find something to do. You may have to remove the child physically by gently undoing the grasp he has on you. The main point of moving away from the child is to give as little attention as possible when he clings. Say nothing. Do not show concern, exasperation, amusement, or any other emotion related to the clinging by facial or bodily expressions. Remember that any reaction is reinforcement because you convey to the child that he is affecting you. It may be difficult to carry out this step, but be persistent. The sooner you convince the child, by ignoring him, that clinging will get him no attention, the sooner the behavior will stop.

Reinforce Appropriate Behaviors as Often as Possible. While you ignore clinging, take every opportunity to praise the child for appropriate behaviors. Any participation in activities, interaction with peers, or other desired behavior should be well reinforced.

If the child participates in a limited way in classroom activities, reinforce his efforts, even if these are only approximations of what you want. As time passes, you can expect more of the child before you give praise.

At first, be constantly on the lookout for things to praise. Once clinging begins to decrease, you can gradually decrease the amount of reinforcement you give. By the time clinging has been eliminated, praise the child as often as you do other children.

Consider what kind of reinforcement is most meaningful to the child. Because the child seems to seek physical contact through clinging, reinforce with hugs and pats as well as with verbal praise.

Provide a Time for Special Attention, If the Child Does Not Cling. Set aside a special time of 5 to 10 minutes per day to spend one-to-one with the child. This time will provide the child with positive, undivided attention. After the first day, provide this time if the child decreases the clinging behavior.

During the special time, make sure the child has your undivided attention. To do this, you will need to have the cooperation of all the teachers. Let the child decide how the five minutes will be spent. Tell him, "I have five minutes to spend just with you." On a clock or watch, show the child when the time will be over. Tell the child that you and he will do whatever he wants. Be prepared with some suggestions, such as taking a walk, reading a book, or playing a game, in case he is unsure of how he would like to spend the time.

Do not expand the time. At the end, tell the child that the special time will be held again the next day.

1. On the first day, have the special time as soon as the child arrives at school. Make whatever arrangements you need to provide the five minutes. At the end of the first session, tell the child that the special time will be held a little later the next day.

2. On the second day, tell the child as soon as he arrives at school that the special time will be held in a few minutes if he does not cling to you but instead gets involved in an activity. Wait no longer than 10 minutes.

    Hold the special time if the child did not engage in clinging behavior. Start out the special time by praising him for expected behaviors. Do not wait the full 10 minutes to give other reinforcement.

If the child is unable to refrain from clinging, do not hold the special time. Tell him that he will have another chance the next day and explain why you will not hold it this day. Shorten the waiting time a bit the next day.

3. When the child has three successive days of special time, lengthen the waiting time to 15 minutes. Continue holding the special time somewhat later every few days. The child should be able to spend increasingly longer periods being constructively engaged in activities and not clinging. If he is not, then slow down the rate of increasing the waiting period to the special time. Pace the timing to ensure success for the child.

4. When there is a marked decrease in the overall rate of clinging, begin having the special time every other day. Tell the child what you are doing and why. Cut back special times even further as behavior changes. Be sure to continue giving the child attention for appropriate behavior and general positive interaction.

Continue Keeping Track of the Behavior. Continue measuring the behavior so that you are aware of improvement. Use the same hour of the day to time clinging as you did during the initial count. Compute the percentage of time the child clings to the teacher in the same way you did during the first three days of observing him, and record these daily percentages on the Percentage Record-Keeping Graph.

MAINTAINING THE CHANGES

Once the child has stopped clinging, continue to reinforce appropriate behaviors periodically. Let the child know what behaviors you value by praising these. If the child tries to cling, ignore it. Be sensitive to the child's need for assurance, but do not offer it by allowing him to cling.

The CD-ROM that accompanies this text contains several hypothetical scenarios designed for you to apply the guidance principles suggested in the various chapters of this book. Go to the Your Turn section of the CD to access these scenarios. Scenarios 7 and 8 are particularly pertinent to this section of the text, Emotional and Dependent Behaviors.

chapter 34

Seeking Attention

For Lisa, the day usually begins in the child care center at 7:00 A.M. She immediately heads for Mrs. Mason, one of the teachers. At three and a half, Lisa is a very precocious and verbal child. She loves to talk to the three teachers in the classroom and converses with any other adult who walks into the room. Throughout the day, Lisa follows a teacher around, asking questions or talking incessantly. She expects attention and responses from the adults.

At first, Lisa's chatter was enjoyable to the teachers. They found her bright and amusing. Recently, the teachers have become aware that they spend an inordinate amount of time with Lisa at the expense of time spent with the other children. Lisa spends little time with her peers, apparently preferring the company of adults. However, when she is with other children, she seems to be quite able to interact.

The teachers have begun to tell Lisa that they do not have time to talk with her, but such statements leave her undaunted. She usually returns within half a minute with another question or statement. Mrs. Mason notices that none of the teachers approaches Lisa. She always seems to approach them. Also, the teachers rarely call on Lisa during group discussion times.

STATE THE BEHAVIOR

The child requires the attention of the teachers more often than is necessary. The teachers find themselves giving time to this child more than to the other children. The requests for attention are usually unnecessary and not related to a specific need, other than for attention.

OBSERVE THE BEHAVIOR

Spend some time observing to gather information that can give you a clue to the behavior.

When do bids for attention usually come?
- At any time of day
- During specific activity times
- During structured activities
- During free-choice activities
- During meals
- During nap
- At toileting times
- When indoors
- When outdoors
- When it is time to go home
- When other children require a teacher's help

From whom does the child request attention?
- Any adult
- A familiar teacher
- A specific teacher

How is attention requested?
- The child asks questions of the teacher.
- The child talks to the teacher about herself.
- The child talks repeatedly about the same subject.
- The child hints at a concern or problem.
- The child asks for help in getting materials.
- The child asks for help when the teacher is talking with someone else.
- The child interrupts when the teacher is talking with someone else.
- The child asks for physical attention such as hugs, being picked up, and help in dressing or undressing.
- The child sticks close to the teacher's side.
- The child calls for attention from other parts of the room.

What else might be relevant?

- Interaction with other children—often such a child does not have satisfactory interaction skills with peers.
- Participation in activities—the child may not get involved in activities because her energies are directed elsewhere, namely toward the teachers.

This informal observation will help you approach the behavior systematically. It will be helpful to know when to implement your plan and who can best implement it.

CONSULT WITH THE FAMILY

Once you have had the opportunity to observe the child's attention bids carefully for a few days, plan a meeting with the family. Discuss that you are concerned because the child does not appear to participate as much in activities and social interactions as she might. Find out if the child has always been drawn more to adults than to children. Also try to discern whether family members are extremely busy and have limited time to spend with their child. In addition, ask whether there has been a recent event in the child's life that has made her anxious and in need of frequent reassurance. Share strategies that you plan to use to change the undue attention bids from the child. The family might be interested in instituting "special time" at home with the child as one way of providing her with unconditional and undivided attention. Continue to keep in touch with the family to let them know of decreases in attention-getting behavior.

CONSIDER THE IMPLICATIONS

It is important to be aware of how the teacher is affected by the child's behavior. All children need attention. When a child requests an undue amount of attention, it is easy for the teacher to get exasperated and then give attention in negative ways. If tired of the constant requests, the teacher may respond in a cross manner. The child is thus reinforced negatively for seeking attention.

The teacher may begin to avoid the child because she already requests such a large share of time. The teacher may rarely attend to this child except when the child is asking for attention. The child thus does not get reinforced for any appropriate behaviors that occur during the times when she is not seeking attention. The child also learns that the only way to get attention is to pester the teacher. The child does this more because she wants the attention. As a result, the child feels negatively about herself as a person, since the teacher's attention is neither spontaneous nor positive.

EXPLORE ALTERNATIVES

There might be a fairly simple resolution to the concern, particularly if a change in the environment can remedy the situation. Consider the following possibilities:

- There may be an unusual event in the child's life, such as a new baby or a death in the family. Perhaps the child is seeking reassurance. Take the time to help the child understand what is happening in her life.*
- There may not be enough materials and activities in the classroom to interest the child. She might be seeking your attention because of boredom. In such a case, be sure to provide the age-appropriate resources to keep the child constructively occupied.
- Materials in the classroom should be easily accessible to the child. Requests for help may be based on a genuine need for assistance. Rearrange the room and storage for materials so that children can be as independent as possible at school.
- From your informal observation, you might have found that the child interacts very little with peers. The cause of seeking excessive attention may be basically poor peer interaction skills. Help the child learn how to interact appropriately with her peers. As she spends more time with peers, she will seek less attention from adults.

If the resolution of the problem does not lie in one of these suggestions, it is time to use a more detailed approach.

STATE THE GOAL

The goal is for the child to seek attention from the teacher in a positive manner and no more frequently than the other children in the class.

APPROACH

The basic approach involves providing attention for appropriate behaviors while withholding it for excessive bids for attention through the following steps:

- Ignore all unnecessary bids for attention.
- Give the child attention at other times.
- Plan a "special time" each day.

*A child who has a history of neglect or abuse will have special needs, including a need for much positive attention. If you know that the child's background includes abusive or neglectful experiences, your role, as a nurturing adult in the child's life, and the attention you give her are very important.

DEFINITION

Seeking attention is any overly frequent and unnecessary verbal or nonverbal demand for a teacher's attention.

STARTING POINT

Before implementing changes, keep track of how often the child requests attention. Decide on a one-hour time block each day to keep a record, and mark on paper each bid for attention. The period should be a time when the child usually asks for attention frequently and the teachers are free to participate. At the end of each day, count up the number of marks and record them on the Frequency Record-Keeping Graph. Keep track for three consecutive days. This provides your baseline.

STRATEGIES

After you have determined the amount of attention-seeking for three days, begin the following approach. These strategies must be followed consistently by all teachers for them to be effective.

Ignore All Unnecessary Bids for Attention. When the child approaches you, determine first whether her request is reasonable and appropriate. If the request is reasonable, then help the child as needed. If, however, her request is an unnecessary bid for attention, tell the child, "I am sorry, but I must do _____ now." Physically turn away or walk to another area of the room.

Give the Child Attention at Other Times. When the child engages in a desired activity, let her know that you are pleased with her behavior. If the child responds to verbal praise, say, with a smile, "I like how you are working!" "Thank you for helping us pick up." "Wow! You're doing _____ really well!" If the child enjoys physical contact, give her a hug or a pat.

Plan a Special Time Each Day. A special time of five minutes per day may be spent on a one-to-one basis with the child. It provides undivided, positive attention to let the child know that she is special and that attention from the teacher can be a positive experience for both. After the first day, whether you provide this special time depends on the child's behavior. You must be able to do your work, and she must do her work until the special time.

During the special time, make sure the child has your undivided attention. You need the cooperation of all the teachers to accomplish this. Let the child determine how the five minutes are to be spent. Say, "I have five minutes to spend with you." Show her on a clock or watch when the time will be over. "We can do whatever you'd like." If the child is unsure of what she would like to do, you might suggest talking, playing a game, taking a walk, reading a book, or another favorite activity of the child's.

Do not extend the time past five minutes. At the end, tell the child that tomorrow you will do this again.

The timing for this special time is important.

1. On the first day, the special time should occur as soon as the child arrives at school. At the end of the first session, tell the child that tomorrow the special time will be held a little later in the morning.

2. On the second day, tell the child immediately that the special time will be held in a few minutes *if* she lets you do your work and she does her work until then. Be specific in telling the child what your expectations are.

   The timing of the special time depends on the information in your initial count. Determine the average time of attention-seeking for the three days. If the child sought attention three times in one hour, the average is 20 minutes. If the behavior was recorded 12 times an hour, the average is five minutes.

   Let the number of minutes of the average time pass after the arrival of the child, and then hold the special time. Continue the special time on that schedule for three days.

   If the child is not able to refrain from unnecessary attention bids during the waiting time, do not hold the special time. Explain to the child why you did not have special time, and assure her that she will have a chance the next day. Shorten the waiting time a bit the next day.

3. When the child has three successive days of special time, begin to lengthen the waiting time by a few minutes. As the child's behavior changes, extend the waiting time every few days. The child should be able to go for increasingly longer periods being constructively engaged in activities and not asking for undue attention. If she does not, then slow down the rate of increasing the waiting time. Arrange the timing to ensure success for the child.

4. When you see a marked decrease in the overall rate of attention-seeking, have special times every other day. Be sure to tell the child what you are doing. Cut back the special times even further as behavior changes. Of course, general interaction should continue.

Continue Keeping Track of the Behavior. Throughout this time, keep track of behavior on the graph. Continue recording the number of attempts to seek attention for one hour a day. This should be the same time of day used during the initial count.

MAINTAINING THE CHANGES

Continue giving the child attention for expected behaviors as you do with all the children. If there is an occasional slip, ignore it. Let the child know that she is special and that you appreciate appropriate behavior. Remember, too, that as the child seeks less attention from adults, she receives reinforcement from other sources, including peers.

The CD-ROM that accompanies this text contains several hypothetical scenarios designed for you to apply the guidance principles suggested in the various chapters of this book. Go to the Your Turn section of the CD to access these scenarios. Scenarios 7 and 8 are particularly pertinent to this section of the text, Emotional and Dependent Behaviors.

chapter 35

Whining

At teacher conferences, five-year-old Eric is a frequent topic of conversation. The teachers feel very frustrated with Eric's constant whining at preschool. Eric rarely talks without a whine and often complains. Common statements include "Teacher, they won't let me play." "Teacher, there's not enough paint for me." "Teacher, I hurt my finger." "Teacher, I want to go outside now." "Teacher, I can't get my belt unbuckled." "Teacher, I can't find my jacket." On closer examination, teachers usually find that there is enough paint, that the finger shows no signs of injury, or that the jacket is exactly where it usually is.

The teachers have been answering Eric in increasingly more impatient and exasperated ways. Often, they turn the other way when they see him coming. They rarely approach Eric to talk to him.

STATE THE BEHAVIOR

The child frequently whines when talking to adults.

OBSERVE THE BEHAVIOR

Spend some time observing and gathering information to gain insight into the child's behavior.

When does whining usually occur?

- At all times of day
- At particular times, such as early or late in the day
- At mealtimes
- At nap time
- During group activities
- During free-choice activities
- During transitions

What message is usually accompanied by whining?

- The child requests help from the teacher.
- The child complains about another child.
- The child wants the teacher's attention.
- The child asks to be held or picked up.
- The child does not want to do something.
- The child wants attention for an injury, real or imagined.
- The child wants a toy that another child is using.
- The child conveys any and all messages to adults.

To whom does the child whine?

- All adults
- A specific teacher
- Children as well as adults
- The parents or other family members

From this informal observation, you should have some idea of when and under what circumstances whining usually occurs. This helps you to implement a systematic approach, because you are able to anticipate whining and thus deal with it more effectively. It also indicates which adults or teachers should implement the plan. If the child whines mainly to one teacher, that teacher should confront the behavior. If the child whines to all adults, all teachers need to be involved in the implementation.

CONSULT WITH THE FAMILY

In most cases, whining is a habit that the child uses in most interactions with all adults. If whining seems to occur only at school, however, deal with the behavior in the school setting, especially engaging in self-examination to see what might be sustaining it. On the other hand, if whining is a concern to both family and teachers, you can brainstorm with the family to come up with ideas for decreasing and eventually eliminating the behavior.

Share strategies that you think will be effective in eliminating whining while encouraging a more normal tone of voice. Stress that the aim is not to decrease the amount of attention the child is getting but to shift the attention from times when the child whines to times when he does not. Keep the family informed of progress toward the goal of eliminating whining.

CONSIDER THE IMPLICATIONS

Whining is a learned behavior. At some point in early life, a child may learn that by whining he gets attention. Perhaps the adults in the child's life do not attend to him consistently when he speaks in a normal tone of voice. He tries alternatives to get attention and discovers that talking in a whining voice usually gets someone to listen. A pattern is established over time. The child wants attention and finds that adults give it more often when he whines. The adults pay attention to the child when he whines because they find the whining annoying and feel a need to get rid of the annoyance. This attention is given in a negative manner, in exasperation or even anger. The child finds that adults usually listen to him when he whines, but that their reaction is usually unresponsive and unfriendly.

A teacher may attend briefly when the child whines, to get rid of the whining, but otherwise ignores him for fear that he might whine again. The behavior pattern is strengthened as the child gets the attention he needs by whining. The price of getting that attention, however, is that the attention is basically negative. As whining becomes more and more a part of everyday communication, the child feels less and less secure about his self-worth because of the reactions of others.

EXPLORE ALTERNATIVES

From your informal observation, there might be some clues to help you deal with the whiner. Consider the following:

- The child may whine primarily to one teacher. This teacher's behavior may encourage whining in the child. The adult may, for example, ignore the child when he talks in a normal tone of voice. A careful self-examination by this teacher, with the help of other staff members, might disclose the underlying events. The teacher can then change the behavior as needed and help the child to stop whining before it becomes a habit. In addition, the staff should consider the strategies discussed in this chapter and use them to deal with whining. These strategies can be used by one teacher or several teachers, as appropriate.

- If the child does not whine with his family but only in the school setting, there is probably some factor in the school environment that elicits such behavior. A careful examination of the child's actions at school might uncover the root of the problem.
- Some children whine when they get tired. Your observations should tell you if this is the case. If so, plan an earlier rest or nap time, or channel the child into quiet activities when whining begins.

In most cases, whining is a long-established habit that is exhibited both at home and at school. For habitual whiners, the following approach should be used.

STATE THE GOAL

The goal is for the child to communicate with adults without whining.

APPROACH

Basically, the approach involves the simultaneous use of two steps:
- Refuse to listen to whining.
- Systematically shape nonwhining behavior.

DEFINITION

Whining is any verbal communication in which the child does not speak in a normal voice but instead uses a complaining, usually nasal, tone.

STARTING POINT

For three days, before implementing any changes, keep track of how much whining occurs each day. You will want to know not just how often the child whines but what proportion of verbal communications are made in a whining voice. Select an hour of the day when you expect a considerable amount of whining. This same hour should be used whenever you count incidents of whining. Each teacher should have a conveniently located pencil and paper with a line drawn down the middle of the sheet. Each time the child talks to a teacher without whining, it should be recorded in one column. Each time the child whines should be recorded on the other side. At the end of the time, combine the counts from all the teachers. Compute the percentage of time the child whines.

$$\frac{\text{Whines}}{\text{Whines} + \text{Nonwhines}} \times 100 = \% \text{ of Whining}$$

If there are no nonwhines, then the child whined 100% of the time. If the child whined 20 times and did not whine 10 times, then he whined 67% of the time.

$$\frac{20}{20 + 10} = \frac{20}{30} = 0.67 \times 100 = 67\%$$

A percentage score gives an accurate idea of how much whining there actually is in relation to all communication. Record this percentage score on Percentage Record-Keeping Graph for three days to provide a baseline.

STRATEGIES

Once you have the baseline, begin the following approach. All teachers to whom the child usually whines must implement these steps consistently.

For the First Week, Whenever the Child Whines, Tell Him Your Expectations. Follow these steps:

1. Get to the child's eye level and say to him, "I cannot understand you when you whine. Please tell me again without whining."
2. If the child restates his comment without whining, say, "Good! Now I can understand you!" Answer his question, or comment on his statement, as appropriate. This attention is very important.
3. If the child repeats his statement with a whine, repeat that you cannot understand him. Praise him if he talks without a whine after your second try.
4. If the third repetition is still a whine, say, "I'll be glad to listen to you when you can tell me without whining." At this point, model for the child what you expect. State in a clear and uncomplaining manner a sentence conveying what the child wants, and ask him to repeat it after you.
5. If, after your modeling, the child still whines, get up and move elsewhere. Any immediate repeats of whining should be ignored. Nonwhining should be well praised.
6. Handle each incident of whining in this manner.
7. At the same time, take every possible opportunity to praise and reinforce appropriate behaviors.

In the Second Week, Give the Child Fewer Cues. After one full week of being directly told that you cannot understand him when he whines, the child should understand that you expect him to talk without whining.

1. If the child spontaneously talks without whining, tell him each time that you like the way he is talking.

2. If the child tells you something in a whine, do not say anything, but look directly at him. Your silence and expectant look should serve as a cue to repeat without a whine.

3. If the child now repeats his statement in a normal tone of voice, let him know you are pleased.

4. If the child again whines, tell him, "I'm sorry, but I cannot understand you," and turn away. If he approaches you after this without a whine, deal with his questions and praise him.

In the Third Week, Withdraw All Cues. If after two weeks the child has stopped most whining, he is indicating that he understands your expectations.

1. Praise the child less frequently for nonwhining behavior. Gradually cut back reinforcement. Reinforce every other time for a few days, then less and less frequently.

2. Give the child attention for other behaviors, as you do with the other children in the class. Continue to be responsive when he talks with you. Remember, the child's habit of whining began when he did not receive adequate attention from adults for talking in a normal tone of voice.

3. If occasionally the child whines, ignore it. Do not respond. He will probably repeat his statement without whining. Then be sure to pay close attention to let him know that you are pleased with his behavior.

 Continue Keeping Track of the Behavior. Throughout this time, continue recording the percentage of whining on the graph. Count original communications only. If the child whines and then repeats himself without whining after the teacher's response, the corrected nonwhining behavior is not counted. By the end of the second week, the percentage of whining should be below 25. If it is not, continue this approach during the second week until it is.

MAINTAINING THE CHANGES

If whining occurs at home, this would be a good time to share your success with the child's family. Encourage and help them to try this approach at home. At school, continue to give full attention to the child when he communicates with you. If he whines, ignore it.

The CD-ROM that accompanies this text contains several hypo- thetical scenarios designed for you to apply the guidance principles suggested in the various chapters of this book. Go to the Your Turn section of the CD to access these scenarios. Scenarios 7 and 8 are particularly pertinent to this section of the text, Emotional and Dependent Behaviors.

chapter 36

Self-Stimulation

It is group time, and Allysa, age four, listens to the story the teacher is reading. After a couple of minutes her eyes wander away from the page and scan the room. She rubs her right knee with her left hand, then starts scratching up her thigh. With her other hand, she pulls up her dress and continues to scratch at the top of her leg. Her fingers move inside her panties and she starts to rub herself. She stares over the teacher's head, continuing to rub herself for the remaining 12 minutes of the story and song. At the end of group time, Allysa gets up with the other children and moves on to the next activity.

Later, during nap, she again self-stimulates, putting herself to sleep. The teachers are uncomfortable with Allysa's behavior but have not said anything to her. The parent of another child has commented on it to the director.

STATE THE BEHAVIOR

The child regularly self-stimulates.

OBSERVE THE BEHAVIOR

Observe the child for a few days to gain some insights into the behavior.

When is the child most likely to self-stimulate?

- Unpredictably, any time of the day
- Throughout the day
- During nap time
- Early in the day
- Toward the end of the day
- During free-choice activities
- When children sit quietly to listen
- During transitions

What usually precedes self-stimulation?

- The child is not engaged in an activity.
- The child plays alone.
- The child seems upset.
- The child seems tired.
- The child expresses disinterest in ongoing activities.

Where is the child when she self-stimulates?

- Indoors
- Outside
- On a nap cot or mat
- In the bathroom
- In the housekeeping or dramatic play area

What happens when the child self-stimulates?

- She is told to stop.
- She is told that what she is doing is "wrong" or "bad" or something "nice children don't do."
- She looks around to see if anyone is watching her.

How long does the child usually self-stimulate?

- Very briefly
- For a few minutes at a time
- For long periods
- Until she is asleep
- Continues even after she falls asleep

How does the child talk about her self-stimulation?

- In negative terms
- In guilty terms
- In a way that calls attention to the self-stimulation
- In a matter-of-fact way

These observations should provide you with some insights into the circumstances under which the child engages in self-stimulating behavior.

CONSULT WITH THE FAMILY

Discussion of sexually related behavior is not a comfortable topic for everyone. If you feel uncomfortable talking about self-stimulation, you may want to have another adult handle this discussion with the family. It is important to talk with the family if the child does not seem to distinguish between private and public settings for the behavior. If the family tells you that they are not particularly concerned and consider the behavior normal, then discuss a common strategy with which both you and the family are comfortable to help the child confine the behavior to an appropriate setting. If the family is upset about the child's self-stimulation, you should discuss their concerns and feelings in an accepting and matter-of-fact manner. You can offer reading material to the family to reassure them that the behavior is normal for young children and to reinforce what you are telling them. Later in this chapter, more detailed suggestions are provided about communicating with family members about self-stimulation.

CONSIDER THE IMPLICATIONS

Self-stimulation is a fairly common act among young children. Body exploration starts in infancy, and the child soon discovers pleasurable sensations while playing with the genital area. But such body play is disconcerting to many adults. They may subtly or not so subtly convey negative messages to the child by consistently removing the child's hands, slapping, or saying "No!" or "Bad!" Such messages can set up conflicting feelings in the child. On the one hand, the child is made to feel guilty about the genital play, while, on the other hand, such stimulation feels pleasurable and soothing. The guilt and shame set up by these negative messages can have a long-lasting impact, affecting adolescent and adult sexuality as well as identity.

Self-stimulation by young children should be considered normal; however, what should be addressed with preschoolers is the issue of privacy and what kinds of behaviors are appropriate in public and private settings. Self-stimulation can be accepted as a private behavior in which the child may engage in a private place.

EXPLORE ALTERNATIVES

It is important to give careful thought to why a child might be self-stimulating, and to the reactions and attitudes of the adults around her, both family and school staff. This topic needs to be handled sensitively.

- A child who has been sexually abused may self-stimulate because she has been stimulated in the abusive situation by an adult. This is *not* a normal reason for self-stimulation by a child. A child who has been abused may give verbal or behavioral clues, talking about or acting out sexual acts that are beyond the normal knowledge or experience of preschoolers. If the teacher suspects that the child is or has been the victim of sexual abuse, she has legal and ethical obligations to report her suspicions after discussion with the director.*

- Be sure that the genital play is not a sign of a bladder or vaginal infection. The child may actually be rubbing herself because she hurts.

- Children react differently to anxiety, and some may respond by self-stimulation to make themselves feel better. If you see a variety of signs of anxious behavior in a child, take time to talk to her and try to find out what is bothering her.

These suggestions alone may help you resolve your concerns about the child who self-stimulates. Continue to the next section if the child frequently and openly engages in this behavior; if this behavior concerns the family; and if others in the school setting, both adults and children, notice and comment on the behavior.

STATE THE GOAL

The goal is for the child to avoid self-stimulation in places designated as inappropriate.

APPROACH

To have the child not engage in self-stimulation in places designated as inappropriate, the basic approach the following steps:

- Discuss the self-stimulation with all staff who are involved with the child.

- Discuss the self-stimulation with the child's family.

---

*A child who has been sexually abused has special emotional needs. The teachers' understanding, acceptance, and support are extremely important to such a child.

- Discuss privacy and social acceptability of self-stimulation with the child.
- Remind the child gently if she self-stimulates in an inappropriate situation or place.

DEFINITION

Self-stimulation involves the child's using her hands to play with, rub, or fondle the genital area. In this case, self-stimulation in public places is considered reason for changing the behavior.

STARTING POINT

Before attempting to change the child's behavior, discuss the matter with other staff. Keep in mind that the behavior you want to change is self-stimulation in a public, inappropriate setting. The child's home, for instance, may be the appropriate place. Decide what is acceptable before starting.

Spend three to five days recording how often, for how long, and in what public circumstances the child self-stimulates. Each time the behavior occurs, clock and write on a piece of paper how long and in what circumstances the child self-stimulated. Use this list to determine when and where the child self-stimulates. At the end of each day, record the total number of incidents of self-stimulation on the Frequency Record-Keeping Graph. On the Duration Record-Keeping Graph, record the average duration for all the day's occurrences. Add up the total number of minutes for all incidents, then divide by the number of incidents to determine average duration:

$$\frac{\text{Total Minutes of All Self-Stimulation}}{\text{Total Number of Incidents}} = \text{Average Duration}$$

These graphs will help you measure progress.

STRATEGIES

While you are collecting initial information, you can begin the first two steps: discussion with staff and family. The last two steps, discussion with the child and reminders if the child does engage in the behavior inappropriately, should not be implemented until afterward.

Discuss Self-Stimulation with the Staff. Our reactions to sexually related matters differ greatly, depending on our own upbringing, experiences, and information. Attitudes toward self-stimulation can vary among the staff from acceptance of the behavior as normal to conviction that the behavior is bad and should be stopped before it does irreparable harm. All staff who work with the child, as well as the director, should be included in this discussion. It might be helpful to invite a professional who is knowledgeable about the topic to join the discussion. At this meeting, the discussion should focus on each person's attitudes about self-stimulation and the person's observations of the child relating to self-stimulation. The outcome of this meeting should be a common agreement about what is and what is not acceptable. The staff should agree on the situations in which self-stimulation is not socially acceptable. Such agreement will depend on the staff's attitudes and opinions and may conclude that general classroom activity is not an acceptable circumstance in which the child can self-stimulate.

Discuss Self-Stimulation with the Family. Just as teachers may have strong opinions about self-stimulation, so family members may react in different ways. Some may accept the behavior as normal and not be concerned, while others will carry a variety of opinions, ideas, and possible misconceptions about the topic. You need to be prepared for a meeting with family and have information about the topic. Written material by a credible authority, which you can recommend for them to read, might also be helpful. Depending on the feelings of the family, the opinions of the staff, and the circumstances in which self-stimulation occurs, there are different avenues you may take:

- If the family is not concerned about self-stimulation and the child's behavior occurs in private circumstances, you need not pursue any course of action.
- If the family is not concerned about self-stimulation but the child's behavior occurs frequently and in public circumstances, you should discuss this with the family. Children eventually learn that some behaviors are not socially acceptable in public and that these behaviors should be carried out in privacy. You and the family can work together to help the child learn this distinction without making the child feel guilty or ashamed.
- If the family is concerned about the self-stimulation but the staff is not, a discussion may resolve the issue. Family members may be reassured to hear you say that the behavior is common. If the family continues to be concerned, you may want to state the school's position that self-stimulation is not a bad behavior and that the teachers will only respond if it occurs in inappropriate circumstances.

- If both you and the family are concerned about the self-stimulation because it occurs frequently in public circumstances, then you should come to an agreement about how you both can deal with it. It is helpful to the child if a similar approach is taken at home and at school.

Discuss the Self-Stimulation with the Child. Once the staff and family have had the opportunity to share information, concerns, and feelings about the child's self-stimulation, and once baseline information has been taken, you should spend some private time with the child to discuss self-stimulation. Listen to what the child has to tell you on this topic also the following points:

- Self-stimulation is a common behavior among children.
- Self-stimulation is a private behavior.
- Self-stimulation should not be done in public but in places designated as acceptable.

Your discussion with the child is intended to be reassuring and not in any way punitive or negative; thus, an accepting approach is vital. Children are very sensitive to underlying feelings, and if what you say is not congruent with what you feel, you may still convey a negative message to the child. If you feel negative or ambivalent about the normalcy of self-stimulation by young children, then it may be better if another staff member talks with the child about this.

Remind the Child If Self-Stimulation Occurs in an Inappropriate Circumstance. The child may continue to self-stimulate occasionally in inappropriate places even after you have had a discussion with her. If this occurs, give her a gentle reminder of your discussion. Be sure that this is done in a discreet way that does not embarrass the child. Remind her that you agreed on circumstances that are acceptable for self-stimulation and that where she is doing this is not one of those places. You may want to redirect the child into an activity if that is appropriate at the time.

Continue Keeping Track of the Behavior. Continue to count frequency and duration of self-stimulation after you have started implementing these strategies, and record them on the graphs. It is quite likely that you will see a quick drop in inappropriate circumstances in which the child self-stimulates. When the graph shows no self-stimulation in inappropriate circumstances for a period of two weeks, you have achieved your goal and do not need to continue recording data.

MAINTAINING THE CHANGES

Once the child internalizes the messages you have conveyed, she will probably discontinue self-stimulating in inappropriate circumstances. In case there is an occasional lapse, a gentle reminder should resolve the situation.

The CD-ROM that accompanies this text contains several hypothetical scenarios designed for you to apply the guidance principles suggested in the various chapters of this book. Go to the Your Turn section of the CD to access these scenarios. Scenarios 7 and 8 are particularly pertinent to this section of the text, Emotional and Dependent Behaviors.

SECTION 6

Participation in **Social and School** Activities

Nonsharing • Bribery • Stealing • Noncompliance • Disrupting Group Time • Leaving the Classr
nning Aimlessly Around the Classroom • Shouting in the Classroom • Dropping Objects to Create N
aring Books • Breaking Toys • Flushing Objects Down the Toilet • Wasting Paper • Destroying the W
thers • Throwing Tantrums • Pouting • Baby Talk • Thumb-Sucking • Pant-Wetting • Clinging • See
ention • • Nonparticipation in Activities • Nonparticipation in Social Play • Shyness at Group Tir
ing with Only One Toy • Infrequent Large Muscle Activity • Infrequent Dramatic-Play Participatio
ng Infrequently • Short Attention Span • Finicky Eating • Overeating • Messy Eating • Hording Fo
ng • Biting • Throwing Objects at Others • Hurting Others • Using Inappropriate Language • Na
ng • Nonsharing • Bribery • Stealing • Noncompliance • Disrupting Group Time • Leaving the Classr
nning Aimlessly Around the Classroom • Shouting in the Classroom • Dropping Objects to Create N
aring Books • Breaking Toys • Flushing Objects Down the Toilet • Wasting Paper • Destroying the W
thers • Throwing Tantrums • Pouting • Baby Talk • Thumb-Sucking • Pant-Wetting • Clinging • See
ention • Whining • Self-Stimulation • Nonparticipation in Activities • Nonparticipation in Social P
ness at Group Time • Playing with Only One Toy • Infrequent Large Muscle Activity • Infreq
matic-Play Participation • Talking Infrequently • Short Attention Span • Finicky Eating • Overeati
ssy Eating • Hording Food • Hitting • Biting • Throwing Objects at Others • Hurting Others •
propriate Language • Name-Calling • Nonsharing • Bribery • Stealing • Noncompliance • Disrup
up Time • Leaving the Classroom • Running Aimlessly Around the Classroom • Shouting in
sroom • Dropping Objects to Create Noise • Tearing Books • Breaking Toys • Flushing Objects D
Toilet • Wasting Paper • Destroying the Work of Others • Throwing Tantrums • Pouting • Baby
mb-Sucking • Pant-Wetting • Whining • Self-Stimulation • Nonparticipation in Activitie
nparticipation in Social Play • Shyness at Group Time • Playing with Only One Toy • Infrequent L
scle Activity • Infrequent Dramatic-Play Participation • Talking Infrequently • Short Attention Sp
cky Eating • Overeating • Messy Eating • Hording Food • Hitting • Biting • Throwing Objects at O
urting Others • Using Inappropriate Language • Name-Calling • Nonsharing • Bribery • Steali
ncompliance • Disrupting Group Time • Leaving the Classroom • Running Aimlessly Around
sroom • Shouting in the Classroom • Dropping Objects to Create Noise • Tearing Books • Breaking
ushing Objects Down the Toilet • Wasting Paper • Destroying the Work of Others • Throwing Tantr
outing • Baby Talk • Thumb-Sucking • Pant-Wetting • Clinging • Seeking Attention • Whining •
mulation • Nonparticipation in Activities • Nonparticipation in Social Play • Shyness at Group Tir
equent Large Muscle Activity • Infrequent Dramatic-Play Participation • Talking Infrequently • S
ention Span • Finicky Eating • Overeating • Messy Eating • Hording Food • Hitting • Biting • Thro
ects at Others • Hurting Others • Using Inappropriate Language • Name-Calling • Nonsharing • Br
ealing • Noncompliance • Disrupting Group Time • Leaving the Classroom • Running Aimlessly Arc
Classroom • Shouting in the Classroom • Dropping Objects to Create Noise • Tearing Books • Bre
s • Flushing Objects Down the Toilet • Wasting Paper • Destroying the Work of Others • Thro
rums • Pouting • Baby Talk • Thumb-Sucking • Pant-Wetting • Clinging • Seeking Attention • Wh

chapter 37

Nonparticipation in Activities

Throughout the class, children are busy with various activities. Four-year-old Sarah stands near the door, uninvolved and seemingly uninterested. A teacher walks by her and smiles. "Come on, Sarah, help me get out the paint." Sarah stands still and the teacher moves on to complete his errand. A few minutes later, he returns and kneels down to Sarah's eye level. He pulls Sarah toward him, puts an arm around her, and talks to her for several minutes trying to interest her in an activity. Sarah, however, stands firm in her refusal to participate. She does not resist physically. In fact, she lets herself be led around the room to the various activities. When she is brought to an activity, she simply makes no effort to become involved.

Since Sarah entered the preschool six weeks ago, she has not actively participated in any activities. The teachers have all spent considerable time with her, gently trying to interest her in what is going on. Nothing has helped. Sarah continues to be passive.

STATE THE BEHAVIOR

The child rarely or never participates in either planned or spontaneous school activities.

OBSERVE THE BEHAVIOR

Spend some time observing the child to gain further insight into this behavior.

If the child occasionally participates in activities, what are these?
- No one particular activity
- Activities in which each child works alone
- Group activities
- Listening to stories
- Looking at books
- Music
- Art
- Dramatic play
- Blocks
- Woodworking
- Outdoor play
- Sand play or water play
- Sensory activities
- Manipulative materials

What does the child do while not participating?
- The child watches other children engage in activities.
- The child looks out the window.
- The child stays near the door.
- The child cries.
- The child holds or plays with a personal possession, like a sweater or blanket.
- The child talks to no one.
- The child follows an adult or particular child around.

What does the child do when asked to join an ongoing activity?
- If coaxed, the child joins in.
- The child verbally refuses to participate.
- The child refuses nonverbally.
- The child turns away.
- The child begins to cry.
- The child pouts.
- The child goes to where the activity is being held but does not join in.

Use the information from your observations to find a way to help the child who does not participate in school activities.

CONSULT WITH THE FAMILY

After observing the child carefully, meet with the family to discuss your concern that the child is not getting as much out of the school experience as she could. Discuss the child's behavior when she is in nonschool settings. Find out what some of her favorite activities and materials are at home. Also ask if the family considers the child to be shy or a careful observer of what goes on around her. Discuss whether the child might have school-related fears that are keeping her from participating. Enlist the family's suggestions for helping the child participate more in school activities. Once you begin steps to change the child's behavior, keep the family informed of progress toward the goal.

CONSIDER THE IMPLICATIONS

A very shy child may find it difficult to join in school activities, especially if the school experience is new to her. This initial hesitation usually disappears after the child has a chance to become familiar with the school routine and develops a relationship with the teachers.

In some cases, a child may discover that nonparticipation in activities results in considerable attention from adults. These adults are anxious that all the children benefit as much as possible from the preschool experience. Concerned teachers may spend time talking to the child. They may coax the child, provide special incentives and privileges, and otherwise try to encourage her to join in. When this is the case, the attention gained by not participating becomes more attractive than the activities. The teachers' attempts to involve the child in school activities only serve to reinforce noninvolvement because of this attention they give the child.

EXPLORE THE ALTERNATIVES

Before assuming that the child's behavior needs to be changed, consider whether one of the following suggestions might remedy the situation:

- The child's reluctance to participate in school activities might be based on a genuine anxiety or fear about school or something related to school. In this case, help the child overcome such feelings. Give whatever attention and encouragement is needed to increase the child's security and trust at school. The approach outlined in this chapter is intended for a child who does not participate in activities because of the attention such behavior brings. Be very careful in deciding whether the child's motive is attention rather than anxiety or fear. The child who seeks attention usually gives clues to this underlying motivation. She looks for adult reaction, responds positively to adult attention, and subtly maintains adult responses once they are given. The child who acts out of fear withdraws from such attention. If the underlying motive is not attention, then you can work on allaying fears and building a trusting relationship.*

- Examine the classroom to be sure that materials and activities provided are suitable for the children. It is possible that the child is reluctant to participate because what is offered in the classroom does not interest her. If this is the case, move the child to a class that is better suited to her interests, or provide more appropriate materials and equipment.

- Check the child's sensory-perception skills. A child may be reluctant to engage in activities because of a hearing or visual defect that makes her reluctant to try. If the child seems to be overly clumsy or if she fails to respond to sounds and noises around her, discuss your concerns with the family, and recommend a physical examination.†

- If the child refuses to participate in only one type of activity, it is possible that she has some kind of misconception about it. Ask the child why she does not want to join the activity. A child may, for instance, not want to finger paint because she was told to stay clean, or she may resist playing with blocks because someone told her that blocks are only for boys. Once you understand the child's reason for refusing to participate in certain activities, then you can try to remedy her misconceptions.

- It should be noted that children cannot and should not be expected to participate in classroom activities constantly. Children, like adults, need time to reflect, observe, think, and rest without being perpetually busy. Some children are more active than others. Some take more time to reflect quietly on what goes on around them than others. Do not mistake a naturally reflective child for an inactive one. A child may participate in activities at times and sit by quietly to watch at other times.

- Be careful not to confuse age-appropriate behavior with nonparticipation in play. At all stages in play development, a child participates in some form of play. She may be by herself giving little attention to others, or she may be totally involved with

*Some children with emotional deficits experience unreasonable fears and anxieties. If a child has an undue fear or phobia related to school, professional help in dealing with the issue should be sought.
†Evidence that a child has a sensory deficit should be noticeable in other aspects of the child's behavior. If you suspect a sensory deficit as the cause of the child's nonparticipation, be alert for other cues to a possible hearing or visual deficit.

others. When a child begins to become aware of her peers, she may spend some time observing others rather than participating. Rather than being nonparticipation, this is the normal development of play.

If none of these suggestions provides a resolution, continue on to the following strategies.

STATE THE GOAL

The goal is for the child to become actively involved in classroom activities on a regular basis.

APPROACH

The basic strategy to deal with the child who does not participate in school activities involves two steps:

- Reinforce the child for engaging in activities by using the technique of successive approximations. This technique is defined later in this chapter.
- Ignore nonparticipation in activities.

DEFINITION

Nonparticipation in activities involves all instances when the child is not constructively and actively participating in school activities, whether these are teacher-planned or self-initiated. Nonparticipation includes standing around, not handling classroom materials, remaining apart from the class during group activities, and refusing to participate when asked. The teachers, as a group, should discuss and add to the definition any other behaviors they consider as nonparticipation. It is important that all adults share the same definition.

STARTING POINT

It is important to collect some initial information with which to compare later changes. Observe the child for a selected hour each day for three days. This hour should be one in which various activity options are available. During the hour, use a time-sampling technique to gather information. A watch or clock and a pencil and paper are necessary to collect this information. Once every five minutes, observe the child for 15 seconds. If the child meets the definition for nonparticipation, make no mark on the paper. If the child is engaged in an activity, make a mark. At the end of the hour, you will have between 0 and 12 marks. Record each day's total on the Frequency Record-Keeping Graph.

Once you have gathered this information, start these strategies. All teachers should follow them consistently to ensure success.

Use the Technique of Successive Approximations to Reinforce the Child for Engaging in School Activities.
The aim of this approach is to convey to the child that she will be given attention when she takes part in school activities and ignored when she does not. Because the child at this point engages in few activities, there may be few opportunities to give reinforcement. Therefore, the technique of successive approximation provides a way to give reinforcement more often. In the technique of successive approximations, the child is reinforced for behaviors that come nearer and nearer to the desired behavior. Participation in school activities is broken down into steps or components. Each step is closer to the desired behavior. At first, the child is reinforced for the first step, which is only an approximation of the desired behavior. When the behavior is consistently achieved, she is only reinforced for the second step, which is a closer approximation of the desired behavior. This continues until the child reaches the desired behavior through successive steps, or approximations. Follow these steps one at a time.*

1. Reinforce only those occasions when the child watches other children involved in activities. Do not react in any way if the child is not observing her peers. Ignore her at such times. When the child watches other children at play and work, reinforce her with a smile, a pat, or a comment like, "It's fun to watch, isn't it?" Do not try to coax the child into joining the activity. Your verbal comments should convey approval for what she is doing. Do not insinuate that it is less than what you want. Stay nearby and continue to convey nonverbal or verbal approval while the child watches other children engaged in activity.

2. Reinforce only on occasions when the child is within five feet of an ongoing activity that she is watching. Again, do not pay any attention to her when she is removed from areas of activity, when she does not watch a nearby activity, or when she observes an activity from across the room. If she watches an activity close by, reinforce her with a hug, a glance, a smile, or a few words to say you like what she is doing. Your actions should encourage this behavior.

This technique is particularly helpful with children who have cognitive deficits or significant developmental delays. A child who does not demonstrate even a rudimentary form of the activity can be helped by use of successive approximations.

3. Reinforce the child only when she is directly at the activity, though not necessarily participating—for example, the child sits with the group at circle time, sits at a table where manipulative games or art projects are provided, or stands directly in the midst of the housekeeping or block area. An activity should be within easy reach. If the child is not in such a position, ignore her. When she is within easy reach of an activity, reinforce her as you did in the previous two steps.

4. Expect the child to show some involvement in the activity beyond observation. This does not necessarily imply full involvement. The child may hold a toy or material, poke at a piece of clay, or stroke a doll. Reinforce her only when she shows partial involvement, and ignore her at other times. If you reinforce verbally, do not imply that she is doing less than you expect. Make comments such as, "That clay feels soft, doesn't it?" or "You're holding a piece of the kitten puzzle!"

5. This step requires full involvement in the activity. The child should participate in activities as often as do the other youngsters in the class. Provide reinforcement for involvement in school activities every time you notice it.

6. Once the child is fully involved, begin gradual decrease of reinforcement. Every few days, cut back the amount of attention you give. Finally, you should provide reinforcement at the same rate as for the other children in the group.

It should be mentioned that if the child skips over steps, reinforce the behavior that is closest to what is desired. It is possible, for instance, that after the first step, in which you reinforce observation of activity, the child suddenly participates partially in what is going on in the class. In this case, move directly from Step 1 to Step 4.

You may find that once you give reinforcement selectively, the child quickly picks up on your unspoken cues and does what is expected. Remember, her behavior is motivated by a desire for attention. Provide attention in a way that requires compliance.

Ignore Nonparticipation in Activities. The process of successive approximations tells you exactly which behaviors to ignore. When you ignore a behavior, be sure you do it fully. Show neither approval nor disapproval for what the child does. React neutrally. If the child's behavior does not meet your expectations, do not speak to her, smile at her, respond to her, or look at her directly. Try not to stay too close to her. If you have to be nearby, make it clear by your manner that you are attending to someone or something else. Watch the child so that you know when to reinforce, but do not let her know that she is the object of your interest or attention.

Continue Keeping Track of the Behavior. Use the graph to record progress. Be sure to observe and record for the same hour of the day that you used initially.

MAINTAINING THE CHANGES

When the child is fully involved in classroom activities, you have reached your goal. Continue periodic reinforcement of her involvement. If you find the child not involved on occasion, suggest an activity for her. Do not give undue attention to nonparticipation. If the behavior recurs, simply ignore it.

The CD-ROM that accompanies this text contains several hypothetical scenarios designed for you to apply the guidance principles suggested in the various chapters of this book. Go to the Your Turn section of the CD to access these scenarios. Scenarios 9 and 10 are particularly pertinent to this section of the text, Participation in Social and School Activities.

chapter 38

Nonparticipation in Social Play

The children at the preschool engage in a variety of activities. Some activities require the cooperation of several children. Five-year-old Aaron works with projects he can do by himself. He works with puzzles, matching cards, building games, and other materials. He never ventures into activities on which other youngsters are working and playing together.

Aaron is a quiet child. He never seeks out other children and is rarely sought out by them. The teachers are concerned about Aaron, who is an only child, because he seems to avoid social contact with peers. Teachers usually seek him out when he is alone, and he seems responsive to adults when they talk to him. Often, when Aaron is working by himself, a teacher will stop and sit by him, talk to him, or work with him on the activity. The teachers hoped that with time, Aaron would begin to join his peers. However, he has been in the preschool more than four months and still avoids social interactions.

STATE THE BEHAVIOR

The child rarely or never interacts with other children or participates in social play.

OBSERVE THE BEHAVIOR

Take a few days to observe the child informally to gain insight into the behavior.

What does the child do instead of participating in social play or interaction?
- The child uses only toys and materials that he can play with alone.
- The child follows adults around.
- The child follows one specific teacher around.
- The child stands or sits in one place, doing nothing observable.

What does the child do when another child or children initiate interaction?
- The child ignores the other youngsters.
- The child responds briefly.
- The child turns away.
- The child moves elsewhere.
- The child seems uncomfortable (shows facial distress or fidgets).
- The child appears relaxed.
- The child becomes aggressive.
- The child offers to share what he is playing with.
- The child accepts a toy or material another child offers him.
- The child calls a teacher to step in.

If the child occasionally interacts with other children, who are they?
- One specific child
- A few children
- Any child in the group who approaches him first
- A youngster he knows outside of school (such as a neighbor or relative)
- Shy children
- Younger or smaller children
- Older or bigger children
- Boys
- Girls

Use the information from these observations to help the child who does not interact with other children.

CONSULT WITH THE FAMILY

A child who avoids interactions with other children is missing out on important socialization opportunities during which he learns the give-and-take of social interchange. Especially if the child is an only child, the family may not be aware that the child seems to avoid contact with peers. Once you have had an opportunity to observe the child's behavior, set up a meeting with the family and let them know of your observations and concerns. Find out from the family what interactions with other children the child has had, and what they have observed in such situations. Together with the family, discuss ideas to help the child become more comfortable in social interactions with age-mates. Once you have begun an approach to change the behavior, keep in frequent touch with the family to inform them of progress.

CONSIDER THE IMPLICATIONS

Between infancy and the time children enter elementary school, they begin to learn how to get along with other people. This ability comes through repeated practice and through positive experiences in dealing with others. Young children move increasingly out of the realm of egocentric concerns, where they can think only of themselves, into a world where other people exist and must be considered. Preschool facilitates this process. One of the main goals of early childhood education is to help preschool-aged children learn social skills. They learn through many opportunities for peer interaction.

Generally, this process of socialization is a natural one. Occasionally a child has difficulty learning how to interact with other children. In this case, the teachers must examine the situation. The child may lack some of the social skills that help him interact. Perhaps he does not interact because he prefers adult attention. If the child lacks social skills and is not given some help in learning these, he continues on to elementary school deficient in social development. The child may avoid other children because adults then pay more attention to him by trying to coax him into interaction. The child, then, will continue this avoidance as long as he gets the attention he wants. Helping the child increase peer interaction requires a careful assessment of the situation. Otherwise, the teachers' attempts to help will not be effective.

EXPLORE ALTERNATIVES

Consider whether some of the following suggestions might provide a relatively simple resolution to the situation:

- Consider the developmental level of the child. Many young preschoolers are not yet very social, often preferring isolated or parallel play. For the most part, two-year-olds and many young three-year-olds are not yet overly interested in or ready for social play. If the child you are concerned about is very young, examine your own expectations rather than the child's behavior. Given time and appropriate guidance, this child should soon emerge from his preference for solitary play into a more social world.*

- The child's avoidance of interaction with peers might be a result of the classroom in which he has been placed. The child might be the youngest and smallest in the group. He might feel overpowered and intimidated by his classmates. In such an instance, move the child to a more appropriate class, if possible.
- A child who is new to your school or to group experience in general may not interact with other children because he does not yet feel comfortable in the new setting. Time, patience, and gentle guidance will help the child become integrated into the group.

If none of these suggestions provides a resolution to the concern, continue on to the following strategies.

STATE THE GOAL

The goal is for the child to interact with other children and participate in social play at school. The child should spend at least one-third of his time during free-choice activities engaged in social play or interaction with peers.

APPROACH

The approach for the child who does not participate in social play includes four steps:

- Reinforce social interaction with other children.
- Reinforce other children for interacting with the child.
- Systematically help the child learn social skills.
- Ignore the child when he does not interact with peers.

The approach used for a particular child depends on the teacher's assessment of the cause of the behavior. If the child does not interact because of a lack of social skills, use the first three steps. If the child's behavior is motivated by a desire for attention from teachers, then use the first, second, and last steps. If his behavior is caused by a lack of skills as well as a bid for attention, follow all four steps of these strategies.

Children with cognitive deficits may be developmentally at a younger stage of development, and nonparticipation in social play may be a reflection of developmental level rather than inappropriate behavior.

DEFINITION

Nonparticipation in social play includes any behaviors that are not involved with other children, such as playing alone, sitting or standing alone, seeking out adults, or talking solely to adults. *Social play* includes playing the same game or with the same materials as another child, talking to peers, sharing, and otherwise interacting with peers in verbal and nonverbal ways. The teachers should discuss and list the behaviors they consider as nonparticipation in social play so they agree on the definition.

STARTING POINT

Spend three days gathering some initial information with which to compare later progress. Select one hour during the day when children are free to select activities and can engage freely in social play. Use this same hour consistently. Use a time-sampling method to measure how much time the child is spending in interaction with peers. You need a watch or clock and a pencil and paper to keep track. Once every five minutes, observe the child for 15 seconds. If the child is participating in social play, make a mark on the paper. You may record a maximum of 12 marks during the hour. At the end of the observation period, record the total number on the Frequency Record-Keeping Graph.

STRATEGIES

After gathering this information, continue to the following steps.

Reinforce the Child's Social Interaction with Other Children.
Whenever you try to increase a particular behavior in a child, frequently reinforce the child to let him know that you value that behavior. Take every opportunity possible to praise the child for engaging in social play. If the child does not participate because such behavior gets him teacher attention, remove that attention. Giving your attention elsewhere quickly changes his behavior. Therefore, there should be ample opportunities for reinforcement, whatever the child's underlying motivation may be.

Carefully choose the type of reinforcement you give. If the child avoids social play because he gets teacher attention that way, it may be somewhat tricky to give attention when he does interact. You run the risk of the child abandoning the social play situation because he thinks you will now attend to him. How you reinforce will depend on how the child reacts. Try various methods to see which works best. Nonverbal reinforcers such as a smile, a pat, or just your presence nearby for a few seconds may be effective. Verbal praise, if carefully worded, may also work. Say, for instance, "You two are baking such a nice cake together," or "Would you like these little stones to put on top of the cake you two are making?" Your praise should include both children and imply that you are not staying with them for more than a brief time.

Reinforce Other Children for Interacting with the Child. Since interaction is an activity requiring at least two people, other children should be reinforced for interacting with the child. Give other children reinforcement through a smile, a hug, a thank-you, or a few words. This should encourage others to seek out the company of the child more often which, in turn, should help him feel more comfortable in social situations.*

Systematically Help the Child Learn Social Skills. Before moving on with this step, confirm your feelings that the child is lacking in social skills by talking with the family. If they indicate that the child has had little experience with other children his age or that he is shy around other youngsters, you are probably correct in assuming that he needs help in social development. You can help him acquire interactive skills through a step-by-step process[†]:

1. For the first three or four days, help the child observe the social activities of other children. Take him by the hand (if he does not object), and go from area to area in the classroom. Verbally point out what the children are doing. Focus on social aspects. Say, for instance, "See, Mitch is the grocery store owner and Charlotte is shopping. She wants to buy eggs and he is getting them for her." "Carmen and Larry are painting next to each other. Larry gave Carmen his red paint because she didn't have any." "Look! Patrick is putting a block on top of the tall tower he is building with Marsha and Salim. It must be pretty funny from the way they're all laughing!" Do this several times a day. It should only take a few minutes each time. Encourage the child to talk about what he sees, as well.

2. Once the child feels comfortable in the observer role, try to get him a little closer to the activities. Scan the room to find one or two children who you think will be cooperative and not reject the child. Do not always choose the same children, however. Take the child to where the other youngsters are working. Watch for a minute or so.

*When children with special needs are included in a classroom, it is important to facilitate their acceptance by the other children. Letting all children know that you value their inclusion of a child with a disability in their play is an important element.
[†]Children with emotional/behavioral, cognitive, sensory, and often other disabilities may need systematic help in learning social skills. This approach can be useful in helping them master greater social competence.

Sit down nearby with the child. Begin to join in the play and then encourage the child to do so also. Verbally describe what each child is doing to contribute to the play. Emphasize the shy child's role. Physically guide him if necessary. For instance, place a block in his hand and help him add it to the block structure.

Do this several times a day. Spend several minutes with the child at the activity. Let him know you are moving on when you are ready to leave. Continue with this step until the child begins to take initiative in joining in the play. This may take some time, but remember that the child is just learning these social skills.

When the child begins to show some pleasure in playing with other children, move on to the next step.

3. Take the child to another youngster or group. Watch with him for a few moments. Then ask, "Would you like to play with them?" If he does, encourage him to join in the play. This time, do not take an active role beyond helping the child become part of the social group. It might be helpful to provide a prop for the child to contribute to the group's play. For instance, give him a piece of rope to serve as a fire hose. Say to the other child, "See, here is the firefighter with a hose to help you put out that fire." Step back and let the child join the play. Provide reinforcement through comments about the play, praise, or a smile.

Do this several times a day. Continue with this step as long as the child seems to need this support from you. As the child joins in social activities on his own more often, withdraw your help in initiating social play.

4. When the child joins other children in play on his own, provide intermittent reinforcement. At first, try to give some form of reinforcement whenever you notice the child engaged in social play. Smile at the child, and give verbal comments. As the child interacts more, he derives more and more pleasure and satisfaction from social encounters with his peers. Reinforcement comes from the situation itself.

OR

Gradually decrease the frequency of reinforcement. When the child interacts normally with other children, you need not reinforce him any more often than you do the other children.

If the Child Avoids Social Play Because He Gets Adult Attention, Withdraw that Attention. When you see the child avoiding social interaction, ignore him. It is natural to go to a child who is isolated from the rest and try to get him involved by talking and attending to him. When the attention you pay him in this way becomes more important than the social interaction he is missing, your reactions are counterproductive. Instead of reinforcing the child when he is alone, ignore him. Do not talk to him, smile at him, or even look his way. Whenever he does interact, be lavish in your attention. In this way, the child knows which behaviors you expect and value.

Continue Keeping Track of the Behavior. Using the same hour of day as during the initial observations, continue counting behaviors. Observe the child for 15 seconds once every five minutes. If he is engaged in social play, mark it down. Do not record during times when you are systematically helping the child learn social skills. Record spontaneous interactions and social play. When the graph shows that the child interacts socially at least one-third of the time, you have reached the stated goal.

MAINTAINING THE CHANGES

Positive peer interactions are in themselves rewarding and should help maintain the behavior once the goal has been reached. Continue giving periodic reinforcement to all the children for engaging in interactive play.

The CD-ROM that accompanies this text contains several hypothetical scenarios designed for you to apply the guidance principles suggested in the various chapters of this book. Go to the Your Turn section of the CD to access these scenarios. Scenarios 9 and 10 are particularly pertinent to this section of the text, Participation in Social and School Activities.

chapter **39**

Shyness at Group Time

With the exception of Todd, the entire class is singing a song. The four-year-old sits quietly with his eyes cast down, his hands folded in his lap, and his face expressionless. The song ends, and the lead teacher demonstrates a new fingerplay. A few children follow her hand movements and repeat parts of words. She repeats the fingerplay, and most of the children follow along. By the third time, all the children, except Todd, participate. The teacher promises to include the new fingerplay the next day. She suggests that the group join in on another fingerplay before she reads the story. All the children participate, except Todd.

Another teacher notices his passivity and moves next to him. She takes his hands during the last fingerplay and guides them in the appropriate motions. Todd makes his arms and hands limp, so the result is ineffective.

Now the lead teacher picks up the book she has selected for the day. The children listen attentively as she tells the story and raise their hands eagerly when she asks a question. At one point she directly asks a question of Todd, but he continues to sit quietly. He makes no move to answer or even indicate that he has heard. After a few moments, another child answers the question. Later, at a staff meeting, the teachers again wonder what they can do to help Todd participate in group activities.

315

STATE THE BEHAVIOR

The child does not participate during group activities. The child does not speak when called on, sing, join in fingerplays, or otherwise contribute to the group.

OBSERVE THE BEHAVIOR

Observe the child carefully during group times for a couple of days to gain insight into his shyness.

What does the child do during group-participation activities such as songs and fingerplays?

- The child sits quietly, not speaking, singing, or moving.
- The child does not participate, but shows enjoyment by smiling.
- The child seems distressed during group-participation activities.
- The child watches the lead teacher and/or the children.
- The child looks away from the others in the group.
- The child tries to move away from the group.

What happens if the child is asked a question or called on in some way by the lead teacher?

- The child says nothing.
- The child whispers an answer.
- The child tries to answer but manages only a few words.
- The child answers only with a yes or no.
- The child answers nonverbally, such as with a nod.
- The child gets upset.
- The child hides his face.
- The child whimpers or cries.
- The child leaves the group.
- The child seeks reassurance from another adult.

Use the information from your observations to help the child overcome shyness during group activities.

CONSULT WITH THE FAMILY

The fact that the child does not participate in group activities may remain something that the family is not aware of because they may not be present during such times. You can, however, let the family know that you have been working on trying to get their child more involved in school group activities, what strategies you have used, and what their success has been.

People are born with different temperaments and dispositions. Some children are outgoing and meet new experiences with anticipation. Others are withdrawn and anxious about what is unknown. Adults cannot and should not try to change innate characteristics. However, they can help children understand themselves better and put their personalities and characteristics to best use. The child who is reluctant to participate in school group activities is probably a naturally quiet and shy child. If the teacher tries to force the child to participate, he may withdraw further because he is intimidated by such an approach. Through a patient and systematic approach, however, the child can be helped to participate and to enjoy that participation.

EXPLORE ALTERNATIVES

Consider whether a relatively simple resolution might not help with the concern.

- Examine the activities you provide at group times. Perhaps the child is reluctant to participate because the activities are too simple, too difficult, or boring. Make sure you provide age-appropriate activities. They should be varied enough to avoid boring the child.
- The child should be in the appropriate class. He may be unwilling to participate because he feels intimidated by older or bigger youngsters. If possible, move the child to a class that is better geared to his developmental level.
- Poor hearing may cause the behavior. If a child cannot hear well, he may react with silence. He may not sing because he does not understand the words. He may not answer questions because he does not hear them. If you suspect a hearing deficit, use a simple test to verify your concerns. Make a variety of sounds and noises behind the child and look for reactions from him. If this informal test confirms your suspicions, talk with the family. Ask that they have his hearing tested.*
- Some children are more reticent or shy than others. How outgoing or reserved they are is largely an inborn characteristic. If the child

Many children, often because of repeated ear infections, have some hearing loss. Be sensitive to this possibility. In addition, a speech or language deficit or delay may be the root of the problem. You should be aware of such a problem from other contexts. Consult with a speech therapist if one is available to come up with strategies to help the child become more fully involved.

about whom you are concerned has a shy disposition, do not try to change that child into an outgoing one. As the teacher, your role is to help the child be more comfortable in the school situation. Gentleness, understanding, acceptance, nurturance, and patience will be most effective in helping the child who does not participate in the group feel more secure.

- Some children are uncomfortable in large groups, and do better with fewer peers. You may consider splitting the children into two or three smaller groups for a while, rather than having all participate in one large group.

If none of these suggestions provides a resolution to the concern, move on to the following approach.

STATE THE GOAL

The goal is for the child to participate in group activities more fully and with enjoyment.

APPROACH

The basic approach to help the child participate more fully in group activities involves two simultaneous steps:

- Systematically help the child increase involvement in group activities.
- Reinforce involvement in group activities.

DEFINITION

Shyness at group time involves nonparticipation in group activities. Participation includes singing, dancing, playing games, discussing and answering questions, and other behaviors. The teachers should discuss and list desired behaviors they consider as participation so they agree on the definition.

STARTING POINT

Take three days to gather some initial information against which to compare later progress. During group times when children have some opportunity to actively participate, measure the child's participation. Because opportunity for participation varies, count chances for involvement as well as actual involvement. Compute a percentage score.

Total the chances for involvement by counting every opportunity for children to participate through the use of voice, hands, feet, or total body. For example, count each song as one, each fingerplay (and every repetition) as one, and each question to be answered as one. Keep track of the number of activities in which the child actually does participate or demonstrate a willingness to participate, such as by raising his hand.

When you have these two counts, you can compute a percentage. For example, if during a group time you play "Duck, Duck, Goose" (1), sing one song (1), do two fingerplays and repeat one of them (3), and read a story in which the lead teacher asks five questions (5), the total chance for involvement is 10. If the child participates in none, the percentage of participation is zero. If he participates in one fingerplay (1) and puts up his hand to answer one question (1), the participation is 20 percent. Someone other than the lead teacher must keep count. At the end of each group time, record the percentage on the Percentage Record-Keeping Graph.

STRATEGIES

Once you have gathered this initial information, you are ready to proceed. One teacher should be chosen to sit with the child during group times and carry out the strategies.

Systematically Help the Child Increase Involvement in Group Activities. If the child feels uncomfortable participating in group activities, help him cope with his feelings by structuring situations that are not as stressful as dealing with the total group.

1. At least once a day sit with the child for a few minutes and read a story to him. Ask many questions as you read. "What is he doing in that picture?" "How many animals do you see there?" "Do you remember what the man said he would do if the rabbit came back?"

   Encourage the child to answer and to expand on his answers. Praise answers, whether correct or not. If the child is incorrect, you might say, "Good! Let's count them together this time." Remember, your aim is to get the child to verbalize, not just to read a story.

   Continue with this step until the child talks freely and shows enjoyment of this one-to-one situation. You may wish to substitute other activities, such as storytelling, songs, card games, or looking at pictures or posters.

2. Invite another child to join the activity. Choose a child who will talk freely but not monopolize the conversation. Use different children in the class on different occasions. Encourage both children to answer questions and make comments. Praise their answers. If the

child you are concerned about tends to answer less freely and less frequently when another child is present, encourage and praise him all the more. Involve the other child in this process, too. For instance, say, "Let's let Todd have a chance to answer now," or "Wasn't he smart to see the butterfly that was hidden in the picture?" When the child seems comfortable talking with another child present, move on to the next step.

3. Gradually add more children to your small group. At first, involve two children other than the one you are concerned about. As the shy child is able to deal with this situation, add one child or two more children each time. Add participants only as the child is able to handle larger groups. By now your small groups should engage in a variety of activities besides story reading. When the child freely converses in a group of six or seven, you are ready for the next step.

4. Continue the daily small-group activities. Make more effort to involve the child during total-group times.

   There are several ways to do this:

   - Sit by the child and smile or whisper your encouragement.
   - Ask the child a question he already answered during small-group times. Remind him of how well he answered earlier if he hesitates.
   - During discussion, ask the child to share something he told you earlier.
   - Encourage the child to bring a prop to the group for discussion. This might be a colorful fall leaf, a rock, a pine cone, or some other object he can share.
   - If the child raises his hand to answer a question, call on him immediately.

When the child seems to participate as well as the other youngsters in group activity, you can gradually decrease and then stop the small group activities.

Reinforce Involvement in Group Activities. As you work on getting the child to feel more comfortable in small groups, encourage and reinforce involvement in total-group activities. Sit with the child at group times. Do not push him into talking unless you think he is ready. Use his reactions during the small-group activities to judge his readiness. Praise any involvement that he initiates. If he follows a fingerplay with his hands, reinforce him. If he sings even one line of a song, reinforce him. Give him verbal reinforcement or a smile, a pat on the knee, or a squeeze. As he opens up more in small groups, you can expect more of him in the larger groups. Encourage and lavishly praise involvement.

Once the child takes part in group activities at the same rate as the other children in the class, gradually decrease and discontinue this individual attention. Continue reinforcing involvement in the same way that you do with the other children.*

Continue Keeping Track of the Behavior. During each group time count chances for involvement and actual involvement or willingness to be involved, as you did earlier. Compute the percentage and record it on the graph. You have achieved your goal when the child consistently participates between 50 and 100 percent of the time.

MAINTAINING THE CHANGES

When the child is involved in group activities to the same extent as the other children, continue to provide reinforcement. Praise appropriate answers or comments. Periodically praise the group for involvement in activities such as fingerplays, songs, dances, and games. There is no need to continue the small-group activities on a regular basis. You may want to plan these for the curriculum at other times.

The CD-ROM that accompanies this text contains several hypothetical scenarios designed for you to apply the guidance principles suggested in the various chapters of this book. Go to the Your Turn section of the CD to access these scenarios. Scenarios 9 and 10 are particularly pertinent to this section of the text, Participation in Social and School Activities.

Keep in mind that the reason a child may not participate in group activities is because he is developmentally delayed or has a cognitive deficit. For this child, you may want to have an alternative activity available that is appropriate to his abilities.

chapter 40

Playing with Only One Toy

"Suzanne, come and try the finger paint. We have green and red paint today because those are Christmas colors." Three-year-old Suzanne briefly looks at the paint but then picks up the doll she has tucked into the cradle and hugs it. "I don't want to," she tells Mr. Chan. Mr. Chan stays with Suzanne a few minutes. He helps her dress the doll, occasionally asking her if she would like to try another activity.

Later, after story time, Suzanne again heads for her favorite doll. Other children cut and glue Christmas ornaments, paint, build with blocks, look at books, blow bubbles at the water table, put together puzzles, and hammer or saw at the woodworking table.

Each of the teachers spends time with Suzanne. They try to coax her to another activity, or they play with her with the doll. Suzanne is uninterested in their offers of other activities, but enjoys their presence and chats happily while they are with her. Since September, Suzanne has shown little interest in other materials in the classroom. She focuses her attention on her favorite doll and the props for playing with it. The teachers try to expand her interests, but so far their efforts have failed.

STATE THE BEHAVIOR

The child spends most of her time playing with one toy or type of toy to the exclusion of other materials in the classroom.

OBSERVE THE BEHAVIOR

Spend a few days observing the child to gain some insight into the behavior.

What type of toy does the child usually play with?
- One that lends itself to isolated play
- One that lends itself to social play
- One that requires muscle involvement
- One that is quiet
- One that requires imagination and creativity
- One that is fairly structured
- One that requires frequent teacher help
- One that produces a tangible end product

What does the child do if her favorite activity is not available?
- The child finds something else to do.
- The child refuses to get involved in an activity.
- The child asks why her favorite activity is not available.
- The child finds an activity that is similar to the one she usually does.
- The child wanders aimlessly about the room.
- The child whines.
- The child complains.
- The child gets angry.

When does the child play with her favorite toy?
- As soon as she arrives at school
- At every opportunity during the day
- During free-choice activities
- During planned activities
- During group times
- During nap time
- When outside

Use your informal observations to help the child expand her interests.

CONSULT WITH THE FAMILY

Schedule a parent conference in the near future. Find out from the family what kinds of activities and materials the child enjoys using at home, and ask what her favorites are. Discuss with the family how the child reacts in new or unfamiliar situations, including when she gets a new toy. Share with the family that you have found the child to limit the type of play she engages in and that you would like to help her try a wider variety of activities and materials in the classroom. Brainstorm with the family some strategies that could help the child broaden her interests. Keep the family informed of successes in reaching the goal.

CONSIDER THE IMPLICATIONS

The preschool classroom and its contents are designed to facilitate young children's social, emotional, physical, and cognitive development. A large variety of materials, equipment, and activities are provided. These are designed and selected to meet a variety of developmental needs. During their preschool years, young children use and interact with most of the materials and activities available to them. They are naturally active, curious, and eager for new experiences.

Occasionally, however, a child does not want to try a variety of activities, preferring to stick with the same toy day after day. When this happens, the teachers feel concerned. The child does not gain as wide a range of experiences as she should. The teachers may attend to the child when she is busy with her one toy and try to interest her in something else by talking about it and coaxing. The child may soon find that she not only gets to continue what she likes doing, but that she also gets considerable adult attention in the process. Therefore, a systematic strategy is needed to expand the child's interest so she will use a greater variety of classroom materials.[*]

EXPLORE ALTERNATIVES

Your informal observations may provide clues to a simple resolution to this behavior. Consider the following suggestions:

- Examine the materials and activities provided in the classroom. Are they truly appropriate for the developmental level and interest of the children? A child may focus on one toy or type of toy because the other items in the class are too simple or difficult. If this is the case, provide more appropriate materials.[†]
- Check to see if there are enough materials for all the youngsters in the class. The child may limit herself to one toy because little else

[*]*Some children with severe emotional deficits may engage in repetitive behaviors because the repetition somehow offers security and reassurance. If this is the case, consultation with a mental health professional is important.*
[†]*A child with a physical disability, whose ability to manipulate materials or get around the classroom is limited, may find success with one particular toy. If this is the case, seek out other materials that she is likely to be able to use successfully and with enjoyment, and support the child in mastering other materials. In addition, you may have to adapt some materials so the child is able to use these successfully on her own.*

is available. Other items may be either too scarce or less appealing, leaving few alternatives. If this is the case, provide more materials.

- Examine the classroom to see if there is enough variety. You may unconsciously limit what the child can use by providing few alternatives. There must be a wide range of materials and activities that help to enhance social, emotional, physical, and cognitive development. If necessary, provide more variety.

- Consider whether the child is in the right class. If the child is younger or older than the others in the class, and classroom materials are geared to the majority, the child may find only a few items that are appealing. In this case, move the child to a more suitable class, if at all possible.

- Sometimes, children use one particular toy over and over again for a period of time because they are trying to master it. Do not mistake such behaviors with the concern described in this chapter. Children often repeat an activity many times because they are working on understanding and accomplishing the task. A child may do the same puzzle over and over until she can do it quickly and independently. Once she has mastered the puzzle, she loses interest in it, since it no longer challenges her. It is typical that a child who repeats an activity to gain mastery stops doing it once she has accomplished her goal.

If none of these suggestions serves as a resolution to the concern, continue on to the following approach.

STATE THE GOAL

The goal is for the child to use a wider variety of materials, spending time with at least five different categories of material each day.

APPROACH

Basically, your approach to the concern involves three steps:
- Systematically introduce the child to different activity areas.
- Reinforce involvement in various activities.
- Ignore involvement in the old, favored activity.

DEFINITION

Playing with only one toy is defined as very limited involvement in classroom activities. The desired behavior is involvement in a minimum of five types of activities during the school day.

STARTING POINT

Take three days to collect some initial information against which to compare later progress. On a sheet of paper, list the activity areas that are part of your classroom (for example, art, dramatic play, manipulatives, blocks, language center, math center, music, and the like). Each day during child-selected activity times, mark down on this paper the activity areas in which the child participates. To ensure that the activities are not ones that the child is flitting in and out of, mark only those in which she spends at least three continuous minutes. At the end of each day, record the total number of areas in which the child was involved on the Frequency Record-Keeping Graph.

STRATEGIES

After gathering this information, start the approach. All teachers should participate so they can plan appropriately and help the child's activities become more diversified.

Systematically Introduce the Child to Activities in Different Areas. At the beginning of each child-selected activity period, before children have a chance to become involved, go to the child and do the following*:

1. Have an activity in mind. At first, choose one that is fairly similar to the activity in which the child has been engaged. Use information from observations to help you determine what activity to select. For instance, if the child has been working only with blocks, try a manipulation toy such as Bristle Blocks. Use this type of toy for about a week.

    During the next week, select a type of toy that is somewhat less similar. Do not, however, aim for the most dissimilar activity. Continue introducing the child to new activities. Choose those that are increasingly different from what she has been doing. Take cues from the child if she indicates an interest in a new activity. Select activities and structure them to ensure success. The child enjoys an activity more if she feels a sense of accomplishment in what she does.

2. Tell the child you have a special activity you would like to do with her. Take her by the hand to the selected activity, and stay for three to five minutes. Help the child get started, and then encourage, praise, and talk with her, as appropriate. Interact with the

A child who has a significant cognitive delay and engages in only a limited repertoire of play activities can also benefit from this approach.

other children in the area also, but concentrate on the child you are concerned about.

3. Reinforce the child for finished products in new activity areas, such as paintings and completed puzzles. Also reinforce sustained interest beyond the time in which you are paying special interest. Your objective is to convey to the child that you approve of what she is doing.

4. If the child does not want to try a new activity but wants to go to her old, familiar toy, let her do so the first time. However, before you let her go, explain to her that you want her to try other activities also. Tell her she can derive enjoyment and satisfaction from these as well as from her favorite activity and that you want to spend time with her each day in new activities. Tell the child that she will be able to play with her old toy only after she has spent some time in a new activity. If possible, remove her favorite activity or close the activity area in which she usually spends her time until she has spent a minimum of three minutes constructively engaged in another area. Give ample attention to her activity in other areas. After this, allow her to go to her old toy if she so wishes. Do not reinforce such activity, however.

5. Continue leading the child to different activities at the beginning of each activity time. Pay special attention to her for the first few minutes, and continue intermittent reinforcement. Once the Frequency Record-Keeping Graph indicates that the child is spending more time throughout the day in other areas of the class, begin to gradually decrease this special attention. Decrease attention to every other time, then to approximately every third time, and so on. Eventually, you should no longer need to lead the child to diverse activities because she should participate on her own.

6. After several weeks of these strategies, when she begins to expand her involvement, introduce the child more often to the areas in which she does not show an interest.

Reinforce Involvement in Various Activities. At times other than the systematic introduction to various interest areas just described, be alert to the child's activities. Whenever you notice the child involved in an activity other than the one she has been engaged in, praise her. Let the child know you like what she is doing. Reinforce as soon as you see the child involved. There is no need to wait three minutes, although this is the time you use to determine whether involvement in this activity is noted on the chart.

Once the chart shows that the child has begun to expand her activities, cut back on the amount of reinforcement you give. Before you do this, however, the child should consistently be engaged in at least five different activities each day. Decrease reinforcement gradually until you give it at about the same frequency as you do for other children in the class.

Ignore Involvement in the Favored Activity. Whenever the child goes back to her old activity, do not reinforce her in any way. Do not speak to her, look at her, or in other ways pay attention to her. Children enjoy and need adult approval and attention. Withhold these when the child engages in the old activity, and give attention freely when she is involved in other activities. This lets her know what behaviors you expect and value. Once the child diversifies her involvement in all school activity areas, you can go back to giving periodic reinforcement.

Continue Keeping Track of the Behavior. Each day, keep track of the number and type of activities the child engages in for a minimum of three minutes. This data should be for the total day, not just for individual activity periods. Each day, record the number of activity involvements in each activity area on the chart. Count the total number of marks for the day, and record this on the graph. This information tells you how to pace reinforcement and the systematic approach to increase involvement.

MAINTAINING THE CHANGES

Continue intermittent reinforcement of involvement in many activities. Once the child is interested in a variety of activities, involvement in these should become self-rewarding. If the child diversifies play on her own, she undoubtedly finds pleasure in what she is doing. There may be times in the future when the child spends an entire day or even several days on one activity. This may reflect total involvement or a striving for mastery of the activity. As long as she does not do this day after day, week after week, the child is involved in school activities as she should be.

The CD-ROM that accompanies this text contains several hypothetical scenarios designed for you to apply the guidance principles suggested in the various chapters of this book. Go to the Your Turn section of the CD to access these scenarios. Scenarios 9 and 10 are particularly pertinent to this section of the text, Participation in Social and School Activities.

chapter 41

Infrequent Large-Muscle Activity

"Come on, Marianne, I'll push you on the swing!" Four-year-old Marianne shakes her head vigorously. She says, "I don't want to," and quickly turns toward the classroom entrance to the playground. There she stands by the door, pressed against the wall. The teacher who offered to swing her approaches Marianne a few moments later. "What would you like to do, Marianne?" she asks. "I wanna go inside," answers Marianne. "Well," says the teacher, "it's time to play outside now. You can slide or climb or swing or ride a tricycle. Would you like to do one of those things?" "No," she says again with a vigorous shake of the head. "Well," sighs the teacher, "how about a story? Shall I get a book and read to you?" "Okay."

Five minutes later, Marianne and the teacher are still sitting on the grass reading. This incident is a common one at the Head Start Center. Marianne has steadfastly refused to use any large-muscle equipment during the half year she has been at the school. She enjoys and participates in other activities freely.

STATE THE BEHAVIOR

The child engages in few large-muscle activities such as climbing, swinging, and riding a tricycle.

OBSERVE THE BEHAVIOR

Take a few days to observe the child's large-muscle activity. You should gain insight into the circumstances under which she refuses to participate in large-muscle activities.

What does the child do during large-muscle activities?
- The child engages in quiet activities such as reading a book.
- The child engages in activities that require potentially little use of large muscles, such as sand play or water play.
- The child sits and watches other children at play.
- The child frequently expresses a desire to do something else.

What large-muscle equipment does the child avoid?
- All equipment
- Climbing equipment
- Swings
- Slides
- Large building materials
- Woodworking equipment
- Any equipment that requires climbing to a height
- Any equipment that involves fast movement

What is the child's relation to other people during large-muscle activities?
- The child talks freely to others.
- The child plays with other children in games and activities not involving large-muscle equipment.
- The child seeks out adults.
- The child avoids adults.
- The child avoids children.
- The child plays selectively with one or a few other children.
- The child plays only with boys.
- The child plays only with girls.

Use the information you gain from these informal observations to help you plan an approach to help the child.

CONSULT WITH THE FAMILY

Once you have observed the child's behavior in relation to large-muscle equipment and activities, set up a meeting with the family to discuss your concerns. Tell them that you want to maximize the benefits of all the school's activities for the child, including strengthening large muscles, promoting balance, and building body control. Discuss with the family whether the child has access to playground equipment at home or in a nearby park that she visits. Find out how the child responds to using such equipment. In addition, explore whether the child may have had an accident, serious or minor, which might be the basis for a fear of heights or speed. With the family, try to come up with some ways in which the child can be encouraged to increase large-muscle activity. Keep the family informed of changes in the child's behavior.

CONSIDER THE IMPLICATIONS

One of the objectives of early childhood education is to enhance large-muscle development. This is done by providing a variety of activities and equipment to encourage stretching, climbing, pushing, pulling, pumping, crawling, balancing, reaching, running, jumping, digging, and sliding. Such equipment is traditionally found in outdoor play areas or gymnasiums. The equipment includes slides, swings, a variety of things to climb on and over, sand and sand tools, tricycles, wagons, teeter-totters, and movable boards and crates for flexible building possibilities. When outdoor play is not part of a program because of space limitations, and a gym is not available, the indoor environment may be modified to include large-muscle activities. Usually children welcome the chance to participate in large-muscle activities and use the equipment with great enjoyment.

Occasionally, however, a child refuses to use large-muscle equipment. A refusal is usually based to some extent on fear. This child loses the chance to exercise her muscles. She also misses activities that are vital to the development of body control, eye–hand coordination, and eventually skills like reading and writing. Involvement in large-muscle activities during early childhood has widespread effects.

Teachers recognize the importance of large-muscle activity. They are concerned when a child consistently fails to participate. They may show this concern by spending time with the child, encouraging her to use the equipment. Unless such measures are systematically carried out over time, they only serve to strengthen the child's unwillingness to try. As long as the child does not use the equipment, she receives considerable adult attention. Giving attention when the child will not use the large-muscle equipment reinforces this behavior.

EXPLORE ALTERNATIVES

Consider whether one of the following suggestions might help to increase large-muscle activity:

- The equipment in the play yard might not be appropriate for the children. A child may be reluctant to use equipment because the steps or rungs are too far apart, the slide is too steep, or the swing seats are too high. Preschool children need a challenge. Equipment should be carefully selected to provide challenge without hazards. Observe all the children in the play area. If many experience difficulty with the equipment, evaluate its appropriateness. Make the necessary changes.

- The child might have a perceptual problem or developmental delay that causes reluctance to use large-muscle equipment. Observe the child to look for frequent and unaccountable clumsiness. The child may be suffering from a vision problem, poor motor control, or another kind of perceptual difficulty. If your observation supports your concern, talk with the family and suggest they have their pediatrician examine the child.*

- The child's unwillingness to use large-muscle equipment may be based to some extent on fear. Talk with the child and discuss her reluctance to participate. You may learn why the child does not want to use the equipment. If her reasons are based on fear, help the child to overcome her fear.

If none of these suggestions provides a resolution to the concern, then start the following program.

STATE THE GOAL

The goal is for the child to use large-muscle equipment a minimum of five times per play period.

APPROACH

The basic strategy to increase participation in large muscle activities involves three simultaneous steps:

- Systematically help the child overcome her fears and gain confidence in using large-muscle equipment.

Large-muscle activity requires the combination and coordination of many skills, including physical, sensory, perceptual, and cognitive. If the child has a deficit in one or more of these areas, playground equipment may be difficult and even overwhelming to master. Be sensitive to children's abilities and disabilities, and provide appropriate equipment and assistance to challenge them. Even children with moderate to severe physical disabilities can use outdoor equipment if it is adapted to their needs.

- Reinforce all use of large-muscle equipment.
- Ignore nonparticipation in large-muscle activities.

DEFINITION

Infrequent large-muscle activity involves the child's reluctance to use large-muscle equipment such as slides, swings, and climbers. Frequent large-muscle activity involves free and confident climbing, swinging, and sliding on equipment, at a rate of at least five times per play period.

STARTING POINT

For three play periods, observe the child for the purpose of gathering initial information. Each time the child uses a piece of large-muscle equipment, make a mark on paper. At the end of each play period, record the total on the Frequency Record-Keeping Graph. To measure usage, count only those instances in which the child uses the equipment as it is meant to be used. For example, the child should not just sit on a swing, but should pump or be pushed so the swing moves in an arc of at least 45 degrees. On the slide, the child should come down freely rather than holding a teacher's hand or the sides. On the climber she should climb at least three feet above ground level. All the teachers need to discuss and define usage as it best fits the play area and equipment.

STRATEGIES

After gathering this information, begin the following program. All teachers should be aware of the procedures and follow them consistently.

Systematically Help the Child Overcome Her Fears and Gain Confidence in Using Large-Muscle Equipment. If the child's reluctance is focused on only one piece or type of equipment, use that equipment in carrying out the following procedure. If she does not use any equipment, start with a climber, preferably one that is not too high and has a short distance between rungs. Decide on a period of time to implement the program. For instance, use the first 15 to 30 minutes of each play period. Use the following process of *successive approximations:* reinforce the steps that come closer and closer to the desired behavior.

1. At the beginning of the play period, take the child by the hand and move toward the climber. If she shows anxiety at being near the equipment, stop a few feet away. Sit or stand at that spot, and

converse with the child. Expect to be stationed at this spot for a couple of weeks. If the child moves away, accept this. No other teacher should pay attention to the child while she is not near the climber unless she is playing on another piece of playground equipment. Giving attention depends on the child being near the climber. If the child returns, talk with her and pay ample attention. Do not, however, discuss the need for her to use the equipment.

2. Once the child consistently spends at least half the designated time near the climber, station yourself right next to the climber. Now pay attention to the child only when she is right next to the climber. Ignore her at any other place. Again, all the other teachers should ignore her when she is not next to the climber.

3. It should not take long for the child to be spending time next to the climber. When she does this for at least half the play period, again change the condition for attention.

   Now give the child attention only when she touches the climber. You may have to place her hand on the climber the first few times. Encourage and praise her when she holds any part of the climber. Focus particularly on the next rung she would hold if she were to climb on the equipment.

4. Once the child touches the climber without help from you, at least five times during the play period, again change the condition for reinforcement. This time, pay attention to the child only when her entire body is on the climber and off the ground. Even if she is only one inch from the ground, praise her. At first, you may have to pick her up and hold her on the lowest rung of the climber. Be encouraging and supportive, and reinforce her enthusiastically. Do not compare her to other children with comments such as, "See, he can climb to the top. Why can't you?" Accept the child's individuality. Let her know that you are proud of her accomplishments even if they do not match those of the other children.

5. When the child consistently climbs onto the climber by herself at least five times during each play period, move on to a new step. Expect the child to climb higher, at least 18 inches off the ground. At first you may have to give verbal encouragement and perhaps physical help. Once the child begins this move unassisted, give attention only when she climbs to that height.

6. When the child consistently and independently climbs to 18 inches at least five times per play period, move to the next step. From this point, plan the steps according to the equipment. The number of additional steps depends on the height or complexity of the material as well as the progress of the child. The final step involves the child's unassisted and free use of the climber at least five times per play period.

7. It is quite likely that the child's newly acquired ease in climbing will extend to other pieces of equipment. If at any point in this process you notice the child approaching and using the swing, slide, or other climbers, encourage her. If the child has not begun using other pieces of equipment by this time, plan a similar but simplified approach. It is very likely that within a few days the child will be using other equipment freely and unassisted.

8. Once the child is at ease and uses all playground equipment at least five times per day, the child has achieved the goal. Gradually decrease the constant attention you have been giving. Eventually reinforce her at about the same rate as you do other children when they use large-muscle equipment.

Reinforce All Use of Large-Muscle Equipment. The previously outlined steps give detailed instructions for the teacher who will be stationed near the climber. The role of the other teachers on the playground is equally important. They help the child reach the goal by supporting the actions of the lead teacher. They should be aware of the child's movements when she is away from the climber. If at any time the child is on or near other large-muscle equipment, they should reinforce such behavior.

Ignore Nonparticipation in Large-Muscle Activities. During play periods, teachers must ignore all behaviors not related to using the large-muscle equipment. Give no reinforcement to other activities. Ignoring focuses the child's activity toward the large-muscle equipment. If attention is given when the child is doing anything other than approaching or using equipment, the wrong reinforcement is given. As soon as the child reaches the goal, the ignoring is ended. The child should receive attention for large-muscle activities in the same way other children do.

Continue Keeping Track of the Behavior. As the program is being implemented, count only the number of times the child uses the equipment independently. Use the graph. Do not count being near, touching, or only partially using the equipment. Draw a vertical line after the baseline, and record the total for each play period.

MAINTAINING THE CHANGES

Give intermittent praise when the child uses large-muscle equipment. If the child occasionally refuses to use the equipment for any reason, simply ignore any behavior other than participation in large-muscle activities.

The CD-ROM that accompanies this text contains several hypo-thetical scenarios designed for you to apply the guidance principles suggested in the various chapters of this book. Go to the Your Turn section of the CD to access these scenarios. Scenarios 9 and 10 are parti-cularly pertinent to this section of the text, Participation in Social and School Activities.

chapter 42

Infrequent Dramatic-Play Participation

Four-year-old Chip has had little interaction with other children. His enrollment in the nursery school eight months ago was his first departure from an adult world. Chip is quiet, polite, and intelligent. He interacts well with his peers, although with some reserve. He approaches activities with interest and is willing to try most new experiences. However, teachers are unsuccessful in getting Chip interested in dramatic-play activities. Chip firmly refuses to be drawn into any play in which he has to assume a role other than that of himself.

In other areas of the class environment, he also shows a reluctance to engage in imaginative situations. He insists that he is riding a tricycle, not a car, when children turn the bike path into a "freeway." The teachers feel uncomfortable with Chip's literal views on life. They worry that he is missing something.

STATE THE BEHAVIOR

The child rarely or never participates in dramatic-play and role-playing activities.

OBSERVE THE BEHAVIOR

Observe the child for a few days to gain some insight into the behavior.

In what activities does the child engage at school?
- Nonsocial activities
- Social games that are relatively structured (like Lotto)
- Manipulative games and materials
- Blocks
- Art
- Clay
- Collage
- Reading books
- Woodworking
- Sensory activities
- Basically small-muscle activities
- Basically large-muscle activities
- A combination of large- and small-muscle activities

How does the child interact with others?
- The child freely talks with adults.
- The child talks with children.
- The child avoids other children.
- The child interacts with only one child or a few others.
- The child interacts mostly when an adult is present.
- The child takes initiative in interactions.
- The child responds when others initiate interaction.
- The child is passive in communications with others.
- The child is aggressive.
- The child is assertive.

Carefully listen and record what the child says, either to peers or to himself, when he is engaged in activities. These informal observations should enable you to help the child take a more active part in dramatic play.

CONSULT WITH THE FAMILY

Families may not be aware that their child shies away from role-playing or other make-believe situations. During a regularly scheduled parent meeting, mention to the family that you have noted that their child tends to play more literal games than imaginary ones. Tell them that because you value activities that help children experience different roles and perspectives, you are trying to increase the child's involvement in activities such as dramatic play. Listen to the family's view on this topic and expand on why you think such play is important. Solicit the family's ideas about how to increase dramatic-play involvement and suggest that they might encourage the child to participate in make-believe activities at home. Keep the family informed of progress.

CONSIDER THE IMPLICATIONS

One of the goals of early childhood education is to teach the child about the world around him and the people in it. The child learns partly by observations about who people are, what they do, and how they act and react. Passive observation is not enough. The child has to assimilate information by making it a part of him. This the child does through role-playing. He not only plays a role, he becomes it. In dramatic play, the child takes on a role and is the daddy, the mail carrier, the grocer, the baby, or the gas-station attendant. He takes what information he has about the role and shapes it according to his perceptions and perspective.

Role-playing is a vital part of the early years; it facilitates the child's socialization. Children role-play naturally. Children begin with fairly simple interpretations when they are still very young (for instance, rocking a doll, turning an imaginary steering wheel). They progress to more elaborate and complex dramatic play involving many roles and interactions.

A child who does not participate in dramatic play should be encouraged to do so. Teachers should refocus their attention on this child to encourage dramatic-play participation. If a child is given attention when he does not role-play, he has no incentive to engage in it. When gaining the attention of adults depends on role-playing, the child will be directed into this activity.

EXPLORE ALTERNATIVES

Consider whether one of the following suggestions provides a way of increasing the child's role playing:

- Role-playing can take place in all areas of the classroom. It is not limited to the dramatic-play area. A child may never enter the dramatic-play section of the room but still engage in a great deal of role-playing. Listen to the child as he talks with friends as well as when he plays alone. Making motor sounds as he runs a block across the floor, stopping his tricycle to get "gas," and putting together Tinker Toys to simulate a swing are signs of potential or actual role-playing.
- Children often use props to help them in role-playing. The preschool classroom contains many items that encourage assuming specific roles, such as dress-up clothes, dolls, grocery items, and trucks. Role-playing helps children assume a sex-appropriate identity.

Most preschool teachers are conscious of encouraging this in a nonstereotyped way. A child may feel that the available props do not meet his interests and therefore avoids the dramatic-play area. It may be that the dramatic-play area is solely feminine in the sex-typed materials that are provided. If this is the case, add some hats, boots, men's shoes, ties, and men's jackets to the purses, dresses, and high heels. Provide props that encourage role-playing of various occupations. Supply props to encompass all the children's interests.

- Examine the variety that the dramatic-play area offers. Change the area periodically to stimulate new ideas and play. A child may avoid the dramatic-play area because it is overly familiar to him. Occasionally add new props to the existing area, or change it into an airport, a restaurant, a barbershop, a campground, or a grocery store.
- Dramatic play is a spontaneous activity that requires blocks of unstructured time during which children are free to select activities. If children are not given the time and freedom to carry out role-play situations, they do not fully develop this activity. Plan time blocks of at least 45 minutes at least three times during a full-time program and at least once during a part-time program. During these times, provide activities and materials from which children can make choices.
- Because dramatic play is often social, involving more than one child, a shy child may participate little in such activities. If this is the case, Chapter 38 may be helpful.

If none of these suggestions provides a resolution for your concern, continue to the following approach.

STATE THE GOAL

The goal is for the child to participate in spontaneous dramatic-play and role-play activities at least twice per day (each for a minimum of five consecutive minutes).

APPROACH

The approach to involving the child in more dramatic-play activities will include four simultaneous steps:

- Provide many opportunities for role-play within the environment.
- Give reinforcement for role-play during free-choice activity times.
- Give selective reinforcement.
- Systematically help the child become involved in role-play situations.

DEFINITION

Infrequent dramatic-play participation involves the child's reluctance to assume a role other than himself in a play situation. Participation in dramatic-play activities means that the child freely joins in role-playing activities and willingly assumes a role other than himself.

STARTING POINT

Take three days to gain some initial information. Watch for all instances of role-playing in which the child assumes the role of another person. Whenever you see the child engaged in such play, keep track of the amount of time he spends there. Include outdoor play in the count, if this is feasible. For each separate instance, write the amount of time on paper. At the end of the day, record the number of role-play situations in which the child was involved for more than three minutes. Use the Frequency Record-Keeping Graph.

STRATEGIES

Once you have this initial count, begin implementing the following steps. For maximum effectiveness, all teachers should consistently follow the approach.

Provide Many Opportunities for Role-Playing within the Classroom and the Curriculum. Classroom materials and room arrangement can encourage and facilitate dramatic play. Examine the room carefully. If the room arrangement has been the same for more than two months, consider rearranging it. Make the dramatic-play area more prominent and appealing. Add new props to the area. Additions to the dramatic-play area can be inexpensive, such as old hats, shoes, clothing items, kitchen utensils, and food containers. The addition of a large, sturdy cardboard box can also stimulate imaginative play. The outdoor play area can be made more conducive to role-play using props such as traffic signs, a length of hose for a gas station or fire department, or a blanket thrown over a climber to make a house.

The curriculum can encourage more dramatic play by providing many opportunities to create and take on roles. If your curriculum revolves around a theme, plan dramatic-play activities related to that theme. For example, children can become astronauts, zookeepers, pilots, doctors, or beauticians, according to your current theme. You could even convert the entire classroom into a home if your theme revolves around the family. Include centers and activities related to cooking, laundering, cleaning, dressing, TV viewing, sleeping, and other family-related activities. Another way to include more dramatic-play opportunities is through individual activities. Add block people and animals to the block area, or plan craft activities in which the children can make a variety of puppets. You may also provide movement activities that suggest new roles.

Reinforce Role-Playing. Keep careful watch on the child during free-choice activities as well as during outdoor play. Whenever the child approaches or watches other children engaged in role-play or participates in role-play, reinforce this behavior. Verbal praise, a smile, your presence, suggestions, or your involvement provide reinforcement. Let the child know that you approve of his behavior. As the child increases involvement in dramatic play over time, focus reinforcement on instances when the child actually engages in role-playing. When the child regularly participates in dramatic play, gradually decrease the frequency of reinforcement until you are giving it at the same rate as you give it to the other children.

Give Selective Reinforcement. While trying to increase role-playing, give selective reinforcement. Minimize the attention you give to the child when he is engaged in other activities. Be careful, however, not to be harsh in implementing this measure. Do not discourage his enjoyment of other areas in the classroom. As the child engages more in role-play, gradually increase the attention you give him for participating in other activities.

Systematically Help the Child Become Involved in Role-Play Situations. The child may increase involvement in role-play on his own because of selective reinforcement and increased opportunities through classroom arrangement and curriculum. For the first week of this approach, use only the preceding three steps. If, by the end of the week, you begin to note an increase in role-playing as indicated on the graph, continue with those steps. If environmental changes and selective reinforcement do not bring about change, begin the following steps to systematically involve the child in role-playing*:

1. Take the child by the hand and lead him to an area where children are engaged in dramatic play. Stay there with him for two to three minutes watching the children. Verbalize what the other youngsters are doing. Insert praise into the conversation. Say, for instance, "Look, the mommy just came home from work. See her lunch

---

*This technique is particularly helpful with children who have cognitive deficits, significant developmental delays, or severe emotional/behavioral challenges. A child who does not demonstrate even a rudimentary form of the activity can be helped by use of successive approximations.

bag? It looks as if the brother and sister are setting the table. Here comes the daddy now, too. Oh, Larry is barking. He must be the dog. Larry, you're a wonderful dog!" Encourage the child to verbalize what he observes.

Do this step once during each free-choice activity time. Continue it for several days or until the child appears comfortable watching other children engage in dramatic play.

2. Next, begin as you did in the previous step. After one or two minutes of observing, tell the child that you and he are going to join the group. As you observe the play, be aware of the following:

   - What role can the child assume in this dramatic-play situation?
   - What will make the child a welcome addition to the play?
   - Is there a prop the child can contribute to make him a more desirable participant?
   - What role can you assume?
   - How can you use your role to make the child more welcome as a participant?

   You and the child might join in the dramatic-play situation in the following way. Quickly find a prop (a grocery container or even a block) and hand it to the child. Take him by the hand and knock on a nearby surface. Say, "Hello. We're here for dinner. We brought a cake for dessert." Help the child place his prop on the table. Ad lib as appropriate to the situation. Encourage the child to participate, and let the other children continue their play in the way they prefer. Your role is to not take over but to blend in as a facilitator.

   Continue this step over time until the child participates in role-play situations freely, with your help.

3. Continue leading the child to dramatic-play situations. Withdraw your support gradually. Take a less active role in the play, while continuing to praise the child and the others for their imaginativeness. You should eventually need to take on no more than an observer's role, while the child participates.

4. By this time the child should engage in spontaneous dramatic play at times other than when you are with him. The graph should tell you if this is happening. When the child meets the goal you have set, begin gradually to decrease your role. Lead him to dramatic play every other time, then every third time, and so forth. Eventually the child should be participating freely and spontaneously in the same way the other children do.

 Continue Keeping Track of the Behavior. Keep track of the duration of role-play involvement, and record on the graph the number of role-play situations that last more than three minutes. Count only spontaneous situations, not ones to which you lead the child.

MAINTAINING THE CHANGES

Once the child freely engages in dramatic play, he should continue on his own because it offers intrinsic satisfaction. When the child feels comfortable with role-playing, he participates in it at his own pace. There may be days when he engages in a great deal of dramatic play and other periods when he leaves it because his attention and energies are focused elsewhere. The child need not engage in role-playing on a daily basis, but when it is right for him. He should do so freely.

The CD-ROM that accompanies this text contains several hypothetical scenarios designed for you to apply the guidance principles suggested in the various chapters of this book. Go to the Your Turn section of the CD to access these scenarios. Scenarios 9 and 10 are particularly pertinent to this section of the text, Participation in Social and School Activities.

chapter 43

Talking Infrequently

"What is it you want, Noah?" Mr. Parker gets increasingly frustrated with five-year-old Noah's tugs at his shirt and grunting sounds. Finally, Noah succeeds in pulling Mr. Parker to the shelf. Noah points upward. "You want something from the shelf, Noah?" Noah eagerly nods his head. After several tries he conveys that he wants the stapler. Mr. Parker, handing it to Noah, says, "Why didn't you tell me what you needed, Noah?" Noah says nothing, and walks to the table. He staples together several drawings, carefully writes his name on the cover and takes the book to Mr. Parker. "Say, that's neat, Noah!" Mr. Parker looks through the drawings and comments on them as Noah stands by, smiling.

A little while later, Noah sits quietly at a table near several children working together on a game. He turns his chair to get a better view of the teachers as they move about the room, talking to and working with the children. One of the teachers sees Noah watching her. After a few seconds she goes to him. She spends several minutes by Noah, talking to him and trying to coax him to talk. Noah obviously enjoys the attention but remains quiet. The teachers know Noah's language ability is quite adequate because they have heard him chatter with his mother. When he is at school, however, he steadfastly refuses to talk. The teachers are resigned and now seldom try to involve him verbally.

The child talks infrequently to peers or teachers while at school.

OBSERVE THE BEHAVIOR

Spend a few days observing the child to learn what you can about his infrequent verbalizations.

How does the child communicate his needs and wishes?
- The child talks when he needs to.
- The child never talks.
- The child uses sign language (such as pointing) to communicate.
- The child tries to find his own solution to challenges rather than ask for help.
- The child cries if he needs something.
- The child leads an adult to what he wants.
- The child asks for his mother or father when he wants something.

How does the child react when spoken to?
- The child answers.
- The child turns away from the person addressing him.
- The child responds nonverbally, such as by nodding.
- The child responds by smiling.
- The child reacts in a distressed way.
- The child responds verbally or nonverbally to only one person or a few people, such as a trusted teacher or a special friend.

What does the child do while at school?
- The child joins freely in planned activities.
- The child is reluctant to participate.
- The child engages only in nonsocial activities.
- The child joins activities when an adult is present.
- The child engages in parallel play.
- The child goes off by himself to play.
- The child seems to enjoy blocks, manipulatives, sensory activities, art, housekeeping activities, games, books, or music.

Note how the child communicates with his family when he is brought to school and picked up at the end of the day. Such observations will give you some insight into the child's behavior so you can help him verbalize more frequently, or at least more freely.

CONSULT WITH THE FAMILY

Whether you feel that there is a physical reason for the child's lack of language usage or that he simply chooses not to speak although he is capable of doing so, it is good to meet with the family to discuss concerns. Recommend to the family that the child be tested if you suspect that he may have a speech or hearing problem. Be supportive of the family and stay in close contact so you can take part in the resolution of this concern. If the child is from a non–English-speaking home, then make all efforts to provide help to the child in learning English. On the other hand, if the child is quite capable of speaking, discuss with the family why they think he chooses not to use language at school. Solicit their suggestions for changing this behavior, then keep them informed of progress toward the goal of having him use language to communicate.

CONSIDER THE IMPLICATIONS

Communication is one of the most important things learned during early childhood. The process of learning to communicate begins in early infancy. The baby has needs that he makes known through crying and movement. As he grows older, he begins to coo and gurgle. At the same time, he hears language and experiences nonverbal communication, which begin to take on more meaning as he progresses. After the first birthday, formal language usage becomes more prevalent as the child learns, understands, and speaks words that other people use. Soon he is expected to make himself understood by speaking the language of those around him rather than by nonverbal means. By two and a half, most children have a sizable vocabulary and are capable of communicating with people outside the family.

When a young child fails to communicate verbally, one is never sure what the child has understood. More seriously, the child's ability to gain fully from his experiences is impaired. For these reasons, a child who rarely or never speaks is of concern to the preschool teacher. Failure to speak may be caused by one of two factors. The child may be physically unable to speak, or the child may be unwilling to speak. In the former case, medical and remedial help must be sought. This chapter addresses an unwillingness to speak. When a child is able but unwilling to speak, he needs help to overcome his reluctance. Teachers must pay careful attention to the child's nonverbal ways of communicating. If teachers respond to the child when he communicates without spoken language, they reinforce his nonverbal communications. Also, the child is not encouraged to speak.

EXPLORE ALTERNATIVES

Carefully consider the following suggestions. One of them might provide a resolution to the concern.

- Check for physiological causes for the child's unwillingness to speak. A hearing problem can cause slow language development. Conduct a simple test by making a variety of noises behind the child and checking his responses. If you feel that he might have trouble hearing, encourage the family to consult with their physician for further testing. Besides hearing difficulties, the child's lack of language might be caused by a throat or mouth abnormality or by brain damage. A physician should examine, diagnose, or refer for diagnosis, and recommend steps to correct the problem.*

- Preschool teachers should be gentle and soft-spoken. Sometimes, however, some of the adults in a classroom can be overpowering to young children. Carefully consider how the adults are interacting with the children and whether their behavior is intimidating to some of the youngsters. A child may react with silence if he perceives the adults in an overpowering role. If you conclude that the child speaks infrequently because of the adults, the teachers as a group need to discuss the concern and consider ways to improve it. A quieter, slower-paced, and less-demanding approach by the adults may encourage the child to speak more frequently.

- A child from a non–English-speaking or bilingual family needs extra help and encouragement in learning English. If such a child is reluctant to speak, plan a systematic approach. Involve the other children in the class to help him gain proficiency in English.

- A child with a speech impediment may be discouraged from speaking freely because others have trouble understanding what he says. Such a child should receive treatment from a speech therapist. The therapist can give guidance to the preschool staff on how best to help the child. Cooperation among all adults who are around the child will help the child reach the goals set for him.†

Many children, often because of repeated ear infections, have some hearing loss. Be sensitive to this possibility.

†*Children with speech and language deficits sometimes learn that it is easier to avoid talking than to risk the frustration and humiliation of not being understood by others. Teachers need to exercise patience and encouragement toward such children to encourage them to talk and experience success in communication attempts.*

- Sometimes children speak infrequently because they have little need to do so. A child whose every need is anticipated and met by parents, grandparents, older siblings, and others during his early development may not speak because speaking has never been necessary. If, from discussions with the family, you conclude that this is the case, and you have ruled out a physiological problem, use the approach outlined in this chapter. Encourage the family to use it as well.

- Consider the child's developmental level. Some two-year-olds are not yet proficient in language usage, and they use a variety of verbal and nonverbal ways to communicate. A two-year-old who tries to communicate through language, even if not always successfully, gains language skills very quickly. Within a few months, the child should be much more competent. If a three-year-old does not communicate effectively, there is cause for concern. A physiological problem or a developmental delay should be thoroughly explored before the steps outlined in this chapter are applied.*

- The child may speak little because his vocabulary is limited. In such a case, plan a systematic approach to expand vocabulary and reinforce new word usage. Use books, word games, picture cards, magazines, and other appropriate means to work with the child individually or in a small group. Gear other activities to achieve vocabulary expansion, as well. Many of the suggestions in this chapter should help you reach your goals for the child.

- Some children are more reticent or shy than others. How outgoing or reserved they are is largely an inborn characteristic. If the child about whom you are concerned has a shy disposition, do not try to change that child into an outgoing youngster. As the teacher, your role is to help the child be more comfortable in the school situation. Gentleness, understanding, acceptance, nurturance, and patience will be most effective in helping the shy child feel more secure.

If none of these suggestions provides an answer to the concern, proceed to the following strategies to help the child increase verbal communications.

STATE THE GOAL

The goal is for the child to use verbal communications freely: to ask questions, answer questions, and make observations and comments.

Children with significant development delays or cognitive deficits may not speak or may speak very little. Encouragement and modeling are important to help these children acquire more proficiency in language skills.

The child should initiate and respond to a minimum of 20 verbal communications of one word or more per hour.

APPROACH

The basic strategy to increase verbalization involves two simultaneous steps:

- Encourage and reinforce speaking.
- Do not reinforce nonverbalization and nonverbal attempts to gain attention.

DEFINITION

Talking infrequently means that the child refuses or is reluctant to ask or answer questions or to otherwise speak verbally like other children of this developmental level.

STARTING POINT

Establish a base with which to compare later progress. Select one hour during the day (or two half-hour periods) when the children are free to select activities and are free to talk as they want. Do not use group periods when children are expected to listen quietly while others speak. Watch the child carefully during this hour and count all verbalizations, whether they are initiated by the child or are in answer to someone else's questions or comment. Count all verbal utterances of one or more words, not just sounds. (*Exception:* If part of your concern is that the child speaks only in one-word communications such as yes and no, then change the goal to include only sentences of two or more words.) At the end of the hour, record the total on the Frequency Record-Keeping Graph.

STRATEGIES

After collecting this information, begin this approach. All teachers should follow the strategies consistently.

Encourage and Reinforce Talking. To get the child to talk, you must convey to him that you expect him to talk. Reinforce him when he does speak. There are a number of ways of doing this.*

It is important to support and encourage verbal communication with all children with disabilities. Children with physical or visual deficits, for instance, may have to rely more than the average person on verbal ability because of other limitations.

1. If the child speaks occasionally, be alert to such instances, and reinforce him as quickly as possible. If the child's verbalization is not a question, respond with attention, enthusiasm, and praise, as appropriate.

2. If the child asks a question, answer or provide the child with what he asked for, if possible. Convey to the child that he is getting the desired response through talking. Having his wishes consistently granted when he speaks reinforces the fact that talking can be effective and rewarding.

3. If the child speaks only in monosyllables, encourage him to expand his verbalizations. If the child who wants a truck from a shelf points and says "That," insist that he describe what he wants. Say, "Tell me what you would like." If he again tells you "That," respond: "Tell me what 'that' is." If necessary, model a sentence for the child, and have him repeat it. This step ensures that the child knows the name of the item he desires. If you consistently expect the child to tell you precisely what he wants or needs before you satisfy his desire, he will begin to use language more spontaneously. Since you expect precise language usage from the child, be sure that you are exact in your verbalizations also. Avoid vague words such as *those, over there, this,* and *stuff.* Use the most exact word available for what you want to say. Do not say, "Put that stuff over there." Say, "Put the game on the shelf next to the window."

4. Look for activities and events that the child particularly enjoys. During or soon after these have taken place, talk to the child about them. If he is intrigued by a fire engine that has stopped outside the school, ask, "What do they use those ladders for?" Encourage the child to respond, and reinforce his response through your interest, praise, and attention.

5. When the child is engaged in activities, sit near him to encourage talking. Children's artwork provides an excellent opportunity for discussion. You can talk and ask questions related to the colors, textures, shapes, techniques, and media the child is using. Make your attention and praise contingent on verbal responses, rather than on the child's art. If the child responds verbally, continue giving attention. If he does not respond verbally, withdraw attention.

6. If the child speaks neither to adults nor to other children very often, begin with encouragement of interaction with adults. Use some of the techniques previously described. Once the child starts to speak more freely with teachers, expand your efforts to include other children. Read the suggestions for increasing peer interaction in Chapters 38 and 42. Use appropriate techniques to get the child into verbal interaction with other children.

7. When you make attention contingent on the child's talking frequently, the child should soon begin to verbalize more often. Increase your expectations as the child's frequency of talking increases. At first, you may be satisfied with a word or two. Later, expect the child to say more before you give reinforcement and attention.

Do Not Reinforce Nonverbalization and Nonverbal Attempts to Gain Attention. While encouraging and reinforcing talking, ignore nontalking. Children enjoy attention and conform to expectations when attention is given selectively to reinforce certain behaviors. To increase talking, give attention selectively to times the child talks. Provide ample opportunity for verbal interaction. To ensure that attention is given selectively, be careful not to provide it when the child does not talk. The following points clarify how to implement this step:

1. If the child asks for something in a nonverbal way such as by pointing, gesturing, or grunting, say, "You have to tell me what you want." If the child tells you in words, give him what he asks for, and praise him. If he does not, say, "I'm sorry, but I cannot help you until you tell me in words what you would like." Wait about 10 seconds without saying anything more, then turn away and move elsewhere. Insist on verbal requests. If you give the child what he wants when he does not verbalize his desire, you reinforce nonverbal communication by allowing the child to successfully get what he wants without asking for it.

2. If you see the child seeking attention, do not give it. He may stand or sit in a corner, not involved in an activity, and watch you, hoping to gain eye contact. Do not go to him to talk. If the child comes to you, look at him expectantly and let him talk first. If he talks, reinforce him with your attention. If he says nothing for about 15 seconds, walk away. Do not communicate displeasure in your manner. Simply convey that if he has nothing to say, you will go elsewhere.

3. Structure situations to encourage talking when the child is engaged in an activity. If the child is busy at an activity go to him and sit nearby. Be silent for 10 or 15 seconds. If the child says nothing, begin a simple conversation. Comment on what he is doing, then ask a question. For example, say, "You're painting your picture in the same color as your sweater. That's nice! Do you see anything else in the room that is red like your sweater and your picture?" Be sure that the question you ask is simple and nonthreatening. Your objective at this point is not to stimulate thinking as much as it is to stimulate talking. If the child does not answer, prompt him. "Look over by the block shelf. What is Angie wearing that is red?"

Any answers you get should be praised with comments such as, "It makes me so happy when you talk to me!" If the child refuses to speak, move away. Try to prompt and encourage verbalization by initiating conversations at appropriate times. If the child does not respond, withdraw your attention. By ignoring nontalking, you insist that the child verbalize before you give him the attention he wants and needs. Such selective reinforcement helps you meet your goal.

Continue Keeping Track of the Behavior. Each day, continue counting the number of verbalizations, and record the total on the graph. This graph illustrates progress toward your goal.

MAINTAINING THE CHANGES

Once the child reaches the goal and talks more freely, continue reinforcing him for his behavior. His verbal requests and questions should be answered promptly and satisfactorily whenever possible. Also let him know periodically that you are pleased to talk with him. Continue to ignore nonverbal attempts at communication.

The CD-ROM that accompanies this text contains several hypothetical scenarios designed for you to apply the guidance principles suggested in the various chapters of this book. Go to the Your Turn section of the CD to access these scenarios. Scenarios 9 and 10 are particularly pertinent to this section of the text, Participation in Social and School Activities.

chapter **44**

Short Attention Span

Rosie, aged three and a half, gets up from the circle with the other children. It is time to move into activity time. Mrs. Peralta just told the children what activities are available to them. The other teachers set out the materials for the activities. Some children stand still and look around briefly. Others move toward a specific interest area.

Rosie rushes toward one of the tables with a big smile on her face. She picks up a pair of scissors and a magazine. She snips into the cover; she then opens the magazine and cuts a corner off the first page. As the teacher tells the children that they will be looking for pictures of animals to cut out, Rosie puts down her scissors and leaves the table.

She moves to the sand table, where two boys are filling and emptying plastic cartons. Rosie looks around, finds an empty juice can, and begins to scoop sand into it. Halfway through, she drops the can and walks away from the sand table.

Mrs. Peralta walks up to Rosie and says, "Rosie, you need to find something to do. Would you like to play in the doll area, make scrambled eggs in the cooking corner, or play with the blocks?" "I want to make an egg," answers Rosie enthusiastically. She is led to the area, where several children are cracking, scrambling, and stirring eggs. The teacher in charge smiles at Rosie and begins to explain what needs to be done. Rosie has already picked up an egg

354

and cracked it. Unfortunately, she had no bowl under her egg. As the teacher turns for a sponge and water, Rosie leaves.

Mrs. Peralta again notices Rosie and talks to her about finding something to do. As the activity time continues, Rosie flits from one activity to another, but never stays in any one area for more than a few seconds. By the end of the period, she has left a trail of unfinished puzzles, undressed dolls, unread books, and other barely touched activities.

This is typical. The teachers hope that catching her when she is not busy will help her focus her attention. This does not happen.

STATE THE BEHAVIOR

The child has a short attention span and does not attend to any task for very long.

OBSERVE THE BEHAVIOR

Spend a few days observing the child to gain more insight into the behavior.

In what activities does the child spend the most and the least time?
- Blocks
- Dramatic play
- Art
- Crafts
- Manipulative materials
- Sensory activities
- Water play
- Sand play
- Books
- Science
- Cognitive games or activities
- Activities for which a teacher is present

How does the child approach and first engage in activities?
- The child reluctantly joins in activities.
- The child eagerly joins in.
- The child observes briefly to see what is happening.
- The child listens to adult instructions if these are given.
- The child does not listen to adults directing the activity.
- The child selects the activity closest to her.

- The child participates in any type of activity.
- The child participates selectively in a limited number of activities.
- The child selects activities in which there is considerable physical movement rather than quiet ones (such as blocks, rather than books).
- The child stands rather than sits at activities where the other children are seated.

How does the child leave activities?
- The child's attention is caught elsewhere, and she walks away.
- The child rushes through the activity, completes it, and walks away.
- The child leaves activities unfinished and rushes away.
- The child leaves activities before even beginning them.
- The child claims she cannot accomplish the task at hand and walks away.
- The child resents being called back by a teacher (to finish or clean up).
- The child returns if the teacher asks her to.

Use the information from these observations to gain a better understanding of how the child engages in activities and for how long.

CONSULT WITH THE FAMILY

A child who seems unable to focus on activities for any length of time most likely exhibits this pattern in school as well as in other settings. As soon as you have had the chance to observe the child carefully, meet with the family to discuss your observations and concerns. If, from the family's report, it seems that the child is able to concentrate on activities for a reasonable length of time, carefully examine your classroom environment, routines, activities, and level of stimulation. Make appropriate changes to encourage more focused concentration. On the other hand, if the child exhibits short attention spans in all settings, then discuss the concern in depth with the family. If you think that the child may have attention deficit–hyperactivity disorder (ADHD), suggest that the family seek medical consultation; keep in mind, however, that ADHD is often overdiagnosed and that this may not be the problem at all. Share with the family your ideas for lengthening the child's ability to attend to one activity, and work toward reaching a common set of strategies that can be reinforced at home and at school. Keep in close touch with the family to share progress toward the goal of lengthening the child's attention span.

CONSIDER THE IMPLICATIONS

The process of learning requires that a young child observe, manipulate, change, and try out objects, events, and human reactions. Learning does not take place fully if the child is not able to spend time gaining some understanding of the world around her. It is fairly common in a preschool setting to find at least one youngster who has trouble focusing on any task for more than a few seconds. The child who has a short attention span never really becomes involved in an activity and never really learns all she could from classroom activities. This is of concern to teachers. The child is not gaining what she could from her school experience. She is not learning one of the skills prerequisite to success in elementary school: the ability to focus attention and complete a task.

Teachers also find short attention spans disruptive because they disturb classroom routine and the other children's work. Teachers may react by trying to stop the child as she flits about the room. The child receives more attention for her restless behavior than for the times when she participates in activities. The negative aspects of the child's activity level are reinforced instead of the positive aspects.

EXPLORE ALTERNATIVES

Before deciding that the concern stems from the child's short attention span, carefully consider the following points:

- A child's attention span is related to the child's age and developmental level, among other things. Attention span increases with age; adult expectations must be realistic. Very young preschoolers are busy people. It is natural for them to move quickly from one activity to another. Therefore, curriculum plans for a class of two-year-olds and young three-year-olds should include very short group activities, enough available options during free-choice times, and fairly frequent schedule changes.

  While young preschoolers change activity involvement frequently, they also have the ability to become engrossed in and concentrate on what they are doing. Young preschoolers do not lack concentration, but for them the periods of concentration last a shorter time than for other children. As preschoolers grow older, they become increasingly more able to attend to a task for longer periods of time. It is typical for a two-year-old to focus on an activity for two or three minutes, then lose interest. A five-year-old should be able to concentrate for 15 or 20 minutes with no trouble. Take into account, however, the nature of the activity. Some activities hold children's attention more than others.*

- Examine the age-appropriateness of the activities offered for the children. A child may not participate for very long in activities because they are not of interest to her. Be sure to provide a wide range of activities to meet the interest and needs of all the children.

- About 3 to 5 percent of children, the majority of whom are boys, are diagnosed as having ADHD. As a preschool teacher, you should be aware of the symptoms of ADHD so that appropriate referrals can be made for the child who has this disorder. Because preschoolers are naturally active, it is very important to differentiate between their normal activity level and ADHD; the two should not be confused.†

A brief discussion of some of the symptoms of ADHD follows.

Deficit in Sustained Attention. The most difficult challenge for the child with ADHD is the inability to maintain attention. Children with ADHD do not have the persistence to engage in and complete tasks that children their age are able to carry out.

Distractibility. As part of their inability to sustain attention, children with ADHD are also easily diverted from a task at hand. They seem unable to pick out and attend to relevant components of the task and instead focus on whatever catches their attention, rather than on the most salient parts.

Impulsivity. Children with ADHD have great difficulty controlling how they respond to a variety of situations. They act on what they want at the moment, without considering the consequences. They often take risks in the process. Tolerance for frustration is also low in children with ADHD.

Overactivity. Children with ADHD seem to be constantly in motion: fidgeting, moving about, climbing furniture and other objects, tapping their fingers or feet, humming, or talking incessantly. Activities requiring them to sit still for any length of time are particularly difficult, if not impossible, for children with ADHD.

Discipline Challenges. As a secondary symptom, many children with ADHD demonstrate other behavioral challenges. They are often noncompliant, aggressive, and hostile and show other signs of conduct disorders.

*Children with cognitive deficits or significant developmental delays will, most likely, also have a shorter attention span than their peers. Teachers need to make appropriate adjustments in available activities, guidance, and scheduling to accommodate a child who is not able to pay attention in class as long as others.

†ADHD, if untreated by professionals, can be seriously detrimental to a child, since it interferes with the ability to concentrate, an important requirement for learning. Teachers should have a good understanding of the characteristics of ADHD and should be familiar with the approach used for any child who is being treated for ADHD.

If you are concerned that a child in your program who exhibits several of these symptoms may have ADHD, discuss your concern with the family, and ask them to consult with their physician or with an appropriate diagnostic agency (such as a Special Children's Clinic, Children's Behavioral Services, and the like). To expand your own understanding of ADHD, you can also read the following excellent research review article: Landau, S., & McAninch, C. (1993, May). "Young children with attention deficits." *Young Children 48*(4), 49–58.

- Another physical reason for a child's short attention span may be related to nutrition. The child may not have eaten an adequate breakfast and as a result is prevented from full participation in classroom activities because of hunger. Or a child may have an allergy or sensitivity to certain foods that cause hyperactive symptoms. Food allergies manifest themselves in many ways, such as a rash, crankiness, and swollen eyes. Some allergies may result in the child's inability to concentrate. If you suspect that the child is affected by what she eats or does not eat, meet with the family. Share your concerns with them, and suggest consultation with their doctor.

- Consider whether the environment itself may be so distracting to the child that it causes the short attention span. Excessive noise, poor room arrangement, and poor traffic patterns within the room may distract the child. If so, consider changes that will facilitate rather than hinder concentration by all children.

If none of these suggestions provides direction for dealing with the behavior, continue to the following approach.

STATE THE GOAL

The goal is for the child to attend to activities as long as other children of the same developmental level. This varies according to the age and development of the child. The child should attend to at least one-fourth of the tasks in which she engages. Two-year-olds should attend for 2 minutes, three-year-olds for 5 minutes, four-year-olds for 10 minutes, and five-year-olds for 15 minutes.

APPROACH

To increase attention span, use these steps:
- Make the environment as conducive to concentration as possible.
- Provide a quiet place where the child can get away from the noise, activity level, and stimulation of the classroom.
- Systematically reinforce the child for attending to activities for increasingly longer times.
- Ignore nonproductive activity.

DEFINITION

Short attention span is a behavior in which the child attends to activities for a shorter period of time than other children of the same developmental level. This may be demonstrated by behaviors such as an inability to sit still, difficulty in focusing on what she is doing, distractibility when she is engaged in an activity, and frequent difficulty in finishing projects.

STARTING POINT

It is important to know how long, on the average, the child attends to activities. Select one hour (or two half-hour periods) per day when the children have access to a variety of activities. This same time should be used for all observations. Keep available a pencil, paper, and a watch or clock with a second hand. For the selected hour, observe the child's movements. Every time she begins an activity, note the time and watch her closely. When she abandons the activity, again note the time. Write down how long she remains in each activity. At the end of the selected period, average the time spans of all activities and record this on the Duration Record-Keeping Graph. Gathering this information for three days provides a base against which to compare later progress.

STRATEGIES

After gathering this information, begin the following approach. All teachers should follow the strategies consistently.

Make the Environment as Conducive to Concentration as Possible.
There are a number of specific ways to make the classroom environment supportive of concentration by the children. Review Chapter 2, as well.*

1. Spend some time simply listening to the class. Are there unnecessarily loud noises? Do voices carry and reverberate more than they should? Are there frequent crashing and bumping sounds? If these noises are present, carefully examine the room for ways to decrease them. There should be a carpet in the block area and in other active areas, such as housekeeping. Dividers between different areas of the room, pictures on the walls, and drapes or curtains at the windows help to absorb sound. If noises come from outside the class, keep doors and windows closed, when possible.

Careful attention to the environment is important for children with a variety of disabilities. Children with ADHD benefit from an environment that is carefully arranged to promote concentration, as do children with other learning disabilities, cognitive deficits, developmental delays, sensory disabilities, and emotional/behavioral deficits.

2. Room arrangement can help children concentrate. Separate quiet and noisy areas. The book section should not be next to the block area, for example. Use dividers to separate interest areas. Create an air of privacy for the children working in the various areas. This decreases distraction from totally unrelated activities. Arrange the room so that traffic patterns do not interfere with activity centers. Children should not have to cut through the middle of any area to reach another one.

3. Be sure that the curriculum is age-appropriate and stimulating. Introduce some new materials, new media, and new activities if you find that children seem to be losing interest. Consult one of the many preschool curriculum and activity books for ideas.

Provide a Quiet Place Where the Child Can Get Away from the Stimulation of the Classroom. A child may have trouble attending because the level of stimulation in that class is, at times, overwhelming to her. A group of children who are busy, productive, and engaged in a number of activities can be noisy and active. Although such an environment is generally considered appropriate for preschoolers, it may prove to be too much to handle for children who are very sensitive to external stimuli.*

One way to help is by giving the child the opportunity to remove herself from the class. It is important that the child be the one who decides when she is overstimulated and needs to leave the class. Find a quiet, less-stimulating area, either inside or out of the classroom, where the child can go when she feels the need for decreased stimulation. An area in the classroom could be a large cardboard box with some throw pillows and one or two simple activities inside it. Alternatively, an area of the room could be partitioned off as the "quiet" area, and rules could stipulate that only one child at a time be allowed in this area. Whatever area in the room is used, however, the teacher needs to ensure that in it there is a decreased level of stimulation from external noise and activity.

If the designated area is outside the classroom, both teachers and the child must understand and agree on the parameters of this technique. First, the staff must agree that the area is appropriate, safe, and always staffed. The way from the classroom to this area needs to be direct and safely reached; otherwise, an adult will have to accompany the child. Going to this area is not a punitive action and should never be considered so by any adults (teachers, secretary, cook, family) or the

A child with ADHD can benefit greatly if there is a place where she can get away from the classroom if its stimulation level gets overwhelming.

child. For her part, the child must let one of the teachers know before she leaves the room. She may not go to any area other than the one designated.

When the child has the opportunity to recognize that she feels overly stimulated by the environment and remove herself from it, she is given the chance to control her environment and her behavior. At the same time, she must fulfill her obligation to go only to the designated area and let a teacher know if that area is outside the classroom.

If you decide that a child needs the opportunity to remove herself from the stimuli of the class as a method of controlling overactive behavior, you need to discuss this approach with all who are involved. This includes the staff, the person to whose office the child will go, the child's family, and the child herself.

Systematically Reinforce the Child for Attending to Activities for Increasingly Longer Times. Children enjoy attention. Give your attention selectively to increase the child's attention span. First, estimate the average time the child spends at activities. To get this figure, average the information you have from the first three days (Starting Point).*

1. When you begin this approach, give guidance and frequent reinforcement to the child as she selects and remains with activities. As often as you can (but at least five times per day), go to the child as soon as you see that she has selected and started an activity. Give her immediate reinforcement. Say, for instance, "That's a pretty puzzle. I'm glad you're working on it," or "You can make such great patterns with these blocks!" Sit next to or stay by the child as she works, and give periodic reinforcement.

    Time your reinforcement according to the average you computed. For example, if the child attended for an average of 30 seconds during the initial three days, reinforce her approximately every 30 seconds as she engages in an activity. Praise and encourage with words, smiles, hugs, hand clapping, and any other reinforcement to which the child responds.

    Stay with the child until she leaves the activity on her own. Do not stop her from leaving or coax her to stay. Offer the child help if you see she gets frustrated with what she is doing. Be sure your assistance is minimal. You might want to direct the child to appropriate activities if she tends to select ones that are too difficult for her. Say, for instance, "That puzzle is very tricky. This one with the ducks should be a little easier. Let's try it."

Systematically helping children with cognitive deficits or developmental delays to increase attention can have many positive benefits.

2. When the child regularly stays with the activity for at least three times as long as during the first three days (one and one-half minutes if the average was 30 seconds), increase the time required for reinforcement. Try expecting 50 percent more time to elapse before you give praise. Approach the child as soon as you note her starting an activity, and give immediate reinforcement. Continue praising and encouraging at the new, increased time interval. Try to give this individual attention as often as possible, but give it at least five times during each day.

3. As the child stays with activities for longer times, gradually increase the interval between reinforcements. If you note a reversal, with the child participating for consistently less time than she has been, increase your reinforcement rate. Your objective is success. If the child has difficulty, change what you are doing so you are again helping the child lengthen her attention span.

4. Keep the final goal in mind. By the time the child is engaging in activities for the minimum time, in at least one-fourth of all activity involvements, your rate of reinforcement should be considerably decreased. Eventually, the child should engage in activities for appropriate lengths of time with only periodic reinforcement from adults. Such reinforcement should be given and continued at about the same rate as it is given to the other children.

Ignore Nonproductive Activity. As you reinforce the child for desired behavior, also let her know which behaviors are not acceptable. Because children want and need attention, they continue engaging in behaviors that earn them attention. They eventually discontinue certain behaviors when they consistently do not get attention for them. In this case, the child has been reinforced by the teacher's reactions for short attention span and nonproductive activities. To withdraw that attention, ignore the child when she is not engaged in an activity. This means not talking to, looking at, or in any other way indicating your concern with the child's behavior. Whenever the child moves from area to area in the room, abandons activities that are scarcely started, or sits by without engaging in activity, ignore her. As soon as she begins an activity, give her appropriate attention.

Continue Keeping Track of the Behavior. Continue to measure and record behavior so that you can keep track of progress. Continue to time the length of the child's activity involvement for the selected hour, and write the average on the graph. As the length of the child's involvement in activities increases, gradually also increase the amount of time between reinforcements. Keep in mind that the goal is for the child to be involved for longer periods in at least one-fourth of the activities she initiates.

MAINTAINING THE CHANGES

Once the child engages in activities at about the same rate as other children of the same developmental level, she should be motivated by intrinsic enjoyment of the activities, rather than by adult reinforcement. Continue assessing the environment to ensure that it is conducive to attention and concentration. Provide periodic reinforcement to the child for engaging in and successfully completing activities. Reinforce at about the same rate as for the other children in the class.

The CD-ROM that accompanies this text contains several hypothetical scenarios designed for you to apply the guidance principles suggested in the various chapters of this book. Go to the Your Turn section of the CD to access these scenarios. Scenarios 9 and 10 are particularly pertinent to this section of the text, Participation in Social and School Activities.

SECTION 7

Eating

Behaviors

Nonsharing • Bribery • Stealing • Noncompliance • Disrupting Group Time • Leaving the Classr
nning Aimlessly Around the Classroom • Shouting in the Classroom • Dropping Objects to Create N
aring Books • Breaking Toys • Flushing Objects Down the Toilet • Wasting Paper • Destroying the V
thers • Throwing Tantrums • Pouting • Baby Talk • Thumb-Sucking • Pant-Wetting • Clinging • See
ntion • • Nonparticipation in Activities • Nonparticipation in Social Play • Shyness at Group Tin
ing with Only One Toy • Infrequent Large Muscle Activity • Infrequent Dramatic-Play Participatio
ng Infrequently • Short Attention Span • Finicky Eating • Overeating • Messy Eating • Hording Foc
ng • Biting • Throwing Objects at Others • Hurting Others • Using Inappropriate Language • Na
ng • Nonsharing • Bribery • Stealing • Noncompliance • Disrupting Group Time • Leaving the Classr
nning Aimlessly Around the Classroom • Shouting in the Classroom • Dropping Objects to Create N
aring Books • Breaking Toys • Flushing Objects Down the Toilet • Wasting Paper • Destroying the V
thers • Throwing Tantrums • Pouting • Baby Talk • Thumb-Sucking • Pant-Wetting • Clinging • See
ntion • Whining • Self-Stimulation • Nonparticipation in Activities • Nonparticipation in Social Pl
ness at Group Time • Playing with Only One Toy • Infrequent Large Muscle Activity • Infrequ
matic-Play Participation • Talking Infrequently • Short Attention Span • Finicky Eating • Overeatin
sy Eating • Hording Food • Hitting • Biting • Throwing Objects at Others • Hurting Others • U
propriate Language • Name-Calling • Nonsharing • Bribery • Stealing • Noncompliance • Disrup
up Time • Leaving the Classroom • Running Aimlessly Around the Classroom • Shouting in
sroom • Dropping Objects to Create Noise • Tearing Books • Breaking Toys • Flushing Objects D
Toilet • Wasting Paper • Destroying the Work of Others • Throwing Tantrums • Pouting • Baby Ta
mb-Sucking • Pant-Wetting • Whining • Self-Stimulation • Nonparticipation in Activitie
participation in Social Play • Shyness at Group Time • Playing with Only One Toy • Infrequent L
cle Activity • Infrequent Dramatic-Play Participation • Talking Infrequently • Short Attention Spa
cky Eating • Overeating • Messy Eating • Hording Food • Hitting • Biting • Throwing Objects at Ot
urting Others • Using Inappropriate Language • Name-Calling • Nonsharing • Bribery • Stealir
compliance • Disrupting Group Time • Leaving the Classroom • Running Aimlessly Around
sroom • Shouting in the Classroom • Dropping Objects to Create Noise • Tearing Books • Breaking
ushing Objects Down the Toilet • Wasting Paper • Destroying the Work of Others • Throwing Tantr
outing • Baby Talk • Thumb-Sucking • Pant-Wetting • Clinging • Seeking Attention • Whining •
ulation • Nonparticipation in Activities • Nonparticipation in Social Play • Shyness at Group Tin
equent Large Muscle Activity • Infrequent Dramatic-Play Participation • Talking Infrequently • S
ntion Span • Finicky Eating • Overeating • Messy Eating • Hording Food • Hitting • Biting • Throv
cts at Others • Hurting Others • Using Inappropriate Language • Name-Calling • Nonsharing • Bri
ealing • Noncompliance • Disrupting Group Time • Leaving the Classroom • Running Aimlessly Arc
Classroom • Shouting in the Classroom • Dropping Objects to Create Noise • Tearing Books • Brea
• Flushing Objects Down the Toilet • Wasting Paper • Destroying the Work of Others • Throw
rums • Pouting • Baby Talk • Thumb-Sucking • Pant-Wetting • Clinging • Seeking Attention • Whi
ng • Biting • Throwing Objects at Others • Hurting Others • Using Inappropriate Language • Na

chapter 45

Finicky Eating

All the children in the class of three-year-olds wash their hands and sit down at the tables for lunch. Kevin surveys the contents of the serving dishes, points at the macaroni and cheese, and says, "I don't want any of that." Mrs. Barton replies, "But Kevin, that's really good. You'll like it. Everyone loves macaroni and cheese!"

Kevin shakes his head and reaches for the milk. He pours himself a cupful, finishes it, and fills his cup again. Meanwhile, he lets carrot and raisin salad, broccoli, chicken, and macaroni and cheese pass him by. Mrs. Barton notices Kevin's empty plate, gets up, and serves a little of each food to him. Kevin pushes his plate back saying, "I hate that stuff," and finishes his second cup of milk.

When he reaches for the pitcher for more milk, Mrs. Barton takes it away, saying, "You can have more milk when you've tasted your food." Kevin protests and begins to cry. Another teacher glances at Kevin, walks to the table, and says, "What's the matter?" Mrs. Barton explains while Kevin continues to sob. The two teachers briefly confer, then Mrs. Barton asks, "Will you try your lunch if I give you some more milk, Kevin?" Kevin eagerly nods his head, and more milk is poured into his cup. He greedily drinks more than half; then Mrs. Barton puts the cup down and says, "Hey, Kevin, remember our bargain?"

Kevin picks up his fork and pushes some carrot and raisin salad around on his plate. He puts some food on his fork, then lets it drop off. Next, he pushes the macaroni and cheese around. Mrs. Barton, who has gone back to her own seat, notices that the food has been moved and says, "Good, Kevin. Keep eating."

Kevin puts down his fork, finishes his milk, and pours himself more. Several times, Mrs. Barton reminds Kevin to eat some more, then finally says, "You won't get your dessert until you eat your lunch, Kevin." When the other children finish their meals and throw their paper plates in the garbage, Kevin throws his plate of uneaten food away as well. He has a dish of ice cream and gets seconds when those are offered.

STATE THE BEHAVIOR

The child is a finicky eater and is unwilling to eat or even try many foods.

OBSERVE THE BEHAVIOR

Spend some time observing the child so you can gain a better picture of his eating patterns.

What foods does the child refuse to eat?
- Raw fruits or vegetables
- Cooked fruits or vegetables
- Meats
- Grain products (bread, cereals) or pastas
- Mixed foods, such as casseroles
- Dairy products (eggs, milk)
- Juices
- Sweets
- Sandwiches
- Soups

What foods does the child enjoy eating?
- Sweets
- Juices
- Dairy products (eggs, milk)
- Sandwiches
- Soups
- Fruits
- Bread

- Meats
- Grain products or pastas
- Raw vegetables
- Cooked vegetables
- No foods

How does the child express his finicky eating habits?
- The child sits quietly without eating.
- The child verbally expresses his dislike for some foods.
- The child makes faces or noises at certain foods.
- The child shows distress when certain foods are on his plate.
- The child cries.
- The child tries to remove food from his plate.
- The child holds food in his mouth for long periods of time.
- The child plays with the food.
- The child tries to throw food on the floor or in the garbage can.
- The child complains that something is wrong with the food.

What happens when the child exhibits this behavior?
- The child eats very little.
- The child eats selectively.
- Teachers talk to the child about the need to eat.
- Teachers coax the child.
- Teachers spoon-feed him.
- The child is often the last to finish meals.
- The child usually has leftovers from his meal.
- The child eats dessert but he does not finish the main part of the meal.
- The child talks often during meals.
- The child talks rarely or not at all during meals.

Use the insights you gain from these observations to help the child acquire better eating habits.

CONSULT WITH THE FAMILY

As soon as you have had an opportunity to observe the child's eating behavior more carefully, meet with the family. If you find out that the child seems to eat most foods without problems at home, examine mealtime routines and the foods that are served at school. Also, with the help of the family, try to find out if there is an underlying reason why the child does not want to eat at school. On the other hand, it is very likely that the child's finicky eating is as evident at home as it is at school. In this case, ask the family about food allergies, the child's likes and dislikes, and his eating pattern during infancy and the toddler years. Also, find out about current mealtime routines and behaviors at home. Discuss with the family what strategies they have tried to increase the child's food acceptance and how successful these have been. Share your ideas for decreasing the child's finicky eating and come up with some strategies that can be reinforced both at home and at school. Once you have begun the plan to change the behavior, keep the family informed about progress toward your goal. The approach outlined in this chapter also suggests ways that family can be kept informed.

CONSIDER THE IMPLICATIONS

Eating is a fundamental human need and activity, one that most children enjoy. Eating is much more than an activity for mere survival. It is a sensory experience, a social experience, an emotional experience, and a source of learning. It is very much tied to the essence of children's feelings of well-being. Children's eating patterns develop from earliest infancy and are shaped by many experiences. Some babies are enthusiastic eaters right away. Their parents expect good eating behavior, and these children easily develop it. Other infants may worry their families because they are colicky, allergic to some foods, or difficult to feed. Such babies may or may not become finicky eaters. Continuing experiences with food and eating contribute to shaping later eating habits.

If a child is considered to be a delicate eater, he probably will be one. In subtle ways, this behavior is shaped as family members show worry over the way he eats, are concerned about how illness affects his eating behavior, and coax him to "try just a little." By the time the child reaches preschool, eating habits are well established, and the child may soon have teachers reinforcing the habits. If a preschooler sits at lunch dawdling and not eating, a teacher inevitably attends to this behavior. If teachers continue to pay attention as the child continues in his finicky eating, such behavior is reinforced.

EXPLORE ALTERNATIVES

Consider whether one of the following suggestions might help the finicky eater:

- Eating is very much affected by environment. When the atmosphere surrounding meals is pleasant, eating is more enjoyable. Examine how meals are conducted. Tables should be attractively set. Conversation should be lively, though low-keyed. Soft background music may also help make meals more pleasant. A relaxed atmosphere may help the finicky eater focus on a wider perspective than his feelings about the food.

- Be sure that the food served is appropriate for preschoolers. Young children usually enjoy plain, unmixed foods. Avoid highly seasoned dishes. Include foods that look and feel attractive. Color and texture variety should be considered as much as nutritional value in meal planning and preparation. It is good to introduce new foods to young children, but most of the time familiar items should be served. Do not introduce more than one new food at a time. Menu-planning guides for preschoolers are available through the federal government, through many local agencies, and from commercial books on the topic. Consult such guides for menu ideas.

- Menu-planning guides can also be of value as you determine how much food to serve. Portions should be realistically planned so there is enough for everyone, but so that servings do not look overwhelming. It is often a surprise to teachers when they realize how little preschoolers eat and how small serving sizes should be. Children can always have seconds.

- A finicky eater may eat better if he feels more control over what he is required to eat. Therefore, serve food family style so children can help themselves. Provide small serving dishes at each table or for each group of six or eight. Allow children to take what they feel they can eat. You may want to set some guidelines for meals to help make this process run more smoothly. Children can certainly be involved in setting rules. You might want to suggest rules, such as "Take only what you can eat because you can always have seconds," or "Take at least a small taste of everything." When children are given control over how much food they should take, they are more likely to eat the food without fuss. Such a self-serve arrangement also encourages autonomy and fosters independence.

- Children tend to be more interested in food they help prepare. Plan periodic cooking experiences, especially ones in which the food is later eaten at a meal. Mealtime conversation can then center on what part each child had in preparing the dish. Children usually feel a great deal of pride in their contribution to meals.

- When a new food is served, avoid introducing it to the children during the meal. Instead, prepare them for accepting the new item by discussing it earlier. Such an introduction can become part of the curriculum. For example, rather than allowing a dish of broccoli to just appear at lunch, plan activities related to the dish earlier in the day. Include a discussion of broccoli during group time to explore its looks, texture, smell, parts, and name. Discuss how it is grown. You may add plastic broccoli to other play food items in the dramatic play area. Broccoli can also become part of a bingo-type game, a classification activity, or a cooking experience. If the children have some experiences with this vegetable before lunch, they are more receptive to trying it when they see it at lunch.

- There is also recent evidence that some food preferences or dislikes may have a biological basis. Some children are more genetically sensitive to certain tastes than others. Therefore, this heightened sensitivity may cause the dislike. In addition, some children's dislike may actually stem from an allergy to a particular food. For instance, one child, who for most of her childhood rejected milk, was later found to have a milk allergy. Her dislike seemed to be a protective reaction.*

Consider these suggestions as you try to change the child's finicky eating pattern. They may suffice in the case of a child who is somewhat fussy in what he eats. If a more systematic approach is needed to handle the concern, then move on to the following strategies.

STATE THE GOAL

The goal is for the child to be more accepting of foods and to at least taste each of the foods served at a meal.

APPROACH

The basic strategy to decrease finicky eating includes four simultaneous steps:

- Make the mealtime environment pleasant and conducive to good eating.
- Reinforce appropriate eating behavior.
- Put stickers on a chart for tasting all items on the menu.
- Ignore all signs of finicky eating.

DEFINITION

Finicky eating means that during meals, the child engages in behaviors such as refusing to eat many foods, dawdling over his food, playing with his food, not swallowing his food, and in other ways displaying poor eating behaviors. The teachers as a group should discuss and list all the specific behaviors to be considered as finicky eating.

Appetite may well be affected in a child with a chronic health problem. Maintain close communication with the family about the child's illness and its symptoms, including any symptoms related to eating behavior and appetite.

Take three days to gather some basic information against which to compare later progress. Since the goal contains two separate parts, two types of information should be gathered. One is related to the number of menu items tasted, and the other is related to the number of behaviors defined as finicky eating. Decide on the meal during which eating is to be observed and measured. Lunch will probably be the most appropriate meal to use. Snacks, breakfast, or dinner may also serve the purpose. A teacher should sit next to the child and observe him carefully throughout the meal. For the first measurement, count the number of different menu items or lunch box items. Keep track of how many the child tastes. Compute a percentage at the end of the meal, and record it on the Percentage Record-Keeping Graph. If at lunch the menu consists of a piece of chicken, potato wedges, tossed salad, carrot sticks, grapes, and milk (six items), and the child tastes the chicken, potatoes, and grapes (three items), then record 50 percent on the graph. The percentage is computed as follows:

$$\frac{\text{Items Tasted}}{\text{All Menu Items}} \times 100 = \frac{3}{6} \times 100 = 0.5 \times 100 = 50\%$$

For the second measure, simply count the number of behaviors that fit your clear definition of a finicky eater. Keep a pad of paper and a pencil with you, and unobtrusively mark down each time the child engages in such a behavior. For instance, count each statement of rejection or dislike of a food as one behavior (such as, "I don't want to eat that"). Consider dawdling as two or more minutes without eating. Go through the list of behaviors that the teachers as a group specified, and define more exactly how they should be measured. At the end of the meal record the total on the Frequency Record-Keeping Graph.

STRATEGIES

Once initial information has been gathered and you have conferred with the family, you are ready to begin. All teachers should be fully aware of the approach and implement it at all meals, even though daily counting is done at only one meal.

Make the Mealtime Environment Pleasant and Conducive to Good Eating. There are a number of ways in which meals can be made more enjoyable. Implement as many of the following suggestions as are appropriate:

1. The classroom environment should be neat and orderly before meals begin. Schedule a cleanup time just before meals so that the

room is put back in order before the children begin to eat. When unfinished games, toys, and materials are left lying about, there is the potential for a great deal of distraction. Avoid this by making sure everything is in its place before the meal.

2. Make the table attractive. Table settings should be neat, not haphazard. If children set the table, spend time teaching and discussing the proper way to lay out plates, cups, napkins, and utensils. Placemats and centerpieces also add to the attractiveness of the table. Children can make placemats and centerpieces during craft activities. Each child's personalized placemat can be made more durable by covering it with clear plastic adhesive or by laminating it.

3. Food should be served attractively. Serving dishes should be of a proper size for ease of handling. Food should be selected and arranged for color, shape, and texture appeal, as well as for nutritional value.

4. Select food that is familiar and appealing to the children. Periodic discussions to find out what dishes children particularly like can be helpful. You might ask the child who is the finicky eater what foods he enjoys, and incorporate them into the menu.

5. Do not treat dessert as a reward or treat, but rather as part of a meal. Dessert, like all other parts of the menu, should contribute to the total nutritional value of the meal. Because highly sugared foods are often of little nutritional value, avoid them. Fruit or milk products make satisfactory desserts. Do not offer dessert as a reward for eating the rest of a meal. Because dessert is nutritious, it should not be withheld. You might even consider putting dessert on the table with the other food items at the beginning of the meal so the children may eat it as they wish. There is no hard and fast rule that dessert must be eaten at the end of the meal.

6. Engage in friendly mealtime conversation. Avoid dwelling on table manners and eating behavior. Instead, talk about whatever interests the children. Encourage children to talk with each other as well as with you. Mealtimes should be happy and relaxed. Pleasant conversation contributes to this atmosphere.

7. Periodically introduce new foods into meals; however, do this only after the children have the chance to familiarize themselves with each one. The more children understand the food before it is served, the more likely they are to accept it. Provide an opportunity to see, smell, feel, and manipulate the new food. Incorporate such introductions into planned activities on the days the food is served.

8. Your informal observations indicate which foods the child enjoys and which foods he dislikes. Pay particular attention to foods he generally rejects. Introduce new but related foods in learning

activities. For instance, if the child generally refuses to eat fruit and you plan to have honeydew melon for lunch, incorporate honeydew melon into the curriculum. Allow children to feel its smoothness and weight, guess at its inner color and texture before you cut it, smell and taste its flesh, observe and discuss its seeds, and classify and seriate it in relation to other foods. Use the seeds in a collage, and paint at the easel with colors matched to the honeydew. The more the child knows about the honeydew before it appears on the lunch menu, the more likely he is to taste and enjoy it. Be sure you let family know that the children experienced a new food that day.

9. Plan frequent cooking and food-related activities for children to experience where foods come from and how they are made. It is hard to relate hamburger to a cow, french fries to potato plants, or spaghetti to wheat and tomatoes. Children can begin to understand some of the origins of food through field trips, gardening projects, and cooking activities. If your outdoor play area and the weather allow, you might plant vegetables. Seeing seeds develop into plants that later are picked and processed can be very enlightening. For instance, few children know that catsup does not grow in a bottle on the store shelf. If you have gardening facilities, you can plant and pick tomatoes and process some of them into catsup.

10. Plan periodic cooking experiences related to the finicky eater's dislikes. The child may be more likely to try a food he has helped to make because he has become familiar with it through his involvement. At the meal at which this food is served, encourage him to talk about the item and his role in preparing it.

11. Eat meals with the children. Your behavior during meals serves as a model to the children.

Reinforce Appropriate Eating Behavior. In addition to the preceding steps for making mealtimes more pleasant, your behavior can let the child know that you approve or disapprove of how he is eating. Sit next to the child during all meals so you can respond to his behavior. Unobtrusively, observe how the child eats. Whenever he is not engaged in one of the behaviors described as finicky eating, give reinforcement. You may do this in one of several ways. You can comment directly on his eating behavior by saying, for example, "You're eating so nicely today!" or "That's the way I like to see you eat!" You can also reinforce the child by talking with him, patting him on the shoulder, giving him a hug, or smiling your approval. As the child learns to eat well, continue to reinforce at least once per minute during the meal. When you count fewer than usual finicky eating behaviors for the meal just finished, tell the child again how pleased you are with him.

As finicky behaviors decrease, you can decrease direct comments about his eating behavior. Continue to engage in mealtime conversation with the child when he displays good eating behavior. At the same time, converse with other children sitting nearby.*

Put stickers on a chart for each meal during which the child at least tastes every item on the menu. Since one of the two objectives of this approach is to have the child taste each menu item, a chart is used to provide incentive for this goal. Before beginning the steps, make a chart similar to the one shown. Include all appropriate meals down the side.

CHILD'S NAME										
Date										
Snack										
Lunch										
Snack										

Talk to the child before the first meal on the day you start this approach. Tell him that you are concerned about his eating behavior and that you really want him to at least take a bite of every item served. If the child has any allergies, substitute an appropriate item for the forbidden food. Show him the chart and some of the gummed stickers you will use. Tell the child that you will sit next to him and will keep track of what he eats. Explain that if he has tasted each of the menu items, he may put a sticker on his chart at the end of the meal. Plan for success for the first few meals by serving items that the child enjoys eating.

During the meal, unobtrusively watch what the child eats. Do not comment on what he does not eat; reinforce lavishly when he does taste a food. Say, for instance, "You've tasted the milk, the meatballs, and the rice! I bet you're going to get a sticker today!" Combine reinforcement for items tasted with reinforcement for nonfinicky eating, as described.

Share daily progress with the child's family by letting the child show them the stickers he has earned.

Ignore Finicky Eating Behavior. This strategy is based on the assumption that this finicky eating pattern is maintained because it has been reinforced by adults. It is important, therefore, to pay as little attention as

---

Sometimes, eating concerns accompany other areas of disability. Encouraging and reinforcing appropriate eating behavior can be beneficial for such children as well.

possible to the behaviors you have defined as finicky eating. At the same time, reinforce appropriate eating behaviors. Never coax or urge the child to eat. Do not use bribes or threats.

1. Whenever the child engages in one of the finicky behaviors, withdraw your attention. Talk to another child or focus on your meal. Pay no attention to the finicky eater.

2. If the child tries to get your attention, such as by talking to you or tugging at your sleeve, turn to him and say, "I'll talk to you when you're eating again." Turn away in such a way that you can still watch the child without being obvious about it. As soon as he begins eating, pay attention to him.

3. If the child makes comments expressing dislike for the food, ignore them. If he tries several times to gain your attention by repeating the comments, say simply, "I heard you." Turn your attention elsewhere. Again, as soon as the child begins to eat properly, pay attention.

4. If the child is slow in eating, do not comment on this, either. When most of the children have finished eating and the child still has food on the plate in front of him, casually ask, "Are you done?" If he says he is finished, have him put his dishes away. If he says he is not done, instruct him to clean up when he is done. Never force the child to sit in front of his food until he is done. This only focuses attention on the negative behavior and sets up a potential stalemate in which the child refuses to eat. You either have to back down from your stand or continue insisting that the child sit at the table.

5. If the child has eaten little during the meal and then tells you he is hungry a while later, do not lecture about his not having eaten. Also, do not provide any food. Simply tell him when the next meal will be. Say, for instance, "Snack will be after we've finished story time and outside play. Then we'll all eat."

 Continue Keeping Track of the Behavior. Throughout the approach, continue to compute the percentage of items tasted and to count the number of finicky eating behaviors and record these on the graphs. Use the same meal each day as you did initially. When you find that the child consistently tastes 100 percent of the items served, begin to withdraw the sticker chart gradually. Start using it at every other meal, then at every third meal, and so on, until the child continues at least tasting every item served without being reinforced by the chart. Within a few weeks, you should achieve this end. Also, gradually decrease frequent reinforcement for nonfinicky eating when the graph shows that these behaviors are consistently near zero. Because finicky eating is a long-established habit, it may take quite a while to reach the goal.

MAINTAINING THE CHANGES

Once the child has stopped finicky eating behaviors and at least tastes every food on his plate, maintain these accomplishments. Continue selective reinforcement of good eating behavior, and ignore any finicky behaviors. It should not be necessary to sit next to the child at all meals. Be sure to give him your attention as you do with all the children.

The CD-ROM that accompanies this text contains several hypothetical scenarios designed for you to apply the guidance principles suggested in the various chapters of this book. Go to the Your Turn section of the CD to access these scenarios. Scenarios 11 and 12 are particularly pertinent to this section of the text, Eating Behaviors.

chapter 46

Overeating

During outdoor play, five-year-old Brenda sits on the grass. She plays with a doll and some doll clothes for most of the 45-minute period. At activity time, she finds a seat at a table and works with manipulative materials. At one point, she gets up and moves toward another table where a craft activity is under way. She sits there for the remainder of the hour. Several times, she asks a teacher when it will be time for lunch.

When the lead teacher announces that it is time to put everything away in preparation for lunch, Brenda stops her activity immediately and goes to the bathroom to wash her hands. She is the first in line to go to the lunchroom. At lunch, she eats three servings of mashed potatoes, two pieces of chicken, four rolls, and two helpings of dessert. The second dessert is from a neighbor who does not like chocolate pudding. Brenda did not touch the carrots and salad that were also part of lunch. Brenda's lack of activity and overeating worry the teachers and her family. Brenda weighs 92 pounds.

STATE THE BEHAVIOR

The child eats more food than her body requires and as a result is overweight.

OBSERVE THE BEHAVIOR

Take a few days to observe the child's eating habits to gain greater insight into what foods and what circumstances are most closely related to overeating.

Of which foods does the child consume more than an average portion?
- All foods
- Sweets
- Bread products
- Meats
- Fruits
- Vegetables
- Mixed foods, like casseroles
- Dairy products

What foods does the child dislike or avoid?
- Vegetables
- Fruits
- Meats
- Mixed foods, like casseroles
- Dairy products
- Bread products
- Sweets

How does the child behave at meals?
- The child serves herself large portions.
- The child usually asks for seconds or thirds of all or some of the menu items.
- The child eats very fast.
- The child eats slowly.
- The child puts large amounts of food in her mouth at one time.
- The child converses.
- The child does not talk much.
- The child talks about food.
- The child seems happy.

Does the child often bring foods from home, such as candy, cookies, or gum?

Do any specific events seem to be related to greater consumption of food?
- The child has been upset.
- The child is rejected by another child or children.

- The child is called names by someone.
- The child is reprimanded by a teacher.
- The child is frustrated in completing a task.
- The child hurt herself.
- The child is hurt by another child.

What is the child's activity level like?

- The child engages in about as much activity as the other children.
- The child engages in more activity.
- The child engages in less activity.
- The child engages primarily in sedentary activities in which she can sit.
- The child runs and engages in other large-muscle activities about as much as the other children do.
- The child avoids large-muscle activity.

Use these informal observations to help you gain a better understanding of the behavior.

CONSULT WITH THE FAMILY

An approach to change a child's overeating must be done with the full cooperation of the family as discussed in the first step of the Strategies described later in this chapter. Discussing a child's, and by implication, a family's eating habits, is a delicate and personal matter. It is, therefore, imperative that good parent–teacher relations exist before such an issue is discussed. If you do begin a course to change the child's overeating, be sure to take the time needed for the first step in the Approach section later in this chapter.

CONSIDER THE IMPLICATIONS

An overweight or obese preschooler may have many areas of need. Extra weight poses a physical health hazard. The overweight child is likely to become an overweight adult and be much more vulnerable to cardiovascular disease, diabetes, and other illnesses. Such a child is also susceptible to social challenges. Other children may make remarks about a child's obesity and leave the child out of group play. She is considered different. In school activities, the overweight child is at a disadvantage. It may be difficult for her to keep up physically, since she is not as agile as her peers. She may run out of breath on walks, tire easily during movement exercises, and prefer sedentary activities to more active ones. Perhaps most serious is the damage that obesity causes to the child's self-esteem. She looks different. Her peers make fun of her.

Overeating may stem from many causes. Factors in one child's background may lead to a pattern of overeating, while in another child there is no such result. By the time the overweight child reaches the preschool years, she is already caught in the habit of eating more than she needs. She usually eats the wrong foods, such as sweets rather than a balance of foods. Eating is one of the most difficult activities to change because of its association with pleasure. If overeating is not changed during the child's younger years when adults still have considerable control over her food intake, it becomes increasingly difficult to alter it later. The preschool staff, in cooperation with the family, can make a contribution to changing the child's eating style. This may help her lead a happier, more normal life.

EXPLORE ALTERNATIVES

It is generally easy to spot the obese overeater, but consider the following points as alternative explanations.

- When you have a child who is considerably overweight in your class, check for any medical reasons for the weight problem. Obesity due to glandular or other bodily dysfunctions is quite rare but should be carefully considered by the child's physician. Discuss your concerns with the family. If they have not already done so, ask them to have their doctor give the child a thorough checkup to eliminate possible medical causes for the obesity.*
- You may have a child in your class who is not particularly overweight but who eats a great deal. Children's appetites respond to internal and external factors. A child may eat a large meal because she engaged in considerable physical activity before eating and worked up a good appetite. Perhaps she is in a growth spurt and her body requires more food intake. Also, the food and mealtime atmosphere may be so enjoyable that she eats more than usual. Consider the child's appetite in relation to her activity level. Remember that metabolism varies from one person to another.
- Consider a child's bone structure when judging weight. A child may appear large because she has a large skeletal frame rather than because she is overweight. Look at fat layers as well as overall dimensions.

*Obesity may be a side product of a chronic illness or a syndrome that affects other areas of development. Teachers should be very familiar with the symptoms and side effects of the health condition and the treatment of such a child in the class.

- Young preschoolers sometimes are heavy because they have not yet lost their baby fat. Toddlers and young two-year-olds often appear quite chubby for their height. Unless their heaviness is excessive or persists into the fourth and fifth years, do not worry about it.

If none of these points pertains to the child's situation, start the following approach to deal with overeating.

STATE THE GOAL

The goal is for the child to decrease eating so she consumes no more food than her body needs, to eat a well-balanced diet each day, and to increase activity level so that she is active in at least half of the time segments counted.

APPROACH

The basic approach to deal with overeating and to decrease weight involves six simultaneous steps:
- Thoroughly discuss the proposed approach with the family and ensure their commitment.
- Discuss the proposed approach and goal with the child each day.
- Monitor food intake at all meals.
- Stress a well-balanced diet.
- Reinforce appropriate eating behavior.
- Systematically increase activity level through an exercise program.

As we will discuss later, it is very important to carry out this approach with the full participation and cooperation of the family. The family can ensure that the child has been seen by a doctor, that there is no medical reason for the problem, and that the doctor approves of the strategies that are going to be implemented.

DEFINITION

Overeating is a behavior in which the child consumes more food than her body needs for proper functioning, resulting in obesity.

It is important to gather some information before beginning. Three measures are discussed below:

1. One of the main indicators of this approach's success will be the child's weight; therefore, weigh the child. Ultimate progress will be gauged by a decrease, or at least a lack of increase, in weight. After this initial weighing, weigh the child once a week, at about the same time of day, and keep a listing of dates and weights throughout the approach.

2. Another important part of the needed information deals with what and how much the child eats. Family members as well as teachers will have to collect this information on a daily basis. Ask the family to keep track each day of what and how much the child eats outside school and to bring you the list the following morning. Combine the list with your own record of what and how much the child ate at school.

   Keeping track of the child's intake is simple. Write down everything the child eats for all meals and snacks. Estimate in tablespoons, cups, or other appropriate measures the amount she consumes. An example for breakfast might be:

   1 slice toast

   2 soft-boiled eggs

   1/2 cup orange juice

   1 cup milk

   When you have food intake information for a full day, classify the food according to the following five categories:

   Meat and meat product group

   Bread and cereals group

   Fruit and vegetable group

   Dairy product group

   Junk food group

   Table 46-1 provides a brief listing of foods that are classified in each of these groups. This table also indicates how much of these foods equals one serving. Using the above example of a breakfast, this meal can be converted into servings as follows:

   1 slice toast = 1 serving, bread group

   2 soft-boiled eggs = 2 servings, meat group

   1/2 cup orange juice = 1 serving, fruit group

   1 cup milk = 2 servings, milk group

   These measures of daily food intake will not be absolutely accurate, but will give you enough information to carry out this

Table 46-1 Conversion Table for Food Serving Sizes for Preschoolers

MEAT GROUP:	any meat, fish, poultry, eggs, peanut butter, or other protein equivalent
One serving equals	1 ounce lean beef, veal, lamb, pork, poultry, fish, seafood, or various meats such as liver, heart, or kidney
	1 egg
	1 frankfurter
	1 ounce cheddar cheese (if it not counted as a milk group food)
	¼ cup cottage cheese (if it is not counted as a milk group food)
	½ cup dried beans or dried peas
	2 tablespoons peanut butter
BREAD/CEREAL GROUP:	whole grain or enriched bread or equivalent
	1 slice bread
	1 roll, muffin, or biscuit
	5 saltine crackers
	2 graham crackers
	1 ounce ready-to-eat cereal
	½ cup cooked cereal, cornmeal, grits, rice, macaroni, noodles, or spaghetti
FRUIT/VEGETABLE GROUP:	any fresh, canned, or frozen fruit or vegetable
	½ grapefruit
	1 medium orange
	½ cantaloupe
	¾ cup strawberries, blueberries, or other berries
	½ cup orange juice, grapefruit juice, or blended citrus juice
	2 wedges honeydew melon
	2 tangerines
	1 cup tomato juice or cooked tomato
	2 medium raw tomatoes
	1 cup cooked brussels sprouts, raw cabbage, cooked collards, kale, mustard greens, spinach, or turnip greens
	5 apricot halves
	1 medium apple
	1 banana
	1 peach, plum, nectarine, or tangerine
DAIRY (MILK) GROUP:	fluid, while, skim, buttermilk, or equivalent
	½ cup milk of any kind
	½ cup yoghurt
	¼ cup undiluted evaporated milk
	2 tablespoons nonfat dry milk
	½ cup custard or milk pudding
	1 cup cream soup made with milk
	½ cup milk used on cereal
	½ cup ice cream
JUNK FOOD GROUP:	all empty-calorie foods such as potato chips, soda, candy, cakes, and other nonnutritive snack foods.

Graph 46-1 Daily Food Intake Graph

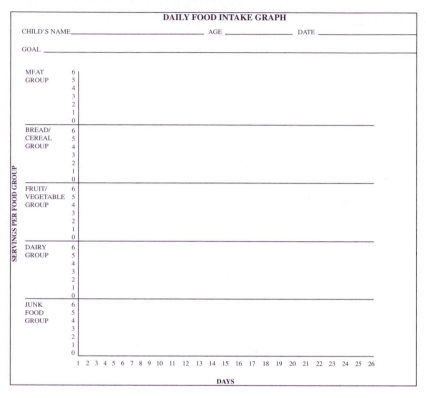

strategy. If you wish, you can also consult one of the many published child nutrition books, which will provide a more detailed listing.

Keep track of daily food intake by using the Daily Food Intake Graph (Graph 46-1). This graph allows you to summarize the child's daily intake in each of the five areas. Add up the converted serving numbers from the information provided by the family and from your listing of the child's food intake at school for the total day and place an X by the appropriate number for each food group.

3. A third measure has to do with the child's activity level. Keep in mind that body weight is a reflection of the balance between caloric intake (food eaten) and *expenditure* (calories expended through movement and exercise). Select one hour or two half-hour periods during the day when the children have ample opportunity to exercise. Outdoor play may be a good time. Observe the child once every minute so that you have a total of 60 observations by the end of the time. If you see the child engaged in any kind of exercise, giver her a mark for that minute. *Exercise* is

defined as any activity that stimulates the lungs and heart to work harder. It includes running, climbing, jumping, repeated bending, swinging, hopping, skipping, fast tricycle riding, and any other relatively strenuous activity that involves the whole body. If the child breathes hard during and after the activity, she is exercising. Do not include instances when the child is sitting, standing, or walking, even if her hands and arms are occupied. Record the total number for each day (from 1 to 60) on the Frequency Record-Keeping Graph.

STRATEGIES

Thoroughly Discuss the Proposed Approach with the Family and Ensure Their Commitment. This approach is effective only if carried out with the cooperation of the family. Unless the child eats less and eats the right foods at home as well as at school, efforts to change overeating are negated when the child is not at school. It may confuse the child. Schedule a conference with the family to discuss the concern. If the family agrees there is an issue and indicates they will work together with the school on resolving it, then continue with this approach.

It is important that the family and teachers work closely together and that they share the commitment to changing the child's eating patterns. This is not an easy task for the family, because it means changes in their food-related behavior as well. Do not rush this step. Spend as much time as needed to talk with the family so that they fully recognize how difficult the task ahead will be. Explore the emotional and social changes this approach brings about for the child and the family. When family eating patterns are affected, the change is not a simple one. Once you discuss all the ramifications of trying to change the child's eating behavior, you are ready to begin.

After you talk with the family and collect the initial measurements, the remaining steps may be implemented. It is important that all teachers and the kitchen staff are aware of the strategies and cooperate in carrying them out. The success of getting the child to change her eating habits depends on the support of all the adults who provide the food.

Discuss the New Eating Approach and Goal with the Child Every Day. Although adults essentially control the child's supply of food, it is important to enlist the child's help in implementing this approach as well. Make a point each day of talking to the child for a few minutes about nutrition, relating your discussions to the steps you have outlined for her. If the child brings up her overweight condition, use such comments as a starting point for your discussion. Otherwise, set aside a time other than at meals to talk about food and eating. Choose topics that suit your knowledge and the child's understanding and interest level. The following are some suggestions:

1. *The need for a balanced diet.* Every day, the child should eat something from the meat, bread and cereal, fruit and vegetables, and dairy products groups. Everyone needs a balance of these four types of food.

2. *Food as a bodybuilder.* How the body and mind grow and develop is related to what is eaten. Eating proper foods in the right amounts is important to growth and development.

3. *Calories.* All foods give the body energy. Some foods have more energy, or calories, than others. If a person consumes more calories than the body uses, these get stored as fat in the body.

4. *Exercise.* The body needs food to get the energy to function. The more energy the body uses, the less there is left over to turn into fat. Some activities like running, climbing, and jumping use more energy than sitting or standing still.

5. *Snacks.* Snacks eaten between meals should contribute to the daily total intake. Some snack foods are more nutritious and have fewer calories than others.

6. *Junk foods.* Some foods are not good for people. If one fills up on foods that have little nutritional value, a person then eats less of the foods that the body really needs.

7. *Food and emotion.* Sometimes when people are upset, they like to eat to make them feel better. It is better not to eat when upset.

Use these suggested topics or add others as appropriate. The point is to give the child information to help change her attitudes toward eating. As an alternative to talking individually with the child, incorporate nutrition concepts into the curriculum so that all the children benefit from them.

Monitor Food Intake at All Meals. To a large extent, adults control what the child eats. Exert that control to decrease eating and encourage consumption of balanced meals. Follow the suggestions listed, and encourage the family to do the same at home. At school, a teacher should sit next to the child at all meals.

1. Encourage small serving sizes. If food is served to the children on individual plates, be sure the serving is small. If children serve themselves from larger serving dishes, help the child take small portions. Rules help enforce your expectations. You may

say, "Take one at a time. You may have seconds." If the child reaches for more than the limit you have set for the first serving, gently but firmly stop her. Tell her, "That's enough for now."

2. If the child has a small first serving, she can have a second small helping as well. This technique of dividing the food into two portions makes it appear like the total is more, and it encourages slower eating.

3. Frequently encourage the child to eat slowly, in direct and indirect ways. Tell the child to slow down, chew slowly, take smaller bites, and wait between bites. Indirectly, you can encourage slower eating. Engage the child in pleasant conversation. Give her the chance to speak, listen, and laugh.

4. Small plates and utensils make food seem more abundant than it is. A small amount of food fills a small plate but looks meager on a larger plate. Small utensils encourage smaller bites.

5. Avoid foods with excessive amounts of sugar and fats. All children benefit from such a move, and the overweight child is particularly helped by this. Avoid sweet desserts. Fruit not only provides a satisfying alternative, but it also contains many of the vitamins and minerals children need. If you use canned fruit, look for the kind that is packed in water or its own juice, or drain off the syrup. If a recipe calls for sugar, decrease the amount. Also use less butter, oil, or shortening whenever possible. Drain the fat off meat such as hamburger, and broil rather than fry foods.

6. Never serve foods that contain empty calories. Soft drinks, potato chips, candy bars, and similar junk foods have little or no nutritional value and contain a large number of calories.

7. Be aware of how much food preschool children need each day. Allow the child to take no more than the required amount for all meals and snacks combined. This requires close cooperation with the family to ensure that the total intake is not excessive. Use the conversion table (Table 46-1) to help you determine how much food is contained in a serving.

   As a rough guide, consider the following percentages of the total daily allowance for each meal:

Breakfast,	20%
Morning snack,	10%
Lunch,	25%
Afternoon snack,	10%
Dinner,	25%
Evening snack,	10%

You may not be able to completely control the child's intake in relation to needs. The preceding information provides a rough guide so that you are at least within a reasonable range.

Stress a Well-Balanced Diet. In addition to monitoring how much the child eats, you also need to keep track of what she eats each day to ensure a balance of foods. This should be coordinated with the family.

The suggested minimum daily allowances for preschool children are as follows:

Dairy (milk) group	4 servings (½ cup each, 2 cups total)
Meat group	2 servings (2 ounces each)
Fruit and vegetable group	4 servings
Bread and cereal group	4 servings

Reinforce Appropriate Eating Behavior. At all times, be alert to appropriate eating behavior and reinforce it often. Whenever the child eats slowly, pauses between bites, takes small bites, takes small servings by herself, refuses second helpings, or focuses on lower-calorie foods, praise her. Tell her during and after the meal that you are pleased with her efforts to change her eating behavior. Be warm and enthusiastic in your praise. Also give attention by engaging her in conversation and listening.

Systematically Increase Activity Level through an Exercise Program. Because exercise burns off calories and because overweight children are usually less active than children of average weight, encourage the child to be more active. Carry out a systematic program of large-muscle activities to combine exercise with fun.

Each day the child is at school, plan an exercise period of at least five minutes per hour. This can be an individual or class activity, as appropriate. The objective is to get the child moving vigorously to burn more calories. The following are some suggestions for such activities:

1. Movement exercises can be designed to encourage stretching, bending, twisting, or any other type of motion that involves the whole body. Encourage the overweight child and, if necessary, help her to carry out the exercises as vigorously as possible. Preschool children enjoy movement exercises that involve use of the imagination (such as "Pretend you're a snake!" or "Let's be popcorn popping"). They also enjoy straightforward instructions (such as "Touch your toes" or "Hop on one foot"). There are many excellent movement ideas in preschool activity books and records.
2. Follow-the-leader activities can also be designed to encourage movement of all kinds.

3. Devise an obstacle course, either inside or outdoors, in such a way that children have to bend, crawl, jump, and climb.

4. There are many props that make exercise fun. Give the children balloons to keep afloat, hula hoops to twirl, balls to bounce and roll, kites to fly, or tires to roll. Provide opportunities for a great deal of movement.

5. If you have a slight incline or hill in your outdoor play area or near the school, play a game with the overweight child that requires her to run uphill (rolling a hoop, for example).

6. Run races. Set the boundaries, and encourage the children to run back and forth. There's no need to name winners.

7. Provide movable outdoor equipment such as large cardboard boxes and plastic crates. Encourage the child to push and pull these items into place, climb them, and use them in other ways.

There are many other activities you can use. Provide a variety so the child maintains interest. If the child particularly enjoys an activity, repeat it. If she dislikes an activity, stop it. Exercise should be fun, not a chore. Your individual attention should be based on the child's activity level. If she stands still, ignore her. If she is active, reinforce her with your comments, praise, attention, and enthusiasm.

 Continue Keeping Track of the Behavior. Continue the record-keeping. Once a week, measure and record the child's weight. Continue to record combined school and home information on what and how much the child eats. If the family is willing, include weekend data, also. If they decide not to write down food intake over weekends, encourage them to continue their awareness of what and how much the child eats. Finally, continue observing and counting exercise segments for one hour per day.

MAINTAINING THE CHANGES

The main objective of this approach is not weight loss. However, if the child eats no more than she should for her age and exercises regularly, her weight should decrease. Measure and record data related to the stated goals: eating appropriate portions, eating balanced meals, and increasing the exercise level so that the child is active for at least half the segments you count. Remember, however, that eating behavior is hard to change and that the child needs your continued support and help to change it. Continue talking about proper nutrition often, and continue to reinforce appropriate eating behaviors frequently. If the child begins to monitor her own food intake, withdraw your role gradually. This may not be achieved until well after the child leaves preschool.

Decrease the hourly exercise periods as the child maintains her own activity at a higher level. Once the child has lost some weight, she should be more inclined to exercise on her own.

The CD-ROM that accompanies this text contains several hypothetical scenarios designed for you to apply the guidance principles suggested in the various chapters of this book. Go to the Your Turn section of the CD to access these scenarios. Scenarios 11 and 12 are particularly pertinent to this section of the text, Eating Behaviors.

chapter 47

Messy Eating

"Zara, use your spoon!" Three-year-old Zara turns to Mrs. Leslie, her hands covered with spaghetti sauce. She tugs on her hair and leaves a smear of tomato in the process. Mrs. Leslie gets up in exasperation and wipes Zara's hand, face, and hair with a napkin. "Now eat with your spoon, Zara." Zara looks at the spoon a moment, then uses it to mix the foods on her plate. Some of the food spills off the plate onto the table.

Mrs. Leslie gives Zara a stern look, and Zara uses her spoon to pick up a carrot stick. On the way to her mouth, the carrot stick drops onto her lap. Zara picks it up, puts it in her mouth, and munches. She wipes at the food residue on her lap with her other hand.

When dessert is served, Zara uses her hand to eat the applesauce and drops muffin crumbs all over the table, herself, and the floor. The teacher who cleans up after lunch can always tell where Zara has eaten; at no other spot is there so much food smeared and spilled on the table, chair, and floor.

STATE THE BEHAVIOR

The child eats in a messy manner, spilling food and soiling herself at meals.

OBSERVE THE BEHAVIOR

Take a couple of days to observe the child to gain a better understanding of how messy eating occurs.

What does the child do that results in messy eating?
- The child has difficulty getting food onto the fork or spoon.
- The child twists the fork or spoon so food spills off.
- The child does not always reach her mouth accurately with eating utensils.
- The child eats with her hands, even if the foods should be eaten with a fork or spoon.
- The child wipes dirty hands on her clothing, in her hair, or on someone else.
- The child has trouble holding finger foods effectively.
- The child knocks over drinks frequently.
- The child spills food off the edge of her plate onto the table.
- The child spills food in her lap or elsewhere on her clothing.
- The child spills food on the floor.
- The child plays with her food deliberately.
- The child mixes food inappropriately on her plate (for example, she pours the catsup meant for the french fries onto the pineapple chunks).
- The child smears food around her plate or on the table.
- The child spits out food.

Is there a relation between what foods are served and how messily the child eats?
- The child is equally messy at all meals.
- The child is more messy when liquid foods, such as soup, are served.
- The child is more messy when soft foods, like spaghetti or mashed potatoes, are served.
- The child is more messy with foods requiring a fork or spoon than with finger foods.

Are there any times when the child eats very neatly, regardless of what is being served?

Use the information from these observations to help you change the behavior.

CONSULT WITH THE FAMILY

After carefully observing the child's eating behavior, meet with the family to share your observations and concerns. Find out about home mealtime routines and whether the family has noted messy eating behaviors. It may be that the child is fed by an adult at all times at home and that she does not have much experience at self-feeding. Discuss your ideas for decreasing messy eating and listen to how the family deals with this behavior at home. Once you have come up with a strategy to help the child learn more appropriate eating skills, stay in frequent touch with the family to keep them informed of progress.

CONSIDER THE IMPLICATIONS

By the time a child passes her third birthday, she usually eats relatively neatly. Spills and misses happen occasionally, especially with difficult foods. For the most part, however, the child eats properly and neatly. When a child has difficulty with eating, there can be one of three underlying reasons. The child could have a perceptual problem or developmental delay that prevents proper coordination. The child might be using messy eating as a way of gaining attention from adults and other children. Finally, messy eating may be caused by a combination of these two factors.

A young preschooler may find that adults give her considerable attention when she eats messily. When this repeatedly happens, the child may conclude that she can get even more attention by deliberately making a mess. Most likely, she is correct. The messier her eating habits, the more adults react. It is easy for preschool teachers to reinforce messy eating by calling attention to the mess, scolding, or expressing concern. Combine nonreinforcement of messy eating with a systematic approach for teaching neat eating habits to overcome the concern.

EXPLORE ALTERNATIVES

Consider whether one of the following suggestions provides an answer to the concern about messy eating:

- A vision problem might be at the root of messy eating. Review your informal observations, and see if the child has particular difficulty in scooping food on the spoon or fork and in reaching her mouth accurately. An optometric examination may reveal a visual impairment that can be corrected. If you suspect that such a problem is involved, discuss your concerns with the family. Recommend that they consult their physician.*

*A perceptual problem can make it difficult to get foods accurately onto a utensil and from plate to mouth. A child with a vision or coordination problem may well demonstrate this difficulty at meals.

- Note how the child holds her spoon and fork, and how she picks up finger foods. If a three-and-a-half or four-year-old uses her full fist, there is reason to recommend further testing.
- The child's age is important when considering how she eats. A young preschooler's coordination is not yet completely developed, and the child is not always adept at the mechanics of eating. Do not expect two-year-olds and young three-year-olds to eat neatly. By three-and-a-half and certainly by four, a preschooler should be able to eat neatly most of the time.*
- Make sure that the environment is such that children are encouraged to eat neatly. Carefully prepared and served food, an attractive table setting, and a relaxed atmosphere convey your expectations for proper eating behavior from the children. When the table and food are presented haphazardly and with little care, you give the impression that you are not too concerned about neatness. In the eyes of the child, this may mean that messy eating is acceptable.
- Dishes and eating and serving utensils should be of an appropriate size for small hands. Provide plates and bowls that are lightweight and small; small, sturdy cups; small, deep spoons; and small forks. These items should fit comfortably in the children's hands and should function efficiently.
- Be sure that food is served in the most appropriate container. For instance, a gelatin dessert can be hard to handle on a plate but is much easier to handle in a bowl and should be cut into small pieces.

If none of these suggestions helps the messy eater, continue to the following approach.

STATE THE GOAL

The goal is for the child to eat neatly, use the appropriate utensils, and not spill food.

APPROACH

This approach is designed on the assumption that messy eating is caused in part by an inability to eat neatly and in part by the attention such behavior brings from adults. The basic strategy includes several steps:

- Systematically help the child learn appropriate eating skills.
- Reinforce appropriate eating.
- Ignore messy eating.

*Children with cognitive deficits may be at a younger stage developmentally, and messy eating may be a reflection of developmental level rather than inappropriate behavior.

DEFINITION

Messy eating is a behavior in which the child spills foods, plays with foods, and eats foods inappropriately. List all the specific behaviors you consider to be messy eating.

STARTING POINT

Take three days to gather some initial information. Do this during lunch, or at snack time, if lunch is not part of the program. Keep a pencil and paper with you as you observe how the child eats. Each time she engages in one of the behaviors listed in your definition of messy eating, unobtrusively mark it down on the paper. At the end of the meal, count the marks, and record the total on the Frequency Record-Keeping Graph.

STRATEGIES

When you have gathered this initial information, start the following approach. All teachers should be aware of and carry out these strategies consistently.

Systematically Help the Child Learn Appropriate Eating Skills.
The way you implement this step depends on which specific behaviors the child engages in when eating. Following are three messy eating challenges and ways to improve them. Use one, two, or all of these as needed to change the child's behavior. Implement them simultaneously. You should sit next to the child at meals to carry out these steps.*

1. *Difficulty getting food on the fork or spoon.* Food may easily be pushed off the plate, or fingers may be used to maneuver the food on the plate if the child cannot get her food on the utensil. Scooping up food is a difficult skill to acquire. If the child has trouble with coordination, it is all the harder. You can help the child acquire the skills and give guidance in the process.

   First, be sure that the child knows which utensil to use if more than one is available. Many foods are easier to spear with a fork, while others need a spoon. Some foods are unmanageable with a fork or spoon and require fingers. Before the child begins her meal, ask, "Which foods will you eat with the fork? Which ones with a spoon? Which ones with your fingers?" Praise correct answers. Present a logical reason for how each food is to be eaten, whether

It can be helpful for children with a variety of disabilities to learn systematically how to control eating utensils more effectively. Children with physical disabilities that affect fine motor control, cognitive deficits, or visual disabilities might benefit from such an approach.

the child's answers were correct or not. For instance, say, "Right. You eat the meat with the fork because you can spear it and pick it up more easily," or "It will be easier if you use your hand for the carrot sticks because you won't be able to pick them up with the spoon." Take only a few seconds for this.

Second, be sure that the food is cut into bite-sized pieces. If food is in chunks that are too large, messy eating is inevitable. Foods like sandwiches should be cut into quarters for ease of handling.

Third, show the child how to use bread, a roll, or other soft finger foods as an aid in scooping hard-to-catch foods on the spoon or fork. For instance, peas are much easier to capture if the utensil approaches them from one side and a piece of bread from the other.

Fourth, guide the child's hand to show her how best to use the spoon or fork. Let her try on her own at first, but help if she fails to capture the food after two tries.

Put your hand around and maneuver the utensil to get the food. Do this as often as necessary. Eventually, the child acquires the feel for using utensils effectively. As the child becomes more adept at scooping up foods with the proper utensil, withdraw your help gradually.

2. *Difficulty getting food to her mouth without spilling.* Most spills occur somewhere between the plate and the mouth. If the child has trouble with this task, provide direct guidance.

At first, take hold of the child's hand as she scoops the food on the utensil. Pause for a moment to make sure food and utensil are evenly balanced, then slowly guide them to the child's mouth. Verbalize the process as you help the child. Say, "First, we have to make sure that the food is on the spoon. Now let's make sure the spoon is straight. Now let's move the spoon very slowly to your mouth. We don't want to spill the food. Now it goes into your wide-open mouth. Close your mouth. Take the food off the spoon. Now the spoon comes out of your mouth and you can chew and swallow. See! You didn't spill one bit!" Guide the child for several days, verbalizing the steps as they happen.

When you feel that the child understands, try decreasing your guidance. Again guide the child's hand, and verbalize the entire process, but remove your hand just before the spoon reaches her mouth. Tell the child that she will get the food into her mouth by herself and praise her well for success.

When the child gets the food to her mouth with no spills for an entire meal, withdraw your guidance further. This time, remove your hand about halfway between the plate and her mouth. Continue verbalizing what is happening and encouraging slow and neat eating.

Next, let the child go alone from the plate to her mouth after the food and utensil are balanced. Then let the child balance the food. Finally, withdraw all physical guidance. Decrease and then stop the verbal comments gradually as the child is able to remind herself of what needs to be done.

3. *Other messy eating behaviors.* Treat other messy eating behaviors in a way similar to the behaviors just described. Examine the behavior you want to teach, break it down into steps, and help the child acquire the process through direct guidance. As the child gains skill in the new behavior, withdraw your support gradually.

Reinforce Appropriate Eating. During all meals, be alert to proper eating behavior and reinforce it lavishly. Whether it is a spontaneous behavior or a step you are teaching the child, let her know that you value neat eating habits. Tell her throughout the meal as well as at the end that she is doing a good job. Give praise according to her ability. At first, you may reinforce only balancing food on the spoon (even if the food falls off the spoon afterward). Later, the child should be able to finish an entire meal with few spills, and you can gear your praise accordingly.

Ignore Messy Eating. If the child is messy because of lack of ability, continue helping her to learn the skills needed to eat neatly. Focus on small successes. If the child deliberately makes a mess by playing with or throwing food, deny the attention the child is seeking. Do the following when the child is deliberately messy:

- Say, "No, you may not spit out milk." Use this statement as a warning with any specific messy behavior. Be sure the child hears you.
- If the child continues this behavior, take any utensils the child may be using out of her hands, pick up her plate and cup, and remove these items. Be sure they are out of the child's reach.
- Turn your back on the child. Do not look at her, talk to her, or otherwise react to her behavior. Ignore whatever she may do.
- After one minute, put her plate, cup, and utensils back in front of her. Make no comments about the messy behavior.
- Continue to help her eat neatly. Find a positive achievement to reinforce as soon as possible.
- Repeat this strategy every time the child deliberately makes a mess with her food.

 Continue Keeping Track of the Behavior. Each day of this approach, continue to count the number of messy eating incidents. Record these on the graph. When messy eating counts are consistently near zero, you have reached your goal. However, expect that accidents may occasionally occur.

MAINTAINING THE CHANGES

Continue periodic reinforcement once the child has reached the goal. Give help occasionally if it is needed. If, at any time, the child reverts to deliberately messy eating behavior, ignore it in the way previously described.

The CD-ROM that accompanies this text contains several hypothetical scenarios designed for you to apply the guidance principles suggested in the various chapters of this book. Go to the Your Turn section of the CD to access these scenarios. Scenarios 11 and 12 are particularly pertinent to this section of the text, Eating Behaviors.

SECTION 8

Multiple

Challenging

Behaviors

chapter **48**

Children Who Present Multiple Challenges

Sometimes, a child presents not just one challenging behavior but several. Such situations often become frustrating because it seems that too much effort is involved in bringing about changes. If your attempts to handle multiple challenges have failed in the past, those experiences probably reinforce the helplessness you feel in trying to deal with them now.

This chapter outlines a systematic approach to dealing with the child who has a number of challenging behaviors. It is important that the staff as a whole follow the suggested strategies. Spend time in a staff conference to discuss these challenging behaviors thoroughly and decide on a specific approach. The time spent in planning a concerted effort will prove to be well spent when your approach begins to take effect.

REVIEW THE BEHAVIORS THAT CONCERN YOU

List all of the child's behaviors that are of concern to you. Do not worry about listing them in order. Record your concerns on paper.

- Review the chapters in this text that deal with the challenging behaviors on your list.
- Consider whether any of the challenging behaviors are similar. One clue to similarity is that behaviors fall under the same general section heading in the table of contents.

403

- Consider whether any of the suggested approaches for dealing with the concerns are very similar.
- Check the behaviors to determine whether any of them are direct opposites. Often the decrease in one behavior leads quite naturally to an increase in another. Infrequent social interaction and hitting are behaviors that illustrate this point. As positive social interactions increase, negative social behaviors such as hitting should decrease. Another example involves concerns with infrequent participation in activities and thumb-sucking. Again, as the child increases participation in activities, thumb-sucking should automatically decrease.
- Check whether any of the suggested strategies are primarily preventive. A preventive approach is based largely on change in the teachers' actions and reactions. Teachers become more aware of what the child is doing and act to stop the child if the child begins to engage in the target behavior. Preventive methods are used either in combination with other techniques or when the child's behavior is expected to stop soon on its own (biting by a two-year-old, for example). Most of the strategies in this book are not preventive but use techniques that lead to direct behavior change in the child.

PRIORITIZE LISTED BEHAVIORS

Reorganize the behaviors you listed. Start with the behavior of greatest concern to you and the child's family. Use the following criteria to decide which behavior to deal with first:

- Any behaviors that lead to a direct hazard to the health or safety of the child or of other children should have first priority. Hitting and throwing objects at others are examples.
- The second most serious category includes behaviors that pose a severe threat to the self-esteem of the child or of other children. Examples are name-calling, infrequent social interaction, and shyness at group times.
- The third category includes other highly disruptive behaviors, such as throwing tantrums and running in the classroom.
- The fourth category includes any behaviors that are an indirect health or safety hazard, such as breaking toys and flushing objects down the toilet.
- Include any other behaviors in the final category, such as wasting paper and baby talk.

As you prioritize behaviors, also keep in mind the magnitude of the behavior. The chapter on hitting, for instance, can include a wide variety of behaviors, from a light slap to a severe punch.

CONSULT WITH THE FAMILY

Once you have focused more clearly on the behaviors you find of concern and have prioritized these, meet with the family to discuss your observations. Families whose children exhibit a multitude of behavior challenges may be happy to hear positive suggestions for making changes, or they may feel defensive and hostile because they feel they are being attacked. Be sensitive to the feelings and needs of the family. Ask for their suggestions for changing behaviors to more appropriate ones, and enlist their ideas to reach your goal. Discuss with them your ideas for changing behaviors and how you plan to implement these. Let the family know that you will work slowly toward reaching your goal rather than trying to change all challenging behaviors at once. Keep in close touch with the family to keep them informed of progress toward the goal.

DECIDE ON THE APPROACH YOU WILL USE

Once you list, examine, and prioritize the challenging behaviors, you can decide what to do first. It is important that you do not try to do too much at one time. Focus on one or at the most two behaviors at a time.

1. Begin with the most serious challenge on your list. If you feel it is necessary, begin with two challenges, combining the most serious with another from the top of your list. To do this, the two behaviors must fit one of the following categories:

   - The two behaviors are very similar. The strategies can easily be combined.
   - The strategies for the two behaviors are very similar and can be combined easily.
   - The two behaviors are direct opposites; as one increases, the other automatically decreases.
   - One of the approaches uses primarily preventive action on the part of the teachers. Use such a preventive approach at the same time you use another strategy only if you feel that you can handle both. For instance, if the first approach you are going to implement requires your attention only at specific times, such as at group time or during meals, then you probably can handle it in combination with a preventive strategy. Remember, do not overreach your time, ability, and resources. Also, do not expect too much from the child at one time.

2. When the one or two behaviors you start on are well under control, begin on the next behaviors on your list. Continue until you deal with all the challenging behaviors.

3. Often, as one behavior improves, other behaviors also change without any specific intervention on your part. This may happen for several reasons. The child may establish a more positive relationship with the teachers and thus feel more inclined to do what is expected. Conversely, the teachers may find the child to be more pleasant and respond to the child more positively. The child's overall behavior may also improve because the strategy builds the child's self-esteem and self-confidence. The child may simply recognize that compliance with the requests of adults is not a bad thing, particularly when adults reinforce such behaviors.

Keep these limits in mind when you deal with multiple challenges. A systematic approach helps you eliminate challenging behaviors. It takes time and effort to carry out several successive strategies. In the long run, however, you save the time, energy, and frustration you would have spent dealing with challenging behaviors. Most important, you help the child grow in the process of socialization. You help the child improve in relations with other people and in the child's feelings of self-worth.

The CD-ROM that accompanies this text contains several hypothetical scenarios designed for you to apply the guidance principles suggested in the various chapters of this book. Go to the Your Turn section of the CD to access these scenarios. The last scenario is particularly pertinent to this section of the text, Multiple Challenging Behaviors.

chapter **49**

Some Final Thoughts

Early childhood is the time when children learn about and begin to internalize the expectations and rules of society. This is a gradual process. During this time, children's behaviors are molded and shaped so that they can function effectively within society. Adults are very important in this socialization process, as they help children learn how to negotiate social relationships in a way that is satisfying and meaningful. You, as a teacher of young children, are especially vital in this process.

Behavioral challenges are an inevitable part of young children's lives. Children are not born with an understanding of social rules and expectations. They learn these gradually through the reactions of other people, especially adults, and through the consequences of their behaviors. Behavioral challenges sometimes also result from events in children's lives that are beyond their control, events often, although not always, stemming from family difficulties. Because young children generally have little control over what happens in their lives, their reactions to such events may show up in the form of inappropriate behavior. The sensitivity and understanding of the adults in their lives can help children build resilience for coping with such difficulties. Generally, the techniques in this book are intended for situations in which a child's inappropriate behavior is something under the child's control, such as when the child is motivated by a desire for attention.

The preceding chapters of this book are intended as a guide for teachers of young children, a stimulus to careful reflection about why children do not behave appropriately. They are certainly not intended as a "cookbook" for dealing with every situation. Every child's behavior is unique because it is triggered by different causes and circumstances. The techniques suggested in these chapters are meant as guidelines to help you think through alternatives and different possibilities. A number of inappropriate behaviors, some very common and others less common, are explored and discussed.

Each of the chapters is built on some assumptions about the circumstances and atmosphere within the early childhood program in which you carry them out. It is expected that the program in which these are implemented is child-oriented, with developmentally appropriate activities and materials, and with positive and nurturing teacher–child interactions. Children are far less likely to behave inappropriately if the environment and activities are engaging and if adults are responsive. The chapters also assume that teachers will carefully examine the reasons why a child engages in challenging behaviors and react accordingly. In other words, if the cause of the behavior is beyond the child's control, then the teacher must look for ways to change those external causes, if at all possible. The chapters also are based on the assumption that children understand what is expected of them, that rules are clear, and that they are consistently implemented. Finally, the book assumes that teachers and families work together in the best interest of the children.

This book uses a format to help you, as the teacher, deal with children's inappropriate behaviors in a clear and focused way. It begins by carefully stating the behavior under question; this serves to zero in on the concern rather than on extraneous issues. Next, it directs you to carefully observe what is going on; before trying to change a behavior, it is important to know when, where, how, with whom, and under what circumstances it is most likely to occur. Consulting with the family of the child is another important step in the process. There are consequences for all behaviors, and the following section in each chapter provides some thoughts about what the implications might be if the behavior continues unchecked. A very important section, encourages you to explore alternatives. This is especially important in considering what environmental changes can help deal with the behavior. Now, if you are ready to implement strategies for changing the behavior, the next sections state a goal, outline a suggested approach, specifically define the behavior, help you gather some baseline information about frequency of the behavior's occurrence, then give details about each step in the approach. Finally, there are suggestions for maintaining changes. These steps are intended to help you proceed slowly and think carefully about what is happening with the child. There are also opportunities for you to reflect on and practice how to help children learn more appropriate behaviors through a set of scenarios, which you will find in the CD-ROM that comes with this text.

Different strategies are suggested for different behaviors in the various chapters, depending on the nature of the inappropriate behavior. Some behaviors require quick action, especially if the child's behavior harms or potentially harms others. Other concerns are about the child's disruptive or annoying behaviors, or about the child's lack of interactions in activities or social encounters. Whatever the behavior, however, it is important to be thoughtful and respectful of the child and his needs. The time required in working through the behaviors in an effective way is well spent if the child's behavior changes to something more acceptable.

By helping children behave in appropriate ways, you are making your classroom a much nicer place for you and for all the children. The child in question, whose behavior has been a concern, will feel better about herself, and will spend her time in productive and rewarding activities. The other children will spend time in a pleasant environment and will receive their share of attention when you are not frequently spending an undue amount of time with one or two challenging children. And finally, you, as the teacher, will feel more successful if you can spend your time on meaningful interactions and in enjoyable activities with all the children.

Behavioral challenges may be an inevitable part of young children's lives, but they do not have to be all-consuming. Careful, thoughtful strategies can guide you in helping children learn more effective, alternative ways of behaving.

g • Nonsharing • Bribery • Stealing • Noncompliance • Disrupting Group Time • Leaving the Classroom
ning Aimlessly Around the Classroom • Shouting in the Classroom • Dropping Objects to Create No
ring Books • Breaking Toys • Flushing Objects Down the Toilet • Wasting Paper • Destroying the W
hers • Throwing Tantrums • Pouting • Baby Talk • Thumb-Sucking • Pant-Wetting • Clinging • Seek
tion • • Nonparticipation in Activities • Nonparticipation in Social Play • Shyness at Group Tim
ng with Only One Toy • Infrequent Large Muscle Activity • Infrequent Dramatic-Play Participatio
ng Infrequently • Short Attention Span • Finicky Eating • Overeating • Messy Eating • Hording Foo
ig • Biting • Throwing Objects at Others • Hurting Others • Using Inappropriate Language • Nam
g • Nonsharing • Bribery • Stealing • Noncompliance • Disrupting Group Time • Leaving the Classroo
ning Aimlessly Around the Classroom • Shouting in the Classroom • Dropping Objects to Create No
ring Books • Breaking Toys • Flushing Objects Down the Toilet • Wasting Paper • Destroying the W
hers • Throwing Tantrums • Pouting • Baby Talk • Thumb-Sucking • Pant-Wetting • Clinging • Seek
tion • Whining • Self-Stimulation • Nonparticipation in Activities • Nonparticipation in Social Pla
ess at Group Time • Playing with Only One Toy • Infrequent Large Muscle Activity • Infrequ
atic-Play Participation • Talking Infrequently • Short Attention Span • Finicky Eating • Overeatin
y Eating • Hording Food • Hitting • Biting • Throwing Objects at Others • Hurting Others • Us
ropriate Language • Name-Calling • Nonsharing • Bribery • Stealing • Noncompliance • Disrupt
p Time • Leaving the Classroom • Running Aimlessly Around the Classroom • Shouting in
room • Dropping Objects to Create Noise • Tearing Books • Breaking Toys • Flushing Objects Do
oilet • Wasting Paper • Destroying the Work of Others • Throwing Tantrums • Pouting • Baby Ta
mb-Sucking • Pant-Wetting • Whining • Self-Stimulation • Nonparticipation in Activities
participation in Social Play • Shyness at Group Time • Playing with Only One Toy • Infrequent La
cle Activity • Infrequent Dramatic-Play Participation • Talking Infrequently • Short Attention Spa
ky Eating • Overeating • Messy Eating • Hording Food • Hitting • Biting • Throwing Objects at Oth
irting Others • Using Inappropriate Language • Name-Calling • Nonsharing • Bribery • Stealin
compliance • Disrupting Group Time • Leaving the Classroom • Running Aimlessly Around
room • Shouting in the Classroom • Dropping Objects to Create Noise • Tearing Books • Breaking T
shing Objects Down the Toilet • Wasting Paper • Destroying the Work of Others • Throwing Tantru
uting • Baby Talk • Thumb-Sucking • Pant-Wetting • Clinging • Seeking Attention • Whining • S
ulation • Nonparticipation in Activities • Nonparticipation in Social Play • Shyness at Group Tim
quent Large Muscle Activity • Infrequent Dramatic-Play Participation • Talking Infrequently • Sh
tion Span • Finicky Eating • Overeating • Messy Eating • Hording Food • Hitting • Biting • Throw
cts at Others • Hurting Others • Using Inappropriate Language • Name-Calling • Nonsharing • Brit
aling • Noncompliance • Disrupting Group Time • Leaving the Classroom • Running Aimlessly Aro
Classroom • Shouting in the Classroom • Dropping Objects to Create Noise • Tearing Books • Brea
• Flushing Objects Down the Toilet • Wasting Paper • Destroying the Work of Others • Throw
rums • Pouting • Baby Talk • Thumb-Sucking • Pant-Wetting • Clinging • Seeking Attention • Whin
ng • Biting • Throwing Objects at Others • Hurting Others • Using Inappropriate Language • Na

Index

Index

Index

Notes